M000235396

Worldview as Worship

Worldview as Worship

The Dynamics of a Transformative Christian Education

EDDIE KARL BAUMANN

WIPF & STOCK · Eugene, Oregon

WORLDVIEW AS WORSHIP
The Dynamics of a Transformative Christian Education

Copyright © 2011 Eddie Karl Baumann. All rights reserved. Except for brief quotations in critical publications or reviews, no part of this book may be reproduced in any manner without prior written permission from the publisher. Write: Permissions, Wipf and Stock Publishers, 199 W. 8th Ave., Suite 3, Eugene, OR 97401.

Wipf & Stock
An Imprint of Wipf and Stock Publishers
199 W. 8th Ave., Suite 3
Eugene, OR 97401
www.wipfandstock.com

ISBN 13: 978-1-61097-108-9

Manufactured in the U.S.A.

All Scripture quotations, unless otherwise noted, are taken from the New American Standard Bible˚, Copyright © 1960, 1962, 1963, 1968, 1971, 1972, 1973, 1975, 1977, 1995 by The Lockman Foundation. Used by permission. www.Lockman.org

Scripture quotations marked NIV are taken from the Holy Bible, New International Version˚, NIV˚. Copyright © 1973, 1978, 1984 by Biblica, Inc.™ Used by permission of Zondervan. All rights reserved worldwide. www.zondervan.com

Scripture quotations marked KJV are taken from the Holy Bible, King James Version, Cambridge, 1769.

Contents

List of Figures

Preface

FOR MOST OF ITS recent history, a fundamental distinction of evangelical education, whether in the church, Christian school or university, has been an emphasis on preparing students to think biblically and apply the Christian faith to every aspect of life. The objective of taking faith and getting students to apply it to both the process of learning and the conduct of life, however, has always been an uncertain goal—not uncertain in the desire and commitment of so many dedicated educators to try to instill these principles in their students, but uncertain as to whether those efforts were producing the desired effect.

As Christian educators we have all experienced the joy of seeing students who have gone on to serve faithfully in various ministries, demonstrating the reality and validity of Christ in various professional endeavors. Unfortunately, we have also shared the heartache of witnessing students who pursue lifestyles and goals apart from the faith. Often these students demonstrate competency and even excellence in areas such as mathematics, the natural and social sciences, the humanities, and even their knowledge of the Bible; yet they have failed to embrace the primary goal of knowing Christ intimately and making him known to a watching world. More distressing is that the rejection of this goal seems to occur with increasing and alarming frequency.

The distinctiveness of a Christian education should not simply be academic excellence, although doing all things for the glory of God should mean striving for academic excellence. Nor should Christian education be the acquisition or indoctrination into a particular catechism of doctrinal statements or theological standards, although doctrine and theology are immensely important. Rather, a distinctive Christian education is one that prepares the disciple of Christ to make the Master "famous"—relevant to the issues and concerns of culture. For Christ to be made relevant to others, however, requires he first be relevant in the life of the believer. This is the primary goal of Christian educators: the integration of faith to learning and life. It is a goal that often is not realized in the lives of many evangelical young people.

The process of making Christ relevant to one's own life and the validity of Christ to the issues of culture is what evangelical educators generally refer to as worldview transformation. Worldview transformation is considered foundational to taking the Christian faith and making it applicable to learning and life. Yet the transformation of one's worldview requires an understanding of what a worldview fundamentally is—something Christian educators have not always done. Christian educators certainly speak the language of worldview, and in doing so we assume a certain familiarity with the concept. This common language and perceived familiarity implies a shared understanding of the process of engaging students in worldview transformation. This perceived familiarity has, in large part, created the difficulty in helping students to take their faith and to apply it meaningfully to both learning and life. It has led many students to reduce the Christian faith to a set of logical propositions or creedal statements or for others to simply view biblical Christianity as irrelevant to the most fundamental issues of life.

Worldview as Worship seeks to define what a worldview is, how it is acquired, and the fundamental principles that make worldview transformation possible. The familiarity in which most Christian educators use the term *worldview* often cloaks the complexity of the concept. The result is that worldview transformation is often reduced to a set of curriculum objectives that fail to address the fundamental characteristics of what a worldview is and how it is acquired or changed. Ironically, this reduction of worldview may create conditions in which true biblical integration, the type that leads to the fundamental and critical step of taking faith and applying it to the issues of learning and life, is actually hindered despite the best intentions and efforts to do otherwise. True worldview transformation can only occur if students, as image-bearers of God, seek to both know and do that for which all human beings are created—to love the Lord with all their heart, soul, mind, and strength, and love others as they love themselves. Without both the knowledge and the opportunity to worship God and serve others, authentic worldview transformation is unlikely to occur. This book is dedicated to demonstrating how worship and service are the vehicles that Christian educators must embrace to facilitate worldview transformation in their students.

While writing a book can be a solitary process it is rarely done alone. My belief that worldviews are developed within communities gives me pause to acknowledge the many people who have contributed to the development of my thinking on this topic. I owe a debt of gratitude to many, and yet in this space can only acknowledge a few.

The value of biblical integration and worldview development has been constantly preached and faithfully practiced by many of my colleagues at Cedarville University. Their examples and subsequent conversations have contributed greatly to the development of my own thinking regarding worldview transformation. In addition, several of my colleagues both read and provided valuable insights to early drafts of this work. I would especially like to thank Dan Estes, Steve Gruber, and Cheryl Irish for their time and contributions to this project.

I owe a great debt to Debbie Jones who patiently worked to help edit and revise my unusually constructed sentences. The style and ideas of this book are mine but undoubtedly it is a much easier read and a better book for the effort she dedicated to make my ideas clearer.

I believe that it is the church, as a community of faith, that God uses to transform believers and to bring them into conformity to Christ—both in terms of how we act and how we think. In this regard I certainly need to acknowledge the contributions of my brothers and sisters of Shawnee Hills Baptist Church. Conversations with my pastors, Jim Riggle, Mark McFadden and Josh Yoder, have stirred my imagination and prompted my thinking. Mark also contributed helpful comments in his reading of the early drafts. A sincere debt of gratitude also goes to the many members of the Adult Bible Fellowship class that I have had the privilege to teach. Their questions, comments, and insights have helped to shape my thinking in ways I cannot even express.

One of the most important decisions a person can make is the person with whom they will journey through life. I thank God for my wife, Teresea, who has been a constant source of encouragement and support even throughout the times I doubted my abilities to complete this project.

Finally, I do not believe that any teacher can truly teach, nor can their thinking develop, without being profoundly challenged and influenced by their students. In writing I often found my thoughts turned to questions, conversations, comments, and insights they have provided me over the years. Often, I would picture specific people and recall particular conversations, many of which are recalled either in word or spirit in this work. It was their desire to develop a more consistent and all-encompassing biblical worldview in their own lives that provided a major impetus to this work.

Introduction

If then, Christianity is a culture rather than a philosophy or a worldview, where do we begin? So much would surely change if the church regarded itself as a way of life and not simply a spiritual retreat or the promoting society of a belief system.

—Rodney Clapp

ONE EVENING MY NINETEEN-YEAR-OLD daughter and several of her friends, all graduates or long-time attendees of Christian schools, were reminiscing about school and talking about the lives of many of their classmates. Most of their friends were Christian school graduates, while several completed public school. Many they discussed were, at some point, avowed believers, while others were not. Like my daughter and her friends, several of their classmates had gone on to college—either Christian or public—while others had entered the military or the job market. Many of their friends were still living at home, while a few were now on their own. Soon the conversation turned to the current lifestyles of their friends. Some of these stories involved unbelieving acquaintances, but a great many others involved their Christian school peers who were living in ways contrary to or in denial of the faith that had been part of their training at home, church, and school. As I listened, I found the stories of their Christian school classmates compelling. Many of their stories were tragic, not simply because they were experiencing the moral repercussions of lives pursued apart from God but also because it seemed that even those who were pursuing socially and morally acceptable goals were pursuing them for reasons that differed little from their unbelieving or public-school educated friends.

A central tenet of Christian education over the last several decades, either in the church or the Christian school or university, has been to produce students who can think biblically. The language of Christian education is filled with phrases that reflect this objective. Christian education emphasizes the integration of faith, learning, and life; it prepares students to view all things through the "lens" of Scripture or simply seeks to teach from a Christ-centered worldview. This emphasis on producing students who can think biblically has developed within a cultural context in which evangelical Christians have come to believe that the prevailing values of the society are increasingly contrary or even hostile to the values of Scripture. The form and language of these cultural conflicts have changed over the years. In the 1980s the threat was secular humanism. In the 1990s these conflicts took on the label of the "cultural war," while more recently these conflicts have been described as a war on faith. The language used to describe this conflict has led the evangelical community to define the struggle as one of a biblically based, unified and encompassing worldview in opposition to the secular worldview of the culture. As sociologist James Davidson Hunter notes, these opposing worldviews have led to "polarizing impulses and tendencies . . . between how these moral visions are institutionalized [into public life]."[1]

Despite the polemic language, many evangelical leaders began to lament a reduction in tensions between the church and the culture. This relief was not the result of a reduction in the power of secularism in the society but rather the result of evangelicals increasingly capitulating to the influences of culture. In 1999, conservative evangelical leader Paul Weyrich claimed that there was no longer a "moral majority" in the United States and that conservatives had lost the culture war. Interestingly, Hunter predicted such a phenomenon in an earlier work when he wrote that "except on issues of abortion, homosexuality, and perhaps the ERA, Evangelicals themselves have adjusted comfortably to the decline in hegemony of traditional moralism and familism."[2] Even Hunter does not speak as prophetically as Harry Blamires, who opens his classic 1963 work, *The Christian Mind*, by noting:

> There is no longer a Christian mind. There is still, of course, a Christian ethic, a Christian practice, and a Christian spirituality. As a moral being, the modern Christian subscribes to a code other than that of the non-Christian. As a member of the Church, he undertakes obligations and observations ignored by the non-Christian. As a spiritual being, in prayer and meditation, he strives to cultivate a dimension of life unexplored by the non-Christian. But as a *thinking* being, the modern Christian has succumbed to secularization. He accepts religion—its morality, its worship, its spiritual culture; but he rejects the religious view of life, the view which sets all earthly issues within the context of the eternal, the view which relates all human problems—social, political, cultural—to the doctrinal foundations of the Christian Faith, the view which sees all things here below in terms of God's supremacy and earth's transitoriness, in terms of Heaven and Hell.[3]

As a result of these trends, many biblical educators have increasingly come to view their role, at least in part, as preparing students to navigate the cultural tensions and moral conflicts or capitulations that result from living in an intensely secularized society. As Christian school pioneer Kenneth Gangel has written, the purpose of a Christian education is to have students "learn a worldview based on [a] solid ethical and moral foundation, and [then] integrate that worldview, consciously or not, into their decision-making process."[4] Many of the early proponents of the contemporary Christian school movement believed, like Gangel, that to accomplish these ends, Christian schools had to teach from a biblical worldview and to promote the integration of faith and learning throughout the curriculum. Their vision, initially put into practice during the 1960s and 1970s, continues

1. Hunter, *Culture Wars*, 43.
2. Hunter, *Evangelicalism*, 193.
3. Blamires, *Christian Mind*, 3–4 (italics in original).
4. Gangel, "Biblical Foundations of Education," 55.

to dominate and direct the purpose and practice of most Christian education today; yet, from the days of Blamires's first pronouncement of the loss of a Christian mind, to the more current observations of evangelical capitulation to the secular, there is a growing sense that these efforts have not produced the desired results.

Christian educators have often observed little difference in the attitudes, aspirations, and beliefs of their students when compared to students in the public schools. Josh McDowell and Bob Hostetler have noted that "it is not that our kids are rejecting Christianity as they know it—they have simply been influenced to redefine it according to their cultural setting. They are putting together their own religious smorgasbord."[5] While it is premature or even wrong to think that the efforts of so many Christian educators have been in vain, it does suggest that the current methods used by most Christian schools to develop a biblical worldview in students may be ineffective and inappropriate.

Worldview as Worship, proposes that the methods used by Christian educators must change if they desire to transform the worldview of their students. To *transform* acknowledges that the process of changing a student's worldview is accomplished by the authority of Christ and mediated through the power of the Spirit of God. Paul commands all believers to be renewed in the spirit of their minds (Rom 12:2), noting that "the new self, which in the likeness of God has been created in righteousness and holiness of the truth" (Eph 4:23–24). This "creation" is neither the work of human hands nor the product of human efforts but is reserved to the sovereign auspices of God. While the product of transformation is under the sole authority of God, he has called his saints into a communal relationship in which they are responsible to one another for engaging in the process of transformation. For this reason, each believer has been provided spiritual gifts or abilities for the common good and edification of other believers (1 Cor 13:7). As gifted and mature Christian educators, teachers have a responsibility before God and an obligation to their students to assist them in their spiritual development. As mentors, they are to guide and direct the process of education. As Christian educators, they are empowered to cultivate conditions that can either assist or hinder worldview development in students.

The analogy of cultivation, and an emphasis on community and the creation of a culture that will foster worldview change, stands in contrast to a more typical evangelical analogy in which a worldview is portrayed as a lens through which individuals orient themselves to the world. In the lens analogy, the sin nature distorts people's perspective and prevents them from viewing the world as God intends. Born as sinners, all individuals possess a nature that prevents them from understanding the world from God's proper perspective. As a result of the sin nature, humanity's orientation to the world is distorted to such a degree that people's interpretations of the world and their resulting desires, motives, and behaviors are also distorted and contrary to God. Consequently, all are dependent upon the qualitative transforming power of Christ—first in justification and then through the renewing of the mind—so that they can engage in the process of "trying to learn what is pleasing to the Lord . . . [understanding] what the will of the Lord is" (Eph 5:10, 17). The prescription is to correct the vision, to gain a new set of lenses,

---

5. McDowell and Hostetler, *Beyond Belief and Conviction*, 14.

whereby the person comes to view the world from a perspective that increasingly aligns with God's vision of the world. Thus, worldview transformation is, in essence, the process whereby the believer is reoriented to the world. In this sense worldview transformation, or learning to think biblically, is an individual process, where the individual believer is the primary focus. While acknowledging that a person lives in a sinful world that has the power to influence decisions in ways contrary to the desires of God, the belief is that the person who is truly transformed can withstand those influences and live a life of thought and deed that corresponds to the will of God.

While we can acknowledge its basic worth, the lens analogy fails to take into full account the biblical emphasis on human beings as communal creatures, and as a result, one's conceptions of the world, or worldview, is communally formed and can also suffer from corporate distortions. This distorted vision comes from living in a sin-affected world and from interacting with others who seek to make sense of this world. In time, these collective visions contribute to us, and we to them, a distorted view of reality, reinforcing each other to maintain and promote an aberrant vision of the world. This collective vision of the world (and the forms it produces) is called *culture*, which helps explain why people who grow up in a similar place and time come to a shared understanding of the world. While not diminishing the autonomy of the individual and recognizing that all people are unique, we generally acknowledge that those who share a common culture come to think about the world in ways that distinguishes them from people of other cultural backgrounds.

The emphasis on the collective development and corporate distortion of reality underscores the idea that worldviews are communal visions. While all individuals are born with a sin nature, the characteristics exhibited by the sin nature are shaped by factors unique to the individual and the influence of the culture. As a result, one's initial worldview is mediated to the person—shaped by cultural influences such as parents, school, media, social institutions, and so, which exert a strong influence on the child. This understanding of worldview means that worldview transformation, just like its initial development, must not only focus on the qualitative change of the individual but also address the collective influence.

Worldview as Worship addresses the need to develop transformative communities and asserts that worldview transformation is best cultivated in a communal environment in ways similar to the initial development of worldview. The idea of worldview transformation acknowledges that individuals possess a worldview long before they are capable of addressing the topic formally. A person's worldview has been powerfully embedded through the process of acting and doing and then having those actions interpreted for him or her by others. This communal view recognizes that one's initial worldview is not learned formally, in some academic sense, but informally, in an apprenticeship relationship with parents, teachers, peers, and the culture in general. By acknowledging that the development of worldview is a communal experience, however, does not imply that we jettison the formal examination of worldview. We are compelled by God to understand the world from his perspective, "taking every thought captive to the obedience of Christ" (2 Cor 10:5). While acknowledging the necessity of a more formal approach to the understanding of worldview, we must also recognize that the formal approach alone may be insufficient to cultivate the type of worldview change desired in our students.

As noted, the lens analogy to worldview transformation focuses on the individual but also tends to view the process as a theoretical or philosophical one. That is, the transformation of worldview is essentially the process of transforming the mind. As a result, the quintessential biblical text for worldview transformation becomes Romans 12:1–2:

> I urge you, therefore, brethren, by the mercies of God, to present your bodies a living and holy sacrifice, acceptable to God, which is your spiritual service of worship. And do not be conformed to this world, but be transformed by the renewing of your mind, that you may prove what the will of God is, that which is good and acceptable and perfect.

The danger of such a perspective is that it seeks to train the person as a Christian philosopher or theologian at the expense of the practical aspect of living in the world. Paul is clear that a relationship exists between the transformation of the mind, which allows a person to ascertain the will of God, and the issue of service. Many Christian educators have also been conscious of this relationship. Christian school pioneer Frank Gaebelein once wrote, "The moment a person takes the position that all truth is God's truth, he is committed to doing something. The Bible knows no such thing as truth that is merely theoretical; in the Bible truth is linked to deed."[6]

It can be relatively easy to proclaim the truth of the biblical worldview. We can engage in the systematic development of grand schemes of thought. Philosophically speaking, we can develop a theology of worldview that is coherent to the point of avoiding even a single logical imperfection. Similarly, we can demonstrate the validity of the biblical worldview by its correspondence to reality. We can even commit ourselves to the practice of faithfully aligning our theology fully and completely into the subject areas that we teach. The virtue of the biblical worldview, however, is not found in the claims of its adherents to its validity. The virtue of the biblical worldview is found in its application to the whole of life, and it is preeminently virtuous because it reflects the One in whom all glory and honor and virtue resides—Jesus Christ. The biblical worldview is valid not simply because it is logically consistent and theologically coherent, the greatest among other philosophical systems or competing worldviews, or even that it best corresponds to the created reality, both in system and in practice. Rather, the validity of the biblical worldview resides in the reality of a person, the Lord Jesus Christ, and the virtue of that worldview is found in the relationship that the followers of Christ have to him—where Christ influences the individual believer and the community of faith in thought, word, and deed in ways that seek to make Christ famous before a watching world.

It is this emphasis on action that the apostle Paul seems to have in mind when he writes, "Whether, then, you eat or drink or whatever you do, do all to the glory of God" (1 Cor 10:31). Paul notes that the proof of the reality of the gospel, from which the biblical worldview emanates, is that it can be lived out in even the most ordinary areas of life. He concludes this thought by encouraging the Corinthian believers to "be imitators of me,

6. Gaebelein, *Pattern of God's Truth*, 35.

just as I am of Christ" (1 Cor 11:1). The reality of the gospel is that it has been and can be lived, first in the person of Jesus Christ and then in the lives of his followers. Paul sought to teach these believers that the reality of the transformative power of the gospel was validated not simply through knowing the teaching of the Word of God but by applying those teachings to everyday life. To this end, Paul offers himself as a model of Jesus Christ so that they would be able to imitate his behaviors in their own lives.

James echoes this same idea when he writes, "But prove yourselves doers of the word, and not merely hearers who delude themselves," and later concludes, "even so faith, if it has no works, is dead being by itself" (Jas 1:22; 2:17). For James, the idea that one can know the truth of Scripture without living that truth in life is a delusion and should cause individuals to examine the reality of their faith (Jas 2:18–26). The title *Worldview as Worship* seeks to capture the essence of Paul's command and James's teaching that every aspect of life represents an opportunity to bring glory to God, to make him famous before a watching world, to proclaim honor or worth to him.

The pattern of Paul's instruction to the Corinthians is revealing. He exhorts them to imitate himself, just as he imitates Christ—behaviors that are consistent with bringing glory to God. It is only after he has encouraged them to live their faith that he begins to instruct them on the "more excellent way" of love (1 Cor 12:31). That is, Paul encourages their imitation of the actions of Christ and himself and then provides the theological rationale for those actions. A similar pattern is presented in Romans 12:1–2, where Paul encourages the Roman believers to present themselves a living sacrifice which is a reasonable act of service. It is through service, that is, engaging in behaviors that are acts of worship, that the mind is transformed. In calling his readers to act in a manner consistent with service and worship, Paul engages believers in the process of transforming their minds, in contemporary language, of worldview transformation, which mirrors the process whereby a person's initial worldview developed: interacting with others, imitating their behaviors, and eventually coming to understand the rationale behind those motives and actions.

Worldview transformation, like worldview acquisition, occurs through the acts of imitation. As a result, worldview transformation is not an individual and theological/philosophical process but is intimately connected to being united with and living in accordance to the community of faith in service and worship to Christ. In this respect, worldview transformation is a process that is lived not in isolation from the world but through interaction with it, so that the virtues of faith are proven to the world by those who proclaim the reality of the relationship they have in Jesus Christ. Thus, for the believer, reflecting Christ is the process of learning the biblical worldview and is the quintessential act of integration.

Worldviews, however, are not just another term describing a life of consistent religious or ethical practice. Worldviews not only provide their adherents with a means for describing the world but also serve to guide them toward a better world. Worldviews provide a narrative or grand story linking how the world is to how the world should be. Postman describes these narratives as "*big* stories—stories that are sufficiently profound and complex so as to offer explanations of the origins and future of a people; stories that construct ideals, prescribe rules of conduct, specify sources of authority, and, in doing all this, provide a sense of continuity and purpose."[7] All worldviews must provide their adherents with such a vision for life. As such, worldview narratives provide a mooring; they direct one's action toward a purpose that is transcendent or greater than the individual. The worldview narrative assures people that their lives and actions have a meaning or purpose consistent with its view of reality.

The biblical worldview shares this characteristic of narrative; it provides a story of how human beings should live in the world. As J. Richard Middleton and Brian Walsh describe,

> It is as if Genesis 1:1–2:3 sets up the initial conditions of the entire biblical metanarrative, consisting in a harmonious world of creatures judged very good by its Creator and a special creature granted agency and historical power, mandated to exercise that power for the benefit of all the rest. The remainder of the Bible consists of the extended story of how we fared historically in this world with this gift and mandate.[8]

The biblical narrative provides the believer with a purpose for living in this world. The temporal life is not, and never was intended to be, simply a staging ground for the eternal. God created a physical world and empowered humanity to manage and care for it in ways that would bring glory to God. The commands of stewardship initially given in the Garden were not revoked because of sin and the Fall. Granted, the pursuit of God's purpose is now more difficult, and the believer who attempts to be a faithful follower of Christ now inherits the additional responsibilities of the "Great Commission" (Matt 28:19–20), but Christ's command to his disciples to "observe all that I commanded you" includes teaching the purposes for which human beings were initially created. Christ does not come to bring in a new law by abolishing the old, but to fulfill the law so that people can be restored to an original state where they can fulfill their true calling, a calling for whom God's righteousness is greater than the righteousness of those who claim to adhere to the law.

This understanding of worldview empowers the believer. Humanity is given the responsibility and power to act as stewards, governing the creation for the glory of God. Humanity is given a type of regency over the creation that caused the psalmist to note, "What is man that You take thought of him, And the son of man that You care for him? Yet You have made him a little lower than God, And You crown him with glory and majesty! You make him to rule over the works of Your hands" (Ps 8:4–6a). As an image-bearer of God the believer is not a victim in this world but an active agent upon it. Middleton and Walsh note this message throughout the Old Testament, where God speaks "to a people submerged in exile—uprooted, homeless, powerless victims of a monstrous empire—the Creator of the universe proclaims that he has granted all human beings (no matter how frail or fragile they might feel) a share in his rule of the earth. Even in exile . . . we have been made royal dignitaries of the earth."[9] It is God's message through the prophet Jeremiah,

---

7. Postman, *Building a Bridge to the 18th Century*, 101.

8. Middleton and Walsh, *Truth Is Stranger Than It Used to Be*, 126.

9. Ibid., 122.

who tells the exiled Jews in Babylon to build houses and plant gardens, marry and raise families, be prosperous, pray and work for the welfare of the Babylonians, noting that they will be in exile for a long while. These commands were not a resignation to their situation but were given as an encouragement to fulfill the plan of God, "plans for welfare and not for calamity to give [them] a future and a hope" (Jer 29:11).

The idea of worldview as narrative is often lost to young people who are exposed to a more traditional understanding of worldview transformation and biblical integration. Having been taught that worldview transformation consists of developing more theologically or logically consistent arguments, the connection of worldview to life is lost. As young people move through adolescence, they begin to envision and plan for their lives. They want to get their driver's license, graduate high school, complete college, start a career, experience love, have sex, start a family, acquire material possessions, and essentially imitate the behaviors of the culture in which they live. As they engage in these behaviors, their actions, as well as their motives and goals, tend to mirror the actions, motives, and goals of the general culture. Missing from the worldview training of most young people is how the biblical narrative differs from the narrative of the surrounding culture and how this difference affects having a driver's license, gaining an education, choosing a career, gaining wealth, having a family, developing relationships, choosing behaviors, and so forth. If young people see no connection between these fundamental issues of their lives and the practice of the biblical worldview, they will default to the motives and practices of the culture, relegating the biblical worldview to a philosophical or academic position with little practical value.

In this respect, the biblical worldview cannot be reduced to a creed or dogma. It cannot simply be the affirmation of a set of propositional statements in contrast or opposition to the general culture. Adherents to the biblical worldview must also think and act consistently with the implications of the biblical narrative. Adhering to a biblical worldview, however, is more than simply acting according to a set of principles; it is acting as an extension of Christ, demonstrating the character of the Redeemer in every aspect of life. Salvation brings a qualitative change, one that Paul described by contrasting the "old man" with the "new man," where the new man is a renewal of the created image of God (Col 3:10). As a result, the actions of believers are not the result of what they believe but who they are. Their actions are an extension of their renewed personhood in Christ. As a result, an education that promotes the development of a biblical worldview cannot simply be preparatory for future action but must allow for believers to exercise the transforming power of God.

Worldview as Worship advocates that worldview transformation is achieved through expression of the renewed image of God in the life of the believer. It argues that the biblical worldview is not simply a creed or set of propositions to which individuals acquiesce, but it is immensely practical and applicable to all areas of life. It maintains that the biblical worldview is an extension of the life of Christ exhibited through his body—the church. For this reason, worldviews are not simply individual but communal—a shared means of interpreting how the world is and a vision for how the world should be. As a result, in the proper expression of the biblical worldview, the individual works in cooperation with the corporate body of Christ. It contends that while worldviews are communally developed and transformed, they are also lived out individually. Genuine faith is the extension of the life of Christ in the believer, so that the behaviors exhibited by mature and maturing believers are exhibitions of the life of Christ who indwells them. To stifle this expression is to actually suppress the development of the biblical worldview in the lives of growing believers.

In order to present this case, the book has been laid out in three sections. Section 1 is a discussion of the nature of worldview and its relationship to community and to the process of education. Chapter 1 examines the fundamental aspects of a worldview by noting that worldviews serve two foundational functions. The first is that worldviews are *descriptive*: they endow the person and the culture with a perspective that allows a person to make sense of the world. The second is that worldviews serve a *normative* function: they impart a vision of the ideal world and the ideal self. As a result, worldviews provide a means of making judgments about how the world is and, more importantly, how the world should be. The chapter also presents the dynamics of how people develop their initial worldviews, a process that is closely tied to the people around them and the culture in which they were born. As we consider what a worldview is and how it can be changed, we must consider the dynamics of its initial development and the context of the culture in which it was formed. Finally, all worldviews must address certain fundamental questions regarding values, the nature of reality, who human beings are, why there is trouble in the world, and how these answers affect how we live. Chapter 1 addresses each of these concerns as well as the biblical worldview responses to these issues.

While many evangelical writers discuss the issue of worldview, there is no consensus on the meaning of the term. For some the term *worldview* is synonymous, or nearly so, with *philosophy*. For others the idea of worldview as philosophy is too formal and does not account for how people can possess or operate from a worldview they cannot articulate. For these thinkers a worldview appears more like an ideology or general pattern of belief. For a third group, to say that all people have a worldview (or are at least developing one) is to include those individuals, such as children, who neither possess a formal philosophy or ideological perspective on life. These theorists maintain that worldviews are more pretheoretical or perceptual in nature. Chapter 2 examines the relationship between philosophies, ideologies, and worldviews. The chapter addresses the qualitative differences between philosophies, ideologies, and worldviews, and the contention that the process of worldview transformation must consider these qualitative differences in order for the process of transformation to be effective.

Chapter 3 discusses the relationship of worldview to culture. When anthropologists or sociologists examine and describe culture, they use many of the same criteria that are employed by evangelicals to the understanding of worldview. Such similarities aside, while the anthropologist attempts to simply understand a culture, evangelicals often engage in cultural understanding as a means of buffering themselves from its influence or identifying how culture can be transformed through the infusion of biblical principles. Engaging in transformation, however, requires an alternative vision of what the culture should be. Chapter 3 provides a description of the biblical mandate for culture and the role of stewardship as it pertains to the life of the believer. It also examines the views of Abraham Kuyper, a pioneer on the relationship of the biblical worldview to education, and demonstrates that the development of a biblical worldview requires a countercultural response on the part of the church to the dominant worldview of the society.

Chapter 4 addresses the role of schools and schooling in modern societies by asking the question, what are schools for? In modern societies, schools have played two critical roles. The first is *role differentiation*, where schools are used as one of the primary vehicles to determine who has access to the economic positions that provide for higher status, prestige, wealth, and power. The second is *social solidarity*, where society entrusts schools with the responsibility of transmitting the dominant worldview of the culture to young people. Schools serve to promote the society's vision of the world and the individual's place in it. Subsequently, to understand the process of contemporary public education, one must understand the dominant worldview that underlies the process of social solidarity. This chapter presents the essential nature of the modernist worldview and the curriculum and instructional methodologies used in schools today to promote the development of a modernistic worldview in students. In essence, the structure of the curriculum and the types of instructional approaches used in schools are embodiments of the values of modernism. As a result, when Christian schools mirror the patterns of curriculum or the instructional techniques in public schools, they may inadvertently be promoting worldview values that are contrary to the biblical worldview they seek to impart. Thus, section 1 ends with a challenge to Christian educators to consider their curriculum and instructional techniques in light of the embedded values that are found in those techniques.

Section 2 is a presentation of the formative principles of a biblical approach to education that encourages the development of worldview transformation. Built upon the foundation of the cultural mandate presented in chapter 3, this section delineates three principles that serve as a means of developing approaches to curriculum and pedagogy that not only allow for the integration of faith and learning but also provide for the application of faith to life. Chapter 5 examines the principle of education for stewardship and the application of this principle before the Fall. Human beings were provided with stewardship responsibilities over the creation, and this responsibility would have demanded that human beings discover realities about the creation in order to manage and govern it for the glory of God. These responsibilities would have included not only learning about the creation but also developing new technologies and methodologies for its governance. These discoveries would necessarily have been passed on to subsequent generations.

While stewardship implies a level of autonomy on the part of the steward, the good steward acts for the benefit of the owner. This requires a close relationship between the steward and the owner. This chapter examines the relationship that human beings have as stewards before God, noting that human beings were created as dependent upon God in all aspects of life (including cognition) so that faithful stewardship is predicated on a close relationship with God. As a result, education before the Fall would have focused on preparing people to engage in stewardship for the glory and honor of God. This is especially appropriate to the understanding of worldview development given that God created human beings with a keen ability to ascertain how the world works (the descriptive function of worldview) but that human beings are dependent upon God for an appropriate understanding on how the world should be (worldview's normative function). The denial of this dependency creates the situation in which human beings must construct their own understandings of what ought to be, resulting in conditions that violate the stewardship mandate and ultimately dehumanize human beings.

While a number of principles in Scripture can be gleaned to develop a biblical understanding of education before the Fall, the reality of human experience is that the pre-Fall period was a very short interval of time. Before long, humanity violated God's initial command, rebelled against his sovereign authority, and, as a result, introduced sin into the world. The entry of sin had profound effects on all human existence, including the practice of education. Chapter 6 explores the effects of the Fall on education by examining the sin nature and humanity's ability to engage in the cultural mandate. Specifically, as human beings create new technologies, artifacts, or techniques to govern the creation, they do so from a particular vision of the world that originates in the sin nature. As a result, the human proclivity to create culture, a characteristic endowed in humanity by God before the Fall, is now corrupted, so that sinful people embed in their creations their sinful visions of how the world ought to be. These corrupted visions can be understood both individually, where the sinner creates sinful things, and corporately, where sinful people acting in concert embed sinful values into the culture. The chapter examines how contemporary American society embeds a sinful vision of the world into culture by embracing the worldview of modernism. As a worldview, modernism provides a descriptive means of making sense of the world while also providing a vision for how the world ought to be, a vision that is then embedded into every aspect of cultural life.

Yet, despite the Fall, human beings were not divested by God of their responsibility to engage the creation as stewards, but now they find that the practice of faithful stewardship is much more difficult in a sin-laden world. For the believer, this requires dealing with the effects of sin so that the creation can once again be managed for God's glory. To do this requires that believers engage themselves in a "ministry of reconciliation" (2 Cor 5:18). This ministry of reconciliation is the second principle that informs a biblical approach to the development of curriculum and pedagogy. This ministry is fundamental to the process of worldview transformation, wherein the effects of sin are dealt with in a fashion that demonstrates God's original intent for how human beings were designed to operate in the world.

The third formative principle of worldview education prepares students to engage in stewardship and the necessary post-Fall ministry of reconciliation by developing the image of God in people. Chapter 7 examines the relationship of the image of God to worldview education and the way transformative education prepares people to reflect the image of God more thoroughly to others. The chapter opens with a discussion of two views of humanity: the biblical view based on the theology of the Protestant Reformers and the classic view based on the work of Aristotle. The chapter contrasts these two views by demonstrating that the Aristotelian view has reduced humanity to primarily a biological and economic entity, while the biblical view promotes a Godly understanding of the dignity and worth of humankind. This reduction of humanity to a biological and economic entity can be seen in the practice of education in contemporary culture, and an education based on a biblical worldview must be careful to not engage in a similar reduction of humanity. By contrast, biblical Christianity represents the "true humanism" by encouraging the development of the whole person into the individual God created him or her to be. This understanding of the whole person extends beyond the individual, having application for the relationship of human beings one to another. Thus, the image of God cannot be understood simply by comparing those traits that individuals share with God (e.g., reason, will, emotion, etc.), but how God's image is reflected by encouraging communal relationships.

Section 3 extends the principles of stewardship, reconciliation, and developing the image of God and begins to develop an approach to education that will facilitate worldview transformation. Based on these principles, a transformative education must develop and promote an alternative worldview vision to the dominant vision of the secular culture. In this respect, the church must represent a type of countercultural response, promoting those aspects of the culture that are biblically appropriate and confronting those that have sin embedded in their development and practice. The need for the church to develop a countercultural response to the dominant secular culture, however, presents another problem in developing an approach to transformative worldview education. Worldviews are not simply philosophical approaches to understanding the world; they are always related to the practice of living in the world. In this sense, the evangelical approach to worldview is one that seeks to develop a response, both for the individual and for the church as a whole, to the surrounding culture and its influence; yet, even a cursory look at evangelical churches, as well as Christian schools and universities, reveals that believers do not demonstrate unanimity in this regard. Some churches and schools are more culturally engaging, others more separatist, while still others emphasize the need to develop discernment in individual believers in order for them to determine what would be appropriate for them as they seek to walk with God in the world. How can believers and churches, which essentially maintain the same doctrinal standards and tenaciously hold to the major tenets of the faith and the authority of Scripture, differ so dramatically in the application of those principles to living in the world?

Chapter 8 surveys this issue by describing three approaches to Christian education—separation, discernment, and engagement—noting the characteristics of each and the effect of their implementation on the practice of worldview education. The chapter concludes by making the case that the engagement model—or a model that seeks to prepare believers to transform culture—may be the most appropriate model for the conditions in which the contemporary church finds itself today.

The reality for the church or Christian school is that not all those who participate in the community of faith are believers who are indwelled by the Holy Spirit. The church and the Christian school are transformative communities, dependent upon the work of the Holy Spirit to bring about this transformation. While educators can engage students in the process of transformation, it is the work of the Holy Spirit to bring about worldview change. The presence of unbelievers within the community of faith presents two particular challenges for developing an approach to transformative worldview education.

First, there must be a definition of the term *Christian education*. Is it something that only a believer can possess (since only people can be educated and only people can be "Christians"), or can it be reflected independently via the curriculum and instructional techniques? If a Christian education can be presented independent of the spiritual condition of the student—that is, it simply reflects a biblical perspective—to what extent does the unbeliever receive (if they cannot "possess") a Christian education? Second, how do the principles of stewardship, reconciliation, and the development of the image of God apply to the unbeliever being educated in a transformative worldview community?

Chapter 9 addresses the doctrine of *common grace* and the relationship of this doctrine to the practice of Christian schooling. In regard to stewardship, common grace can be understood in light of the biblical mandate to be stewards that was given to all humanity before creation, a mandate not revoked as a result of the Fall, so even unbelievers can benefit from understanding stewardship from a biblical perspective. The principle of reconciliation notes that cultural transformation involves demonstrating the value and utility of God's approach to acting in the world as compared to the sin-laden approaches of fallen humanity, so even unbelievers can benefit from participating in the world according to the principles of God. Finally, even though fallen individuals are not restored to the place God intended for humanity, the biblical worldview exhibits a more dignified view of humanity than its secular counterparts. As a result, even unbelievers experience a greater sense of their worth and dignity as human beings (and can treat others with comparable worth and dignity) by being educated from a biblical perspective.

Chapter 10 concludes the book by providing foundational principles for creating a transformative worldview community that goes from theory to practice. Having observed that worldviews are qualitatively different from philosophies, the transformative worldview community must not only seek to understand the biblical worldview but also to put it into practice. Biblically, the process of putting faith into practice is often referred to as worship. Paul, in his writings, never uses the traditional Greek word for worship (*proskyneo*, to fall down in submission). Rather, in Romans 12:1–2 he refers to worship as the process of presenting oneself as a "living and holy sacrifice" (*thusia*, an offered sacrifice), which is "your spiritual service of worship" (*latreia*, service to God or others). When advocates of worldview transformation focus on Romans 12:2 ("be transformed by the renewing of your mind") they often fail to consider that Paul notes that this transformation takes place within the context of worship that serves others. Paul concludes the book of Romans by explaining that the type of service he has advocated in 12:1–2 involves the believer's relationship to the church, to the society and government, and to other believers. In essence, Paul's call to worship is one in which the church seeks to make God famous before a watching world. The practice of presenting oneself to God as a living sacrifice, or emptying oneself for the service of others, is based in the principle of *agape* love that is foundational to the entire Christian ethic of life. Once *agape* is understood as the foundational ethic for the believer's practice in the world, the practice of worldview transformation demands an educational community that will prepare people to use their stewardship resources and talents in a manner that provides for the betterment and well-being of others.

This understanding means that Christian education, in general, and worldview transformation specifically, must move from a model based in the student metaphor to one of apprenticeship—where learning is practiced with the purpose of seeking to emulate the Master. This model focuses on the role of the teacher as the experienced and mature believer and the students as the engaged and active apprentices. It is a model that not only encourages the integration of faith, learning, and life with the academic disciplines, but also encourages this integration across disciplines, doing so by engaging students in the application of stewardship, reconciliation, and the development of the image of God to real-world situations. As such, the model also encourages the utilization of the varied gifts and talents possessed by students across academic disciplines, promoting the practices of cooperation and collaboration as a means of utilizing the diversity of abilities found in the community of faith. In this respect, the model seeks to emulate the body of Christ as described by Paul in 1 Corinthians 12, where the Holy Spirit provides the church a diversity of gifts for the edification of the entire body.

My hope is that readers, as they become aware of the qualitative nature of worldviews, will begin to contemplate not only how worldview is developed and transformed in their students but also how it has developed and can be transformed in their own lives. Even though writing a book assumes a level of expertise, my motivation to investigate and write about worldview change has been prodded more by my need and desire to work out my own transformation than to claim any particular expertise. In this regard, I acknowledge my own dependency on God to provide me a glimpse of his reality. My desire is that this presentation will stir sufficient discussion among biblical educators to discern a "more excellent way" of engaging in worldview transformation.

Recognizing how much power our initial worldviews have and how recalcitrant they are to change should propel us back to Christ and our dependency on him. Recognizing the recalcitrance placed on us by our initial worldviews in regard to how we think and act should not stifle the motivation to engage in worldview transformation but enhance it. Understanding the strength and the process of the initial development of our worldviews should help us better understand the conditions under which we, as educators, can engage our students to facilitate worldview transformation. As believers, the body of Christ in this present age, we are called to be his stewards, his agents of reconciliation, his exhibition of what it means to be created in the image of God before a watching world. Only in Christ can we expect to bear much fruit. Only in Christ can we fulfill our obligation to be both "salt and light." And only in Christ can we expect to fulfill these obligations in the way expressed by the prophet Micah:

> He has told you, O man, what is good;
> And what does the Lord require of you
> But to do justice, to love kindness,
> And to walk humbly with your God? (Mic 6:8)

SECTION ONE

Defining Worldview and Its Development

1

Worldviewing: What Is a Worldview?

The most important things . . . we can know about a man is what he takes for granted, and the most elemental and important facts about a society are those that are seldom debated and generally regarded as settled.

—Louis Wirth, *Ideology and Utopia*

IT IS A WARM August morning, and like thousands of Christian schools throughout the country, the administration, faculty, and staff of Mt. Carmel Christian School gathers in the chapel to begin its annual faculty orientation sessions. Many of the teachers arrive early to help themselves to coffee, juice, and donuts and to take time to get reacquainted with colleagues they have not seen since the end of the previous school year. The five new faculty members, who were required to report to school two days earlier for New Faculty Orientation, huddle together feeling a bit anxious and out of place. For most of them, this is their first teaching job. Occasionally, a veteran member of the faculty or one of the administrators or staff they met earlier in the week greets them and welcomes them to the school. Most of the teachers know that introductions will be coming, so they wait until the group introduction to make personal acquaintance with the new members.

Mt. Carmel is an established Christian school of about six hundred students in grades kindergarten through twelve. The school has been in existence for just over twenty-five years, starting out as an extension of a local church and eventually growing into its own facilities, becoming an independent, nondenominational school about twenty years ago. Mt. Carmel is directed by Dr. Sage Solomon, who has served as superintendent for the last seven years, having started as a teacher in the early years of the school. The rest of the administrative team consists of Dr. Paul Paraclete, the high school principal, and the elementary school principal, Mr. Edward Edify. At last spring's annual Faculty-Board Dinner a number of the faculty received twenty- and twenty-five-year service awards, a testimony to the stability and reputation of the school. Mt. Carmel is known in the area for its excellent facilities, its high academic standards, and its diligence in teaching all subject areas in light of the Word of God. This year's five new teachers represent something of an anomaly. The school has not had this many new teachers in several years.

Faculty Orientation Week is fairly standard at Mt. Carmel. Veteran teachers who have experienced this week several times wonder why they must go through a review of policies and procedures each year, and sometimes they find their minds wandering to the more pressing concerns of getting their classrooms ready for the start of classes next week. There are lesson plans to write, boxes to unpack, bulletins boards to put up, and a myriad of other tasks that need to be done to get the school year off to a good start. Each year, however, the administration plans some type of in-service activity for orientation week. Dr. Solomon places a high priority on the professional development of his faculty. In the past he has arranged for experts to present training sessions on teaching methods, critical thinking, cooperative learning strategies, curriculum alignment, assessment, and other relevant topics in an attempt to enhance the expertise of the faculty. While not all the presenters have been dynamic or practical, for the most part, the faculty appreciates Solomon's efforts and have benefited from the in-service sessions.

After a time of praise and devotions, Solomon addresses the group: "Each year during our faculty orientation we try to address some aspect of school development in order to enhance the ministry of Mt. Carmel Christian School. Every spring, the administrators discuss the needs and vision of the school and consider how we can best prepare our students to receive the Lord's direction for their lives. This year, after much thought and prayer, we have decided to focus on the development of a Christian worldview in our students. In order to facilitate this we will be changing our normal in-service format this year. We will not only discuss the development of a Christian worldview during this week, but we will also meet several times throughout the year to evaluate our own understanding and ability to teach from a biblical perspective. I hope you are as excited as Mr. Edify, Dr. Paraclete, and I are about the possibilities that the Lord has for us."

Arnie Antiquity, secondary social studies teacher and twenty-year teaching veteran of the school, listens attentively. After earning his degree from a Christian liberal arts university, teaching for twenty years at Mt. Carmel, and attending annual Christian school teacher conventions, he knows that developing a Christian worldview in students is important and is continually presented as a goal of Christian school education. What else are they going to tell us? Arnie thinks. As far as his own teaching, Arnie is fairly confident that he already presents history to his students from a Christian perspective. Like all the teachers at Mt. Carmel, he uses textbooks and materials by Christian publishers and is careful to point out when historical figures have either embraced or violated biblical truth and what the historical and ongoing consequences are. He glances at many of his colleagues, making quick evaluations of their teaching abilities and commitment to Christian education, and is convinced that they also understand and present their content from a biblical perspective. Arnie wonders if the emphasis on worldview is a response to the unusual number of new teachers, thinking this may be a way to reaffirm the "Mt. Carmel way of doing things." In any case, Arnie then realizes that Solomon's comment about meeting "several times throughout the year" explains why the academic calendar has two in-service days planned for each semester.

Solomon continues: "In order to facilitate our discussions, we have asked Dr. Venerable Wise from Reformation Christian College to assist us this year. Many of you know Dr. Wise from our teacher conventions, and some of you were students of Dr. Wise when you attended Reformation Christian. He teaches Philosophy of Education and some of the methods courses. I am sure his presentations will significantly assist us, and we will benefit from his instruction—Dr. Wise."

Wise walks to the front of the chapel and begins to address the faculty: "In order to get our discussion started this morning, I would like you to break into groups of three or four teachers. Please organize your small groups to include both elementary and secondary teachers as well as one of the new teachers. Your task is to answer the question, 'What do we mean by a Christian worldview?'"

Arnie quickly looks around the chapel in an attempt to join some of his friends. There are a few minutes of confusion. He thinks Wise's direction to distribute the new faculty among the groups confirms his hypothesis about socializing them into the Mt. Carmel culture. The elementary teachers, because of common interests and the collegiality developed from sharing the same students and a common schedule, sit together. The secondary teachers begin to do the same. A few teachers approach the new faculty and invite them to join a group. The administrators move throughout the room helping pair up new faculty members with veterans and blending secondary and elementary teachers. Arnie pairs with his friend Byron Bunsen, the high school science teacher, and the two wait, knowing that one of the administrators will see them together and pair them with some of the elementary faculty. Sure enough, Edify brings Donna Dewey, one of the sixth grade teachers, and Rita Rookie, the new third grade teacher to join them. After about five minutes, the groups are formed and they begin to engage the task.

Being the veteran of the group, Arnie feels compelled to lead the discussion. "What does it mean to develop a Christian worldview in our students?" Arnie asks, not quite repeating Wise's question verbatim. "I know I have always tried to do this in my classes," he continues. "In presenting history as 'His Story,' I try to show how God works in the development of history to bring about his plan."

Byron chimes in, "Teaching science is a natural, I think. I can focus on creation: how God made all things. I can contrast the biblical creation view of the origin of life in Genesis with the evolutionary model. I can also show that God is a God of order and that the universe has been created as an orderly system."

"Having to teach all the subjects makes integrating a biblical worldview more difficult for me," admits Donna. "In some areas I feel that I can teach a biblical worldview fairly easily. Obviously, in Bible this is easier, but in other areas, such as science or mathematics, I tend to struggle. Maybe it's because, as an elementary teacher, I received little subject area training in some of the academic disciplines to feel confident of my ability to do integration. In other content areas I find it hard to make relevant and meaningful connections for my students. For example, in math class, apart from stating that 'God is a God of logic and order' or that 'math is the language that God used in creating the universe,' I find very few ways of applying the biblical worldview to the subject. Some of the examples given in the textbook seem contrived, and make little sense to my students. For example, when presenting measurement, the text suggests word problems to convert the value of 238 sparrows from farthings to cents using the farthing reference from the King James

Version in Matthew 10:29, or to convert pints of oil to its equivalent one-fourth hin from Exodus 29:40."

Rita has been quiet to this point, but feeling a bit more comfortable with her new colleagues and wanting to participate in the group, she eases into the dialogue. "I know that I am new, but I recall a discussion in college about this subject." Her colleagues' attentiveness makes Rita more assertive. "I remember one of my professors saying that the purpose of a Christian education should be to prepare people to become Christians that can take their faith and live in a world that is hostile to the idea of truth. It seems this would also be relevant to teaching from a biblical worldview."

Byron piggy-backs on Rita's comments, adding, "Last year we had several disciplinary problems with students. Nothing particularly serious occurred, but I recall in teachers' meetings that a number of the faculty expressed disappointment that there seemed to be little difference between students at Mt. Carmel, who profess to be Christians and were receiving a Christian education, and typical students in the public schools. For many of our students, evidence of 'fruit' or spiritual development is lacking in their lives."

Arnie remembers those discussions and assumes this apparent lack of spiritual development might have provided some of the impetus for the administration to focus on worldview development. He then adds, "Like you say, Byron, the behavior stuff was not serious, and, to some extent, it could be overlooked because kids are kids. But I agree that the attitudes and values of our students don't seem to be much different from students who don't attend Mt. Carmel. We are constantly having issues over appropriate dress, music, and language. However, what bothers me more than their behavior is that our students' goals and aspirations are not much different from their public school counterparts. Most want to go to college to get a good job and have a comfortable lifestyle. They see the necessity of doing just enough to get a good grade and feel compelled to learn only what will be 'on the test.' When they are in church mode, they give all the right answers, but when you ask them to think biblically, they really struggle."

"I recall reading that Christian schooling is like operating a greenhouse," adds Donna. "Just like a greenhouse, the Christian school acts as a safe environment where students can engage in the study of the world, learn to discern what is right and wrong, embrace what is permissible or God-honoring, and choose to avoid those things that are not. Like young plants, our students need to be nurtured until they are strong enough to survive, and hopefully thrive, in an often hostile environment."

"Well, I am a bit uncomfortable with the analogy of comparing our student to plants," Arnie responds. "Still, I think you have addressed an important point. Maybe key to developing a biblical worldview in our students is defining what they need to thrive in the world. I also have read the greenhouse analogy, and those writers that use it are not unanimous in what it means. For some it is the avoidance of culture. For others the Christian school becomes the place for learning to discern right from wrong, biblical from unbiblical. Others use it to describe an environment for developing in students the ability to go out into a hostile, secular environment and make an impact on the culture for Christ." Arnie pauses for a moment, his colleagues waiting for him to gather his thoughts. "Maybe developing a biblical worldview in our students will require us to identify what specific beliefs and ideas a Christian must embrace to be able to think biblically and what it means for a Christian to thrive in the world."

Discussions such as these are common in circles where Christian educators, whether they are Christian school teachers, pastors, or youth ministry workers, are seeking to understand how their worldview influences not only their teaching but also the development of a biblical worldview in their students. Belief is foundational to all educational endeavors. Whether a teacher can articulate it or is conscious of it, these beliefs influence how teachers structure and practice their craft. These beliefs influence the planning of daily lessons, the development of goals and objectives, and the planning and implementing of instructional methods to meet these goals. Good teachers have beliefs about the importance of education and its ability to change and enhance the lives of their students. It can be argued that when teachers lose their belief in the ability of education to transform and enhance lives they also lose the power to influence students.

The purpose of education in general and the craft of teaching specifically require a vision of who students will be when they have completed their course of study. The process requires an evaluation of who the students are now, and who they should eventually become. This type of evaluation drives the educational process and often prompts calls for educational reform. It is a process that requires not only an assessment of the students specifically but also an evaluation of the society and the role students will eventually assume. Thus, education is predicated on a vision, one not only for the students but also for the entire society. In this sense, education provides the knowledge, skills, and dispositions needed to prepare students to be productive contributors to society. Understood this way, education is driven by a sense of the way things are and by a vision of the way things should be.

This foundational belief in the power of education to form the individual is not simply a belief among educators but one shared by society as a whole. The history of education in the United States reveals the utopian belief of those who developed American public schools that public education could be a tool to craft a more perfect society. As the "common school" movement in the United States approaches the end of its second century, the beliefs of the original architects of public schools—that schools could be used to help resolve many of the fundamental political, economic, and social issues facing the nation—are expressed with as much vigor today as they were nearly two hundred years ago. When Lyndon Johnson sought to achieve the "Great Society" in the 1960s, declaring war on poverty and the problems it produced, he said, "The answer to all our national problems comes down to a single word: education."[1] In the early twentieth century, social engineers sought to use schools as the institution to perfect the nation by "consciously directing the evolution of the society."[2]

More recent calls for educational reform share a similar belief. Whether these reforms are based in the Reagan administration's recommendations in *A Nation at Risk*, the first Bush and the Clinton administrations' *Goals 2000* agenda,[3] or more recently in George W. Bush's *No Child Left Behind* legislation or Barack Obama's Race to the Top ini-

---

1. Perkinson, *Imperfect Panacea*, i.
2. Tyack and Cuban, *Tinkering toward Utopia*, 2.
3. *Goals 2000: Educate America Act* (PL 103-227), signed in 1994.

tiative, all are based on a belief that schools can be used as a mechanism for the nation to meet the fundamental challenges facing society. Foundational to the formulation of these reform proposals, both past and present, is an evaluation of the current state of schools and whether the nation's vision for the future is being accomplished. Key to any such assessment is an evaluation of how things are and a vision for the way things should be.

At the core of these calls for reform is the issue of worldview. When teachers assess student performance or potential, when they identify student strengths and weaknesses and interpret particular behaviors as acceptable or not, they do so from a set of assumptions that allows them to understand and evaluate the student. Implicit in their frame of reference is that certain types of potential and levels of performance, abilities or talents, and behaviors are of greater value than others. Those of greater value are to be encouraged and developed, while the marginal or less desirable ones are discouraged. Students are encouraged to develop behavioral patterns and, more importantly, ways of thinking that mirror the expectations and values of the society. The societal appraisal of these desired abilities and talents, expectations and values, as well as the definition of acceptable levels of performance, forms the basis of the curriculum. For example, each society must decide which academic disciplines will receive the limited instructional time, energy, and resources available and which will receive less attention or be ignored altogether. When political, social, and economic leaders decry the performance of students and teachers in public schools and advocate reform strategies that will allow schools to prepare students to become better contributors to society, they do so from assumptions about how schools should work and what skills, abilities, and behaviors students must possess to be contributing members of the society. At the core of a society's collective ability to assess the relative worth of these factors is a worldview.

As James Olthuis writes, worldviews are "a vision 'of' life and the world [and] simultaneously a vision 'for' life and the world."[4] Worldviews provide a dual focus. They are *descriptive* in that they allow one to assess what the world is like. They are also *normative*, allowing the formulation of an idea of what things should look like and what actions might be taken to bring about the desired end. For example, when parents conclude that a child has done something wrong and must be disciplined, their actions will include

1. an assessment of the child's inappropriate behavior (descriptive) based on a standard (normative);

2. an appraisal of what behaviors are acceptable and should be encouraged for the present and the future (normative);

3. what corrective actions are acceptable before God and society (descriptive) to bring about the desired behavior.

Underlying these evaluations are tacit assumptions about the child's value as a human being, the way the world operates (both presently and in the future), the reasons for the misbehavior, and the effectiveness of various means of correction. All of these are determined by worldview.

---

4. Olthuis, "On Worldviews," 156.

While a worldview allows people to make descriptive and normative judgments about the world, worldviews are not simply the possession of individuals. Brian Walsh and J. Richard Middleton contend that worldviews are a communal way of thinking about how the world is and how it should be, and it can be argued that true community is only possible when there is a shared vision of the world.[5] The writer of Proverbs notes this idea of a corporate vision for life when he writes, "Where there is no vision, the people are unrestrained" (Prov 29:18). It is this understanding of the corporate nature of worldview that causes Christians to struggle with being in the world but not of the world (John 17:13–16), and leads Paul to write that Christians need to be transformed by the renewing of their minds so that they can know and do the will of God (Rom 12:1–2). While Americans pride themselves on being individualists, believing that they are free to decide for themselves how they should think, people from other nations observe that Americans generally think like other Americans. In other words, the range of possible ways an individual comes to understand the way the world is and the way the world should be is framed by a particular set of assumptions that non-Americans can categorize as "American" thinking.

For Christian educators, and for the evangelical community as a whole, understanding the communal nature of a worldview underscores the frustration and difficulty that is often experienced when attempting to develop a biblical worldview in ourselves and in our students. By being in the world but not of the world, Christ tells us that while we are physically present in the world, we need to separate ourselves from the influences of perceiving and evaluating life characterized by the world. By urging believers to be transformed by the renewing of their minds, Paul assumes that the influences of the world have already affected us and that our ability to understand and do the will of God is compromised until we are able to free ourselves from the prevailing ways of thinking in the culture and to bring our own values, attitudes, and beliefs into conformity with biblical truth. In short, as Christians we must develop a way of viewing our culture from a scriptural perspective. In so doing, the church must also realize that developing a biblical worldview may well mean swimming upstream against the common or typical descriptive and normative visions of life that are accepted as normal.

Worldviews provide, for the majority of individuals in a society, not only a descriptive and normative vision of life, but also a framework for developing ways of operating in the world. Worldviews represent a "lens" for looking at life and a method for determining appropriate ways to function in the world. For example, all societies must develop institutions and social norms to address the realities of living in a communal context. The principles of how those institutions and social norms are developed can be based on a biblical understanding of those aspects of life or on some other vision for life, but a society cannot ignore these aspects of social reality. In similar fashion, all societies must develop norms and institutions for the education and development of the next generation. Failure on the part of society to prepare the next generation to be contributing members would constitute an overall threat to the society and to the coherence of the worldview on which the very definition of a contributing member is based. Whether a society chooses to address this reality

---

5. Walsh and Middleton, *Transforming Vision*, 32.

through a formal institution like school or through some other avenue will depend on the descriptive and normative understandings of the society, that is, on its worldview.

For evangelical Christianity to function as an appropriate expression of the biblical worldview, it must address the issue of educating young people simply because the character of communal life makes education a feature that cannot be ignored. In order for the biblical worldview to serve as a coherent vision for all of life, it must provide for a description of how the world is and normatively a vision for how the world should be. This description must then lead to a definition of what it means to be an educated citizen of the kingdom and an appropriate contributor to the society in which God has placed us. Failure to accomplish these tasks would represent a threat to the internal coherence of the biblical worldview (or at least how evangelicals formulate and practice it). This formulation must also provide Christian educators with the tools necessary to develop models of curriculum, means of instruction, and types and aspects of evaluation to assess the effectiveness of their teaching and their schools in light of the biblical worldview. In so doing, the biblical worldview serves the normative function of providing a vision and direction for what Christian schooling should be and should become.

In the process of developing a biblical approach to education, however, we must acknowledge and respect the tremendous power of the surrounding culture with its non-biblical worldview. As believers who are still "in the world," we must be aware of the impact that the values, attitudes, and practices of the surrounding culture have had on Christian schooling (i.e., organizational structure, curriculum considerations, teaching methodologies, etc.). As believers who are also called to be "not of this world," we must be constantly mindful of the encroachment of nonbiblical values on our schools and consciously embrace and promote a curriculum and methodology consistent with a biblical vision for what a Christian education should be. To accomplish this, we must develop an understanding of the type of education that a Christian school should provide—one that prepares students to be active participants in a community of believers living as responsible citizens in the world, a community devoted to the development of a biblical perception and understanding of the world and committed to a biblical vision and practice in all areas of life.

This is a book on worldview and education, specifically the biblical worldview as it relates to biblical education and Christian schooling. While it will be important in our discussion of this relationship to adequately define the concept (the fundamental components of a worldview) and provide a brief statement about the biblical formulation of these components, it is not intended to be a full development of the biblical worldview. Rather, we will examine the role Christian schools specifically, and Christian education in general, can have in the overall communication of a biblical worldview to the society at large and in the development of a biblical worldview in students. As we shall see, the power of any worldview to adequately fulfill its descriptive and normative functions will depend, in part, on its internal coherence and its ability to address all aspects of human life and endeavor.

WHAT IS A WORLDVIEW AND HOW DID I GET ONE?

A worldview orients us to life. As such, a worldview is a given; it is not a luxury, but a necessity. In essence, to not have a worldview would result in a consistent disorientation to life. While animals behave from instinct, human beings must choose how they will live, and their behavior reflects the choices made that are the results of a particular vision of life or sense of perspective.[6] For example, honey bees are born knowing the "dance" that communicates where the source of nectar can be found to the other bees of the hive without ever having to learn it. In contrast, to acquire the folk dances of a human culture a young person needs be formally taught the dances, which are reflections of the cultural development of that particular group.

The orientation to life that a worldview provides allows the members of a culture to see certain realities as significant, and to ignore or be oblivious to other ones. Worldviews serve as a means of placing the occurrences of life in perspective; they serve as a type of lens through which individuals view the world. Worldviews are also a type of filter, a mechanism for attaching significance to things deemed important and worthy of attention, while ignoring those things of little importance. In this sense a worldview provides a means of integrating all of life and provides a framework to interpret life or make sense of experiences. Worldviews also allow individuals to judge life according to an ideal of what life should be.

This dual purpose is reflected in the definitions of worldview by many Christian thinkers. Ronald Nash describes a worldview as "a conceptual scheme by which we consciously or unconsciously place or fit everything we believe and by which we interpret and judge reality."[7] Nicholas Wolterstorff writes, "a people's world view is their way of thinking about life and the world, coupled with the values they set for themselves in the context of that way of thinking."[8] Richard Wright notes that worldviews serve as "a comprehensive framework of beliefs that helps us to interpret what we see and experience and also gives direction in the choices that we make as we live out our lives."[9]

Wolterstorff notes that in any specific academic discipline, the theories used that govern acceptable thinking and practice must correspond to two criteria. The first criterion, which Wolterstorff identifies as *data beliefs*, relates to the areas of knowledge acquisition: what will be permitted and used as acceptable knowledge or information. For example, in thinking about the resurrection of Christ there have been a number of theories that have tried to explain the resurrection as something other than God actually raising Christ from the dead (e.g., the theft theory). These theories are more acceptable to a person who does not believe in God or does not believe in miracles because prior experience and other data suggest that people who die are not resurrected. Thus, data suggesting the validity of someone stealing the body of Christ from the tomb is more acceptable than data supporting the conclusion of a bodily resurrection. To the Bible-believing Christian, however,

---

6. Ibid., 31.

7. Nash, *Faith and Reason*, 24.

8. Quoted in Walsh and Middleton, *Transforming Vision*, 9–10.

9. Quoted in Phillips and Brown, *Making Sense of Your World*, 29.

data suggesting the literal bodily resurrection of Christ is more easily accepted because, as Wolterstorff notes, all data beliefs are subject or accountable to a second criterion, a larger body of theories or ways of looking at the world, which exists in the background called *control beliefs*.[10]

Wolterstorff continues by stating that control beliefs are dominated by faith-based assumptions, that they are taken for granted, rarely debated, and form the basis of people's values. Control beliefs are thus presuppositions or assumptions made beforehand that essentially cannot be proven or are taken to be true without having to be defended or supported. Returning to the example of the resurrection, a man who could be labeled a naturalist would have difficulty accepting data that supports a bodily resurrection of Christ because his control beliefs may deny the existence of God (and thus there cannot be a God to raise Christ from the dead); or he may deny the existence of miracles. Evangelical Christians, whose control beliefs include the existence of an omnipotent God who reserves the right to intervene in human history when he so chooses, have little difficulty accepting data that suggests Christ's bodily resurrection. It is through these control beliefs that Wolterstorff says humans interpret and make meaning of the world. It is also these control beliefs and the values derived from them that are reinforced by a particular communal group that help constitute a person's worldview.

The question then becomes, how do one's control beliefs come to be? Developmental psychologists have long understood that children, even at the earliest ages, are engaged in the process of attempting to make sense of the world around them. Jean Piaget viewed children as naturally curious about their world and in the process of trying to understand the world by actively seeking out information to help them make sense of it. For Piaget, their curiosity causes children to initiate actions or engage in personal experiments, wherein they manipulate things, observe, and interpret the effects. Because children were observed to engage in this process, Piaget used the analogy of children as "little scientists," orchestrating a process whereby they casually (and later purposefully) view things that occur, develop crude hypotheses, and then engage in further experimentation and variation to formulate a more complex understanding of their world. For Piaget, the development of a person's understanding of the world and, by extension, the development of that person's worldview is, for the most part, an individual and active process. W. Gary Phillips and William Brown note, "Worldviews are never passive; they are by their nature confrontational. My worldview is a confrontation of my presence in the world. I must orient myself to my world and make sense of it or lose the desire to exist as a human being."[11]

The Russian developmental psychologist Lev Vygotsky tempers this highly individual or autonomous process of cognitive development by noting that complex mental processes, of which the development of worldview would qualify, begin as social activities, having their roots in social interactions. Vygotsky believed that the development of one's understanding of the world is mediated through interaction with people that are more knowledgeable and competent in the world. This process starts with the parents and

10. Wolterstorff, *Reason within the Bounds of Religion*, 63.
11. Phillips and Brown, *Making Sense of Your World*, 29.

the family and, over time, is extended to the members of the immediate community (e.g., other adults, teachers, peers, etc.) and then to the society at large. For example, newborns are ignorant of the meaning of things that they encounter in the world and are dependent upon their parents and others to help them understand the importance of things and incorporate these into their understanding. Through a process that Vygotsky called *internalization*, children take in knowledge from their social contexts (which would constitute a type of *data belief*), as well as the significance of that knowledge and the value of certain things (which would serve as a type of *control belief*), and these become part of their individual way of thinking about the world. Vygotsky notes:

> In the buzzing confusion that surrounds the infant during the first few months of her life, parents assist her by pointing and carrying the child close to objects and place of adaptive significance (toys, refrigerator, cupboard, playpen), thus helping the child to ignore other relevant features of the environment (such adult objects as books, tools, and so on). This socially mediated attention develops into the child's more independent and voluntary attention, which she will come to use to classify her surroundings.[12]

For example, children may watch how their parents discuss beliefs (e.g., of politics, religion, or the relative merits of chocolate versus vanilla ice cream) and through this process not only learn how to argue for their beliefs, but also learn to value particular ways of arguing. That is, they may deem "good" arguments as those based in logic and substantiated by facts or those that are made with the most force, persuasion, or appeal to emotion. Vygotsky also noted that the types of tools that individuals use in a culture, how they use them, and for what purpose all provide a set of fundamental data that reflect the overall value system of the society. When children learn to text message, they not only learn how to send messages to friends, but they also become socialized into the fundamental values of speed and efficiency that are found in the culture that develops such a technology. The sense of priority and purpose that significant people around children attach to objects, time, ideas, and so on eventually become internalized and become their own way of viewing the world. As Vygotsky wrote, "every function in a child's cultural development appears twice: first, on the social level and later on the individual level; first between people (interpsychological) and then inside the child (intrapsychological)."[13]

This is not to say that everything human beings perceive or their entire understanding of the world is determined solely by or predicated solely on the culture into which they are born. The great debate among philosophers of knowledge in the eighteenth century was whether the mind was an instrument for understanding or using real world experiences (as expressed in the views of British empiricists like John Locke and David Hume) or an instrument designed to organize and discover reality (as proposed by the Continental rationalists such as René Descartes and Gottfried Wilhelm Leibniz).

The gestalt psychologists of the early twentieth century emphasized that human beings have certain inherent mental processes that predispose them to perceive and or-

---

12. Vygotsky, *Mind in Society*, 128.
13. Ibid., 56.

ganize information in similar and predictable ways. Gestalt psychologists proposed that certain principles or patterns of perception are common to all human beings regardless of their cultural background. These patterns of perception allow human beings to organize their experiences, to create structured wholes that are greater than the sum of their parts. For example, a series of lights going off in a particular order in reality are single lights flashing at predetermined intervals. Looking at them, however, a person perceives a flow of light or motion, so it appears that the light is moving in a particular direction, say from left to right. From observations such as these, gestalt psychologists concluded that human beings, irrespective of their culture, are given to perceive things in ways that may not constitute what is truly there. Thus, gestalt theorists have noted that perception is often different from reality. What these perceptions provide are the basic units or building blocks from which people organize their understanding of the world.

Vygotsky's theory indicates that cultures take these basic perceptions of the world and organize them in ways that allow them, as groups, to explain and develop cultural tools to interact with the world in particular ways. As such, the ways in which individuals interact with the world are highly tied to the culture in which they have been raised.

Both Piaget and Vygotsky emphasize the importance of social interaction in cognitive development, but from different perspectives. Piaget believed that interaction with the world (including others) created a sense of disequilibrium, a cognitive conflict that motivates individuals to change their understanding of the world in order to minimize or alleviate that conflict. This cognitive conflict, which Piaget labeled *cognitive dissonance*, is uncomfortable, creating the desire for resolution. For Piaget, the development of understanding is based on the processes used to reconcile the cognitive conflicts created by interaction with the world. A person's current ways of understanding the world may be insufficient to adequately comprehend a new set of circumstances or ideas. The resolution of these conflicts results in cognitive changes that will serve to comprehend future events or ideas. To Piaget, cognitive development (and we will claim worldview development) has its source in the reconciliation of these conflicts.

Vygotsky, on the other hand, suggests that cognitive development is fostered by social interactions with people who are more capable or advanced in their thinking—for a child, people such as parents and teachers. For Vygotsky, the world and people in the world provide many of the situations or conflicts that must be resolved if individuals are to develop cognitively. Piaget would agree; however, Vygotsky goes further in noting that the ways that human beings resolve these situations, the *tools* they use to mediate or resolve these conflicts, are also provided and modeled by those they view as more competent than themselves, and thus they are assisted in their cognitive development though their social and culture relationships.

These tools to which Vygotsky refers—including ways of thinking, the language or speech and thought, value systems, etc.—form the basis from which individuals develop solutions to these conflicts. Because people from a similar background use similar cultural tools to develop their understanding of the world, they begin to develop a communal identity—whether it be national, ethnic, religious, socio-economic, etc.—which helps to account for why people of similar backgrounds tend to have similar ways of thinking and similar value systems. For example, Vygotsky and Alexander Luria noted that literate and nonliterate cultures tend to think about the world differently and that many of those differences are tied to language. When shown pictures of a hammer, hatchet, saw, and log, members of literate cultures tended to group hatchet, saw and hammer together, noting that all were "tools." Nonliterate cultures, often lacking the abstract concept "tools," would group objects based on concrete or nonabstract factors, so "log" would be included with the hammer, hatchet, and saw since "tools" do not exist independent of their use on the log. For reasons such as these Vygotsky concluded that language plays a fundamental role in how people in a culture come to think about and perceive the world around them.[14]

For Vygotsky, because factors such as language and other cultural tools for interacting with the world are provided to people by their culture, the social mind has primacy over the individual mind in a unique way. Society is the bearer of a cultural heritage without which the development of the individual mind would not be possible. Peter Berger and Thomas Lickmann also note this relationship, stating that the reality of life is intersubjective, that it is shared with others.[15] Berger and Lickmann believe that members of a culture assume that there is a common knowledge shared by others, so similar significance is attached to certain things.

When others do not possess this common knowledge, which may be true of those traveling to a foreign culture, a type of culture shock may well occur. For example, in an unfamiliar culture a tourist may experience an inability to communicate with others since they do not know the language. There can be other types of mental dissonance created from a lack of intersubjective knowledge. In some cultures two men walking down the street arm-in-arm would be viewed as perfectly normal; a member of their culture would probably take little note of it. For many Americans the same situation might appear unusual, causing them to take a keener interest (descriptive). Similarly, people of a particular culture tend to share similar beliefs regarding what constitutes the "good life" and what should be prioritized (or minimized) in terms of an orientation toward the future, the value of the individual, the characteristics of a "good person," and so on (normative). The idea of a shared cultural heritage that underlies the development of the mind in Vygotsky's theory or the development of an intersubjectivity of reality proposed by Berger and Lickmann underlies the communal or corporate nature of worldview thinking.

The purpose in referencing Piaget and Vygotsky, both developmental psychologists whose theories are rarely attached to the development of worldview, is to emphasize both the passive (or receptive) and the active, dynamic natures of worldview development. All people possess a worldview; its development begins at birth through our primarily receptive interaction with the social environment. While we are active agents that initiate interaction with the world (as indicated by Piaget), the resolutions of those interactions tend to be structured for us by the cultural context into which we are born (as emphasized by Vygotsky). These resolutions begin primarily with our parents and other family members and extend out to the community and the society at large as we grow older so that the

---

14. Wertsch, *Vygotsky and the Social Formation of Mind*, 34.
15. Berger and Lickmann, *Social Construction of Reality*, 23.

development of our worldview occurs in a particular cultural or psychosocial context. As a result, the internalization of a particular view of the world can become largely unquestioned yet provide the means for interpreting and judging the world.

As less competent individuals, infants, children, and often adolescents are not equal contributors to the social interactions in which they engage. Thus, society can influence their understanding of the world much more than they are able to change the predominant worldview of the culture. Consequently, as individuals come to define themselves (i.e., who they are and who they should be) they do so in terms of the values and priorities communicated to them by significant adults and the institutions of a society. They will also tend to reflect these values and priorities in their interactions with peers. Infants and young children are almost exclusively recipients of a worldview that is provided to them by the culture, while adolescents and adults may have more of an interactive relationship with the dominant worldview of the culture. As Olthuis describes a worldview, it acts as "the set of hinges on which all our everyday thinking and doing turns."[16] Theologically, the culture into which an individual is born and, because of the receptive nature of worldview, the initial way they come to understand themselves in the world are directed by the sovereign will of God. The predominant worldview of the culture will largely control what is considered normal in terms of dress, use of time and resources, mannerisms, appropriate foods, the treatment of and by others, what is believed to be the "good life," and the categories and ways of thinking about the world that Vygotsky or Berger and Lickmann suggest when they describe the relationship of society to the development of worldview.

On the other hand, the development of worldview is also a dynamic process as reflected in Paul's admonishment in Romans 12:1–2. Many Christian writers also assert that our way of looking at the world can be changed, our worldview altered, by a critical appraisal of the adequacy of that worldview. This suggests that worldviews are dynamic entities and that they can be changed and brought more in line with a biblical perspective. The theories of Piaget and Vygotsky suggest that what prompts an alteration in worldview is some type of event or interaction with the world that the current worldview fails to adequately integrate or explain.

Piaget called this process *disequilibration*, and claimed that it was an inherent desire to avoid this state of cognitive dissonance for a state of equilibrium that motivates a change in a person's understanding of the world. To achieve equilibrium individuals alter their understanding of the world, changing their perspective so that they have the cognitive ability, the cognitive tools, that will allow them to make better sense of the world. Piaget saw this altering of their understanding of the world as a *qualitative* growth, so that they do not simply know more (quantitative) but they come to know or understand the world differently; however, simply creating a sense of cognitive dissonance, which calls into question the adequacy of an existing worldview, is not sufficient to initiate change in a worldview. Resolution to cognitive dissonance can also be achieved through acceptance of the new event or interaction as an additional manifestation of the current understanding. In this scenario the existing worldview is strengthened quantitatively because it is

16. Olthuis, "On Worldviews," 159.

now capable of explaining another aspect of the world that it was previously unable to explain, thus rendering the existing worldview more impervious to change. Finally, resolution of cognitive dissonance can also be achieved when an individual simply refuses to deal with it, cognitively ignoring the new information. In such a case, no qualitative or quantitative change in cognitive development occurs. In accepting the dissonant event for a broader view or rejecting it altogether, there is no qualitative change in cognition, which is characteristic of worldview transformation.

While Piaget notes the process that individuals engage in to resolve cognitive dissonance, another consideration is that the frames of reference or the mental categories on which individuals rely are not independent but are developed within a cultural context. That is, in the process of resolving dissonance, individuals rely on the judgment of the community, either directly or through the internalized cultural tools and the values and beliefs of the culture, to engage in and evaluate whether successful resolution has occurred. Thus the individual is not cognitively autonomous but remains, in large part, dependent upon the community, not only for the development of the initial worldview but also for worldview transformation to occur.

While all believers receive and are empowered by the Holy Spirit, whose ministry includes guiding the believer in all truth (John 16:13), The Holy Spirit's ministry is most often exercised within the community context. For this reason Christians are commanded to "test the spirits" (1 John 4:1) and to remove false teachers from the community (1 Tim 3:5; 3 John 10). Righteousness is to be imitated (3 John 11); in fact, Paul often called for others to imitate him (1 Cor 4:16; 1 Tim 3:10). This imitation occurs within a social context. Older believers are to teach the younger (Titus 2:1–5), not just in doctrine but by modeling a godly lifestyle. Likewise, spiritual gifts are given for the edification and preparation of the community of believers (1 Cor 12:7; Eph 4:12; 1 Pet 4:10), yet no one is given all of the gifts so that believers are dependent upon each other for their spiritual development. It is for this reason that they are told to "stimulate one another to love and good deeds, not forsaking our own assembling together" (Heb 10:24–25).

Thus, for transformation to occur, what is needed is not random events that stimulate the questioning of the existing worldview but the development of *cultural tools* (to borrow a phrase from Vygotsky) to resolve the conflict. It follows that the transformation to a biblical worldview requires a set of cultural tools, or ways of thinking, that will allow the believer to resolve cognitive conflicts. Insofar as the biblical worldview differs from the dominant secular worldview of the surrounding culture, resolution will also require a type of countercultural critique. A biblical transformation requires an evaluation of the values and cultural tools of the dominant society in light of the descriptive and normative aspects of worldview expressed in the Bible. While it is the individual who experiences and ultimately resolves the cognitive conflict, the community provides the cultural tools, expertise, and necessary support for the development of a biblical worldview. From this perspective a countercultural critique of the dominant secular culture is not enough. What may also be required is a type of countercultural community that has developed, and continues to develop, cultural responses based on a set of qualitatively different cognitive tools (i.e., a different worldview) that provide a foundation for understanding and evaluating the world and a vision for what life should be.

As previously mentioned, many writers use the analogy of a lens to discuss worldview, a particular way to see the world. Applying the lens analogy gives insight regarding our perception of the world. Since the lenses that we possess are essentially given to us because we are members of a particular culture, a poor set of lenses would not necessarily be perceived as poor. Since we have viewed the world only through the poor lenses we tend to see this poor vision of the world as normal. As a result, we see little need, or have little incentive, to change our worldview. Cognitive psychologists call this *status-quo bias*, it is the tendency of people to retain what they know or think they know even when gains could be made by selecting an alternative.[17] By extending the lens analogy, the recognition of a need for change could occur when we take off the glasses and notice that they are scratched beyond repair or when our acuity has significantly changed so that the current glasses are useless and need to be replaced. The lens analogy also provides a means of understanding the necessity for worldview transformation. The idea of creating dissonance can help explain how challenging a person's initial, unconscious perspective (we give little attention to our glasses when they are clean and functioning properly) can serve as a catalyst to worldview transformation (my glasses no longer work well and I need new ones). Without the tools to correct our vision, however, we may become skeptical of everything we see (I know I can't trust what I see because my vision is faulty, but I have no alternative), or take solace in a set of arguments or creedal positions that do not significantly challenge one's vision, values, or behavior in light of the dominant culture.

The process of developing an alternative vision for life is predicated on coming to understand that the existing vision of life is faulty. Realizing that my lenses are poor may occur when I continually trip or walk into things, indicating that my glasses are not serving their designed function. Recognizing faulty lenses or initiating the process of worldview change is possible by enlightened unbelievers. Since God created the world to operate properly according to certain principles, when sinful people, in the process of developing culture, create cultural institutions that are contrary to those principles, those institutions will contain the seeds of their own demise. Thomas Kuhn's principle of *paradigm shift* resembles this process, where a new theory emerges and is accepted by the community as a better explanation for the world than previous theories.[18] In time, the older explanation is discarded and the new theory becomes the accepted perspective through which experts view the world and also develop a new vision and set of questions to engage the world. The astute unbeliever can perceive this tension even if he or she fails to adequately perceive a proper alternative. In addition, the believer, under the ministry of the Holy Spirit, can be directed to truth (John 16:13). The Holy Spirit prompts the believer to see the inadequacy of his descriptive vision and also assists in the development of understanding of a new normative vision. It is this dependency on the Holy Spirit that Paul suggests when referring to the transformation of the mind in Romans 12:1–2.

17. Samuelson and Zechhauser, "Status Quo Bias in Decision Making," 8.
18. Kuhn, *Structure of Scientific Revolutions*, 17.

While I do not offer these steps as a developmental model for changing worldview, the process of developing a new worldview may encompass aspects of each of these stages. Many teachers desire to develop in themselves and their students the highly systematized type of worldview that is characteristic of a mature biblical thinker; however, to do so may require allowing students to experience the struggles and possible skepticism that seem necessary to go from biblical worldview novices to mature biblical thinkers.

BASIC QUESTIONS FOR ALL WORLDVIEWS

To this point we have defined worldviews as a way of explaining not only what life is like but also what life should be like. These two aspects reflect the descriptive and normative functions of a worldview. Worldviews allow us to place things in perspective and to make value judgments about the world around us. In this sense, worldviews are foundational to our thinking. We have also seen that all people have a worldview—it is part of the essence of being human—and that the development of worldview is a socio-psychological process. The worldview we initially assume is largely determined for us by the dominant perspective of the culture into which we are born. As we interact with people who are more competent because of experience and greater socialization in the dominant worldview, we begin to assimilate the cultural tools (i.e., the values, attitudes, language, customs, etc.) that allow us to interact with the world and people in predictable and meaningful ways. This perspective suggests that there are people who have a more firmly and systematically developed sense of worldview. This is the more developed sense of worldview that we would expect of theologians, philosophers, and other experts in their particular fields of study. The lens analogy, however, points to the status quo bias tendency to regard our way of seeing the world as normal. This suggests that people whose worldview is less systematic or who may not be able to articulate the particulars of their worldview still possess one to which they hold with some degree of conviction. The existence, description, development, and power of these less developed types of worldviews will be discussed in chapter 2.

Worldviews provide a way of describing the world and formulating a vision for life. Consequently, how we parent our children, how and why we educate young people, how we treat the environment, how we set up our legal, political, and healthcare institutions, and how we treat others in social interactions are all derived from our worldview. Foundational to these issues of practice are certain assumptions, faith statements about reality, which form the basis of our cultural responses. Thus a worldview develops at two levels—the foundational beliefs that form the critical core of the worldview and the outward manifestations in the world we experience that emanate from this core. While not all the members of a society are able to articulate these core beliefs, as members our worldview thinking is highly influenced by these beliefs or faith statements. They constitute a large part of the set of cognitive tools that we use to make sense of the world. In any communal group, however, there are those members who have developed more highly systematized responses to the basic questions that all worldviews must answer to produce the outward cultural manifestations that make social life possible. In this section we will examine these basic questions and begin to examine the biblical worldview responses to them.

We should note that the six foundational questions we are about to examine, and their answers, are not really separate questions. The answers provided to one question will have ramifications for many, if not all, of the other questions. As a result, the examination and articulation of the core beliefs of any worldview can be difficult, for in trying to reduce the complex interconnectedness of the responses to these basic questions, some of the richness of the whole is lost. What individuals believe to be an important or worthy goal in life (to answer the question of what is valuable) will directly affect how they behave (which is part of the answer to the question of the moral or ethical life) and also what they consider to be valid or appropriate ways of knowing about the world (which is a reflection of the question of the nature of knowledge). This means that the six basic worldview questions are not listed in any particular order of significance. Since all are foundational, one is no more important than the other. In order for us to develop a greater sense of the nature and scope of the core beliefs of any worldview, we need to examine these questions as separate entities while remaining aware of the potential hazards that isolating these questions can create.

Since all worldviews provide a vision for what life should be, questions of value or levels of worth or significance must be assigned to attitudes, values, ideas, behaviors, and so on. Certain aspects of life are deemed to be of greater value while others are regarded as of less. Thus, the first worldview question: *What is important or of value?* Theories of value are a part of virtually every philosophical system; they attempt to answer questions regarding what is good, important, beautiful, or ethical. Within this context a person considers and answers the question, What is the good life? When young children describe what they want to be when they grow up and get encouragement from a parent or teacher, they are attempting to develop their vision of the world within this framework of values. Such questions extend beyond issues of morality and ethics, but include areas such as what is beautiful (aesthetics), what are the highest priorities (both personal and societal), or the beat means of resolving issues involving competing values.

In general, theories of value can be divided into two groups. The first major group includes those systems that consider value questions as objective, having absolute and knowable standards of beauty or truth. Objective theories of value often place these standards of value as independent of human experience. For example, Plato believed the physical world could be judged as beautiful based on an absolute or ideal state of beauty that could be known through the development of reason. The second group consists of those systems that consider questions of value as subjective, either having no absolute objective standard of value or, at least, not having one that can be known by human beings. In subjective systems, standards of value are dependent on human experience or, at times, personal taste. For example, the statement "beauty is in the eye of the beholder" essentially states that what one considers beautiful is a construct of personal attitudes and dispositions and that these can be radically different from one person to another yet still have equal validity.

I once was watching the astronomy series *Cosmos* on PBS. The series, narrated by astronomer Carl Sagan, opened each episode of the series with the statement, "The cosmos is all there ever is, ever was, and ever will be." Sagan's statement reflects the heart of the second foundational worldview question: *What is ultimately real?* This area of philosophy is called *metaphysics* and includes discussions of the fundamental nature of reality and being. It is the study of "ultimates," of first and last things. Is reality essentially spiritual (as Plato believed) or physical (as Aristotle maintained)? Is there a supernatural component to the universe so that miracles are possible, or is the universe mechanistic, a big machine that works solely according to natural law (making miracles technically impossible)? The statement by Sagan that begins each episode of *Cosmos* reflects an impersonal and mechanistic universe. It is a universe that, for him, operates according to the laws of time, energy, matter, and (possibly) probability or chance. This perspective, known as *naturalism* or *philosophical materialism*, allows its adherents to make statements regarding the origin of things according to natural processes. Further, there is a relationship between the question, what is real? and the question, what is of the highest value? From the perspective of naturalism, the good or valued is that which corresponds to natural law, or there may seem to be no real reason for the existence of values in the world since values are essentially personal and have no basis in reality in an impersonal universe. Whatever one believes to be good, therefore, may be valid.

The third foundational question to all worldviews is the nature of knowledge: *How do I know what is true?* This area, known to philosophers as *epistemology*, attempts to address how we evaluate beliefs, whether they are warranted or not, what we will consider as acceptable evidence to defend a belief, and whether something counts as knowledge or belongs to some other category (such as superstition). For example, if I said to you, "seeing is believing," I would be making an implicit assumption about the nature of knowledge—that what is real and can be known is empirical or knowledge based on sense data. All worldviews must address questions regarding the importance and reliability of reason and logic, sense perceptions and intuition, and the best ways to obtain truth. Worldviews must address questions such as, Is the scientific method the only reliable means to truth (as it is to the philosophical materialist), or are there other sources of truth that need to be considered (e.g., biblical revelation)?

Similarly, this worldview question must address how conflicts between accepted sources of knowledge are resolved. In the previous example, a person could believe in knowledge obtained through the scientific method and from a revealed source of truth, like the Bible; however, what if these two sources of knowledge conflict? How will conflicts in knowledge sources be resolved? A worldview provides the means of determining the most credible sources of knowledge, the conditions of credibility, and the most reliable or valid sources of information. Any theory of knowledge must address these types of questions. The area of epistemology is complex, yet all people and cultures maintain a dominant epistemological belief as part of their worldview.

On a recent trip to the mall I passed a pet shop that had a T-shirt on display that said "Dogs are People Too!" (to avoid discrimination there was a comparable version for cats). This innocent caption gets at the heart of the fourth worldview question: *What is the nature of humanity?* To philosophers this is the area known as *philosophical anthropology*, which attempts to answer such questions as, do human beings possess free will or are their choices the result of material or spiritual forces? Are human beings physical and temporal beings or essentially spiritual and possessing eternality? Others define humanity as simply having more of a specific characteristic, which would allow for the possibility that dogs and cats are people too. For example, if loyalty is a characteristic of humanity and a dog behaves in a manner that is viewed as more loyal than some people, could that dog be considered, in this regard, more "human," or do human beings possess some qualitatively different trait (like a soul or a spirit) that separates them from animals?

In a similar manner, worldviews must answer such questions as, Is there life after death, or is physical death the end of existence? When we advocate a pleasure principle of "eat, drink, and be merry for tomorrow we die," we are making assumptions about the nature of humanity (that human beings are essentially physical-material beings) and about the nature of reality (that there is nothing beyond this life). In such a belief system the value of anything could be reduced to what pleasure it can bring, and the value of anything, including education, reduced to its ability to satisfy certain desires such as to obtain wealth or gain more leisure time. A belief that human beings are essentially physical or material beings could also render the development of the mind or the soul as secondary or inconsequential compared to more temporal considerations.

As we have seen, a worldview provides a means for describing what the world is like and also for developing a vision of what the world should be. Since an inevitable gap exists between the real world and the envisioned ideal, worldviews must provide a means of answering another question: *What is wrong?* And its correlative: *What can be done to remedy the problem?* These constitute the fifth question that all worldviews must address. One evening while watching television, I observed a public-service announcement in which a celebrity delivered ten seconds of "sage wisdom" by telling me that if I applied a particular principle in my life, I could help eradicate some fundamental problems faced by individuals and society. The commercial ended with the little phrase "The More You Know." The worldview message of these spots is that the fundamental source of the problems of our society—racial prejudice, economic disparities, domestic difficulties, substance abuse, various injustices—is ignorance. The corollary is that the answers to human difficulties can be found in education.

In most Western societies, schools and education have been a fundamental part of the proposed solution to a number of the social, political, and economic ills that trouble society. It should be noted, however, that such a response to social problems is predicated on a belief that human beings, when they think and behave rationally, are essentially "good" (or at least disposed to do that which is right) or "neutral" (whereby they can be taught to be that which is right). It also reflects a belief that humans are essentially rational and, given proper knowledge, they will essentially make sound judgments. Further, it assumes that sound judgments are those that promote a view of harmony and tolerance between individuals (which also reflects a sense of what is valued). A view of human nature that would assert that humans are basically selfish, having the ability to choose to freely do things for their own benefit with little regard for the effects on others or that humans might use their talents, abilities, and power of intelligence to justify the preferences of their own will would diminish the value of education as a primary vehicle for individual or social reform, or (at least) change what we believe a good education to be.

Finally, based on the answers provided to all of the previous questions, worldviews must ultimately answer this question: *How should we live?* This is the area of philosophy or theology normally addressed by *morality* or *ethics*. Most people are more aware of this area because it affects their lives directly and daily. We make moral judgments about ourselves, about others (both individuals and groups), and about situations past, present, and future. Ultimately, however, worldviews must address the source of the values from which these moral judgments can be made. As we saw in the question of what is of value, moral laws or ethical perspectives can come from a variety of sources. For example, is morality ultimately a personal choice, so that living according to my convictions, regardless of the consequences, constitutes an ethical life? This would be the position of existentialist thinkers. On the other hand, is that which is right ultimately a societal question, whereby if 51 percent of the people (or their chosen representatives) think something is right or good, it thereby becomes such? Determining right by societal preference might be the basic issue in some people's defense of a woman's legal right to an abortion and in defenses of Roe v. Wade (i.e., if a majority of Americans respond positively to a woman's right to choose). Likewise, this question seeks to answer questions regarding whether morality should be based on some universal moral imperative deduced from human reason. For example, should all people be treated as an end in themselves and never as a means to an end (as advocated by philosophers such as Immanuel Kant)? The question further attempts to answer whether or not there are absolute and universal moral standards that transcend human experience and time and to which all human beings, regardless of culture, are expected to conform. This would be the position of most religious systems and would include standards such as the Ten Commandments.

THE BIBLICAL WORLDVIEW: ANSWERS TO THE BASIC QUESTIONS

The six foundational questions that all worldviews must answer provide the basis from which all adherents of that worldview begin to address the fundamental questions of life. How a society or culture responds corporately and how individuals think and live individually in relation to issues of life are reflections of the predominant worldview of the culture. For example, issues of how government should work and what it should do and expectations on issues of the economy, education, health care, entertainment, and so on start with a basic understanding of what is real, what is valuable, what it means to be a human being, how we assess what is true, and what is the nature of the problems that are found in society. It can be argued that a worldview is not truly a worldview unless it provides adequate answers to these basic questions. A worldview that fails to provide adequate answers to these questions is inherently unstable and cannot continue without creating problems for and eventually the downfall of the individuals or cultures that insist on maintaining it.

As Christian educators, when we seek to teach students a biblical worldview, we implicitly or explicitly maintain that the Bible provides sufficient answers to the foundational questions that confront all worldviews. We also are acknowledging a belief that the Bible provides us with sufficient insight to address issues of government, education, economics, arts, entertainment, and all the other areas that are part of the dynamics of human beings living with each other under the authority of God. In essence, when Paul writes that "whether, then, you eat or drink or whatever you do, do all to the glory of God" (1 Cor 10:31), he indicates that there is no area of life, no matter how routine, that is not affected by our understanding of God as we come to know him through his Word. How the biblical worldview begins to address these more corporate concerns will be the focus of our attention in chapter 3. For now we will examine the biblical response to the foundational questions fundamental to all worldviews.

The first foundational question of worldview centers on the issue of *what is important or of value?* The Bible is clear that God is the absolute and only standard of value. The value of all other things is derived from and is relative to him; they are reflections of the ultimate value that is God. John Piper notes that God "must be for himself if he is to be for us. . . . If God should turn away from himself as the Source of infinite joy, he would cease to be God. He would deny the infinite worth of his own glory. He would imply that there is something more valuable outside himself. He would commit idolatry."[19] The desire to elevate humanity to the place of ultimate authority over life, to make humanity the arbiter of all things, is a characteristic that is deeply embedded in our sin nature. It is a desire to usurp God's place of supremacy over our lives and to overtake his throne as it relates to our lives. While proper education will help develop the individual to his potential, that potential must always be defined in terms of how that individual, created in the image of God, reflects the only true and absolute value, which is God.

Because God is the absolute and only true value, everything that does not reflect God's glory is to be devalued and relegated to a secondary position in our lives. Thus, a biblically based education is one that assists students to develop their full potential as reflections of God's glory. This would be in contrast to a view of education, prominent in our society today, that defines the individual in terms of economic potential, where becoming a "good person" is secondary to or synonymous with becoming a good or productive worker. While goodness based on the absolute value of God will certainly make the person a good worker, this goodness will transcend the workplace and may even cause the individual to be an economic liability when reflecting the absolute character of God puts her in conflict with unbiblical interests. For example, a worker may be acting more ethically when calling attention to practices in the workplace that are unjust or violate principles of good stewardship. These behaviors, however, may force the worker to confront superiors or possibly to disclose the practices of the company to a larger audience. These "whistle-blowing" behaviors may not be viewed as conducive to the ethic of being a good worker, but they are more aligned with a standard of goodness, justice, or stewardship based in God.

19. Piper, *Desiring God*, 47–48.

By stating that the God of the Bible is the absolute and only value, we are also explicitly stating that values are real and that they are not constructed from human understanding. While human beings do engage in the process of trying to make sense of their world and while sin does negatively influence this process, human beings are not autonomous entities that create their own set of values based on individual or cultural criteria. They are dependent on God to understand what is good, what is right, what is beautiful. They are dependent on God to reveal himself to them, and from that revelation to construct and apply a theory of value to things in the world. As dependent creatures, human beings must rely on God in constructing their understanding of the world. Because human beings were created dependent, there is a reliance on God for their construction and understanding of the world that was a part of humanity's make-up even before the Fall.

Here the lens analogy for worldview breaks down or is in need of modification. When I go to the optometrist to have my eyes checked, an eye test is conducted during which a series of lenses is given to me; my doctor asks me to identify which lenses give me a clearer vision of the chart. Based on my assessment, my doctor adjusts the lenses, progressively moving me closer to normal vision. This process, however, is predicated both on my knowing what "normal" vision looks like and my ability to discern that which is normal from that which is blurred. Worldviews do indeed serve as a type of lens; however, from the biblical perspective we are all born finite (a condition that would have been true of Adam) with a sin nature (which has affected all humanity since Adam), so our ability to know what is normal or true is faulty and requires that we be shown the nature of truth. This makes us all, even Adam before the Fall, dependent on God for an understanding of what constitutes a normal vision. Essentially, we are unable, starting from ourselves, to develop a sense of normal or to be sure that any conceptualization of normal that we might develop is correct.

For example, aesthetically, the biblical perspective of God as the absolute and only value calls into question the more subjective idea that "beauty is in the eye of the beholder." Jonathan Edwards once wrote that his wife Sarah was the most beautiful person he ever knew (a view one might suspect to be motivated by a desire to maintain a good standing with his wife). Portraits of Sarah Edwards do not show her to have been a woman of particularly striking appearance, even judging by the standards of beauty of that time. Edwards though, defined his wife's beauty in terms of the holiness that characterized the way she lived her life. It was his view of holiness as a reflection of the absolute and most definitive characteristic of God that caused Edwards to use it as the basis for making his aesthetic judgment. Furthermore, his view of beauty did not originate in Edwards himself. It was a perspective of beauty based on the revealed character of God. While not all art or music needs to reflect explicit "God-themes," good art, music, literature, behavior, science, or any other area of human life may be viewed as having value from a biblical perspective if it seeks to put into practice Paul's admonition of Philippians 4:8–9: "Finally, brethren, whatever is true, whatever is honorable, whatever is right, whatever is pure, whatever is lovely, whatever is of good repute, if there is any excellence and if anything worthy of praise, dwell on these things. The things you have learned and received and heard and seen in me, practice these things, and the God of peace will be with you."

The second foundational question all worldviews must address is, *what is real or what is the nature of reality?* Biblically, we see that God, who preexisted in perfect freedom before all time and space, creates, sustains, judges, and redeems for his ultimate glory. Since God existed before all things, he has no imposed duties, nothing that compels him to do anything. No standards of conduct and no obligations exist outside of himself to which he must conform. God was not obligated to create the world, nor was he obligated to redeem humanity when they fell, but in all things he chooses to act in a way that gives him pleasure and leads to his glory (cf. Rom 11:33–36; 9:19–24). From the perspective of Scripture we biblically learn that God is perfectly sovereign and that he is free to do what pleases him.

That God preexists and that he creates for his own pleasure means that God exists independently of his creation. This places the biblical worldview apart from transcendental worldviews that see God as part of all things. In Ralph Waldo Emerson's declaration, "The currents of the Universal Being circulate through me; I am part or parcel with God,"[20] he reflects the view that there is no difference between the spiritual and the material, that all things are part of the same substance. By maintaining the preexistence of God and the reality of spiritual things, the biblical worldview stands in contrast to that of the naturalists or philosophical materialists who deny any reality beyond the physical or material world. Also, that God chose to create and that he calls this creation "good" means that the created world is valuable, an externalization of his perfect character, and not to be minimized or rejected as in some Eastern worldviews where the physical universe is merely illusion, and reality consists of spiritual nothingness. In an unfallen world we would see all created beings act out the perfect character of God. This suggests that the creation is valuable and worthy of our attention and study, to be valued, not despised, to be cared for as God has charged humanity (Gen 1:28; 2:15). In recognizing the value of the creation, however, we must not allow the created order to supersede the value of the Creator himself, a propensity Paul tells us is true of those who reject the reality of a transcendent God (Rom 1:25).

The biblical view of reality acts as a remedy for the propensity of the sin nature to make humanity the focal point of history. The biblical worldview communicates God in his proper place of significance. God's being the highest and greatest good makes the glorification of God, the extension of his honor and glory, the theme of all history. The process of the redemption and reconciliation of all creation, which God chooses as the means to bring the greatest honor and glory to himself, becomes the focal point of history (Rom 8:19–22; 1 Cor 15:24–28; Col 1:28). It is a focus in which humanity, created as the image-bearers of God, is an integral part but not the exclusive focus. Without this perspective, human beings are inclined to presume that the story of creation, fall, and redemption is the story of God's exclusive work for humanity. The biblical view of reality changes the near-sightedness of believing that God's redemptive history focuses wholly on humanity. It also acts as a cure for the arrogance of a secularized view of history that centers exclusively on the accomplishments of humanity in terms of building wealth, power, prestige, and self-glorification, a view that God illustrates as insanity (Dan 4:28–37). It should also

20. Emerson, "Nature," 10.

act as a means of reorienting human beings to conform to the biblical mandates of stewardship and reconciliation given to them in Scripture.

The Bible tells us that human beings are created in the image of God (Gen 1:26); this understanding forms the basis for the biblical worldview response to the third foundational worldview question: *What is the nature of humanity?* Created in the image of God, humanity bears the likeness of its Creator—a likeness we reflect before others so that we become the tangible or concrete representation of God. This aspect of our nature also separates human beings from the rest of creation, so that we stand in an authoritative position over creation (Gen 1:28; Ps 8:4–8). By stating that humanity is created in the image of God, the Bible teaches that I have an obligation to reflect God to others just as others have a biblical obligation to reflect God to me; however, being created in God's image does not simply refer to our positional standing before God and above the rest of creation. As beings created in God's image, the Bible teaches that our fundamental makeup is such that we are designed to have a qualitatively different relationship with God and with others created in that image than we are to have with the rest of creation. We are to live for God and for others in a way that places all other relationships with the creation as secondary (Matt 22:37–40). Stating that human beings are created in the image of God, however, then raises the question, How are we, as human beings, like God?

Cornelius Plantinga notes that human beings reflect the image of God in three ways. First, humans, like God, have "responsible dominion" over the created world.[21] In Genesis 1:28 the cultural mandate to humanity is to increase in number, to subdue the earth, and to rule over every living creature. This charge to rule over the creation does not give humanity the right to exploit it in ways that allow us to simply please ourselves but includes the idea of stewardship—caring for that which belongs to another with the interest of the owner in mind. The idea of stewardship or responsible dominion stands in contrast to a more naturalistic or modernistic worldview that sees nature as something to be conquered, as exemplified in the American mythos of "taming the frontier." Ann Coulter once stated in a television interview, "God says, 'Earth is yours. Take it. Rape it. It's yours.'"[22] Unfortunately, through an improper understanding of the teaching of responsible dominion or stewardship Christianity has, at times, contributed to the Western attitude that treats the environment in a destructive manner. This has led some critics, for example, historian Lynn White Jr., to conclude that Christianity bears a "huge burden of guilt" for the present ecological crisis.[23]

Second, we bear the image of God in our ability to live in loving communion with each other and with God. This aspect of the image of God refers to our social nature, to the fact that we are incomplete or cannot experience our full humanity apart from a relationship with God and with others. Just as God is triune in his nature and therefore can love, enjoy, communicate with, and experience the other members of the Godhead, so human beings, as his image-bearers, are designed to be able to experience these same

---

21. Plantinga, *Engaging God's World*, 30–31.

22. Coulter, *FoxNews* interview, December 22, 2001.

23. White, "The Historical Roots of Our Ecological Crisis," 1201.

characteristics in their relationship with God and with others. For this reason we are told not to avoid or forsake assembling or fellowshipping with other believers (Heb 10:25). Paul writes that one of the distinguishing marks of the mature believer is the ability to demonstrate unity with other believers and to love them (Eph 4:13–16). Christ distinguishes this aspect of unity, or living in communion with others, as a characteristic of true believers. Because God is one, the Lord claims the characteristic of unity within the body of Christ as a criterion by which the world can judge the validity of Christ, the church, and the gospel message (John 17:21).

Finally, Plantinga notes that we bear the image of God by "conforming to Jesus Christ in suffering and death, the ultimate example of self-giving love."[24] The image of God means that as human beings we have the capacity to give of ourselves, to place the needs of others before our own needs. We have the ability to demonstrate care and compassion to others, even when there is no foreseeable gain for us in doing so. Jesus notes this characteristic in humanity when he says, "Greater love has no one than this, that one lay down his life for his friends" (John 15:13). While the sin nature corrupts this aspect of the image of God in such a way that we now are prone to place our own desires above those of others, the sin nature mars the image of God in humanity but does not destroy it. Christ infers this in teaching the disciples about prayer, noting that even those who are evil still know how to give good gifts to their children (Luke 11:11–13). Because the image of God is not lost in sinful humanity, God can still hold humans accountable for obedience to the original mandate of responsible dominion or stewardship.

Being in the image of God does not equate human beings with God or imply that human beings *are* God. The image is not an exact reproduction; thus, as created beings we possess certain fundamental limitations that distinguish us from God. The greatest of these are the limitations imposed on humanity as a result of their finiteness. Just as finiteness causes us to depend on God for a proper understanding of the world, we are also dependent upon God to know how to bear his image to others and to the rest of creation. Finiteness preceded the Fall, meaning that even before the Fall, humans were cognitively dependent on God for their understanding. The cultural mandate to be stewards requires that humans not only commune with God so that we can know his will for the creation but also learn about the creation itself so that we can implement God's will. Our finite nature also makes us dependent on others. Unlike God, who can bring about all things through the power of his will (1 Chr 29:11; Dan 4:35), as limited creatures humans find that we often need to cooperate with others to achieve God's will. This, combined with our limited understanding, makes us dependent on others to learn about the creation and obliges those of us who are more knowledgeable to teach for the benefit of the individual and the welfare of others (Luke 12:48; Phil 2:3–4).

At this point it should be noted that we have not addressed the Christian response to the fundamental worldview questions in order. Specifically, in addressing the biblical response to the nature of humanity, we have skipped the biblical response to the question of the nature of truth and the way we can know it. That God exists and is the absolute and

24. Plantinga, *Engaging God's World*, 34.

only real value means that there is an absolute truth that exists in the universe. That God created a physical world and created humanity in his image to have responsible dominion over that creation means that not only is there a spiritual dimension of reality but that the physical creation also has value as a reflection of the character of God. This does not constitute a type of pantheism, believing that everything that exists is an extension of God, but an understanding that creation, while separate from God, is a declaration of his power and majesty (Ps 19:1). Also, since human beings are created in the image of God, they are empowered with certain attributes that allow them to have fellowship with God and others.

The fact that we have been given the responsibility of managing the creation as stewards indicates that there is knowledge that can be gained from the creation that is real and can be objectively communicated. Our stewardship responsibility also suggests a dependence on God for gaining a greater perspective on truth and for using the knowledge that we gain to indeed manage the creation as stewards. Obviously, educators are in the "knowledge business," and questions regarding what is true and how we know that which is true are of vital importance. Combining these questions with the biblical doctrine of the image of God highlights important implications for the Christian educator—regarding the nature and scope of the curriculum and the type of teaching methodologies used. Being created in the image of God is fundamental to how human beings will live and work. As a result, the concept is either distorted or attacked by many theorists who wish to reject a biblical view of education or simply ignored by those insensitive to the ramifications on curriculum and instruction from such a high view of humanity.

As we have seen, worldviews provide both a means for explaining the world and a vision for determining how life should be lived. The result is an inevitable discrepancy between these two positions or functions. This leads to the fourth foundational worldview question: *What is wrong?* From the biblical perspective the answer to this worldview question is the entry and continued existence of sin, humanity's rebellion against God, into the world. Sin is any transgression of thought, attitude, or action that opposes the will of God and attempts to diminish or take from God the glory that is due him. Sin produces and sustains the existence of evil in the world, its effects going beyond the person who engages in the sin, rippling through all of creation so that all things are affected by human rebellion against God (Gen 3:14–24; Rom 8:19–21). Because of sin, humans become the enemies of God and the objects of his wrath, following our own desires in opposition to God's will (Rom 5:9–10; Eph 2:3–4).

What is it about sin that causes God to oppose it so vehemently? Why does God sacrifice his only begotten Son, Jesus Christ, as a remedy for the problem of sin (to answer the correlative question—*what can be done to remedy the problem?*)? Human rebellion is no threat to God; he remains totally omnipotent, omniscient, and omnipresent. God's sovereignty is never in jeopardy, so there is no rebellion, whether by Satan and his followers or by human beings, that can succeed. What God resolves will be done, for there is no force in the universe that can oppose his will (Ps 115:3; Isa 46:9–10). God was not required by any mandate or principle to create. He is, and was, and always remains totally self-sufficient, living in harmony with himself since eternity past. Any motivation to create is solely the result of his will. We are told, though, that our sin can grieve the Holy Spirit of God (Eph 4:30) and that the sin of all humanity can cause pain in the heart of God (Gen 9:6). Do I individually or do human beings collectively possess the ability to disrupt the contentment of God? If God does not do what I want, can I punish him like a spoiled child by sinning, thus causing him some pain, some pang of heart, some loss of joy—even if I cannot get my own way? If God and his glory are of ultimate value, does my sin constitute a threat to God's glory by my ability to somehow disvalue God?

The simple answer to these questions is no—sin is no threat to God in any way. God's sovereignty is not threatened by human rebellion. His glory is not diminished, nor is his happiness dependent on human conformity to his will. In contrast, however, Piper notes that our own happiness is totally dependent on the delight that God has in himself. According to Piper, "The very thing that can make us most happy is what God delights in with all his heart and with all his soul,"[25] namely himself (cf. Isa 43:6–7; Jer 32:40–43; Rom 8:28). Understanding that sin does not represent any real threat to God underscores the idea that a holy and loving God truly has in mind the best interests of human beings, as the recipients of his love, when he sets standards for holy and righteous living. Sin inhibits the display of God's glory in human beings as the image-bearers of God—and creates conditions or effects that prevent the display of God's image in others.

If we understand humanism to be the elevation of human beings to their highest state, to allow humans to be all they can possibly be, then biblical Christianity represents, according to theologian J. I. Packer, the only true form of humanism.[26] Humanity was never more human than it was in the Garden before the Fall, and believers will experience true humanity again when they are ultimately sanctified, freed from their sin nature, at the return of Christ. Until that time, biblical Christianity maintains that human beings can become more complete image-bearers of God in Christ and that they can experience life more abundant in Christ (John 10:10). From this perspective the reason sin is so destructive is that it dehumanizes people, making them less than what God intends them to be. That God grieves and finds sin distressing is not because it causes him any discomfort or ruins God's personal peace, but because God loves humanity and wants the best for them. Since God is the ultimate value in the universe, he grieves when people act in ways that are not in their best interest, when they sacrifice the best for themselves for something that can never truly give them what they ultimately desire or need. Understood this way, when God gives a command not to engage in a particular thought, attitude, or action, he does so because, as the Creator and having full knowledge of what is best for humanity, he understands that having these particular experiences will diminish their own peace and happiness, and make them less than what he intended. It in the end, sin is ultimately not in the best interest of human beings.

Understanding sin to be a dehumanizing process means that whenever a sin is committed, it has at least four effects. The first, and the one that traditionally comes to mind, is that sin separates humanity from God. Because of the holiness of God, human rebellion

---

25. Piper, *Desiring God*, 53.

26. Packer and Howard, *Christianity: The True Humanism*, 15.

and moral impurity make it impossible to stand before God on the basis of personal merit. The sin nature desires to be autonomous from God, to seek its own way of determining what is right and wrong (Rom 3:10; Gen 3:5). To sin is to implicitly ally with Satan, whose goal is to overthrow God and place himself on God's throne (Isa 14:12–15). As a result, the punishment of hell that was created for Satan and his angelic followers is extended to rebellious humanity. The *Westminster Confession of Faith* begins with the statement that "the chief end of man is to glorify God and enjoy him forever." Sin takes the glory and adoration that is due to God, which humans were created to give him, and tempts them to hoard that glory for themselves. In the process, no positive end is produced. Martin Luther wrote that sin "takes from God and from men what belongs to them and gives neither God nor men anything of that which it has, is, and is capable of."[27]

Taking from human beings that which belongs to them in God is the dehumanizing aspect of sin and is sin's second effect. Sin robs sinners of their humanity, acting to erode the image of God in them. To say that sin dehumanizes is to assert that as humans engage in sin, they become less able to fulfill the created purposes that God has for them—loving God, loving others, and caring for and developing the creation for his glory. While sin is a transgression against God, it is also a transgression against humanity and against the creation as a whole. In this sense we can make a differentiation between sin and immoral behavior. Certainly immoral behavior is a sin; however, when individuals engage in immoral acts they engage in actions that use other people, either directly or indirectly, to meet their own desires. Their actions reduce the other people to objects, dehumanizing them in some way, so that the victims can be used as items or things to meet the desires of the sinner.

This tendency to diminish others to objects, reducing their uniqueness as image-bearers of God, is the essence of what Martin Buber called "I-It" relationships, where the sinner ("I") reduces others to objects ("It") to satisfy one's own desires.[28] Motivated from our sin nature, we tend to reduce others to objects, failing to see them as image-bearers of God; consequently, we tend to view them as things that may be used for our own benefit. Since immoral behavior dehumanizes another person, it constitutes a sin. Further, engaging in immoral actions is also detrimental to those who perform such actions since the process desensitizes them, making them more capable of engaging in similar actions against others in the future (1 Tim 4:2). These immoral actions violate the scriptural principle of placing or esteeming others as greater than ourselves (Phil 2:3), of placing the needs and development of others above our own, of treating each individual as an image-bearer of God, relations that Buber characterized as "I-Thou" relationships, where the former "It" is now viewed by the other person in all of his nor her humanity as "Thou."[29]

The dehumanizing of those engaging in sin is the third effect of sin, the effect that renders sinners less capable of exhibiting the image of God in their own lives. This expands the concept of sin beyond that of simply immoral behavior. In immoral behavior there is

27. Luther, "How Christians Should Regard Moses," in *Luther's Works*, 35.369.

28. Buber, *I and Thou*, 102–3.

29. Ibid., 59. "When I confront a human being as my You and speak the basic word I-You to him, then he is no thing among things nor does he consist of things."

always a victim, a person against whom the action is directed. In sin the perpetrator of the sin, the sinner, is always a victim of dehumanization. In essence, to sin is to dehumanize one's self. Since sin can be a thought or an attitude, in addition to an action, we can engage in sin, and in so doing, will damage our reflection of the image of God. This will occur whether or not we act on that thought or attitude and produce an action against another that will constitute an immoral act. For this reason Christ said that not only is our act of murder or adultery wrong, but to engage in the thought or attitude of hate or lust that produces the moral wrong also makes us equally guilty before God (cf. Matt 5:21–30).

When human beings engage in sin, they attempt to meet God-given or God-permitted desires in ways that are contrary to his will, and, in so doing, bring harm to themselves and often to others. The need for rest can become sloth. The desire to meet material needs can become greed. The God-given desire for food can become gluttony. In each of these cases, the sin causes the person to become less an image-bearer of God, less a reflection of him to others. For example, God has given the desire for sexual activity to human beings, and because of this, sexuality is neither wrong nor detestable. However, God gives guidelines on the proper context for the expression of sexual desire and provides parameters for engaging in sexual activity, attitudes, and thoughts. Human beings who experience the desire for sexual activity can look at these parameters as restrictions and conclude that God is some type of "celestial kill-joy" who does not desire for them to be happy. For example, I might conclude that God is not looking out for my welfare or interests and, because he is not, I need to do what I think is right or good for me. This conclusion might lead me to engage in sexual activity in any context that seems "right in my own eyes" (Judg 21:25). On the other hand, I might conclude that because God is bigger and stronger than I am and has threatened me with hell if I disobey him, it is in my best interest not to engage in sexual activities outside of these rules. Either conclusion comes from the perspective of deciding for myself what is good or evil, usurping God's authority in my own life by reserving for myself the right to decide what is right or wrong, what is in my own best interest.

If, however, we ask the question, why has God given certain parameters for the fulfillment of sexual desire?—keeping in mind that God's desire for us is that we be all that we are intended to be in him—we might come to an entirely different conclusion. In focusing on the fulfillment of my sexual desires, those desires become the focus of my thoughts, attitudes, and possible actions. Consequently, I am inclined to look at those that can fulfill these desires as objects to satisfy me. Those people are no longer image-bearers of God in my eyes, but they are reduced to objects that can be used to satisfy my desires. While I may not engage in the act of adultery with another woman, if I entertain such thoughts, I become disposed to looking at that woman as an object. Such thoughts also create in me an attitude that will predispose me to look at other women as objects in the future and to evaluate the relative worth of a woman by how well she satisfies some set of objectified standards on what a woman should be—standards that may be based in my desire to achieve sexual satisfaction. Conversely, understanding that God created humans as sexual beings means that the purpose of biblical sexuality is to enhance the expression of the image of God in the marriage relationship. For this reason Scripture uses the marriage relationship to illustrate the unity within the Godhead and the relationship of Christ and the church (Gen 1:26–27; 2:23; Eph 5:22–33).

Finally, because human beings are given responsible dominion or stewardship over the creation, each act of sin produces a ripple effect, so that all of creation is affected by our sin. This is the fourth effect of sin—that it creates a separation between human beings and the creation that they are to nurture and develop for God's glory. We are not dismissing or diminishing the fact that Adam's sin immediately brought a cursing of nature by God as a consequence of his sin (Gen 3:17–19), but acknowledging that, as a result of sin we now desire to use the creation to meet our own desires, outside of the concerns of God. The creation, therefore, suffers from and reacts to the mismanagement by humanity. Problems of pollution, endangered species, waste management, resource depletion, and other environmental difficulties can often be attributed to poor stewardship. Because of this mismanagement, all of the creation also awaits the liberation from the bondage of sin imposed upon it, a condition that will occur when humanity is restored to its ultimate glory in Christ (Rom 8:20–21).

The dehumanizing effects of sin are not limited to the thoughts, attitudes, and actions of individuals, but they are also experienced at the corporate or communal level of society or culture. Just as sin hinders the expression of the image of God in individuals, sin in a society acts as a type of moral wrong, creating actions that victimize individuals (or groups of individuals) in the society and reducing them to a status that is less than God intends. As sinful individuals create society and social structures, they do so in a way that often allows them to fulfill their desires at the expense of others. Thus, individuals and groups can become oppressors, and others can be oppressed. Two examples are the advantage of whites over blacks in apartheid South Africa and the justification of abuse towards slaves by labeling them as property in the antebellum South. The oppression often creates the desire in the exploited groups to gain power to meet their own desires, which may result in greater social conflict and tension.

The final question of concern for all worldviews is the question of ethics: *How should we live?* The biblical response is that every action, attitude, rule, policy, thought, or project, whether done individually or corporately, is morally correct only if it is in accordance with God's purpose to glorify himself. "Whether, then, you eat or drink or whatever you do, do all to the glory of God" (1 Cor 10:31). Paul tells the Philippians that "whatever is true, whatever is honorable, whatever is right, whatever is pure, whatever is lovely, whatever is of good repute, if there is any excellence and if anything worthy of praise, dwell on these things." Paul goes on, however, to note that actions should follow such thoughts and attitudes: "The things you have learned and received and heard and seen in me, *practice these things*, and the God of peace will be with you" (Phil 4:8–9, emphasis added). To act in accordance with God's will, which brings glory to God, is also to act in such a way as to experience true humanity. In this context, a biblical worldview means that every aspect and issue of life, including those of education, will need to be brought into alignment with the expressed will of God. As we engage in the study of the goals and objectives of education, we will need to engage in the process of evaluating contemporary educational practice, including the predominant practices of Christian schooling, from the perspective of the biblical worldview. This will include evaluating whether these goals, objectives, and practices prepare teachers to develop the image of God in their students so that they can bring honor and glory to God by participating and practicing his will.

CONCLUSION

As we have seen, the development of worldview is a communal process. As we interact with others in the world, especially those more competent in the world than ourselves, we begin to develop ways of viewing the world that may not be conscious but that affect our ways of thinking and our value systems, even to the point of deciding what is normal and best. In this sense worldviews may seem to be more caught than actively taught. This reality does not mean that changing a worldview cannot be done through direct teaching, but it suggests that the changing of a worldview will be a process that requires an active and supportive community engaged in progressively developing and implementing a biblical worldview. Scripture tells us that the changing of our way of thinking is foundational to doing the will of God (Rom 12:1–2), but an understanding of the communal aspect of worldview helps illustrates why gifts are given to all believers to be used to spiritually develop or edify the church body (1 Cor 12:1–30) and why we are told not to forsake our own assembling together (Heb 10:25).

These passages, of course, apply to the church as a body of believers. While a Christian school is not a church, it does constitute a body of believers where the core questions of a worldview are addressed and where the answers to those core questions should be actively applied to understanding all areas of life. This may include aspects of the worldview not normally addressed by the church. The Christian school and university may currently be the best places to address issues of social concern, of the humanities, and of the natural and social sciences, and to develop leaders trained in the biblical application of world-view. These leaders, whether they be pastors, teachers, or other lay persons, would then be able to help educate and edify their congregations specifically and the body of Christ in general, in ways that would lead to personal and social transformation—which is the charge given to the church.

2

Philosophies, Ideologies, and Worldviews

The nature of man is richly diversified. There is not only the diversity of basic need but there is also a profuse variety of taste and interest, of aptitude and endowment, of desires to be satisfied and of pleasure to be gratified. When we consider the manifold ways in which the earth is fashioned and equipped to meet and gratify the diverse nature and endowments of man, we can catch a glimpse of the vastness and variety of the task involved in subduing the earth, a task directed to the end of developing man's nature, gifts, interests, and powers of engagement with the resources deposited by God in the earth and the sea.

—John Murray, *Principles of Conduct*

O N A BRISK LATE October morning Arnie arrives at school early as is his custom. Arnie is a creature of routine, he likes to get to school early so that he can plan the day, get materials ready for his classes, and generally not feel rushed. Even when fully prepared, he likes to get to school, have an extra cup of coffee in the teachers' lounge, read the newspaper, and fellowship with some of the other "early birds" on the staff.

As Arnie walks into the lounge, he finds two of his colleagues already there. Manfred Median is the long-time high school mathematics teacher at Mt. Carmel. Barry Baroque teaches music to high school and middle school students. Both Manfred and Barry are "political junkies," often coming to school early to discuss issues in the news over coffee. Barry and Manfred are close friends who engage in animated discussions since they tend to have differing political views. Manfred is a conservative and long-time member of the local Republican Party. Barry is a self-described "left-leaning independent." Arnie knows them both well. Both are active in strong, Bible-believing churches. He also believes that each man's testimony and walk with Christ are exemplary and that both seek to apply their faith to their political views. Because Arnie is the social studies teacher, both try to convince him of the veracity of their positions since, as Manfred once said, "I have to make sure you present those young minds with the correct view." Since Arnie respects both men and enjoys the dynamics of their discussions, he often listens and participates.

It is an election year so Manfred and Barry always seem to have something to discuss. Manfred has jokingly lamented that "school is getting in the way of my political discussions." The issue this morning is a proposition on the local ballot that would impose greater restrictions on local manufacturing plants that dump waste into the river running through town. If adopted, the proposition would increase taxes on local manufacturers to aid in cleaning up the river. In the town of Mt. Carmel there are several large manufacturing plants. Opponents of the bill believe that the clean-up initiative is aimed primarily at the paper mill, which is the town's largest employer. As Arnie walks into the lounge, he notes that today's discussion has already begun with vigor.

"The bill simply seeks to make the environment cleaner and the water we drink safer," contends Barry. "There also has been some evidence of increases in certain types of disease down river, and the EPA recently noticed a decrease in certain species of fish and other small organisms. Biblically, I think the bill is simply recognition of our need to be better stewards, to take greater care and show more concern when we do things that threaten the environment and place others at risk."

"No one denies that we need to be good stewards," counters Manfred, "but stewardship is not the only principle of note here. Part of our biblical command is to have dominion over the creation and develop it. What this proposition will do is make the industries in town, particularly the paper mill, less competitive. Passage of this bill would result in increased cost of production for the mill, which would make their products more expensive. Local businesses must already comply with federal EPA regulations, and the plants are already in compliance with those guidelines. Business leaders argue that this bill threatens their ability to compete, and its passage will result in layoffs, or even relocations, to stay competitive. Many of our students have parents that work at the mill. If they get laid off, that could result in our enrollment going down, and even if this bill passes, it is not going to improve the environment. Since this proposed legislation would not apply to the companies up river, only our town will be affected. You might, and I emphasize *might*, be right if the proposition were statewide and affected the communities up the river. Until it does, I think the proposition is a bad idea."

"I can't believe what I am hearing," counters Barry. "Are you suggesting that we should not be better stewards of God's creation because someone else is not doing their part? Even if what you say about competitive advantage is true, it does not negate the fact that the plant is a health risk to many people downstream. The types and concentrations of chemicals being released are a major factor in what is at issue. The only reason that the plants are in compliance to EPA standards is that the standards have been lowered over the last few years in order to make business more competitive. This bill only purports to bring these plants back into conformity with previous standards. I really think your argument is shortsighted. Eventually we will have to do something about all the companies, up and down the river, who are dumping harmful chemicals into the water supply. The longer we wait, the more difficult and more expensive the clean up will be. Plus, what do we say to those people down river who are being placed at risk by our pollution—sorry, but our economic livelihood is more important than the health of your kids?"

"There you go again," starts Manfred. "It is not simply an issue of jobs versus health. Let me see if I can explain this to you." Suddenly, the bell rings, signaling the approaching of first period. "Of course, just when I am about to set you straight, you are saved by the bell," laughs Manfred as he gets up to head for class. "For now let's just say that we have differing worldviews on this."

As Arnie walks to class he contemplates Manfred's last statement—do they really have different worldviews? They are both Christians and seek to apply biblical principles to their daily lives, yet their ways of looking at issues are vastly different. Is one position more biblical than the other? Can two committed Christians have different worldviews? Does this mean there is no such thing as "*the* biblical worldview," or do Manfred and Barry simply have different perspectives within the same worldview? Is it even possible to espouse two perspectives from the same worldview? In light of Mt. Carmel's current emphasis on biblical worldview, Arnie's mind races with these questions, and he resolves to think them through more deliberately.

The term *worldview* and the earnest attempt to help young people develop a more biblically oriented approach to understanding the relationship of faith to authentic living has become an important concern for many pastors, youth workers, and Christian school educators. Helping young people develop discernment and skill in applying the truths of Scripture to the fundamental issues of life is a goal for all Christian educators who desire their students to live as faithful followers of Jesus Christ. According to their worldview, Christians believe that the Bible can be applied to all areas of life. Issues of life goals, career choices, entertainment or recreational activities, and political perspectives are aspects of life that can be aligned with Scripture. Christians, while demonstrating a great deal of likeminded viewpoints in many areas, nevertheless have fundamental differences in many others. As people who aspire to be devoted followers of Christ and integrate every aspect of life with the standards of the Bible, fundamental differences in some of these areas may seem difficult to resolve. Can two Christians be faithful to the truths of Scripture and come to fundamentally different views on issues of art and music, environmental issues, or politics? Does the faithful application of Scripture demand uniformity of thought, or does a diversity of viewpoints represent an improper understanding on the part of some? Does a correct interpretation of the Word lead to a relative conformity in application to the issues of life, or does a multiplicity of responses represent the effects of sin in the lives of some?

As Brian Walsh explains, "The ascendancy of 'worldview' language as part and parcel of the vocabulary of the intellectual evangelical community in North America is intriguing because apart from anthropologists describing non-Western cultures, 'worldview' language has not been a dominant motif in the North American academic tradition."[1] Given humanity's robust descriptive power to explain the development of his understanding of the world and of his own self, it is interesting to note that the term *worldview* does not find its way into much literature outside of evangelical circles. David Naugle, in his book *Worldview: The History of a Concept*, notes that the most prominent proponents of the concept of worldview, outside of North American evangelicals, are European (and primarily German) philosophers. In fact, the English word *worldview* comes from the German *Weltanschauung* or "world" (*Welt*) "perception" (*Anschauung*). George Marsden,

---

1. Walsh, "Worldviews, Modernity, and the Task of Christian College Education," 13.

in explaining the adoption of worldview language among evangelicals, cites the influence of the late nineteenth- and early twentieth-century Dutch theologian Abraham Kuyper, who developed

> a style of Christian thought that emphasizes that crucial to the differences that separate Christian worldviews from non-Christian ones are disagreements about pre-theoretical first principles, presuppositions, first commitments or basic beliefs. . . . The prevailing view now emphasizes that Christian thought and non-Christian thought, being founded on some opposing first principles, reflects wide differences in total worldview.[2]

Kuyper and other evangelicals of that period observed the growing influence of a school of thought known as positivism that began in the mid to late nineteenth century. *Positivism* is the term used to describe a group of epistemological theories that view science as the only source of true knowledge and the scientific method as the only way to acquire reliable knowledge. August Comte, who popularized and systematized the term, argued that societies evolved from a theological or religious stage, through a metaphysical stage, and finally to a scientific stage wherein the scientific method would be used to develop and reform political, educational, economic, and other social institutions. Comte, and other positivists, proposed that, in order to be considered "intellectual," individuals needed to embrace the epistemology of the scientific method as well as the understandings of the world it produced. The spirit of modernism, and eventually positivism, led many nineteenth-century evangelicals to try to reconcile the findings of science, most notably evolutionary theories, with religious faith.[3] By the end of the nineteenth century positivism found its way into theology. Many Protestant theologians and thinkers attempted to apply a more scientific method to theology, using modern critical methods of textual interpretation to study biblical texts and the history and development of religious thinking. This approach to biblical interpretation, which became known as *higher criticism*, emphasized the importance of comparing the Bible with other literature rather than the over literal or historical interpretations of Scripture.

In regard to the sciences, many evangelicals of the time assumed that if absolute truth existed (and they believed that it did), that a scientist (believer or unbeliever), using the objective tools of inquiry (the scientific method) would discover truth that would point to the reality of God. What became clear to Kuyper and other evangelical thinkers was that the assumption of an objective science, which would align Christian and secular thinking in a biblical way, had to give way to a new model of understanding sensitive to the differences of how Christians and nonbelievers come to know truth. This new view emphasized that Christians and non-Christians thought differently about fundamental first principles or presuppositions and that these differences influenced the conceptual formulation of truth, how truth can be known or pursued and, ultimately, how truth should be used. In essence, Kuyper proposed that the inquirer's general assumptions about reality affected

---

2. Marsden, "The State of Evangelical Christian Scholarship," 355.

3. Jacoby, *Freethinkers*, 136–37.

the practice of science, so that the scientific method was not value neutral but influenced by the worldview of each scientist.

By the late nineteenth century, the first principles from which the majority of non-Christian intellectuals worked were based primarily in the beliefs of naturalism (the belief that material things represented the only real means of explaining reality) or phenomenology (the belief that sense data and its interpretation form the basis for knowing truth). Francis Schaeffer argued that prior to the late nineteenth century the dominant view of truth in the Western world was based in a Judeo-Christian way of thinking, which not only held the theological and ethical teachings of the Bible, but also maintained a belief in special revelation (as found in the Bible) as a legitimate and valid means of establishing truth. By the late nineteenth century, the theories and methods of people like Darwin, Marx, Nietzsche, and Freud began to overtake the Judeo-Christian view of truth. These men questioned the primacy of Scripture and special revelation in favor of naturalism and phenomenology.[4] As the Judeo-Christian view of truth lost its dominance to a secular, material view of the world, many evangelical scholars began to examine the presuppositions and their consequences that separated Christian thinking from non-Christian thinking. From this examination, the emphasis on worldview thinking among evangelicals began to develop.

EVANGELICAL ANTHROPOLOGISTS

Within this historical context the fundamental difference and the relationship between the use of the term *worldview* by anthropologists and by evangelical Christians becomes clearer. When anthropologists use the term *worldview*, they tend to do so from the perspective of conducting research and doing field work in order to understand another culture. When anthropologists enter the field, they bring certain assumptions about how the world is and how it should work, which are a product of the culture in which they grew up. If they are to understand the new culture, however, they must realize that their perspective is tinted by their own cultural upbringing and that these assumptions cannot be used to understand the practices of the culture that they are studying. They must understand that their worldview assumptions are not necessarily shared by the culture they are studying. In fact, their views are a minority perspective. In order to function within that culture as anything other than a separated observer, the anthropologist must come to understand the presuppositional belief system, the worldview of the culture in question, as well as the influences those beliefs have on the daily practices of life. Discerning and understanding these presuppositions also requires that anthropologists examine the nature of their own worldview and be able to articulate the assumptions they make about the world, contrasting their assumptions to the culture they are seeking to understand.

When the Judeo-Christian view of the world fell from dominance in the West, evangelicals increasingly found their perspective to be the minority perspective in the culture. Just as anthropologists find that they need to understand the dominant position of the society they are studying as a means to interact with that culture, so also Christians need

---

4. Schaeffer, *Escape from Reason*, in *Complete Works*, 1:225–36.

to understand the dominant presuppositions of the society in which they live. In addition, just as anthropologists need to define their own assumptions about what is normal and how the world works, evangelicals, as the minority position, must develop a better understanding of their own worldview in order to contrast it with the dominant worldview of the culture in which they find themselves immersed.

Although the anthropologist metaphor illustrates the relationship of a minority worldview to the dominant perspective of a society, the evangelical and anthropological perspectives of worldview differ in some very important ways. For evangelicals, a systematic and complete understanding of the biblical worldview serves as a buffer or a shield against the influence of the dominant worldview of the culture in which the church finds itself. Both the anthropologist and the evangelical discover that they have a need to develop an understanding of their own worldview and the worldview of the culture they are studying in order to compare and contrast the two. Though anthropologists may come to such a study with an assumption of cultural neutrality or be unwilling to judge their own worldview perspective as inherently superior to the culture they are studying, the vast majority of evangelicals do not share this view, assuming that their worldview is absolutely true. Since the nonbiblical, dominant worldview of the culture is inherently inferior to one developed from a proper biblical understanding, being firm in the superior biblical worldview should serve to guard believers against the influence of the dominant, secular culture.

Secondly, the evangelical and anthropological views differ in terms of how individuals interact with the other culture. When anthropologists begin the study of a culture, they come into that culture voluntarily; that is, as a researcher of the culture, the anthropologist willingly enters into the study. They are free, in many respects, to control the amount and degree of interaction with the culture, from becoming completely immersed to remaining essentially an outside observer. In addition, they come into that culture with an existing and, more or less, developed worldview. The worldview they bring with them to the study of the new culture has usually been developed independently of the culture they are studying. Having been raised independently of the culture, the anthropologist does not have to give significant consideration to the interaction effects of the new culture's worldview with the development of their own. In other words, there is little to no blending of their worldview with that of the culture they are studying. As a result, they do not have to seriously consider the problem of where their worldview begins and that of the other culture ends. As a result, the task of comparing and contrasting their worldview with that of the other culture is somewhat easier. In addition, anthropologists have the ability to disengage from the study of the new culture and return to their native culture when they so choose.

By contrast, the evangelical shares none of these characteristics. Evangelicals must seriously consider the interaction effects of the dominant culture with the development of a biblical worldview, in essence what blending exists between the worldview of the dominant culture and their understanding of the biblical worldview. Evangelicals find themselves, for the most part, involuntarily placed within a particular culture (God's sovereignty notwithstanding). While anthropologists choose the culture they desire to study, evangelicals do not. This involuntary component is often the result of being born into a particular culture and having been raised to understand the world from the perspective of that culture. S. D. Gaede, in his book *When Tolerance Is No Virtue*, contends that a believer's values and behavior mirror those of the general culture, noting that "one consequence of this is that Christians, by default, wind up duplicating the politics of their peers. . . . For example, studies have consistently shown that North American Christians tend to 'vote their occupation.' That is, if you know their occupation—along with their region, class, and educational background—you can pretty closely predict how they will vote."[5] While not all evangelicals conform to this generalization, nor conform to it equally, the amount and degree of cultural influence can vary according to factors such as type of family, strength of the family's Christian influence, age when the person came to know Christ, strength, biblical integrity, and regularity of attendance at their church or Christian school, to name a few. While some factors can reduce the influence of the dominant culture on the believer, others may increase its influence. Regardless, because of the dominant culture's influence on the Christian, the development of a biblical worldview will be more interactive than studying a culture from the outside as does an anthropologist.

Whereas the anthropologist enters a culture as a mature individual with an essentially fully developed worldview, a person born into or raised within a dominant culture does not. As a result the believer must develop a biblical worldview that contrasts with the dominant culture while still being immersed to some degree in that culture. Thus, when considering the development of a biblical worldview in a student, the amount of interaction with the dominant culture becomes a significant issue. The involuntary immersion of the evangelical into the dominant culture also means that the believer does not have the luxury of disengaging from the culture. While the amount and degree of cultural interaction may be controlled, the fact is that the culture in which believers find themselves is *their* culture. This means that, unlike the anthropologist, remaining an outside observer is practically impossible.

Finally, evangelicals must concern themselves with the issue of transformation when addressing the issue of worldview. Generally, anthropologists do not seek to become permanent members of the studied culture. Even when they do seek to function more fully within the culture, they approach this interaction as a minority seeking to be socialized into the majority. Likewise, anthropologists, if they are true to their discipline, do not desire to transform the culture they are studying. New believers, on the other hand, desire to become integrated members of a subculture (the church) and to develop a worldview that is different from the dominant worldview of the majority. Society attempts to socialize a person into being a fully functional member of the society based on its vision of what a good person should be. In contrast, the church attempts, in essence, to de-socialize or transform the person to a new set of values and away from the nonbiblical worldview where appropriate. Similarly, anthropologists do not seek to transform the studied culture, assuming cultural neutrality to be an important value and imposition of an individual's

---

5. Gaede, *When Tolerance Is No Virtue*, 55.

own view on the majority to be inappropriate. The church does not share these assumptions and actively endeavors to transform believers.

The church maintains the superiority of the biblical worldview, and since Christians hold to the belief that they are called to live lives of obedience to the Bible, the issue of transformation, both of the individual and the culture as a whole, has importance. While the believer or groups of believers may differ as to what transformation means, all evangelicals maintain that transformation individually begins with the receiving of Christ as Savior. In addition, all believers must develop an understanding of what it means to be "in the world but not of the world" (John 17:14–15) and how to serve as "salt and light" (Matt 5:13–16) in the culture, where the application of these metaphors can range from the church serving as force to prevent deterioration or decline to the church actively seeking to transform the dominant culture.

Consequently, when evangelicals approach the issue of worldview, they come to it with two foundational concerns. First, a biblical worldview is implicitly viewed as being superior to any other worldview that is not based on the Bible; therefore, the assumption exists that there is a biblically superior answer to any question or concern regarding thought or culture, even if the question or concern has not yet been sufficiently articulated. Acknowledging that a fully developed biblical position on every cultural issue has not yet been articulated by the evangelical community serves as the impetus for people within the church to develop thoughtful responses to issues of culture. This does not mean that an antithesis must always exist between the world and the church. John Calvin notes that when believers approach the works of unbelievers in science, medicine, art, the humanities, and so forth, that they should

> let that admirable light of truth shining in them teach us that the mind of man, though fallen and perverted from its wholeness, is nevertheless clothed and ornamented with God's excellent gifts. If we regard the Spirit of God as the sole fountain of truth, we shall neither reject the truth itself, nor despise it where it shall appear, unless we wish to dishonor the Spirit of God. . . . Those men whom Scripture [1 Cor 2:14] calls 'natural men' were, indeed, sharp and penetrating in their investigation of inferior things. Let us, accordingly, learn by their example how many gifts the Lord left to human nature even after it was despoiled of its true good.[6]

While Calvin acknowledges that the human apart from Christ can produce works that demonstrate evidence of the image of God, he is not so optimistic as to believe that unsaved humanity produces works in culture that bring glory to God. Even when humanity produces good deeds in the culture, they are works that "limp and stagger"[7] in the pursuit of the good; since unbelievers are motivated by their own ambitions, "their virtues are so sullied that before God they lose all favor," so that anything in them "that appears praiseworthy must be considered worthless."[8] Similarly, Hoeksema acknowledges that unbelievers may engage in the principles and practices of proper societal living. A ra-

6. Calvin, *Institutes of the Christian Religion*, 2.2.14, p. 273.

7. Ibid., 2.2.13, p. 272.

8. Ibid., 2.3.4, p. 294.

tional being who observes the natural laws that God has woven into the created universe would come to discover these in the process of making sense of the world; however, "such a person does not seek after God, nor aim at Him and His glory." As a result, he uses his knowledge and social efforts to rebel against God, leading to "evil effects upon himself and his fellow creatures."[9] The net result is that even when Christians adopt the works of unbelievers in the arts, sciences, humanities, politics, and so on, they must be clear that these adoptions correspond to biblical ways of thinking. In some cases the believer may have to modify the use of the works of unbelievers, understanding that having been created in the image of God, unbelievers may discover and utilize many of the how's embedded in the way God created the world without understanding and thus corrupting the why's.

All believers, because they possess the Holy Spirit who ministers in their lives, have some semblance of or capacity to develop a biblical worldview. Just as all people are acknowledged to have a worldview, so all believers are recognized to possess the seeds of a biblical worldview because of the ministry of the Holy Spirit leading them to truth (cf. John 16:13–15). One component of the difference between the natural and spiritual person is the ability to discern spiritual things (1 Cor 2:14–15). The development of spiritual discernment in believers results from such things as the quality of their relationship with God through Christ, the effect of the ministry of the Holy Spirit in their life, their relationships to other believers in the church, and the effects of ambitious study focused on integrating the sciences, arts, and humanities with the Word of God.

The second foundational concern of worldview development is the relationship of believers to the source of their development, which are others in the community of faith. By stressing the need to provide responses to culture, a more complete, integrated, and articulate biblical worldview is needed for those of the community of faith. Evangelicals acknowledge that some people have more fully developed biblical worldviews than others. While implicitly acknowledging that all believers have the capacity to develop a biblical worldview, the idea that those of greater maturity have more fully articulated worldviews has led many to advocate that the development of a person's biblical worldview can be greatly enhanced by studying with those who are more spiritually mature and expert in their particular disciplines. This point is especially held by many advocates of the Christian school movement. For example, Richard Edlin writes, "In short, if this is God's world, then it can only properly be understood in the light of His revelation. . . . It can be attempted in a God-centered Christian school system that leads students to study the world and their tasks in it in response to the God who created, redeemed, and sustains it."[10] Ellen Black notes, "The teacher's primary responsibility in the Christian school is twofold, to be both the spiritual leader and the academic leader. Teachers who do not embrace a biblical worldview are incapable of teaching the whole child, for God created humankind with a mind, body, and soul."[11] Ronald Nash advocates for the Christian university by stating,

9. Hoeksema, *Protestant Reformed Churches in America*, 372.

10. Edlin, *Cause of Christian Education*, 34.

11. Black, "The Teacher," 147.

"The evangelical college can offer an approach to education that helps the student become a whole person that enables the student to tie all the important aspects of her intellectual, moral, spiritual, and religious life together."[12]

The development of a biblical worldview in students is one of the more prominent objectives of Christian schooling. For the Christian educator this objective poses two critical concerns. First, how do experts define a worldview? If a primary goal of Christian schooling is to develop biblical thinking in students, it would be good to know what biblical thinking is, how it relates to the academic disciplines and its application to the real world. The idea that all believers are capable of having a biblical worldview but that some people have more extensively developed patterns of biblical thinking means that teaching involves the process of turning novices into those who more closely resemble experts. If this is the case, knowing the characteristics of what expert thinking looks like will be a critical component in developing strategies to assist students in their growth from novices. Also critical in developing more expert-like worldview thinkers is an understanding of the characteristics that separate experts from novices. Since all people have a worldview, and some people have one that is more fully developed and articulated than others, it is important to identify the factors that produce transformation and growth in a person's worldview. Is the ability to articulate a fully developed worldview the only significant characteristic of an expert in worldview or are there other factors that need to be considered? To address these concerns, the first task must be to define the term *worldview*.

THREE PERSPECTIVES ON WORLDVIEW

Brian Walsh notes that, while the term *worldview* is often used by evangelicals, not all evangelicals who use the term are referring to the same thing. A survey of evangelical literature reveals at least three distinct uses of the term. Walsh characterizes the three uses of *worldview* as being a synonym for theology, being a "theoretical construct," and being "pre-theoretical in character."[13] To Walsh, how individuals conceive a worldview will affect how they proceed in understanding its development, which will also have ramifications for the ways in which they think that it can be changed.

For some evangelical writers the term *worldview* becomes almost a synonym for theology or a more formally articulated religious philosophy or system of thought. From this perspective a worldview is similar to a series of statements, creedal formulations, or dogmatic propositions that are coherently organized and based in Scripture, understood to be founded on principles that are divinely inspired, infallible, and inerrant. Walsh understands this to be essentially the meaning attached to the biblical thinking of Francis Schaeffer, whose writings in the late 1960s through the 1980s did much to influence many evangelicals in their conception of worldview. For David Noebel, "the term *worldview* refers to any ideology, philosophy, theology, movement, or religion that provides an

---

12. Nash, *Closing of the American Heart*, 161.

13. I am indebted to Brian Walsh's article "Worldviews, Modernity, and the Task of Christian College Education," 13–32, for helping me develop my thinking on these differences. While I have borrowed his categories and have borrowed some of his examples, I have attempted to go beyond the brief explanation he gives for the three categories he portrays in his article.

overarching approach to understanding God, the world, and man's relationship to God and the world."[14] J. P. Moreland and William Craig write, "Philosophy can help someone form a rationally justified, true worldview, that is, an ordered set of propositions that one believes, especially propositions about life's most important questions."[15] Nash seems to maintain a similar definition of worldviews, noting that "the philosophical systems of such thinkers as Plato, Aristotle, Spinoza, Kant, and Hegel [constitute] worldviews."[16] While Nash maintains that all people have a worldview, the vast majority of people do not have the well-formulated and articulated worldviews common to or characteristic of philosophers or theologians.

Nash's idea that every person operates from a worldview, even if it is not formally developed compared to those of philosophers and theologians, leads to a second way that worldviews are described in evangelical literature—worldviews as theoretical constructs. From this perspective, worldviews serve as personal, suppositional or hypothetical visions of how the world is or should be. This is essentially the perspective on worldview taken by James Sire in his influential book *The Universe Next Door: A Basic World View Catalog*. Sire portrays worldviews as "systems of thought." Like Nash, Sire also notes that few people have "articulated philosophies" or have a "carefully constructed theology," but that all human beings operate from "universes fashioned by words and concepts that work together to provide a more or less coherent frame of reference for all thought and action."[17] Sire acknowledges that the number of worldviews to choose from is not infinite (i.e., there are a limited number of basic worldviews from which one can choose), but within those possibilities, individuals must make choices. For this reason Sire notes that worldviews are either adopted consciously or unconsciously, from an examined life or an unexamined one. But, like Socrates, Sire believes the examined life is more worthy of living.[18]

A tension is created when worldviews are thought to be personal choices but to be also limited to a range of possibilities. While Sire presents what he believes to be the dominant worldview positions in Western society, he notes that worldviews constitute a personal choice. He believes that the criteria of internal consistency, adequate handling of data, and the ability to adequately explain those aspects of reality that the worldview claims to explain are critical in making a choice.[19] In the end, though, Sire maintains that "a world view should be subjectively satisfactory. It must meet a sense of personal need."[20] The need for a worldview to be "subjectively satisfactory" suggests that all worldviews are distinctly personal and, thus, equally valid. Sire tries to escape this subjectivity by noting that only truth will ultimately satisfy; therefore, it is the desire for truth contrasted with the sense that something in a chosen view of reality is an illusion that creates the type of disequilibrium that motivates individuals to investigate and make changes in worldview

14. Noebel, *Understanding the Times*, 8.

15. Moreland and Craig, *Philosophical Foundations for a Christian Worldview*, 13.

16. Nash, *Faith and Reason*, 24.

17. Sire, *Universe Next Door*, 16.

18. Ibid., 19.

19. Ibid., 213–16.

20. Ibid., 216.

in the first place.[21] This explains Sire's contention that worldviews need to be personally discovered and that doing so is a "significant step toward self-awareness, self-knowledge, and self-understanding."[22]

These first two uses of the term *worldview*, however, deviate from its original use in the German, resulting in a loss of much of the power and descriptiveness of its original meaning. Although, outside of evangelical literature the concept of worldview is rarely mentioned, the term originates in the writings of several German philosophers and social thinkers of the late eighteenth and early nineteenth centuries. For the majority of these writers the idea of *Weltanschauung* (world-outlook) has a pre-theoretical character. *Weltanschauung* describes a global *Schauung* or outlook and is used to describe the characteristic way a people or culture conceive the world. Because of the corporate or group orientation of a *Weltanschauung*, the concept of worldview is distinct from science, philosophy, or even theology in that it can be held by all people regardless of their intellectual capabilities or academic backgrounds. From this perspective, a worldview is held by a majority of the people in a culture and forms the dominant way of making sense of the world for members of that culture As a result, people who engage in the process of developing a worldview more systematically (as suggested by the perspective of worldviews as philosophical systems) and those who engage in the process of trying to explain new phenomenon they encounter in the world (via the process suggested by Sire) do so within the parameters of a particular way of looking at the world. From the perspective of these German proponents of *Weltanschauung*, the development of any formally articulated system of thought, or even a subjectively consistent system of belief, is done within a context where the dominant worldview of the society serves as the background from which individuals will develop their ideologies, philosophies, or theologies. In this way the primary worldview of the society is prejudicially predisposed by members of that society to be the best or "right" perspective. As a result, no formally articulated set of propositions, system of thought, or subjectively coherent framework of belief can be understood or evaluated apart from the global world outlook from which it was developed.

This pre-theoretical character of worldview means that a worldview cannot be seen as synonymous with a philosophy or a theology, or even an ideology, but rather operates more closely to a "mythos"—a pattern of beliefs or characteristics that are expressions of the prevalent attitudes of a group or culture. Philosophies and theologies represent highly articulated and essentially personally held systems of thought. Ideologies describe the manner or content of thinking for an individual or culture, yet these are still essentially systematic ways of thinking about the world that may not be held with the same degree of intellectual rigor that would characterize a philosophy or theology. By contrast, a worldview is a guiding narrative that is maintained on an even more fundamentally basic level. Like a mythos, a worldview can be articulated but it need not be and still can have power to influence thought and behavior. For example, most Americans hold to some conception of the mythos known as the "American Dream" and may even articulate

21. Ibid.
22. Ibid., 17.

aspects of the American Dream as symbolizing the ideals of "life, liberty, and the pursuit of happiness" (however those are defined). While their conception and articulation of the American Dream may not entail much more than that, their development of the ideal life as Americans is still driven by the pursuit of that mythos. The worldview of the culture, which is encapsulated in the common vision or mythos, serves to define what the good life is and operates as a means of evaluating the goals, attitudes, and actions of both the individual and collective responses in the world. As a result, the worldview of the culture is expressed symbolically through art, music, science, and all other aspects of life—both individually and corporately.

While both ideologies and worldviews operate from a set of faith statements about the world, ideologies are more suppositional; that is, they assert what is true and the facts that are known or can be used to maintain it. On the other hand, a worldview is more pre-suppositional, its power coming from an implicit belief in what constitutes truth, which precedes logic or analysis. Thus, the pre-theoretical nature of a mythos, which is the first evidence or articulation of the worldview of a culture, means that it is foundational to the development of an ideology or philosophy. The worldview, and its resulting mythos, is an expression of the beliefs of a group that have their origins in the group's ways of perceiving the world, which are assumed, for the most part, without question. They are the "real" (i.e., normal) ways of seeing things. The power of the worldview and resulting mythos comes from the community's adherence to its core beliefs: current members of the culture operating in them and developing them; new members being socialized into them. These core beliefs are what allow the mythos to develop and constitute the perceptual and essentially religious core of a worldview.

In essence, a mythos is a cultural expression that arises from the perceptual filter of a worldview and provides many of the initial cognitive tools and materials needed for the development of an ideology (and ultimately a philosophy). In this sense, a mythos acts as a foundation for the members of that culture. The mythos provides the normative formulation of what constitutes the good life in that culture. This aspect has made worldview attractive to some anthropologists who have used the concept to explain how so-called primitive people operate from a set of presuppositions that function to integrate and explain experiences and the responses to those experiences in the life of the culture. These conceptual presuppositions were not systematized into a way of thinking that would be characteristic of an ideology or philosophy in Western thinking, yet they form a powerful belief system for members of the society.[23]

THE RELATIONSHIP OF THE THREE VIEWS

It may appear that the three views of worldview presented in evangelical literature vary simply in degrees of quantity. In other words, a philosophical approach represents a greater articulation of a worldview than the theoretical or pre-theoretical approaches. Because Christian writers have used the term *worldview* to denote any of these three posi-

23. For a further examination of the relationship of mythos and the pre-theoretical nature of a worldview in anthropology, see Howell, "Ojiba Ontology, Behavior and World View," 19–52.

tions, understanding the differences between them becomes difficult and may, practically speaking, seem a waste of time. On the contrary, considerable benefit, beyond simply an academic understanding, can be gained from noting the differences between these views. The greatest benefit is an understanding of the fundamental dynamics necessary in developing a person's worldview. Since believers are commanded to be transformed by the renewing of their minds (Rom 12:2) and to bring every thought into alignment with Christ (2 Cor 10:5), understanding the dynamics that assist or impede one's ability to obey these commands is critical, especially for educators who desire to empower students to fulfill God's commands for transformation and renewal. While there are similarities between philosophies and worldviews that make understanding the distinctions between them difficult, the critical differences between them make the synonymous use of the terms incorrect. If evangelicals are to develop a more thoroughly biblical worldview in their students, they must become familiar with the essential features and critical differences between a philosophy, ideology, and a worldview.

Gaining an understanding of the differences between a philosophy and a worldview is complicated by the fact that philosophies are more articulate and well-reasoned forms of a worldview. The idea that philosophies are quantitatively better expressions of worldview is not completely false. Because of this relationship it is tempting to approach changing a worldview by developing a more articulated philosophy of life. This seems to be the most common approach to worldview transformation practiced by Christian educators. While this approach may have some efficacy, it seems naive with regard to some of the qualitative differences that separate worldviews and philosophies. Understanding these qualitative differences constitutes a critical component to developing an effective approach for transforming worldview.

Philosophers and theologians often possess pre-theoretical conceptions of the world shared by other members of the culture, which are predicated, in large part, on certain foundational assumptions or presuppositions regarding the nature of truth, the nature of reality and the universe, and the essential character of humanity. The pre-theoretical nature of worldview means that, for many people, answers to these questions are sometimes difficult to articulate because their worldview has been insinuated from the culture without any real critical engagement. Regardless, worldview writers generally insist that all people have a worldview, whether they can articulate the answers to these fundamental questions or not.

A fundamental task of philosophers is to engage in the difficult task of articulating these answers. In general, philosophers seek to develop systems of understanding that are consistent with how the world is and how it should be. Unfortunately, in the process of gaining this greater understanding of the worldview through the process of diagnosing and articulating, something seems to be lost along the way. A price is paid for this greater articulation: fragmentation begins to occur, often resulting in several coherent but seemingly competing philosophies emerging from the same worldview. Also, because philosophies develop out of worldviews, there is no distinctive point along the continuum where one can say a worldview ends and a philosophy begins. This blurring of worldview and philosophical boundaries helps explain why some writers present worldviews as a type of theoretical conceptualization of the world.

Figure 1 attempts to graphically portray the three perspectives of worldview—the pre-theoretical character of worldview, a theoretical conceptualization of the world, and a philosophy—generally described in evangelical literature. The model examines the distinctions between the three characterizations of worldview. In order to explain the model we will use the example of the development of political-economic thinking found in American society.

Figure One:
Relationship of Philosophies, Ideologies, and Worldviews

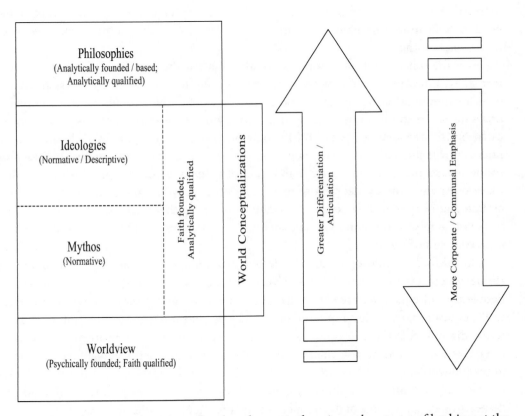

Philosophies are attempts to develop theoretical, universal systems of looking at the world that establish their credibility through the use of analytically founded and analytically qualified statements.[24] A good philosophy seeks to develop a theory of the nature of reality (metaphysics), the nature of knowing and establishing truth (epistemology),

---

24. I am indebted to James Olthuis for my understanding of the distinctions of these three views of worldview. While Olthuis informed my thinking on these distinctions, I have taken his views and developed them. Credit for comprehending the qualitative distinctions between the three views of worldviews should be his. I assume blame for any weaknesses in the development of his idea.

the meaning of life or existence (ontology), and the nature and types of values and the way humanity should live in relation to these values (axiology and ethics). Stating that philosophies are analytically founded assumes that the basis of a philosophy (the underlying principles and structural integrity of the system) can be presented in terms of propositional statements. These propositional statements form the basis of an argument. The argument can be maintained, debated, questioned, or rejected based on the validity of the logic or evidence that support it. The analytical nature of a philosophy allows for the identification and separation of component parts within the philosophy as well as for delineation of the nature and relationship of its component parts. Philosophers maintain that the integrity of a philosophical system is based on the degree to which it either logically corresponds to the real world or is rationally or internally coherent with the rest of the philosophical system. By maintaining that philosophies are analytically founded, the philosopher rejects ways of thinking that are characterized more by personal preference or intuition, maintaining the role of reason and logic as the primary vehicles for understanding.

On the other hand, philosophies are also analytically qualified, which means that change within a philosophy or from one philosophy to another is a process mediated by critical evaluation using logic and reason to evaluate the strength of the arguments that support the philosophy. Maintaining, modifying, or rejecting a philosophy is predicated on the supporting strength of its logic or evidence. Being analytically qualified, a philosophy is judged by critical analysis and must meet certain conditions of validity or soundness to maintain its strength and integrity. The analytically qualified nature of a philosophy also implies that philosophies possess not only internal consistency but also a certain degree of objectivity or generalizability, meaning that the truth of the philosophy rests not simply with the individual adherent but can be applied by others and to others as a reflection of reality.

In this sense philosophy and theology (since many theologians attempt to answer similar questions in light of biblical revelation) are specialized disciplines in which all people cannot equally engage. To engage effectively in these disciplines requires special skills, education, and a level of intelligence that permits a person to function effectively in the discipline. While this does not mean that lay people cannot perform effectively in philosophy or theology, it does mean that they are at a distinct disadvantage compared to people who are trained as experts in those fields. Since philosophies are generally developed, argued, and maintained by experts, they tend to be held individually and can demonstrate a fair degree of divergence within a particular worldview.

The analytically qualified nature of philosophies also suggests that reason, evidence, and logic will be the primary vehicles in the transformation of a philosophy or in the adopting of a new one. If worldviews are synonymous with philosophies, then the primary way to change a worldview would be through the use of well-reasoned arguments. Both the strength of the objective evidence used to develop the argument and the logic with which the evidence is presented are the primary instruments in effective change. This understanding of worldview leads to a type of *worldview apologetics*, where the objective validity of the worldview is presented, using reason, evidence, and logic to question the validity of any competing worldview.

Often, however, well-reasoned arguments are not sufficiently convincing to people, and in the end (as Sire suggests), people must find a sense of personal satisfaction with their worldview. If individuals are not convinced by the objective nature of the philosophical/worldview argument, it could be concluded that they are thinking (and acting) irrationally. We might be quick to acknowledge this possibility when we present the validity of the biblical worldview to someone who does not acknowledge it, believing that the only rational response would be to embrace the validity of the biblical argument. In contrast, we might be less apt to embrace this position if we were confronted by another well-reasoned, logical argument that contradicted the biblical worldview. In such a situation we might find that we have no response to the challenge being presented, yet we would also be disinclined to sacrifice our position simply because the alternative argument was better than our own. In such a case we could also be accused of being irrational, yet we might defend ourselves (either to our opponent or in our own mind) by stating that, while we don't have an articulated response ready at the moment, we believe that one is available, and we maintain, by faith, that given time we or someone else could sufficiently answer the concern.

The acknowledgment of such a reality underscores the idea of worldview as a theoretical construct or world conceptualization. Theoretical constructs are articulations of beliefs about the world that someone maintains on faith. When believers are instructed to "always [be] ready to make a defense to every one who asks you to give an account for the hope that is in you" (1 Pet 3:15), they are to have an articulated argument ready, the source of which is based on faith. In this sense, the source of validity for the argument is not the logic or evidence presented but the faith that underlies the argument; the strength of the faith is not necessarily eroded by the lack of articulation in the argument or the strength of an opposing argument.

Identifying faith as the basis of validity suggests that there is a level of apprehension from which philosophies arise. This level of apprehension forms the basis of theoretical constructs. Theoretical constructs, or world conceptualizations, are faith themes or beliefs about how the world is and how it should be. While they are less articulated than philosophies, they share the characteristic of being analytically qualified: how the world is and should be can be stated in propositional or positional terms, and thus individuals maintain the view that their belief is founded in reason, evidence, and logic (especially in a culture that places a high regard on these characteristics).

World conceptualizations often lack the systematic coherence of a philosophy or theology and are typically stated more in terms of position statements on particular issues than in terms of unified systems. For example, a person might state, "I am a Republican because the Republican Party is more pro-life." In this case the person would effectively see herself as a Republican even if she did not fully espouse all the aspects of the Republican Party platform or a particular party candidate. Furthermore, the analytically qualified nature of a world conceptualization also means that differences or inconsistencies, if they exist, can be resolved through greater articulation based on reason.

World conceptualizations, however, differ from philosophies because they tend to be faith founded rather than analytically founded. Faith founded means that these positions are held with a certain degree of trust in the underlying foundation of the belief even if the belief cannot be fully articulated by the person. Trust in the world conceptualization is based on a level of allegiance to or confidence in certain principles that are accepted on faith. This level of allegiance is typically found in people who are more knowledgeable advocates of the position (i.e., those people who are operating more like philosophers). For example, the old bumper sticker that stated, "God said it, I believe it, and that settles it," was not a call to abandon theology or a rational faith, but an acknowledgment that even if presented with a rational argument that the adherent could not answer one's faith would not be shaken, having confidence that a pastor or some other knowledgeable proponent of the faith could adequately provide a counterargument. World conceptualizations may also reflect a type of commonsense way of looking at how the world is and how it should be in which *common* is an acknowledgement that most reasonable people view the world essentially the same way as the person making the claim. Of course, the term *commonsense* often defines the typical beliefs of the person or group holding the world conceptualization and can be used as a way of reinforcing their assertion.

The faith-founded nature of a world conceptualization also differs from a philosophy in that philosophies tend to be developed and maintained more as individual entities, whereas world conceptualizations are developed and maintained corporately. The person holding a particular world conceptualization rarely holds that view alone but does so with the encouragement and reinforcement of the particular community in which the common view is held. This community could be the society at large (e.g., we are all Americans) or a subculture (e.g., a local church).

The strength of one's allegiance to a community is what helps to preserve the foundation upon which the world conceptualization is based. A marginal member of the community would have a weaker sense of the truth of a particular way of looking at the world and be more easily persuaded away from a particular world conceptualization than a person who is more fully integrated into that community. The encouragement and reinforcement of the community strengthens the faith foundation upon which the world conceptualization is built in the individual. Socio-cultural motivation theorists note people's identities are highly tied to identification with a particular group and that the more they desire to be a part of or maintain inclusion in a particular group, the more their identity will be bound up in participation with that community in terms of both actions and thought.[25] The writer of Hebrews seems to note the power of the community to strengthen and reinforce beliefs when he writes,

> Let us hold fast the confession of our hope without wavering, for He who promised is faithful; and let us consider how to stimulate one another to love and good deeds, not forsaking our own assembling together, as is the habit of some, but encouraging one another; and all the more as you see the day drawing near. (Heb 10:23–25)

25. Woolfolk, *Educational Psychology*, 356–57.

Consequently, a "good argument," one that would cause a person to change his world conceptualization, would not simply be more reasonable or have greater evidence but must also be aligned to the beliefs and themes held by the community. For example, someone presents research demonstrating that children whose parents come from higher socio-economic backgrounds generally have higher IQ scores, do better on standardized achievement tests, matriculate and complete college at higher rates, and, as a result, are more productive in their adult lives. From this research, they contend that the community should divert some school funding resources away from schools that tend to serve poorer families to those that service wealthier families based on the argument that the community would get more from their educational investment. While a great deal of research and logic might be used to substantiate the proposal, and critics might lack sufficient evidence to oppose it, most people might reject the proposal on a fundamental belief that all children deserve a quality education. The idea that all children should be provided equal access to a quality education comes from a faith-founded belief in the equality of all individuals. The belief in equality for all and the resulting influence on social policy represents a strong conviction that can be highly resistant to other claims of logic or reason. World conceptualizations, therefore, help account for statements such as "That can't be true" or "I simply refuse to believe that" when people are confronted with arguments that oppose their way of looking at the world.

On occasion people do, however, hold beliefs that are contrary to the accepted beliefs of their communities. While uncommon, there appear to be certain characteristics associated with those individuals who maintain positions contrary to that of the group. The first is that the greater the difference in the individual's beliefs from those of the community, the greater the need for the individual's belief system to resemble the more analytically founded and analytically qualified characteristics of a philosophy. This may be because philosophies are generally developed and held individually, so that individuals who choose to dissent or "go it alone" must develop their convictions in a way that not only convinces themselves but can also address concerns from other members of the community. Second, the greater the difference between the beliefs of the individual and the world conceptualization of the community, the greater the sense of cognitive distress or doubt created in the mind of the dissenter. Since personal identities are highly tied to identification with a particular community, the more a dissenter separates from the fundamental beliefs, priorities, and practices of that community, the more she might feel a sense of alienation from both self and the community.

In some respects these two characteristics tend to exacerbate the problem faced by dissenters as they view their niche within the community. For example, in the opening scenario Barry Baroque is a self-identified, left-leaning independent. As an evangelical he maintains the plenary inspiration and authority of Scripture, the virgin birth, the reality of the consequences of sin, the deity of Christ, Christ's blood atonement for the penalty of sin, and Christ's bodily resurrection and ascension into heaven. Clearly this places Barry within the community of faith and, if consistent with his beliefs, an active member of a local church community. However, his more liberal political beliefs might separate him from the rest of a more politically conservative evangelical community. As a committed believer he would naturally seek to support the validity of his political positions on Scripture and scriptural principles. This would help to reinforce the correctness of his beliefs in his own mind, which would also serve to strengthen the sense of alienation he has from the more politically conservative church community. This sense of alienation would be magnified by factors such as the strength of his sense of connectedness to his church community, the response of the church community to Barry's opposing beliefs, or the magnitude of the difference of Barry's beliefs from those of the community. Barry's responses could include changing his beliefs so that they align more closely with the group, seeking solace in identification with a subgroup within the body (such as other more liberal members of his congregation), or an ideological subgroup (other evangelical progressives via print, the Internet, etc.), or simply leaving that church community to find another with whom he can more closely identify.

World conceptualizations serve as a transition between the formally articulated, analytically founded and analytically qualified area of philosophies and the more foundational concept of worldviews. The nature of world conceptualizations is such that those who hold one do so with some degree of reinforcement and encouragement from a community, while philosophies are highly individual by nature. The closer one gets to understanding the nature of worldviews and how they differ from philosophies, the more critical the role of the community in which individuals are members. The basis of this claim is that worldviews are held communally and that the development of a worldview occurs within a cultural context. Thus, while examining how world conceptualizations serve as a transition from philosophies to worldviews, the increased importance of community in the development of worldview will unfold. In addition, the closer individuals get to a worldview, the less conscious they actually need to be of its existence. The claim that all people have a worldview whether they can articulate it or not illustrates this point—since a worldview need not be held consciously to affect a person's outlook on life and behavior. Still, the individual is the one who possesses the worldview, so the effects of the development of a worldview on the individual must be considered.

As a transition from philosophies to worldviews, the role of world conceptualizations can be divided into two parts. The first of these is ideology. An ideology serves to classify a group of individuals who maintain a basic system of thought even while there may be philosophical distinctions arising from that ideology. For example, being a political conservative would constitute a type of ideology for it associates one with other conservatives. However, there can be multiple of versions of conservatism arising from the basic ideology, and to label a person as a conservative does not constitute a specific philosophical label. Versions of an ideology tend to be associated more with individuals; that is, they are more characteristic of philosophies. For example, a person may be primarily a social conservative while another more a fiscal conservative. Persons viewing themselves as social conservatives would find their primary ideological voice in other, like-minded social conservatives.

As a type of world conceptualization, ideologies are characteristically faith founded and analytically qualified. The leading proponents of an ideology, those who come closer to approaching a philosophical level, can give more well-articulated, evidenced, reasoned arguments for their ideology. These individuals are often championed as the spokes-persons for the ideology; however, the arguments they present are founded in certain assumptions that constitute the faith-founded nature of a world conceptualization. For example, to be a conservative means that individuals maintain a set of assumptions about the world that would separate them others who would be considered liberal. Both individuals can give well-reasoned articulations for their positions, which are convincing to members of their ideology (although members of a competing ideology might question how anyone could possibly think that way). Even so, the analytical qualifications that constitute their arguments generally are not enough to persuade someone from the opposing position to accept the competing ideology (except, possibly, on a particular issue). Because ideologies have a faith-founded component, changing ideologies constitutes a type of identity realignment. Identity realignment is usually accompanied by identification with the members of the new ideological group.

The analytically qualified arguments of an ideology are manifestations of two aspects: the descriptive aspect (how the world is) and the normative aspect (how the world should be). Both the descriptive and the normative are functions of a worldview, which raises the question—what is the relationship between the two? Most philosophies seek to answer these two worldview questions, and individuals who do so are often viewed as philosophers (in the loose sense of the term). Note that the level of conscious awareness decreases in the transition from a philosophy to a worldview. Consequently, in ideologies the descriptive and normative functions, while still articulated, are articulated more loosely. This may result from the fact that as people settle into and identify with a particular ideology, there is less need to defend their reasoning since they are associating with a group who share the same beliefs. Only those who serve to defend the faith of an ideology against a competing ideology, those identified as philosophers or ideologues, need to have the most well-articulated arguments. For the rest, there is a level of comfort that comes from a shared-belief understanding that allows for the expression of positions or opinions in a way that is characterized by the phrase "preaching to the choir," where a lesser degree of support and logical rigor is needed because the speaker and listener share similar assumptions.

Since philosophies are highly individual and ideologies constitute more a group identification the transition to worldviews means that large groups of people will become identified with a particular worldview—to the point that observers can start to note that worldviews are reflected by societies and eventually cultures. For example, as noted earlier, Americans tend to hold to the notion of the American Dream, which often includes the ideas of "life, liberty, and the pursuit of happiness" (Thomas Jefferson), or "a chicken in every pot, and a car in every garage" (Herbert Hoover). The American Dream is an example of the second type of world conceptualization—the mythos, or the first cultural manifestation of the worldview. A mythos explains prevailing patterns of beliefs and the prevalent attitudes and values of a society. Both conservatives and liberals, as Americans, would share the fundamental values and views of the world that are espoused by the mythos (although it is interesting to note that in political rhetoric one side will try to portray the other as being somehow in opposition to the mythos). While ideologies serve to differentiate certain segments of the society from other segments (e.g., a conservative and liberal might detail different agendas for achieving the American Dream), the mythos tends to bind members of a society together. When people engage in the task of trying to identify what makes someone an American, they tend to identify the larger set of group attitudes and values that tend to bind Americans to the society as a whole.

Most Americans have little consciousness of what makes them American, and when asked what one has to believe to be an American, they have trouble articulating the attitudes and values that are essential core components to their identities. In this respect, a mythos is not really descriptive. In living as an American among other Americans, one does not need to be conscious of being American, since everyone is operating with similar basic assumptions about how the world works. The analytically qualified descriptive function is not as important. In fact, the ability to describe what it actually means to be an American may require separating oneself to some extent (literally or figuratively) from other Americans so that one can more objectively look at what it means to be an American. The more immersed one is in American society, the less conscious one needs to be of these characteristics, yet all the while may operate in ways characteristic of and consistent with the assumptions that make this way of life normal for Americans. This constitutes the faith-founded aspect of the mythos and makes it part of the world conceptualization. In this sense, the mythos is more normative. It serves more to tell someone what they should be, what the good life is, and how it can be achieved. The power of the mythos comes from the fact that it is encouraged and reinforced by the society in general as *the* way of looking at the world. The power of community, seen in ideologies, is magnified since the mythos is held by a larger majority of people in a society.

In essence, to oppose the mythos is to stand against the society as a whole. When the hippie movement of the 1960s espoused a set of values and a lifestyle that differed from the mainstream values and lifestyle of American society of that time, they were considered a counter culture, which placed hippies in an adversarial relationship with the rest of the society. Likewise, when critics of multiculturalism note that emphasizing the distinctiveness of different cultural groups will deteriorate the common heritage or culture of the United States, they tend to reflect a fear of eroding the mythos that makes a common life possible.

The largely unconscious and powerful nature of the mythos makes it difficult for members of a group to envision alternative ways of life. The more closely associated individuals are with the common culture, the less able they are to see the validity of alternatives, especially in relationship to their own lives. Those more fully vested in a culture may be less willing and less able to entertain alternative visions of what the good life may be than those members of the society who are less vested, enfranchised, or assimilated because for those more vested, the mythos provides both meaning and reinforces the practices of their life. Simply stated, the mythos is the filter that defines normal, and only the act of consciously separating from the mythos allows evaluation of it. The understanding that the mythos of a culture allows one to operate within the vision and values of that culture without much conscious attention sets the stage for understanding the nature of a worldview.

A worldview is foundational to both philosophies and world conceptualizations. Worldviews represent faith perceptions of the world. They are held with little or no conscious attention, so that almost all theorists of worldview note that whether individuals are conscious of it or not, whether they can articulate it or not, they all operate from a particular worldview, even to the point of noting that worldviews are a "human necessity."[26] The idea of human necessity underscores the belief that to function as a human being requires having a worldview; however, the development of the self always occurs within a social context, such as the family, the local community, or the larger society. The necessity of a worldview, along with the idea that the worldview develops within a social context, underscores the idea that worldviews are communal and that, in very large measure, people can only experience their true humanity within a social (relational) context. The context in which individuals can experience this sense of community can be through identification with the larger, more dominant, socio-cultural context or a close identification with a subculture or countercultural group. Clearly, worldviews are active and powerful, and the powerful and unconscious element of worldviews separates them from philosophies and world conceptualizations.

The unconscious element of worldview allows theorists like Walsh to describe worldviews as pre-theoretical in nature. The pre-theoretical quality of a worldview supports characterizing them as psychic founded and faith qualified. Stating that worldviews are psychic-founded acknowledges that they are systems of perception—and understanding that leads many writers to use the analogy of worldviews as lenses. The lens analogy, while appropriate, is incomplete, only clarifying part of the worldview function. A lens takes visual stimuli and put it into some sort of perspective. In this sense, the lens analogy works well, for a worldview is the unconscious perspective from which people interpret the world. A second analogy often employed to describe worldviews is that they function as a type of filter. From this perspective, worldviews serve to help us determine what to pay attention to and what should be ignored. In fact, the idea that worldviews are unconscious means that to ignore (which, in reality, is a conscious process) really means that a worldview causes people to *not* see certain things while demanding that they pay attention to others things.

Claiming that worldviews are psychic founded or perceptual in nature underscores the idea that they operate almost intuitively. Thus, a worldview allows individuals to possess a type of knowledge or understanding of the world and to maintain a sense of conviction that precedes reason. Since the development of a worldview begins at birth and since people are primarily cultural receivers during the fundamental years of worldview formation, alternative visions of the world are not considered or even recognized. Since a worldview defines who they are and who they are supposed to be, the worldview largely defines reality for them. Since the acceptance of this view of reality is implicit, it is unconsciously assumed to be true because they have never known any other way of looking at the world. To question the validity of their worldview would be extremely difficult, and to change it would require a redefinition of themselves and of the world. All worldviews are,

26. Phillips and Brown, *Making Sense of Your World*, 26.

therefore, faith conceptions, constructions of normalcy that are maintained with a tenacity that is more affective than reasoned and with a sense of conviction that is essentially religious in character.

Because worldviews are held with a sense or religious conviction they are faith qualified in nature. Worldviews are based in certain unproven (and possibly unprovable) assertions or presuppositions about the world that are taken on faith and form the basis for the structure of a belief system. Initially, these presuppositions are assumed because they are the only ones presented as individuals are socialized into the culture. Since a worldview is vital for human existence and if true humanity is developed and experienced in a relational context, then worldview development is an act of socialization. To change a worldview will require not only a "better argument," which may appeal to reason, but also a change in the object and direction of faith. Worldview transformation requires a new vision and an experience with the community of that vision which is more than rational. Christ told his disciples "to love the Lord your God with all your heart, with all your soul, with all your strength, and with all your mind" (Luke 10:27). The reality is that a commitment to God is more than simply a reasoned choice; it is one requiring and affecting every aspect of life. In essence, believers must essentially redefine who they are, who they should be, what is real, what is important, and so on, and must do so in a way that not only informs their thinking but also affects how they live in the world. A change in worldview is a change in the total belief system, underscoring the idea that worldviews are faith qualified.

Based on the worldview foundation, the mythos is the first conscious articulation of the worldview. Anthropologists use mythos to describe prescientific primitive cultures. Yet, can the idea of mythos be applied to more scientific and technologically sophisticated societies? Walsh notes that the answer increasingly given by sociologists, historians, and theologians is "yes." Sociologist Langdon Gilkey writes:

> Social existence involves and depends on a shared consciousness, a shared system of meaning. This shared system of meaning is structured by symbols that shape or express the understanding of reality, of space and time, of human beings and its authenticity, of life and its goods, of appropriate relations, roles, customs and behaviour, symbols which together constitute the unique gestalt, the identity or uniqueness, of that social group. To be a member of any community is to be aware of, participate in, and to be oneself shaped, energized, and directed by this common mythos.[27]

Walsh concludes that "it is this common shared consciousness, this shared system of meanings that gives rise to a historical way-of-being-in-the-world, and which constitutes the identity of a particular people or culture. This constitutes the essence of what is meant by worldview."[28] For example, the American Dream provides the mythos or vision for people in the United States; it is a vision that is given a type of official sanction in some of the literature of the founding fathers. It is a vision of the world that Democrats and Republicans proclaimed with equal conviction and intensity and in recent decades has

27. Gilkey, *Society and the Sacred*, 43.
28. Walsh, "Worldviews, Modernity, and the Task of Christian College Education," 17.

come to be defined chiefly in economic terms. For example, regardless of political party, the vision for America proclaimed by candidates of either party includes a platform of increased economic growth or improving the standard of living, a standard of vision and behavior that comes from a mythos in which economic considerations are of primary importance. It would be considered political suicide to endorse a platform of slowing, suspending, or reducing economic growth, and one could argue that the lack of success of so-called third parties is due, in part, to platforms that are not in line with the larger vision or mythos of the nation.

While it may be tempting to equate a worldview with the mythos of a culture, the mythos itself is predicated on certain faith-based assumptions of reality. These faith-based assumptions of the world are what constitute a worldview and give rise to mythos and increasingly more reasoned and articulated manifestations of the worldview. The pre-theoretical nature of a worldview provides the means for answering the most fundamental questions of life, answers that can be stated and analyzed propositionally (as they are in philosophies or theologies). These answers provide guidance to groups of people and cultures for the direction of life and the basic themes by which they live, and they do so in such a way that they are largely taken for granted as true.

The pre-theoretical nature of worldview can be seen both positively and negatively. Positively, this view maintains that worldviews function as a source of unity for the culture as a whole. They provide a sense of shared vision or purpose as well as the basic groundwork for decision-making within the culture. This sense of worldview makes a coherent cultural life possible. Worldviews also serve as the foundation for future theorizing. Thus, as people in the arts, sciences, humanities, and so forth develop their explanations and propose their visions of how things should be, regardless of their academic discipline, they do so from a fundamental set of presuppositions that constitute the worldview. This positive aspect of worldview is foundational to the inducement by evangelicals to develop a biblical worldview. The development of a biblical worldview is considered empowering in the quest to fulfill the biblical obligation to bring "every thought captive to the obedience of Christ" (2 Cor 10:5).

Negatively, this view asserts that worldviews operate unconsciously, that they are deeply rooted in each group's perception of the world. They provide the means to judge and label people, cultures, or ideas that disagree with one group as primitive, backward, or unenlightened. They predispose one group to view its worldview as the "best," and provide for a negative or suspicious view of other groups and their visions of the world. This understanding of worldview emphasizes how they are deeply rooted and unconscious, making them particularly powerful and resilient to change. It underscores the difficulty individuals have in developing an objective view and analyzing a culture when they are immersed in it. This makes Paul's use of the words, "transformed by the renewing of your minds," particularly cogent because transformation implies a metamorphosis to a higher qualitative state.

IT TAKES A CHURCH COMMUNITY TO CHANGE A WORLDVIEW

The idea that worldviews are held in community, or by a group from which individuals develop a strong sense of identity, not only underscores the biblical doctrine of the church as a corporate entity, but also underscores the need to develop a biblical worldview as part of a communal process. Bruce Milne notes that the New Testament describes the church in many ways that project this sense of community.[29] The analogy of the church as the body of Christ supports the idea that it represents an organic, living entity, not simply an institution. John 15:5 notes that for believers their life flows from Christ, that they are in a dependent relationship with him but they are also in a communally dependent relationship as members of the body (Rom 12:5). Therefore, their growth and development as believers, as well as the development of their brothers and sisters in Christ, is tied to interdependence in the body and the body's dependence on Christ. The church also has a special relationship with Christ as his "bride" (Eph 5:27), and in that capacity, it has the relationship of being a chosen or special people (cf. 1 Pet 2:9; Titus 2:14; Rom 1:1). As servants, believers minister as members of the kingdom of God (cf. Col 1:13) and ambassadors of that kingdom (2 Cor 5:20).

Milne notes the error of equating the kingdom with the church. The church is not the means by which Christ ushers in his kingdom; however, when the church lives in submission to Christ and obeys his will, it becomes an instrument of God's rule. By living in submission to the authority of Christ, both individually and collectively, the church demonstrates God's authority over the earth. Also, while the church waits for the full coming of the kingdom, it is able, by the ministry of the Holy Spirit, to embody an experience of the kingdom in mutual love and service. Milne concludes, "In the community of the Spirit, where the vast diversities of human experiences are overcome and the diverse members discover a unique unity in the family of God, the kingdom is truly pre-visioned and anticipated."[30]

The submissive church embodies the kingdom experience to a watching world and illustrates why the church exists as a community that encourages and prepares believers for good works and why individual Christians are not to separate themselves from it (Heb 10:24–25). The church serves various functions in the life of the believer and to the world. These can be summarized as worship, fellowship, service, and witness. As a worshiping community, the believers' responsibility and privilege are to praise God (Heb 13:15; 1 Pet 2:9). In fellowship, they affirm their commitment to those with whom they have been joined together by Christ, whom each believer is responsible for and responsible to. As a servant community, believers have been gifted and empowered by the Holy Spirit to serve others. This service is designed to promote growth and development in the body of Christ and in the community at large. When the church acts in this capacity, it serves as a testimony of Christ and a witness for Christ in the world. As a result, the church is empowered to supply answers related to questions of religion and faith and also to demonstrate the ability of the gospel message to impact all areas of life.

29. Milne, *Know the Truth*, 260–65.
30. Ibid., 264.

"One cannot keep evangelizing the world without interfering with the world's culture. . . . To divide life into areas of sacred and secular, letting our devotions take care of the former while becoming secular reformers during the week, is to fail to understand the true end of man."[31] In this quote, Henry Van Til expresses the need of the church, as an evangelizing community, to be able to show the truth, the value, and the utility of the gospel in all aspects of life. Van Til's emphasis on community contrasts with the ethos of individualism that is characteristic of American culture. Peter Schmiechen notes that this sense of individualism threatens the community of the church and, ultimately, the ability of the church to fully realize its mission because issues of faith become matters of personal choice and personal application, even by members of the church.[32]

This emphasis on individualism means that faith becomes separated from other aspects of communal life; faith becomes concerned with either the avoidance of the problems associated with culture, or the ability to live Christlike individually within the culture. An individualistic Christianity divorces Christian living from the body life of the community, living as a Christian in the world is relegated to issues of personal purity, personal charity, the use of time and talents, issues of relationships (e.g., marriage, parenting, or friendship), and so on. In addition, this individualistic emphasis detaches the Christian faith from critiquing the culture and developing biblical responses to it. In essence, Christians become individual responders to unbiblical culture rather than corporate creators of a more biblical culture.

Raymond Williams sees cultures are "signifying systems"; they "provide a collection of language and other signs that make sense of the otherwise chaotic and unrelated events of our lives."[33] As a signifying system, the church provides a set of principles and ways of interpreting the world. These principles provides the church, Rodney Clapp believes, with a particular language that sets it apart from the rest of the culture, and it provides a narrative or "grand story" of how things are, have come to be, and will end. Within this narrative of church culture individuals descriptively understand who they are and normatively understand who ultimately they are to be.[34]

Conversely, Walter Brueggemann suggests that the church as a subculture not only provides a countercultural message to its members but also provides the context from which the church can engage in a "prophetic criticism" of the dominant culture.[35] As a countercultural group, the church has the ability to confront or to criticize and, when appropriate, to dismantle the dominant consciousness of how the questions of life are envisioned and practiced by the culture. This dismantling is not reserved simply for members of the church as a means of strengthening the allegiance of its members to the counterculture, but more importantly, it allows the church to reject and delegitimize the message of the world. In turn, this alternative consciousness of life allows the church to nurture and energize its members to live in anticipation of the newness of life God has

31. Van Til, *Calvinistic Concept of Culture*, 43–44.

32. Schmiechen, *Christ the Reconciler*, 10.

33. Williams, *Sociology of Culture*, 13.

34. Clapp, *A Particular People*, 172–86.

35. Brueggemann, *Prophetic Imagination*, 9.

provided in Christ, for the future that is to come, and of the relevance of the gospel message to all aspects of life.[36]

Placing too much emphasis on the Christian school or the Christian university for the responsibilities of the church is dangerous. The Christian school is not the church and cannot assume its leadership responsibilities in the world. The church serves as the community of faith, as the body of worship, fellowship, service, and witness. While the Christian school cannot, and should not, seek to replace the church as the primary vehicle for the development of a biblical worldview in its members, there are certain characteristics of Christian schools, as a collection of believers representing expertise in various academic disciplines, that place it in a unique position to assist the church in developing a biblical worldview.

Granting that the biblical worldview applies to all areas of life, that all truth is God's truth, and that there is no aspect of life in which God is uninterested, then no aspect of life is morally neutral. The sciences, the arts and humanities, business, politics, and the helping professions are all aspects of life that fall under the auspices of a biblical worldview. While the local church may have individual members in many, if not all, of these arenas, the contemporary mission of the local church does not provide for the training of scientists, business leaders, poets, teachers, doctors and nurses, lawyers, etc. The Christian school (defined as K-12, undergraduate, and graduate education) provides servants to the local church to engage in the development of the biblical worldview in these more specialized areas. As such it provides the context from which the church as a counterculture can train its future leaders in the church's vision of life in these special areas, as well as help to integrate into these areas the overall gospel message. By training its future leaders, the Christian school enables the local church to engage in the prophetic criticism of the culture. It energize the church to develop biblical responses in the sciences, arts, humanities, and so on that assist believers to counter the dominant culture by providing a biblical framework from which to develop alternatives to the dominant culture.

36. Ibid., 3.

3

Worldview and Culture

Religion is the substance of culture and culture is the form of religion.

—Paul Tillich

IN THE FIRST TWO chapters we learned that a worldview is a type of lens that we use to make sense of the world around us. Worldviews allow us to make sense of the world through their descriptive function; that is, they help us interpret our experiences in the world; they tell us what the world *is* like. Worldviews also tell us what constitutes the good life, the types of appropriate goals and aspirations for ourselves but also for society or the world as a whole. In this sense, worldviews serve an idealistic or normative role—telling us how the world *should* be.

These descriptive and normative functions are couched within a cultural framework. As people develop their understanding of how the world is and how it should be, they do so from perspectives provided to them from the culture in which they live. While there can be levels of disagreement between individuals or groups over how to achieve this normative vision for the world (e.g., conservatives and progressives may disagree about how to achieve the best possible society), these types of disagreements are generally variations of philosophies and ideologies within the predominant worldview of that society. Also, what people tend to see when they examine objective knowledge, expressed in philosophies, theologies, theories, or ideologies, is only a small part of the worldview that produced them. Sociologist Peter Berger notes that "objective knowledge" constitutes the "official" interpretations of reality held by the experts of the society who can best articulate them; however, the knowledge base that maintains them, the interpretative schemes, moral maxims, and traditional wisdom shared by the majority of people in the culture, is pre-theoretical. It is the implicit understanding of reality—the ways of seeing the world, that are essentially held by faith and are shared by the majority of people in the culture.[1] It is this socially shared knowledge that leads us to see worldviews as a communal understanding of the world.

1. Berger, *Sacred Canopy*, 20–21.

Because worldviews represent a collective vision of the world, they constitute a common consciousness for the members of a society. As individuals interact with other members of the society, their social interactions are mediated through an integrated pattern of shared knowledge, beliefs, and behavior, which constitute the social mores of the culture. Our ability to live successfully in the society is predicated on this shared system of knowledge, beliefs, and behaviors. This understanding allows us to see that worldviews are cultural entities, that worldviews must ultimately find expression in the ways individuals live, from the most refined expressions of cultural life (e.g., the arts, humanities, and sciences) to issues such as how and what we eat or what we wear. These expressions of life can be carried out for the glory of God or in ways that do not glorify him. Consequently, when human beings are born into a particular culture, they immediately begin an immersion process in which they learn the appropriate values, attitudes, and behaviors of the culture and make them their own. From this perspective all education, and schooling in particular, is part of a socialization process preparing the individual to be a successful and contributing member of the society, and all education becomes worldview education.

This chapter will examine the relationship of worldview to culture. We will examine what culture is and how it is an expression of an underlying worldview. We will also examine the biblical mandate to be culture creators and the effects of the Fall and the sin nature on humanity's ability to be obedient to that mandate. This discussion will provide the background to examine the relationship of schooling to the development and perpetuation of the culture, and ultimately its worldview, and the role Christian schools and Christian educators should serve in the perpetuation or transformation of this worldview in the life of our students.

CULTURE AS THE EXPRESSION OF WORLDVIEW

Among people who study the idea of "culture," there is no single accepted definition of the term. Most scholars, however, would agree that culture can be defined as the "patterns of knowledge, skills, behaviors, attitudes, and beliefs, as well as material artifacts, produced by a human society and transmitted from one generation to the next."[2] Culture represents the sum total of the religious, intellectual, social, political, economic, moral, and aesthetic accomplishments of a group of people. Common to descriptions of culture is that they are best understood as goal oriented—possessing a set of behaviors, beliefs, and hopes of the group that direct the group toward a particular vision or goal of life. In this sense cultures propose or embody a social ideal. As Clifford Geertz states, "Culture is best seen not as complexes of concrete behavior patterns—customs, usages, traditions, habit clusters—as has been the case up to now, but as a set of control mechanisms—plans, recipes, rules, instructions (what computer engineers call "programs")—for governing of behavior."[3]

While evangelicals have adopted the language of worldview, it is a term used in other academic disciplines, most notably the fields of anthropology and sociology. When anthropologists and sociologists describe the effects of culture in its members, they note

2. Pai and Adler, *Cultural Foundations of Education*, 21.

3. Geertz, *Interpretation of Cultures*, 44.

that culture provides "the standards and controlling mechanisms with which members of a society assign meanings, values, and significance to things, events, and behaviors."[4] This process, known as "symboling," examines the inherent value of objects or actions as perceived by the culture. As Leslie White and Beth Dillingham note, the process of symboling occurs through "thinking, feeling, and acting, and produces corresponding products such as ideas, acts, and objects. These patterns are reflections of *unique worldviews* and value orientations belonging to *individual societies*."[5] Cultural anthropologists use the term worldview to denote this function for culture. As Pai and Adler state,

> There is probably no definitive answer explaining why a particular culture assigns certain meanings and worth to a given set of events, objects, or acts. But we can reasonably assume that the dominant worldview of society is the major source of meanings and values. In turn, a prevailing worldview of a culture results from certain experiences that have enabled a group of people to successfully solve the problems of daily life. In a very important sense, a culture is a conception of what reality is like and how it works.[6]

The anthropologist views culture as inclusive of all aspects of life. This concept of culture runs contrary to the idea of "high culture" (as distinguished from "folk" or "popular" culture)—which refers to a process of individual education and refinement and, by extension, the products of such processes (e.g., works of art, music, and literature) that characterize those who embody the "ideal" of the culture—the literate, urbane, or self-conscious.[7] Whereas high culture is evaluative and exclusive (not all people are cultured and those trained are deemed better than those who are not), the anthropological view of culture is descriptive, normative, and inclusive: it serves to direct the goals and explanations of life for all members of the culture. Kathryn Tanner notes that the evaluative and exclusive view of high culture produces a view of culture that is *singular* rather than plural. This means that there is a high culture that is shared in varying degrees among "cultured" people separating them from the less-cultured members of the society. It provides those cultured members a sense of spiritual, artistic, and intellectual refinement, which also provides its possessors a greater sense of self and cultural control. It also produces a view of culture that is focused on the individual or subgroups of the culture and not on the culture as a whole.[8] In this way the singular view of culture can be used in an ethnocentric sense to define a particular culture as the high (or higher) culture and look with disdain upon other cultures or subgroups of that particular culture. This view of culture separates those who possess more high culture within a society from those who merely possess folk or popular culture. From the singular perspective, education serves to foster the development of individuals, initiating them into a particular social standing (usually a more highly encultured group) and separating them from the less "cultured" members of the

---

4. Pai and Adler, *Cultural Foundations of Education*, 22.

5. White and Dillingham, *Concept of Culture*, 27 (italics added).

6. Pai and Adler, *Cultural Foundations of Education*, 23.

7. Smelser, "Culture: Coherent or Incoherent," 4.

8. Tanner, *Theories of Culture*, 5.

society. This view is based on the belief that those who have been sufficiently enculturated possess and typify the ideals of the culture.

A more inclusive view of culture, encompassing a more descriptive, normative, and inclusive understanding of communal life, provides several basic elements that are important for an understanding of the relationship of culture to worldview. This understanding informs the power that culture has on shaping a person's worldview and why one's worldview is so resilient to change. Understanding the relationship of worldview to culture will become critical to the formulation of a biblical approach to viewing Christian education's role in culture and to developing a biblical worldview in students.[9]

The first, and possibly the most basic, tenet of anthropology applicable to understanding the relationship of worldview to culture is that _culture is a human universal._[10] All and only human beings have culture. It is a universal principle that separates human beings from animals and is thus part of God's image borne by all humanity. As a human universal, culture is characterized as the process whereby human beings act on nature in ways that distinguish them from nature. The result is that culture becomes an "artificial, secondary environment" that humanity superimposes on the natural.[11] "Rivers are nature, a canal culture; a raw piece of quartz is nature, an arrowhead culture; a moan is natural, a word cultural."[12] The idea of culture being a human universal imposed on nature makes the development of culture part of the biblical mandate to humanity given by God in the Garden, a concept that will be developed in the next section.

Second, though culture is universal, it is not universally shared. All people have a culture, but they do not share the same culture. Thus, anthropologists highlight the _diversity of human cultures._ Cultures are plural, not singular, as in the high culture view. Culture helps human beings understand and adapt to conditions in the environment, thus geographic location will have a significant impact on worldview and cultural development. The types of foods eaten, clothing worn, and attitudes and behavior toward the scarcity or abundance of resources are aspects of culture that develop within an environmental context and are shaped by the impact of historic forces and contribute to the diversity of human cultures.

Consequently, no culture will have a monopoly on characteristics that conform to a biblical understanding of the world. Some cultures, admittedly, may be more biblical (i.e., aligned more closely with the characteristics and commands of God) even if they do not base their mores and practices expressly on the Bible. For example, in regard to issues like interdependence and the importance of interpersonal relationships, Latin and Native American cultures may demonstrate a more biblical perspective in these areas than the more independent and goal-oriented Anglo-American culture. This despite the latter's

---

9. Ibid.

10. I am indebted to Tanner's book, _Theories of Culture,_ for these "basic elements" of culture. The characteristics and basic descriptions of these characteristics are from her work. I have taken liberty to amplify or slightly modify these descriptions to portray my understanding of their relevance to our understanding of worldview.

11. Malinowski, "Culture," 621ff., quoted in Niebuhr, _Christ and Culture,_ 32.

12. Niebuhr, _Christ and Culture,_ 33.

closer alignment with Christianity. This does not suggest that interpersonal relationships that characterize, for example, Native American cultures arose from an understanding of the biblical concept of interdependence. In many cases the cultural characteristic preceded exposure to Christian influences; however, cultural characteristics developing prior to Christian influence suggests that human beings, as image-bearers of God and developers of culture, can create cultural forms that have vestiges of biblical principles. It also suggests that even societies with a historically strong biblical influence can produce cultural mores and institutions contrary to biblical principles due to the presence of the sin nature in its members,

Third, *cultures vary within social groups*. A single culture consists of a variety of different groups within a culture. This variety does not preclude the existence of dominant ideals in the culture, but simply variations in the practice of those ideals. Viewing worldviews as communal helps explain how differences in ideologies and philosophies can come from the same worldview. For example, demographic trends among people of similar race, class, age, or gender suggest group variations within the dominant ideals of the society. Groups such as advertisers or politicians often use these trends to court certain segments of the population.

Fourth, *a culture tends to be conceived as an entire way of life*. In this sense, the definition of a culture used by anthropologists and sociologists is similar to the understanding of worldview as defined by evangelicals. In explaining this particular aspect of culture, Tanner notes that culture includes "everything about the group that distinguishes it from others, including social habits and institutions, rituals, artifacts, categorical schemes, beliefs and values."[13] While evangelical worldview language does not normally include culture manifestations such as rituals and institutions, the ideas of categorical schemes, beliefs, and values are foundational parts in almost all definitions of worldview.

Fifth, *cultures are associated with a social consensus*. To be a member of a cultural group means that one shares certain fundamental beliefs with other members of the culture. This is an idea not readily apparent in the typical understanding of worldview, but is critical to the development of strategies for teaching and transforming worldview in students. While a culture may consist of a number of different subgroups (e.g., evangelicals would represent a subgroup of Americans), and while each of these subgroups demonstrates certain characteristics that distinguish them as a subgroup, there are still certain fundamental beliefs that are shared with the larger cultural group. For example, socio-economically upper-class Americans differ from lower social class Americans in certain characteristics, yet it can be presumed that both groups value democratic government and a respect for personal freedom that are fundamental to the culture of the United States. Subgroups in a culture are reinforced by the culture at large to maintain certain fundamental beliefs, even while holding beliefs that may differ from other groups within the culture.

Sixth, *culture is understood to constitute or construct human nature*. Here is another point often absent in the evangelical literature on worldview critical for understanding the

---

13. Tanner, *Theories of Culture*, 27.

process of worldview transformation. As noted, from infancy children begin to construct their understanding of the world from the perspective of the culture into which they are born. In this respect they are products of their native culture. Their way of understanding the world is a result, in large part, of the family, community, social institutions, peers, media, and so forth that act on them in such a way as to socialize them into the culture. This socialization results in members holding certain fundamental beliefs that are characteristic of the culture as a whole. Sociologists and cultural anthropologists argue that what constitutes human life, apart from the biological, can only be understood in terms of the relationships that human beings have with other humans. The idea that human nature is, in large part, a construct of culture has biblical support, demonstrated as early as the first chapters of Genesis. We often note that humanity, created in the image of God, is more than simply physical; for example, we note the triune nature of God and point to the triune nature of humans as body, soul, and spirit. In Genesis 2:18, however, when God spoke, "It is not good for the man to be alone; I will make him a helper suitable for him," we see the social aspects of humanity being expressed by God in the need to complete man by creating a relationship with one similar to himself.

The fact that evangelical worldview literature tends to ignore the cultural construction of human nature may be the result of certain beliefs that are particular to evangelical thinking. In describing the characteristics of white evangelical thinking, Michael Emerson and Christine Smith note that white evangelicals mentally possess a "cultural toolbox" from which they tend to view the world. This toolbox is based on three "tools" or principles that shape the development of white evangelical subculture and its responses to the surrounding culture. They identify these tools as a belief in "accountable freewill individualism," "relationalism" (i.e., attaching central importance to interpersonal relationships), and "anti-structuralism" (i.e., an inability to perceive or unwillingness to accept social structural influence).[14]

Applied to the understanding of worldview development and change, these factors would contribute to a white evangelical emphasis on worldview as an individual possession (i.e., each person must develop his own biblical worldview, and he will be accountable to God for how he lives out his worldview—accountable freewill individualism). Anti-structuralism minimizes or denies the strength of the prevailing culture to influence worldview development (since these cultural forces would hamper free-will individualism). For example, as noted in chapter 2, Sire, in *The Universe Next Door*, treats worldview as a personal choice. Thus, Sire sees worldviews as personal systems of belief without explicitly acknowledging the power the cultural context has on the development of worldview. While Sire notes that one must choose a worldview that is "subjectively satisfying," he fails to acknowledge how the predominant worldview of the culture would contribute to what would constitute a satisfactory response for an individual.[15]

Although culture has significant influence over the formation and development of worldview, human beings are not simply byproducts of their culture. Tanner's seventh

14. Emerson and Smith, *Divided by Faith*, 76.
15. Sire, *Universe Next Door*, 216.

point acknowledges that *cultures are conventions in the sense that they are human creations*. Human beings create the cultures they live in. While culture is a powerful determinant of how people think about their world, the work of people in the world alters the culture and thus alters how people subsequently think about the world. This aspect of culture must be considered in the process of transforming worldview. Because worldviews influence the explanation of both how the world is and also how the world should be, a worldview by its very nature must have a component that is behavior oriented.

To treat the concept of worldview as simply a rational way of understanding or explaining the world, without the behavioral component, leads to an insufficient conception of worldview. Because worldviews include a vision for how the world should be, any plan for the development of a biblical worldview must include a vision that will serve to both direct and evaluate the behavior of the believer in the world. Cultural change occurs as members of the culture seek to implement the worldview ideal, to figuratively close the gap between the normative vision and the current descriptive vision provided by the worldview. As members of the culture seek to implement the worldview ideal (both individually and corporately), they also change the descriptive component, causing periodic evaluations of the current state of the world in light of the worldview ideal. This evaluation serves as the basis to inform subsequent behavior. Thus, any plan for the transformation of worldview must have a vision of how the world should be that will drive subsequent evaluations and behavior. Considering the communal aspects of worldview, however, means that the development of such visions and action plans cannot simply be individual. It must be a shared vision, acted out by individuals but promoted and reinforced by the community. Such actions provide the seeds of change within the culture that allow the worldview to develop and grow for those who adhere to it.

It is understandable that evangelicals, given their predisposition toward explaining the world from the perspective of freewill individualism, relationalism, and anti-structuralism, are wary of a more social-structural explanation for the development of worldview. To some, a structural perspective on culture, where the power of the culture to influence the development of worldview is deemed preeminent, suggests a type of social determinism—where the society decisively shapes the character and thought patterns of its members. Some may believe that such a perspective means that the patterns of thought and action resulting from the initial worldview are resistive to change, and thus it denies the efficacy of freewill individualism. In reality, one can acknowledge the power of culture in the formation of worldview and its resistance to change without denying the power of individuals to alter the worldview. While most subsequent behavior that emanates from a worldview seeks to bring the descriptive evaluation of the world in line with the normative, individuals acting on the world can also bring about changes to the normative aspect of worldview. When this occurs, there can be qualitative change to the existing worldview causing fundamental shifts in the worldview for the entire culture. As a result, the idea that individuals can change the culture and, subsequently, the way that a culture looks at the world, means that the cultural aspect of worldview, while tremendously powerful, is not omnipotent.

Consider the development of modernity and the rise of confidence in scientific thought. Throughout Europe, prior to the seventeenth century, life was understood and its purpose defined in religious and spiritual terms. Truth was based on the revelation of God in the Bible and the authority of the church. Throughout the sixteenth and seventeenth centuries many thinkers (e.g., Bacon, Descartes, Galileo, Copernicus, and Kepler) tried to incorporate both scientific thinking with the teachings of the church. When these views came into conflict (e.g., with Galileo and Copernicus), the church sought to censure them. In 1687 Isaac Newton published his *Mathematical Principles of Natural Philosophy*, a book that radically influenced Western society. Newton, by demonstrating the universal laws of gravitation that could mathematically explain all motion both in the heavens and on earth, established science as the new means by which the world could be understood and new knowledge discovered.

Newton's work not only led to a revolution in science, but to the scientific methodology being used as the dominant means to understand all of social life as well. It gave rise to a type of optimism that everything in nature could be known and that progress was the natural trajectory of human development. Through Newton, the ideas of the modern world of the nineteenth and twentieth centuries began to develop. Thus, while powerful, culture does not act as an unalterable determiner of a people's perceptions and thoughts about the world, and individuals can transform their own thinking and influence the way an entire culture perceives reality. As Tanner writes,

> The character of one's culture is contingent but one's conformity to it is not. Individuals may influence the culture of their society through their activities— altering its constitution, furthering or hampering its continuation over time. Their capacity to do so is implied by the conventional character of the culture. But this agency on the part of individuals is always subsequent to, and predicated upon, their prior formation by the culture into which they were born. They first became the people they are by being formed by the culture of their society, by internalizing as children, in the process of being socialized, an already existing culture. A culture they simply found themselves a part and could have done nothing themselves to produce. At least initially, individuals are almost the "passive porters" of a culture.[16]

Changing our understanding of worldview from a primarily individual process to a group process derived through culture allows a better understanding of the power of the prevailing culture on the thinking of evangelicals who find themselves members of a secular, naturalistic society. This means the task of transforming a person's worldview must consider the power of the dominant culture on individuals. As noted in chapter 2, evangelicals did not really begin to adopt the language of worldview until the late nineteenth and early twentieth centuries, and only when evangelical Christianity was confronted by forces that radically changed the dominant worldview of the culture. Because the Judeo-Christian worldview lost its status, biblical explanations of the world are relegated to a type of subcultural status. Evangelicals must now make a type of cross-cultural comparison between their understanding of truth and that of the prevailing culture. Often, when the term *worldview* is employed, it is used to make such comparisons. In this sense, to think

16. Tanner, *Theories of Culture*, 29.

with a "Christian mind" is to think counterculturally. Failure to do so will result in a type of secularized Christian thinking, where biblical terminology is used to adapt or adopt the more dominant vision of the culture. The result is a compromise or corruption of the biblical normative vision and failure to understand the world from a biblical perspective.

The secularization of the Christian mind produces the need for an emphasis on *biblical integration*. As the term is commonly understood, integration means bringing the products of the various academic disciplines into faithful alignment with the theological or doctrinal teachings of the Bible. This emphasis on integration supports the need to correct the separation that has occurred between faith and learning as a result of secularization. In this respect integration represents an essential component of Christian education—the fusion of the Christian mind with the academic subjects taught and all other aspects of personal and school life.[17] Biblical truth constitutes the beginning point, the foundation through which everything else is evaluated. Biblical integration, from this perspective, represents the filter from which we evaluate all life experiences.[18]

Implicit in the view that faith, learning, and life must be biblically integrated is the idea that the Christian faith has lost its predominant status in the culture. Francis Schaeffer notes that for much of the history of Western civilization, even nonbelievers operated within the framework of a Judeo-Christian perspective. Believers and nonbelievers shared similar concepts of right and wrong, truth and falsity, concepts that were rooted in a biblical worldview. No longer is this the case. Such concepts are rendered "nonsense statements," indicative of the lack of influence the Christian perspective has on society.[19] The biblical perspective's loss of prominence within the culture has facilitated the focus on integration among evangelicals; however, this integration must be accompanied by praxis—an implementation and application of faith to cultural behavior. Without such praxis there may be the integration of faith and learning but a failure to apply the biblical worldview to the issues of life.

A cultural perspective of worldview provides the means to understand the full consequences of a biblical worldview in the life of the believer. Since worldviews are orientations to all aspects of life, a biblical worldview will move beyond simply changing the ways or categories of personal thinking, beliefs, and attitudes. From these must also follow the production of actions and artifacts of culture that are consistent with its vision. In essence, a worldview that does not produce behaviors that are consistent with it is an inadequate worldview. A cultural perspective of worldview stands as a challenge to evangelicals to produce a type of subculture that will remain biblically consistent in both thought and action as it approaches the issues of cultural life, even though it may not always be distinctive in terms of practice.

A cultural perspective of worldview also provides a way to understand the power and consequences of the secular worldview of the culture. Thus, people will generally accept the normative vision and descriptive interpretations of the world that align with the

17. Hasker, "Faith-Learning Integration: An Overview," 3.

18. Campbell, "Integration of Learning into Faith," 36.

19. Schaeffer, *The God Who Is There*, in *Complete Works*, 1:7.

predominant worldview. When confronted with the normative and descriptive aspects of the biblical worldview, the discrepancies between these two worldviews can create dissonance. This dissonance is enhanced when the dominant worldview is also aligned with the desires of the sin nature. In this case the sin nature and nonbiblical worldview reinforce each other. As a result, individuals experience a type of alienation, not only spiritually in their relationship to God, but also personally in their relationships with others, with nature, and even with themselves. This spiritual alienation is the result of the sin nature's desire to be autonomous from God.

The result is that individuals are motivated to develop culture that will render the motivations, thoughts, and actions of the sin nature as "normal." This normalization will, in the short run, allow individuals and societies to live apart from God. This compromise, however, cannot be maintained indefinitely without significant consequences both individually and corporately. The existence of dissonance suggests a need for change and provides a means to understand the nature of transforming worldview and the types of resistance that believers can expect to encounter when attempting to change it. Thus, to transform one's worldview means challenging the accommodations in the culture that have normalized the sin nature, a situation shared by others in the culture who also embrace a like investment in normalizing their sin nature. This examination requires confronting motivations that are rooted in the sin nature—motivations in which individuals have a deep vested interest and which they may not desire to examine. Such an examination may require wholesale changes in a person's attitudes, values, goals, and, ultimately, behaviors.

Of course, this sense of dissonance is predicated on a belief that the concept of culture is fundamental to the understanding of worldview and that the connection of worldview to culture is, in fact, a biblical one. The biblical relationship of culture to worldview can be found by examining the cultural mandate given to humanity in Genesis.

THE BIBLICAL CULTURAL MANDATE

Two passages in Genesis will serve as a focus regarding the relationship of the biblical worldview to culture:

> Then God said, "Let Us make man in Our image, according to Our likeness; and let them rule over the fish of the sea and over the birds of the sky and over the cattle and over all the earth, and over every creeping thing that creeps on the earth." And God created man in His own image, in the image of God He created Him; male and female He created them. And God blessed them; and God said to them, "Be fruitful and multiply, and fill the earth, and subdue it; and rule over the fish of the sea and over the birds of the sky and over every living thing that moves on the earth." (Gen 1:26–28)

> Then the Lord God took the man and put him into the garden of Eden to cultivate it and keep it. (Gen 2:15)

Richard Mouw has described these passages as the "cultural mandate," God's charge to the first parents to "transform untamed nature into a social environment" through the process of cultural formation and development that fits God's design.[20] It is a call to "responsible dominion," or stewardship, where God gives to humanity the responsibility for managing and developing the creation. As seen in the command of Genesis 2:15, God placed Adam in the Garden both to keep it (i.e., maintain, preserve, or do no harm) and to cultivate it (to improve it by labor, care, and study). God's charge that was particular to Adam in Genesis 2:15 is representative of the command to keep and cultivate all of the earthly creation that was given to all humanity in Genesis 1:26–28.

The cultural mandate of Genesis 1:26–28 is introduced by the principle that humanity is created in the image of God. Just as God is the authority over all creation, he assigns to humanity the responsibility of stewardship dominion over the earth. Henry Van Til notes that stewardship dominion requires humanity to "take responsibility for keeping the earth, for respecting the integrity of kinds, and times, and seasons. Let human beings discover the character of other creatures and do what they can to assist these creatures to act in character."[21]

It also extends to the development of aspects of culture found in Genesis chapter 4. Here Abel is a "keeper of flocks" (animal husbandry); Cain, a "tiller of the ground" (agriculture); later Jubal is "the father of all those who play lyre and pipe" (music); and Tubal-Cain, "the forger of all implements of bronze and iron" (metallurgy). While the Fall has corrupted the motivation and use of the talents and abilities given to humanity to develop culture, the cultural mandate of Genesis 1:26–28 and Genesis 2:15 reveals that the development of these areas in Genesis 4 is not simply a result of the Fall. In essence, humanity was commanded to develop the creation before the Fall occurred. After the Fall, God's expectations to humanity did not change nor was the cultural mandate revoked, but their ability to fulfill the mandate was corrupted by the effects of sin on humanity and the rest of creation. Thus, the development of culture is not an effect of the Fall, although the motivations and the forms that culture production now takes bear the marks of the Fall.

The word *steward* comes from the English term *sty ward* or the "ward of the pig sty." It is a medieval term for the trusted servant whom the feudal lord placed in charge of the pigs, property of considerable value. The more traditional meaning of steward as the "man over the house" is similar to the role Joseph served in Potiphar's house (Gen 39:1–6). Different from simple *servanthood*, stewardship is the responsibility given to one trusted to use the resources of the owner apart from specific instructions as to how they are to be managed. While general principles for their use are implied by the owner, the steward is given considerable latitude.

This understanding of the cultural mandate calls into question the popular perception of the idyllic perfection found in the Garden of Eden. A popular understanding of Eden is of a place in which Adam and Eve had little real work to do, aside from keeping the Garden and naming a few animals. The idea of work seems foreign to the idea of paradise. Genesis

---

20. Mouw, *When Kings Come Marching In*, 16.
21. Van Til, *Calvinistic Concept of Culture*, 28.

1:26–28 presents the basic requirements of the stewardship mandate. In this passage the commands given to humanity are injunctions to (1) "be fruitful and multiply" (the procreation command); (2) "and fill the earth," and (3) "subdue it." The first part of the command is fairly direct, the procreation command, to have children and populate the earth. The second denotes that humanity was expected to spread out across all the earth, so that the commands of stewardship would be applied to all of creation. It is this command in which the decedents of Noah were in violation after the flood so that God confused human language, forcing humanity to disperse across the earth (cf. Gen 11:1–9).

The third phrase "and subdue it," though, challenges the idea of a paradise that did not have to be brought under subjection. Often evangelicals are guilty of imposing a view of perfection that is nonbiblical. In this case the perfect creation was not one that had no further need for its completion (i.e., perfect in the sense that nothing more could be done to it), but one that perfectly matched God's intent for humanity and the rest of creation. The creation was not one that would be completely self-sustaining; it would require some type of work on the part of Adam (as indicated in 2:15) and future generations in order to tame it and, therefore, fulfill God's command.

The second part of the cultural mandate is stated in Genesis 2:15, in which Adam is commanded to both cultivate and keep the Garden. The command to cultivate is to engage in a process of developing or improving. Adam's command was to improve and develop the perfectly created Garden. To this end God provided Adam with the time, talents, gifts, resources, and abilities needed to develop the Garden. From this perspective, to "cultivate," or the principle of stewardship dominion, is to add value or to develop the creation in such a way that the steward brings greater glory to its owner—God. The act of cultivating becomes an act of worship, where an individual's actions are governed by a desire to glorify God by how one acts and cares for the creation.

A similar illustration of this value-added idea of stewardship dominion is given by Jesus in the parable of the Talents (Matt 25:14–29). Here each servant or steward was entrusted with talents of gold—one five, another two, and the last one. The first servant took the wealth and doubled it from five to ten talents. The second also doubled the value of the talents entrusted to him—from two to four. Only the last servant, who simply buried the talent in the ground for fear of losing the value of the talent, was called a wicked servant. This servant was admonished by the master, who said the least he could do was to "put my money in the bank and upon my arrival I would have received my money back with interest" (Matt 25:27). Note, the master did not prescribe to the servants the manner for using the talents entrusted to them. The servants were given considerable freedom to manage their talents in any way that would increase their value for the master. The good servants were those who took care of the original talents, while also working to develop and increase their value. The wicked and lazy servant preserved the talent's original value but failed to work to develop and add value for the master's glory.

The cultural mandate given to humanity in Genesis 1:26–28 and 2:15 suggests that, like the servants in the parable of the Talents, Adam specifically and humanity in general have been entrusted with something of value (the earthly creation of God) that they are to manage as stewards, with all the freedom and authority granted by the Master to administer the estate, for the purpose of bringing greater glory to God by adding value to his earthly creation. Thus, it is God's expectation that the products of human endeavor, whether they be the arts, language, literature, science, mathematics, technology, customs, manners, institutions, and so on can be used to bring glory to God. These products of human endeavor are the results of choices that individuals and cultures make in the allocation of time, talents, energy, and resources—choices that indicate an underlying value of either bringing glory to God or bringing glory to one's self.

Van Til notes that cultures seek to meet the needs of human beings living in a social context. These needs include nutrition, material goods, aesthetics, reproduction, and so forth. In addition, human beings, even before the Fall, possessed needs and desires that would have been based on proper or godly motivations. An omnipotent God, in order to provide human beings with the resources to meet all those needs and desires, could have created an environment of unlimited resources. Instead God, in his sovereignty and infinite wisdom, did not create such an environment. Rather, by placing humanity within a world of limited resources, God forces humanity to choose how they will use those resources.[22] Humans must prioritize, and prioritizing takes place within a certain frame of reference: the attitudes, beliefs, customs, and social mores that are part of the culture.

In worldview language, the ability to prioritize comes from the vision of how the world should be. The sense of how the world should be guides the use of limited resources toward the achievement of a particular vision of the world. For example, a cultural vision that values the qualities of speed and efficiency could be expected to divert limited time, materials, human and capital resources to the creation of technologies that would be cultural manifestations, or artifacts, of those values (e.g., telecommunication technologies). Naturally, the process of using resources in that way will preclude the use of the same resources in another way. Thus, the achievement of cultural goals involves choice, and choice is never morally or ethically neutral; it is inherently religious in character in that it sees certain ends as good (and, therefore, worthy of the investment of time and material resources), and others as less valuable or even bad. As Van Til states, "Since man is a moral being, his culture cannot be a-moral. Because man is a religious being, his culture too, must be religiously oriented."[23]

From a biblical perspective, culture becomes the sum of human effort to subdue the earth together with its total achievement in fulfilling the creative will of God.[24] Cultural efforts unearth the treasures of creation and bring them into service for the glory of God. As a consequence, the use of resources in this way also brings enjoyment, enrichment, and satisfaction to humanity as they exercise their God-given and created role. Humanity's steward relationship to God places individuals in a covenantal relationship with the Creator to manage his creation in ways that will bring glory to him. Being in the image of God, endowed with creativity and rationality, humans are morally responsible for their actions and duty bound to function as stewards. As stewards, humans exercise

22. Ibid., 27.
23. Ibid.
24. Ibid., 30.

dominion, the privilege to mold the creation according to their will while still functioning within the realm of truth. In order to fulfill their calling, human beings must learn about the creation, for subduing cannot be done without a proper understanding of the characteristics of the creation for fear of violating the injunction to do no harm. Stewardship also requires an intimate relationship with the Creator, for as human beings seek to glorify him, they must understand the One they desire to glorify.

Van Til understood religion—in this context, worldview—to be at the heart of culture. Religion provides culture with its foundation by providing the moral precepts of value-based choices that precede all manifestations of culture.[25] When Adam introduced sin into the world, humanity's desire to be autonomous from God led to a perversion of the cultural mandate. Humans no longer sought to glorify God through the creation but to glorify themselves. This led to a new "religion," a new worldview, in which the creation is used as a vehicle to gratify and glorify the desires of human beings apart from considering God and his glory. Because of this distortion of the cultural mandate, the institutions and practices of a culture can be, more or less, pagan.[26] Sinful humanity develops culture that is an extension of its fundamentally flawed spiritual-moral character. Just as a species can only reproduce biologically that which is essentially its own species, so, too, sinful humans can only create cultures that are extensions of their sinful being.

The development of culture apart from the desire to fulfill God's stewardship mandate means an understanding of culture as an extension of humanity's sinful condition. As a result, there must be a critical and conscious effort on the part of each believer to evaluate how practices that are considered normal in the culture may be vehicles for the normalization and gratification of the sin nature. For the believer, to accommodate cultural practices that are contrary to a biblical perspective is to engage in cultural practices that hinder his ability to live a life that glorifies God and serves as a testimony of the church to the world. As Van Til writes,

> It is certainly folly for God's people to think that they can live in two separate worlds, one for their religious life and devotional exercise, and the other usurping all other time, energy, money—an area in which the priests of Secularism are calling the numbers. One cannot keep evangelizing the world without interfering with the world's culture. . . . To divide life into areas of sacred and secular, letting our devotions take care of the former while becoming secular reformers during the week, is to fail to understand the true end of man.[27]

For this reason, Van Til concluded that the biblical understanding of culture and a biblical worldview are inseparable. A worldview must cover the whole range of human existence and is manifested in the culture that humans create. That humans create culture is not a post-Fall characteristic of humanity, but is part of the creative image of God in humanity and the pre-Fall cultural mandate. Just as human beings did not completely lose the image of God when they chose to sin, they also did not have their responsibility for be-

25. Ibid., 39.
26. Ibid., 42.
27. Ibid., 43–44.

ing stewards of the creation revoked because of the Fall. For this reason, humanity is still held morally accountable to God for the culture it creates and for the way the creation is used; however, because of humanity's sinful condition, human beings are unable to create culture in a manner that will ultimately bring glory to God. Yet there is hope, for in Christ individuals are restored to God, not just in their vertical relationship to the Father but also in their horizontal ability to be cultural creatures that can serve their Master in the world and demonstrate renewed stewardship dominion over the world for God's sake.[28]

KUYPER AND CHRISTIAN EDUCATION

At the inaugural convocation of the Free University of Amsterdam, Abraham Kuyper said, "There is not a square inch in the whole domain of our human existence over which Christ, who is sovereign over all, does not cry 'Mine!'" Free University was founded by Kuyper in 1880 and was built on the premise that all of human knowledge and endeavor must serve the glory of God and be informed by Scripture. Kuyper, in the tradition of the Protestant Reformation, insisted that God considered all of life, not just religion, important, and that Scripture provided the foundations of all human life. For Kuyper, a "life and world view" was an "all embracing system of principles from which we obtain a peculiar insight into three fundamental relations of all human life: [namely] (i) our relation to God, (ii) our relation to man and (iii) our relation to the world."[29] Kuyper believed that it was the role of Christians to engage in the development of an understanding of how all areas of creation related to the truth of God and that this knowledge would inform how they are to live in the world.

Kuyper believed that there were two great worldviews that competed for the allegiance of humanity—modernism and Christianity. These worldviews formed the basis of a "conflict of principles" in which modernism proposed the absolute sovereignty of humanity and Christianity asserted the absolute sovereignty of God. For the Christian, this sovereignty means that the truth of God can be found and must be taught, not only in religion but also in the sciences and social sciences, arts, humanities, and all areas of human learning and endeavor.[30] This integration is the biblical obligation of believers to reach an unbelieving world. To Kuyper, Christians had a relationship to the world that was based on their relationship to God. This relationship was not limited to the vertical relationship between God and humanity (i.e., reconciling individuals back to God) but was also to demonstrate the horizontal relationship—how biblical Christianity applies to living in the world. For this reason he was particularly critical of those Christians that sought to withdraw from the world. Commenting on Kuyper's view, D. M. Lloyd-Jones wrote, "The Christian is not only to be concerned about personal salvation. It is his duty to have a complete view of life as taught in the Scriptures. . . . We must have a world view."[31] Christians are to be broad minded, seeking to cultivate a more liberal-arts view

28. Ibid., 45.

29. Kuyper, *Calvinism*, 11.

30. Ibid., 12.

31. Rodgers, *Incarnation of the Antithesis*, 11–12.

of education, not limiting their understanding to theology, and thus leaving other areas of human understanding in the hands of unbelievers, They are to be conscious of the fact that Christians have been called to understand all things of this world.

Any study of the world that is done from the perspective of biblical understanding must be conducted not merely for the benefit of the individual, but for the preparation of believers to promote the common good for all of humanity. Thus, any understanding of the relationship of the truth of God to any area of human endeavor that is limited to a person's individual understanding is in violation of the principles of Scripture. Kuyper insists that a biblical worldview will imply that all knowledge relates not only to humanity's relationship with God, but also to humanity's relationship with others and to the nonhuman world. As a result, any biblical understanding of the physical and social sciences, arts, humanities, and so forth that does not lead to faithful and appropriate behavior in the world is not truly biblical. Kuyper notes that the guiding principles of loving God and one's neighbor serve as the basis of the relationship between knowledge and action. For Kuyper, love serves as the basis for all life so that to obey and love God requires working for the best interest of others. In essence, one cannot claim to love God without also serving others (cf. 1 John 4:20).

For this reason, Kuyper, as a proponent of biblically based action in the world, was a staunch advocate of the relationship of Christianity to education. He worked for the formation of the Free University of Amsterdam, which sought to develop the relationship between education and action in the world. As Kuyper proposed, God's sovereignty extends to all aspects of life and humanity. Having been created in the image of God, humanity has been given intellect and wisdom to discern not only *how* God has put things together, but also *why* and *for what purpose*. He was critical of believers who advocated that Christians had no place in higher learning outside of theology because (as some Christians claimed) Scripture condemns human learning. Kuyper acknowledged that the Bible makes statements such as "Your learning and wisdom have made you perverse" (Isa 47:10) and "he who increases in knowledge increases in woe" (Eccl 1:18) and that "the wisdom of the world is foolishness to God" (1 Cor 3:19). However, he also notes that the Bible teaches that "the excellency of knowledge gives life to those that have it" (Eccl 7:12).

These passages differentiate wisdom that originates in the fear of God from learning that originates in sin, "which tempts humanity to disconnect learning from God, to steal it from God, and finally to turn it against God."[32] This dichotomy, he believed, led to societies that have turned from the truth of the word of God, not just in terms of religion and morality but also in the understanding and practice of the sciences, arts, and humanities. While human learning apart from the principles of Scripture may accurately discern the "how" of God's creation, since unregenerate humanity still retains part of the image of God, it cannot discern the "why" and "for what purpose" because of the effects of sin in darkening their understanding.

---

32. Kuyper, "Common Grace in Science," in *A Centennial Reader*, 447.

In contrast, an education based in biblical principles would provide both a thorough understanding of how the creation works and (when grounded to biblical principles of application) the relationship of Christian thought and action to the world. The ability to engage in such a view of education is predicated not only on a thorough understanding of content knowledge but also on rigorous theological thinking. To Kuyper, the motivation to engage in academic knowledge and understanding of the world and the purposes for which that knowledge and understanding are used should be based in a desire to convey an "aggressive testimony to the sovereignty of God over every area of experience."[33]

Kuyper's view of the relationship of Christianity to education stemmed from a theology based in the principles of Reformation thinking, specifically Calvinism. While Kuyper inherited the Reformation impulse to transform culture, he never lost sight of the fact that engagement with culture is not, in and of itself, an evangelistic activity. Kuyper understood that Christians could not transform culture in such a way that it would create social systems that would lead people to Christ. In this sense Kuyper does not advocate Christian reconstruction—the belief that the church can and should recapture every social institution for God and create a type of theocracy. Rather, Kuyper was hopeful that Christian contribution and the participation of believers in the culture would serve to pre-evangelize, to demonstrate the validity of and model God's intended purpose for all relationships that had been damaged as a result of the Fall. It was Kuyper's belief that such activity on the part of believers would prepare the hearts of unbelievers to see the relevance of God in all aspects of life, and thus prepare their hearts for the gospel. Regardless of this pre-evangelizing consequence, Kuyper believed that Christian contribution and participation in culture were part of their calling by God, and were acts of obedience as part of being faithful to the commands of Scripture.

SCHOOL AND CULTURE

As previously noted, worldview directs the development of culture so that the institutions and many of the artifacts produced by a culture are the reflection of the dominant worldview that underlies that culture. In this sense, all mainstream institutions in the culture are directed by the dominant worldview of that culture. Arnold DeGraaff and his colleagues note that "political activities, legal, economic activities, marriage, family and child rearing practices are all expressions of a confessionally led way of life. Thus, each culture presents a coherent, meaningful pattern that finds its unity in the dominant vision of life."[34] In addition, worldviews not only provide a way of interpreting how the world is but also provide a vision of the way the world should be. This allows members of the culture to develop a vision for what a perfect institution in the culture might look like. For example, individuals can have a vision of the perfect school, but this vision will, in large part, still be a reflection developed from the alternatives that are part of the predominant worldview.

---

33. Rodgers, *Incarnation of the Antithesis*, 30.
34. DeGraaff, Olthuis, and Tuininga, *Japan: A Way of Life*, 145.

Even though the social institutions and practices of a culture are manifestations of a particular worldview, as people operate within those institutions, they can contribute to the development and possible modification of the worldview. Since the mainstream institutions in a society emanate from the dominant worldview of the culture, they are reflections of the dominant worldview of the culture. There is, however, an interaction effect. As the individual institutions of a culture interact to influence the development of other institutions in the culture, they can affect the practice of those institutions and, ultimately, change the worldview as a whole. For example, certain practices of schooling within the United States are considered a normal part of how school is done. These include things like age-graded classrooms, the awarding of letter grades as an indication of learning, and the requirements of the curriculum to graduate from high school, to name just a few. David Tyack and Larry Cuban have called these types of practices the "grammar of schooling" and note that these persist in schools because they allow teachers to execute the responsibilities that school boards, principals, and parents expect them to perform in a predictable manner and with relative ease.[35]

This grammar of schooling, however, is a product of the influence of other aspects of the culture which, over time, have affected the rationale for the existence of schools and the methods used to perform their function. For example, in the United States the economic need of a trained and differentiated workforce and the need to maintain political and social stability have led to extending the benefits of schooling to an increasingly larger segment of the population. The benefits of education, at one time reserved almost exclusively for white males born into more affluent families, have become increasingly available to other groups. Extending the benefits of schooling to an increasingly large number of people has also created the need to identify those students who are better "equipped" (i.e., as a result of intellectual aptitude, motivation, disposition, work ethic, or talents in a particular area) for those vocations that the society has deemed worthy of greater status (as indicated by the prestige and compensation normally associated with those positions)—positions that a greater number of people would seek to pursue based on the incentives provided by the society. The need to identify such students in an increasingly egalitarian educational environment led, particularly in the years following World War II, to an increased emphasis on a more college-oriented high school curriculum and standardized testing as a means of identifying those most capable of success in college. That is, to use schools, increasingly, as a means of social efficiency, by sorting students.[36]

This increased emphasis on identifying those students who possess the necessary skill set to make greater contributions to the overall well-being of the society (increasingly defined in economic terms) suggests that schooling, like every other manifestation of culture, is a reflection of the worldview of that culture. A nation that embraces a normative vision of the good life as primarily economic will ensure that its schools socialize students and prepare them to be participants and contributors to that vision. The society will also demonstrate concern when its schools are believed to be failing to prepare people for

---

35. Tyack and Cuban, *Tinkering toward Utopia*, 86.
36. Spring, *Sorting Machine*, 43–51.

this vision of life. Thus, the Reagan administration, in the 1980s, believed that the United States was *A Nation at Risk*—at risk of losing its economic preeminence in the world—and that the schools were responsible for the situation. During the 1990s the administrations of President George H. W. Bush and William Clinton embraced *Goals 2000*—designed in part to ensure that American students would lead the world in mathematics and science achievement (academic areas with high economic viability). In recent years the administration of George W. Bush has engaged in educational policies to ensure that "No Child [is] Left Behind"—raising the question, "Left behind what?" The answer to the question is found in the foreword of the law: "In a constantly changing world that is demanding increasingly complex skills from its workforce, children are literally being left behind."[37]

If schools are social-cultural institutions, they are reflections of the dominant worldview of the culture that created them. That is, they are institutions that help to socialize and prepare young people to live in the dominant culture. If schools are social-cultural institutions created by sinful individuals, they will reflect the nature of those that created them. From this perspective believers should not be surprised if schools prepare people in such a way that the sin nature is normalized to reflect the sin laden objectives of an unbelieving culture. Thus, the institutions of a society will be reflections of the false perspective that corresponds to the sin nature of the people that created them. While those institutions may pursue worthy, and even biblical, goals, they do so from a perspective and in a way that does not promote a biblical perspective. These effects would not simply be limited to the structure and operation of government, but to any institution that is a result of the dominant worldview. What the properly functioning school must do, from this perspective, is to prepare young people to accept the false perspective of the world as the real one—to accept the false normative vision of the world as the legitimate vision. From this perspective, the structure and operational practices of any institution are designed to normalize this sin-laden perspective.

Even so, we have also seen that worldviews are dynamic; they can be changed. For this reason any institution in the culture can be both a reflection of the worldview of the culture and an influence on the development or change of the overall worldview of the culture. In light of this reality, the next focus will be on the institution of schooling as the basis for understanding the impact that schools can have as both an agent for socializing students into a particular worldview and for changing worldview.

---

37. Bush, "Foreword," i.

4

Worldview and Education

There is no such thing as a neutral educational process. Education either functions as an instrument that is used to facilitate the integration of the younger generation into the logic of the present system and bring about conformity to it, or it becomes the practice of freedom, the means by which men and women deal critically and creatively with reality and discover how to participate in the transformation of the world.

—Richard Shaull, Preface to *Pedagogy of the Oppressed*

IT IS THE WEEK before Thanksgiving. The administrators of Mt. Carmel Christian School have decided that for this year, rather than attend the regional Christian school teacher's convention, the faculty and staff will meet for two days to discuss the development of a Christian worldview in their students. Since teacher orientation week, smaller groups have met to discuss various issues regarding worldview development. These have normally been short segments of weekly teacher's meetings at either the high school or elementary faculty meetings. This is the first time since orientation week that the faculty has gathered as a whole to discuss these issues.

After Dr. Solomon gives a few announcements and opens the meeting in prayer, Dr. Wise of Reformation Christian College takes over the meeting. "I am so glad to be with you again and have been looking forward to these next two days. During our sessions at the beginning of the year, we tried to define what a worldview is and what factors shape our worldview. Over these next couple of days we will begin to consider the differences between a Christian and the secular worldview of our own culture—especially as it relates to issues of education. Then we will begin to determine what a biblical view of education would really look like."

Arnie's attention strays from Dr. Wise. It has now been several weeks since the election, and Arnie is still bothered by the conversation between his friends Manfred Median and Barry Baroque in the teachers' lounge. The bill to mandate tighter emissions controls and raise taxes to clean the river failed. To the business people in the community and for many of the employees and families (several of whom send their children to Mt. Carmel), this was cause for celebration and relief. Business leaders had warned that the bill would force companies to lay off employees or close their plants entirely. There had been a late push by several environmental groups (including one which Barry Baroque and other members of his church belonged) to gather support for the measure. Many people in the community considered these environmentalists a fringe group that did not represent the best interests of the community. Barry's group of "evangelical environmentalists" was seen as being out of step with the rest of the evangelical community.

While Arnie cannot help but think that the economic concerns surrounding the bill were important for businesses, the community, and ultimately the school, his thoughts go back to that day when Manfred closed the conversation with Barry stating, "We have differing worldviews on this." To Arnie, the claims of the evangelical environmentalists had biblical support, made sense to him, and caused him to think about the role of the Christian in stewardship issues; however, these arguments were countered by many Christian leaders in the community with respect to humanity's dominion over the creation. They argued that the environmentalists were taking a narrow view and not seeing the bigger picture—of which the economic concerns were a major part. These Christian leaders countered that the bill put the interest of plants and animals before human beings, and for this reason, the bill was inherently unbiblical. Arnie has wondered how, if both groups supported their positions with biblically valid arguments, they could have differing worldviews.

Arnie's attention returns to the session and a brainstorming activity that Dr. Wise is conducting with the group. "So, the question is—who cares about the education of your students—who has a vested interest in what you do here at Mt. Carmel?'" After a few moments people from around the room call out responses.

"Well, parents, for sure," notes one teacher.

"Administrators seem to care," says another, and with that several elementary teachers laugh and look at Mr. Edify, confirming to Arnie the rumors of some lively discussions about student assessment that had gone on in some of the elementary faculty meetings.

"Pastors," one voice says a bit tentatively.

"Well, students are supposed to," notes another, a comment greeted with good-natured laughter by the rest of the group.

Dr. Wise writes these responses on the white board at the front of the room. "All right, good answers, but I guess what I really want to know is who has a vested stake in the quality of your grads—that is, who cares how they turn out?"

"Business people, employers," chimes one teacher.

"I would think that the government cares how they turn out, what they learn," cites another. "Well, parents and teachers certainly do; they are on your other list." Arnie calls out, "I would think that taxpayers care, even if they are not parents, since they are members of the community and our graduates affect the overall health of the community."

"Good, very good," notes Wise, writing these responses down. "We could spend more time thinking about possible constituent groups for your graduates, but we have enough to work with here." Pausing for a moment to reflect on the responses listed on the white board, Wise continues, "I guess my next question, just in looking at this list, is do these groups care about *your* graduates, or do the groups we have listed have a vested stake in *all* graduates—not just yours but also those of the public schools?"

After a few moments of discussion, the consensus among the teachers seems to be that the groups listed do have a vested interest in all graduates, not just those of Mt. Carmel.

"What about pastors?" one teacher asks. After a few minutes of discussion, the conclusion of the group seems to be that if pastors have a vested stake in the moral and spiritual development of students, they also have this concern for the students in the public schools. Several note that most pastors have young people in their congregations who are students at both the Christian and the public schools.

"Well, this raises some interesting ideas," says Wise. "You seem to be suggesting that many people, including unbelievers, have a vested interest in your graduates, and that the constituent groups you serve as a Christian school also have a vested interest in the graduates of the public schools." This conclusion seems to cause a few teachers to look a bit bewildered. Wise continues, "I guess it raises the question, do all these constituent groups have the same agenda for students—are schools expected to accomplish similar results in the lives of students? What do you think?"

After a few minutes to clarify the question and discuss the meaning of "agendas," teachers start to note some of their observations. "Well, I think that the government would want good citizens, regardless of whether they are from Christian or public schools," says Manfred Median. "I just think that what we do here at Mt. Carmel accomplishes that goal better than what happens at the public schools here in town."

"Good," says Wise. "Can anyone else add to this?"

Others note that business leaders want good employees: people who are reliable workers and who come to the job with the necessary skills to be productive. One teacher mentions that parents want their children to be successful, whether they are the parents of Mt. Carmel students or the parents of public school students.

"What does 'successful' mean?" asks another. This started a lively discussion that parents generally wanted their children to be prosperous and happy, but that different parents and families might define these terms differently. "Well," Wise asked, "these are all very insightful comments, but I am still perplexed. You have listed many constituent groups and their interests. It seems that many of these groups desire different outcomes from schools. While there certainly is some overlap, there are agendas or interests that conflict with the goals or interests of others. Given that we can't accomplish everything in school, who decides what we will do and what will be excluded?"

Arnie begins to think about this question. The discussion led him to examine the goals and agendas of schooling, causing him to conclude that, in many ways, schools are reflections of the goals and values of the society. Noting that unbelievers and believers have similar vested interests in the graduates of both public and Christian schools causes him a bit of uneasiness, though. If schools are a reflection of society and if the society has a vested interest in the graduates that schools produce, then what really is the difference between Christian and public education? His friend Manfred expressed his opinion that, at least in the area of citizenship, Mt. Carmel did a better job creating good citizens than the public schools. Others suggested that Mt. Carmel's graduates make better employees than their public school counterparts. Arnie concludes that both propositions would be difficult to prove. Still, is the only difference that Christian school graduates are quantitatively better prepared than those of the public schools? Arnie wants to think that there is more to the differences between Christian and public schools; he wants to believe that a Christian education is more than having Bible class and being better at training students in math or science, reading and writing, than the public schools.

WHAT ARE SCHOOLS FOR?

The overall health and robust nature of a culture depends upon the strength of its sense of unity. In other words, the ability of the culture to function and flourish depends on its ability to socialize its members into a basic vision of how life is and how life should be. From these will flow the various ideologies and philosophies for how the good life may be achieved. Cultures often tolerate, and may even encourage, disagreements between ideologies and philosophies within a culture, if those disagreements are extensions or manifestations of the same worldview. For example, schools in the United States may tolerate or encourage political expressions that gravitate around the dominant worldview—ideologies that are conservative or liberal, republican or democratic—but would be less tolerant of views that call the dominant worldview into question—anarchist, socialist, or fascist ideologies. That a culture will tolerate variations of ideologies from a particular worldview demonstrates that unity does not have to constitute uniformity, that a common normative vision of life can be achieved without the need to have all people embrace a similar means of implementation.

The typical high school curriculum demonstrates this point. The conventional high school government course is not one that teaches all forms of government, and even when it addresses issues of comparative government, it does not teach that all systems of government are of equal utility or intrinsically equal value. In the United States, government courses are typically primers for the functional and moral superiority of representative democracies, serving to reinforce the functions and authority of government, as well as the appropriate mechanisms by which citizens can bring about change. While variations of ideology may be, to a greater or lesser degree, tolerated or encouraged, they are done so with the implicit understanding that appropriate expression of political thought and practice must occur within this particular framework. Philosophies and ideologies that advocate revolution or violent uses of force to achieve political ends are not encouraged and usually not tolerated. A similar discussion may occur in a high school economics course. These courses promote the functional, and in large degree, the moral superiority of market economies over other types of economic systems. While disagreements may arise over the extent to which government should be involved in regulating markets, the fundamental acceptance of the virtues of markets is generally unquestioned.

Some degree of countercultural expression can be accepted or tolerated within a culture if those dissenters represent a small group, stay on the fringe, or do not impose a significant threat to the overall vision of the culture as a whole. For example, the United States has had communist, socialist, and neo-Nazi political groups, and these groups have even placed candidates on the ballot in elections. These groups have been tolerated by the culture as a whole, as long as they remain relatively small and functioned within the framework of the law; however, in times of crisis, when a countercultural group was perceived as a greater threat to the culture, the degree of tolerance for those groups waned. For example, in a time of war certain groups may experience greater distrust or even hostility from the general public or come under greater attention or scrutiny from other law enforcement groups, not because they have committed a crime, but because of the perceived threat that they now represent. In other societies similar experiences have been noted. In the former Soviet Union, farmers often possessed small parcels of land that were not part of the large communal farms managed by the state. These small private plots were recognized to generate a greater yield per acre, and it was understood that the individual farmers would sell their produce in a makeshift market system. This system was known and tolerated by the state because the level of market activity was perceived as small and not considered a threat to the state-run agricultural system as a whole.

As the above illustrations suggest, societies have an interest in promoting the dominant worldview of culture, and schools serve as important agents in that process. The government teacher that passionately and routinely advocates for revolution or the economics instructor that ardently and consistently criticizes market capitalism and promotes socialism would find herself at odds with many of the parents in the district, as well as the administrators and other officials in authority over her. Sociologist Emile Durkheim, in his book *Education and Sociology*, posited that education was a critical component in creating the moral unity necessary for social cohesion and harmony. To Durkheim, "Society can survive only if there exists among its members a sufficient degree of homogeneity; education perpetuates and reinforces this homogeneity by fixing in the child, from the beginning, the essential similarities that collective life demands."[1] The development of a moral sense, an adherence and commitment to its central values and ideals, is foundational to the society. He believed this survival requires a transformation in the student: "Society finds itself, with each new generation, faced with a *tabula rasa* very nearly, on which it must build anew. To the egotistic and social being that has just been born it must, as rapidly as possible, add another, capable of leading a moral and social life. Such is the work of education . . . it creates a new being."[2] Durkheim also notes that these collective moral values are extensions of the predominant vision or worldview of the society: "From these facts it follows that each society sets up a certain ideal of man, of what he should be, as much from the intellectual point of view as the physical and moral; that this ideal is, to a degree, the same for all citizens."[3]

The assumption is that some degree of consensus on the foundational goals and values of the society exists, and that these represent the normal or preferred state of affairs within the society. The members of a society, as a collective, have a vested stake in preserving this vision of life, and thus Durkheim concludes, "Education must assure, among the citizens, a sufficient community of ideas and of sentiments, without which any society is

1. Durkheim, *Education and Sociology*, 70.
2. Ibid., 72.
3. Ibid., 70.

impossible."[4] Society entrusts schools with the enculturation of the values deemed necessary for the overall health, well-being, and perpetuation of the culture. Consequently, schools or the public's attitude toward schools can be barometers of how the society as a whole, or particular groups within a society, view the overall health and well-being of the society. When society perceives that all is going well, members of the society give little serious reform attention to the schools (with the exception of professional academics and educators who make their living proposing reforms). However, when society perceives that all is not going well (if people perceive that certain moral, political, or economic conditions threaten the stability of the nation), schools often become the focal point of efforts to rectify or reform the situation.

For example, during the Red Scare and the perceived threat posed to the United States by the Soviet Union in the 1950s, schools came under intense pressure to combat communism. This pressure led to close analysis of teachers and the textbooks used in schools to ensure that the American way of life was being presented and preserved. With the Soviet launch of the Sputnik satellite in 1957, many political and economic leaders in this country believed that the Soviet Union had a considerable lead in developing students proficient in science and mathematics as compared to the United States and that this gap was created by the lack of academic rigor and inattention to mathematics and the sciences in schools. In 1958, President Dwight Eisenhower outlined a proposal for using schools as an instrument to promote and secure the national defense. His recommendations eventually were passed as Title V of the National Defense Education Act, which greatly increased funding for the teaching of science and mathematics in schools as a means of developing human resources to fight the Cold War.

During the Johnson administration schools were used as an instrument to promote racial harmony and civil rights and to fight the war on poverty. In 1964, Congress passed the Economic Opportunity Act, and in 1965, the Elementary and Secondary Education Act. Both sought to use the power and resources of the federal government to combat perceived threats that social and economic inequality posed to the social fabric of the nation. During the economic recession of the early 1980s, the Reagan administration, through its 1983 report *A Nation at Risk*, blamed public schools for America's difficulties in competing economically with other nations, such as Japan and West Germany, in world markets. The report stated that "if only to keep and improve on the slim competitive advantage we still retain in world markets, we must rededicate ourselves to the reform of the educational system for the benefit of all."[5] Schools were called upon to increase academic standards, improve the quality of teachers, and reform the curriculum, as instruments of the United States' economic policy. Interestingly, during the period of economic prosperity that characterized most of the 1990s there was almost no mention of the great job schools were doing in order to help create and secure this economic prosperity.

These illustrations simply seek to demonstrate that schools are often viewed as serving the interests of the majority of a society's citizens in a number of areas. They

---

4. Ibid., 80.

5. National Commission on Excellence in Education, *A Nation at Risk*, 7.

underscore the idea that the people of a society, as a whole, share a vested interest in the graduates produced by America's schools. Thus, education serves a "collective function" for which Durkheim notes, "it is impossible that society should be uninterested in [its] procedures." For Durkheim it was imperative that the society should act this way and take a guiding interest in education:

> The child, it is said, belongs first to the parents; it is, then, their responsibility to direct, as they understand it, his intellectual and moral development. Education is then conceived as an essentially private and domestic affair. . . . [However] as we have tried to establish, education has a collective function above all, its object is to adapt the child to the social milieu in which it is destined to live [and] it is impossible that society should be uninterested in such a procedure.[6]

Durkheim used an interesting analogy to emphasize this point. "Just as the priest is the interpreter of his god, the teacher is the interpreter of the great moral ideas of his time and his country."[7] In this analogy, the priest serves as the intermediary between God and the laity. The priest receives the teachings of God and the church and serves to bring the word of God to the people to inform them of God's expectations for them. The priest is not free to teach whatever he desires; he must bring his teaching into conformity with the will of God, whom the priest has vowed to serve and to represent. In addition, the laity comes to the priest to learn the will of God, to seek forgiveness and absolution, and to be made acceptable to God so that they may join in a blissful relationship with their Maker. The priest has a moral and spiritual obligation to present the members of his parish to God worthy of his acceptance. The alternative is that those ill prepared are ultimately condemned in the eyes of God.

In a similar fashion, teachers serve to present the ideas, ideals, goals, and expectations of the society to the students entrusted to them. Teachers are not at liberty to teach whatever they want but must present the expectations of the society (as embodied in the curriculum) and train students, fulfilling their obligation to the state, which has appointed them or deemed them acceptable to serve (by virtue of the license to teach granted by the state). Teachers serve to deliver the content of curriculum and develop the habits of performance and mind, as well as the dispositions and attitudes that will allow students to become competent adults and earn their way in society. In this sense, teachers have a moral obligation to present graduates who are worthy and acceptable to the society as a whole. Failure to do so means that the student will be condemned to live on the fringes of society without access to all the advantages the society can provide.

Thus schools are asked to perpetuate in the life of the student the intellectual, political, social, and economic interests of the society as a whole, and the whole society has a vested interest in this function being accomplished by the school. The intellectual function of schooling serves to ensure that the basic cognitive skills deemed necessary for success in the society (e.g., reading, writing, mathematics), as well as the necessary content that will ensure the transmission of cultural literacy (through subjects such as sci-

---

6. Durkheim, *Education and Sociology*, 79.
7. Ibid., 80.

ence, literature, history, etc.), will be passed to the next generation. The political function of schooling serves to perpetuate allegiance to and participation in the existing political/economic order of the society. Thus, not only are the structures of political and economic life taught, but patriotism and loyalty are also cultivated. The social function of schooling serves, among other things, to cultivate the appropriate values and respect for roles and standards of behavior that will allow students to have the abilities to navigate appropriately in the economic, political, and social roles of the society. Robert Dreeben calls this function of schooling the creation of *social solidarity*—"the norms that are appropriate for economic and political life in a modern world"[8] Interestingly, Dreeben notes that such learning comes not as much from the explicit content of the curriculum but from the behavioral and organizational patterns used to govern and operate schools. Thus, the development of social solidarity is as much a function of the *how* students are taught as *what* specifically they are taught.

Social solidarity ensures a reasonable level of social stability in the society. This stability is necessary to complement the other role that schools serve in modern societies, the function of helping to determine role differentiation. In modern societies some vocations are granted higher prestige, status, power, and monetary reward, while others enjoy fewer of these benefits. Obviously, there are tremendous incentives for people to aspire and secure those positions of higher status. With many people competing for these positions, a tremendous threat to social solidarity exists—how to ensure that the individuals with the talents and abilities necessary for these high status positions are selected while the lower status roles, equally vital for the health and functioning of the society, are still performed. To do this, society needs a means of sorting people via a system that is perceived as fair and equitable by the majority of society's members. While schools are not the sole determiner of who will eventually rise to assume the positions of higher status in the society, school does serve as a powerful institution for identifying who has the abilities and talents necessary for access to these positions and, consequently, who does not.

Role differentiation, particularly in modern industrial societies, is primarily an economic function of schooling. It is the task of identifying and training individuals to fulfill the roles necessary as part of the division of labor in modern societies. In this role schools are asked to help promote the economic efficiency of the society. For example, there may be only a few people who have the cognitive skills and dispositions to successfully perform the role of a surgeon, while the prestige, status, and rewards provided to surgeons creates an incentive that ensures fairly high interest in becoming one. The talents, skills, and abilities necessary to be a successful teacher, nurse, or accountant may be more abundant in the population, and those of general laborer more abundant still. It would be quite costly simply to allow anyone who wanted to become a surgeon to attempt to become one. Efficiency demands not only allocating the best possible people for the role of a surgeon, but also a means of ensuring that the other roles society needs are filled. Because the skills necessary to be a teacher, nurse, or general laborer are relatively more abundant, these roles generally are granted less status, prestige, and monetary rewards.

---

8. Dreeben, *On What Is Learned in School*, 5.

The creating of fewer higher status roles provides the incentive for those with the requisite skills to pursue these vocations but also has the potential to create disharmony and potential bitterness toward those who are rewarded more lavishly. Schools, though, are seen as institutions to which the members of society come to compete for access to these roles. Schools, through the process of grading, testing, and other types of instruction and assessment, are seen as relatively fair or impartial institutions of sorting. As long as the majority of people accept the relative equity of schools in the process of sorting, most people determine that they have "had their shot"—that they either did not have the skills or abilities to aspire to the positions of higher prestige and reward or that they found something more rewarding they would rather pursue. Of interest is that when a significant number of the members of the society perceive that the schools are not adequately performing the function of role differentiation, other segments of the society rally to hold schools accountable to perform this expected function. For example, when schools are accused of grade inflation, making grades become a less powerful means of sorting, there are calls for other mechanisms (e.g., proficiency exams, college entrance exams) to help sort and determine access to subsequent levels of education.

Perceived as impartial sorting institutions, Walter Feinberg and Jonas Soltis note that schools are viewed as contributing to the development of *human capital* in students.[9] In economics *capital* refers to the resources that enhance the ability to produce in the future. Just as modern industrial societies see the need to invest in machinery and equipment to stimulate future production, the belief is that they need a similar investment in the development of human skills. Thus, education is perceived to have economic value for the society at large. As economist Theodore Schultz noted, in its role of identifying and training new talent, schools enable society to make effective use of the innovations in technology and means of production as a vehicle of economic advancement.[10] Economically, the return on a society's educational investment is viewed in terms of the increased productivity that students will contribute to the society at large. While education may enhance the student's opportunities and social or material well-being, in the end, a society's investment in education is prompted by a desire to enhance the greater health and well-being of all its members, not simply by an altruistic gesture toward the welfare of the individual.

As Durkheim suggests, the health of a society demands some degree of consensus on the dominant goals, values, and vision for the society. The members of a society all have a stake in preserving and promulgating this vision. Schools represent a significant agent of the society for disseminating this vision. Society requires its schools to promote and develop a general understanding of its dominant worldview and the overall culture of society. In this role, schools reflect the dominant values of the society and generally do not create a set of new values. Schools, by serving the intellectual, political, social, and economic interests of the society, give students a powerful message concerning the goals, values, and vision of that society. In addition, schools help provide students with the proper framework for asking the questions of *Who am I?* and *Who should I become?*

9. Feinberg and Soltis, *School and Society*, 27.

10. For a fuller discussion on the economic value of education see Schultz, *Economic Value of Education*, 1–20.

as well as the guidelines for the proper means of answering these questions. Given the importance that a society places on socializing each new generation into the society, schools would understandably reflect the dominant worldview of the society. Evangelicals generally argue that the dominant worldview of society specifically, and of Western culture in general, is a secular worldview. Consequently, the worldview of society that is rooted in the practices of schooling may be at odds with the goals, values, and vision of the evangelical community expressed in the home and the church.

As Durkheim's analogy of teachers as priests suggests, teachers are agents of the state, given authority to prepare students for the needs of the society. As students enter kindergarten, they move from being treated as specific individuals and as members of the smaller social unit of family to being treated as members of a larger group—a class. Teachers serve as the primary agents of this transformation. In essence, they begin the process of socialization into the greater values of the society. While all students experience some level of dissonance, some degree of disconnect between the values, attitudes, and practices of home and school, they are expected to conform to the values of the school rather than the home. The degree of dissonance that the student (and the family) experiences in this socialization is minimized to the extent that the school and the family reflect the greater goals of the society. In other words, the more overlap between the vision of the home and the school the less intrusive the school appears to families. This phenomenon is seen not only in the content of what is taught, but also in the overall objectives and methodologies of the school (i.e., behavioral expectations, instructional techniques, etc.). All of these reflect the political, economic, social, and intellectual goals of the school and reflect of the worldview of the society in which the school resides.

Thus, to understand the purpose of schooling requires an examination and an understanding of the prevailing worldview of the culture. The secularism that we find in our society is an extension and reflection of the dominant worldview of Western culture—the modernist worldview.

SECULARIZATION AND THE "GODS OF OUR AGE"

> How did the West decline from its triumphal march to its present sickness? . . . The mistake must be at the root, at the very basis of human thinking in the past centuries. I refer to the prevailing Western view of the world which was first born during the Renaissance and found its political expression starting in the period of the Enlightenment. It became the basis for government and social science and could be defined as rationalistic humanism, or human autonomy: the proclamation and enforced autonomy of man from any higher force above.[11]

Trying to identify and define the roots of the secularism in modern society is a slippery task. Solzhenitsyn identifies its sources in the historical periods of the Renaissance, which dates to about 1470 for the Italian Renaissance and the European Enlightenment (circa 1700). Brian Walsh and J. Richard Middleton, in their book *The Transforming Vision*, also note these periods of history as the beginnings of the Western secular worldview,

---

11. Solzhenitsyn, *A World Split Apart*, 11.

for they are the periods during which modernity (the modern world) began. For Walsh and Middleton, modernity is "the process of the increasing secularization of life."[12] This is not the view of secularism or "secular humanism" that prompted many evangelical social critics, including those of schools, in the 1970s and 1980s to advocate for greater involvement of parents in monitoring the public schools as well as an increased emphasis on Christian and home schooling. Most of these critics ascribe the rise of secular human-ism to the rise of evolutionary theories, specifically Darwinism in the mid-nineteenth century,[13] the writings of John Dewey or the development of the Humanist Manifestos of 1933 and 1973.[14] While these men and movements have given modern expression to the secularization of Western culture, the roots of modern secularism appear much earlier.

As previously mentioned, by the late seventeenth century, there rose the belief that science and reason could replace revelation and religious authority as the chief method for understanding and gaining new knowledge of the world. The influence of Newtonian physics gave rise to a faith that all aspects of human social life could be explained via the scientific method, inductive reasoning and mathematics. This belief fostered the conclu-sion that human beings, starting from themselves, could acquire knowledge that would lead to the progress of humanity. Thus, secularization starts, at its core, with the principle of human autonomy: the idea that humanity is no longer subject to, or denies the valid-ity of, the revelation of God. This sense of human autonomy did not initially deny the existence of God, but as Walsh and Middleton note, fostered a belief in God as a Creator that made

> mankind—unlike nature—neither limited by nor answerable to the law of God. Instead of being a dependent creature, responding to God's Torah in all creaturely activities, mankind is defined in terms of *freedom from* law. Here we reach the core of modern secularism: the postulate of *human autonomy*. In the modern world view, man becomes a law (*nomos*) unto himself (*autos*).[15]

The achievements of Newton lead modern thinkers from the seventeenth century onward to view the universe as mechanistic, and this understanding of nature could be applied to humanity as well. The imagery of the universe as a machine suggested that human beings, rather than being born a particular way, could be constructed accord-ing to knowledge and will. Rather than accepting the Christian view of original sin and a corrupted nature, modern thought proposed the perfectibility of humanity. Through an understanding of natural law, humans could perfect their environment and, thereby, perfect themselves. John Locke, in his *Essay Concerning Human Understanding* (1690), argued that human beings are a *tabula rasa*, or blank slate, in which the social environ-ment shapes one's beliefs, actions, and knowledge. As a consequence of this belief, there are natural laws that exist among beings, much as they exist in physics, and through the

---

12. Walsh and Middleton, *Transforming Vision*, 117–18.

13. Morris, *Christian Education for the Real World*, 68–69.

14. LaHaye, *Battle for the Public School*; and Noebel, *Understanding the Times*, 7–25.

15. Walsh and Middleton, *Transforming Vision*, 119.

understanding and application of these laws human beings can be molded into the type of people society needs.

Rather than the cyclical views of history maintained by the classical Greeks and Romans, historian J. B. Bury concludes that the Enlightenment maintained, "an interpretation of history which regards men as slowly advancing . . . in a definite and desirable direction, and infers that this progress will continue indefinitely."[16] The scientific and technological achievements of the Enlightenment and the Scientific Revolution fueled the idea of the inevitability of progress and the idea that the more humanity learned, the greater would be its power to control nature and bring about human will. This belief led to the idea of scientific rationalism—the belief that knowledge would lead to greater efficiency, consistency, predictability, and human control. Scientific rationalism provided humanity with a new set of tools to utilize in the development of culture apart from the desires of God and, as a result, created a new set of idols or "gods" that would define who human beings were ultimately to be.

As noted, human beings are culture-creators, given that privilege and responsibility as part of God's original stewardship mandate. What humans create is an extension of who they are and what they believe the world should be. Created in the image of God, without the Fall, human beings would have created social/cultural environments that would have been an extension of their desire to please God and add value to the creation for his glory. With the Fall, however, humanity lost its desire and capability to please God, replacing it with a new desire to focus on and please themselves. The Fall created a dilemma for now-sinful humanity. While humanity, in its sin nature, seeks to please self and use the resources at its disposal to do so, humanity was not created to be a servant of self. Fallen thought not only leads to fallen action but also creates the need to develop ways of thinking that justify, or normalize, the dissonance between what sinful humanity desires to be and who God created humanity to be. Over time, these justifications become shared with others who have a like interest in normalizing their sinful desires. These resulting worldviews are passed on to subsequent generations as explanations for understanding the way things are and visions for the way things should be that are in alignment with the sin nature, which means over the course of time, the sinful nature of humanity fulfills its divinely endowed desire of cultural creation by creating culture that justifies the sin nature. As a result, the examination of culture, and of the worldview expressions that are embedded in culture, provides evidence of the character of the sin nature through the values embodied in the culture.

The normalization of sin has allowed human beings to construct cultures in a manner consistent with its selfish ambitions. In Western civilization, since the time of the Renaissance, the sin nature took the form of *homo autonomos*—man becoming a law unto himself. Walsh and Middleton quote the fifteenth-century writer Pico della Mirandola's *Oration on the Dignity of Man*, in which God addresses Adam in the Garden and says, "We have given you, Oh Adam, no visage proper to yourself, nor any endowment properly your own, in order that whatever place, whatever form, whatever gifts

---

16. Postman, *Building a Bridge to the 18th Century*, 26.

you may, with premeditation, select, these same you may have and possess through your own judgment and decision."[17] Mirandola uses the creation story to justify the concept of autonomous human freedom. By the seventeenth and eighteenth centuries this emphasis on human autonomy fostered the belief that nature is something to be controlled and manipulated for humanity's benefit. Noting the difference between the Renaissance and the Enlightenment, Herman Dooyeweerd writes that, by the Enlightenment, "proudly conscious of his autonomy and freedom, modern man saw 'nature' as an expansive arena for the exploitations of his free personality, as a field of infinite possibilities in which the sovereignty of human personality must be revealed by a complete *mastery* of the phenomena of nature."[18]

The fundamental spiritual consequence of secularization and the normalization of sin is that it denies the spiritual nature of human beings and humanity's dependency on God to provide a vision of how the world should be. In order to preserve humanity's autonomy, sinful people must develop an alternative vision, create alternative "gods," to provide direction. As these alternative gods are worshipped, as they inform the direction of culture creation, they will embed in the practices of culture the sin nature from which they were created. Walsh and Middleton, in describing the worldview of modern humanity, refer to three "gods" of the age: scientism, technicism, and economism.[19]

By identifying these traits as "isms," Walsh and Middleton differentiate them from simply science, technology, and economics. Scientism is the belief that the control and manipulation of nature can be brought about through the process of science. The belief in the power of science to create means for operating on the world that will result in making the world better is called technicism—the belief that scientific discoveries can be transformed into implements of human power. Economism is a belief that material well-being and prosperity are the chief goal of humanity. As "isms," science, technology, and economics are transformed into doctrines: faith statements about the power of these to describe the world human beings live in and bring about the world they want. Since worldviews are faith statements, essentially religious in nature, these become the false gods in which modern humanity, as least in Western cultures, has placed its faith and trust.

Humanity's desire to be independent of God, to truly become *homos autonomous*, requires a knowledge and understanding of the world that will empower mankind to pursue its desired goals. For Walsh and Middleton the first god is scientism—"the absolutization of science, the elevation of human scientific prowess to a place of salvific or redemptive significance."[20] "In science we trust" becomes the cry of modern man. Scientism not only places great faith in the power of human reason to discover truth about the natural world, but also claims that human reason is the only way of knowing, and that the natural world is the only thing that can be known. Scientism maintains that ignorance or irrationality is evil—the cause of the problems in the world. As such, the solutions to the problems in the world must come through greater knowledge, research, and education. Knowledge

17. Quoted in Walsh and Middleton, *Transforming Vision*, 118.

18. Dooyeweerd, *Roots of Western Culture*, 150.

19. Walsh and Middleton, *Transforming Vision*, 131–46.

20. Ibid., 122.

provides the power and the ability to act, and the scientific method provides the power to know in a way that will produce beneficial results. As noted, the science of understanding the nonhuman world eventually gave way to the use of science in understanding human beings. Academic disciplines that dealt with the issues of humankind (e.g., psychology, sociology, economics, history, etc.), were eventually transformed to incorporate the scientific method; the humanities gave way to methodologies that transformed them into the social sciences.

Scientism, as an expression of the sin nature, reflects certain theological flaws that place it at odds with a biblical worldview. While many and varied, two of these flaws are of particular significance. First, scientism is predicated on a belief in a machine-like universe—a universe in which there is no God or, if God does exist, he is not necessary for understanding the universe. This creates a world governed exclusively by natural laws. Once those laws are discovered, they can be used to manipulate the order of things in the universe. Applying this paradigm to the social sciences reduces humanity to the realm of objects—in which certain laws of learning, motivation, behavior, and so on can be discovered and then manipulated to bring about desired outcomes. The failure to produce a desired outcome is not a flaw of science per se but rather a belief that society simply has not yet learned enough to bring about the desired outcome. This leads to the second theological flaw, also a direct outgrowth of the character of the sin nature: a belief that science can produce a type of human omniscience. In other words, given the best minds, time, and research, human beings can solve the problems that plague humanity.

Despite its elevated position, science, of itself, does not have the ability to effect change in the world. What science does is discover those laws that will allow humanity to create the knowledge from which tools can be made to manipulate the world. From science comes technology or the application of science to practical purpose. However, a belief in science or scientism also fosters a belief that the technologies that result from science will help to solve the problems of humanity and make the world better. Walsh and Middleton identify this belief as the god of technicism. Technicism allows for the proliferation of technology into mainstream culture as a means of controlling the environment. Technicism is embodied in the advertising slogan used for nearly a quarter century by General Electric: "GE—we bring good things to life." It is interesting to note that good things are not spiritual, emotional, or social things; rather they are material things. Furthermore, access to the "good life" is predicated on access to technological innovation. From this standpoint, modern or advanced nations are regarded as such because of their level of technological development and dissemination to the general populace. The dissemination causes many aspects of the character of technology to become values for the culture as a whole. For example, technological innovations encourage and reinforce values of speed, efficiency, precision, and convenience. Eventually these values are translated and applied to other areas of life.

Theologically, technicism holds out the promise of human omnipotence. Scientism sees nature as mechanistic and subject to natural laws, while technicism gives humanity the power to engage in nature's manipulation and control. The basic research of science, which reveals truth about the world, leads to the applied research that empowers humanity to command it. In addition, technicism cultivates a belief in the inevitability of human progress. Science provides a seemingly endless supply of new information about the world, while technology takes that knowledge and uses it to provide humans greater control of that world. Thus, there is the belief that each generation of humanity is more advanced, reaching a higher state of perfection and inching ever closer to utopia, than previous generations. With this advancement comes disdain for that which is older and less powerful, those technologies that have become obsolete.

Technicism rejects the type of devolution of culture described by Paul in Romans 1, where people worship the creation rather than the Creator, by replacing a spiritual definition of the good life with a material one. Technicism defines the best ways to do things in terms of efficiency, speed, precision, and convenience. Thus, the best ways to teach and promote student learning are those in which students are manipulated (for their own benefit), to learn the most material (efficiency) in the fastest way (speed) that can be accurately measured (precision). Every teacher who has been subject to teaching reforms knows that, in order for these reforms to be successful, they must be implemented with the least amount of effort by teachers (convenience). While these values may be advantageous when dealing with things, they become particularly dangerous in dealing with human relationships. They cause people to become objects subject to manipulation for desired outputs, and the expectation of inevitable progress makes human relationships seem almost disposable when those relationships no longer fulfill expectations.

While scientism provides a means for describing how the world is, and technicism the means of acting on the world, neither provides a sufficient direction to answer the critical worldview question of how the world should be. For this reason Walsh and Middleton label the final god, economism, the "golden head." Economism answers the question of how the world should be: where individuals (in a world of seemingly endless possibilities) should allocate their time, energy, talents, and resources. Economism is the belief that economic growth is the ultimate end for which society should aim. As economist John Kenneth Galbraith once noted, "A rising standard of living has the aspect of faith in our culture."[21] Innovations in science and technology are driven by the pursuit of that which is profitable or by the goal of protecting a person's or nation's ability to pursue its economic ends. For example, economism informs the selection between options such as a cure for AIDS or erectile dysfunction, mass transportation or SUVs, social services or military spending. Granted these are bifurcations, but there is no denying that much can be revealed about a person and a society by where they place their resources. As Jesus said, "For where your treasure is, there your heart will be also" (Matt 6:21).

Theologically, economism is the reification or the embodiment of self-interest. Adam Smith, considered the father of modern capitalism, writes, "It is not from the benevolence of the butcher, the brewer, or the baker, that we expect our dinner, but from their regard to their own self-interest. We address ourselves, not to their humanity but to their self-love, and never talk to them of our own necessities but of their advantages."[22] Smith believes

21. Quoted in Ibid., 138.
22. A. Smith, *Wealth of Nations*, 1:13.

each individual, acting in his own self-interest, creates an "invisible hand" that works for the greater good of all, justifying the autonomous use of resources as a means of promoting the common good.

From such a position, stewardship issues begin to fade from consideration. Although science can produce knowledge about how the world is, it cannot answer the question of how to act on that knowledge. For example, science can reveal that atoms can be split but not how that knowledge can or should be used. Economism provides pragmatic alternatives to answer this question. Should society use this knowledge to produce energy (if it is profitable to do so and there is a large enough market), or to produce weaponry (as a means of preserving and sustaining the society's way of life from the perceived threat of other nations)? Economism may answer these questions, but not necessarily in ways that promote a biblical view or application of stewardship. In fact, stewardship might dictate that although atoms can be split, the potential dangers prescribe that society not act on this knowledge at all (the command to do no harm). In private life, economism and the autonomous use of resources may trump stewardship considerations even for the individual Christian. While faithful believers would acknowledge the necessity of giving their tithe, decisions regarding the remaining ninety percent are subject to the autonomous control of the individual. As long as those resources are not used for immoral activities (e.g., drinking, gambling, smoking, etc.), their use is deemed acceptable.

An example of the concepts of scientism, technicism, and economism wielded together can be found in contemporary marketing and advertising. A belief in the power of science to understand phenomena in the natural world, of which human beings are considered a part, prompts the study of human nature. The social sciences of psychology, sociology, and economics conduct investigations on the nature of human beings as it relates to particular areas of those disciplines. Psychology might discover aspects of human responses to certain types of stimuli; sociology may delve into the natural desire of individuals to conform to social groups and align themselves with the dominant attitudes and values of a community; economics may explain the nature of incentives and people's response to those incentives. The answers to such questions can be combined with other information and technologies to create devices and techniques designed to persuade people to embrace or act on a particular message (which is evidenced in a belief in technology or technicism). This knowledge can be used to help persuade people to stay in school, to buy beer or soda, or to persuade and act in any other way that a client of an advertising agency might want.

What economism ultimately leads to is a vision of the good life that is defined in naturalistic and economic terms. By removing God or his active involvement in the world from worldview considerations, there is no concern with the afterlife or consideration of his agenda for life in this world. Devoid of a spiritual concern and removed from biblical focus, human nature is defined in naturalistic terms; humans are reduced to being a part of nature and can be understood as any other natural phenomenon. As psychologist B. F. Skinner proclaimed, "A scientific view of man offers exciting possibilities. We have not yet seen what man can make of man."[23] Consequently, only this life is of concern. As a result, the "good" person is defined in terms of economics, with human value increasingly attached to human productivity or potential for productivity. Educationally, the idea of teaching the good person and developing the good worker become melded to the point of being nearly synonymous.

As stated previously, worldviews are not philosophies and worldviews can give birth to a number of different ideological and philosophical perspectives; these perspectives can often seem contradictory in nature. The Enlightenment worldview gave birth to the type of materialistic capitalism experienced in contemporary American society, but the human-centered belief in the power of reason, the power of science and only science to explain the natural world, and the belief in the perfectibility of people and human society are not only central to materialistic capitalism, but also foundational to Marxist communism. Aleksandr Solzhenitsyn suggests the same:

> As humanism in its development became more and more materialistic, it made itself increasingly accessible to speculation and manipulation, at first by socialism and then by Communism. So that Karl Marx was able to say in 1833 that "Communism is naturalized humanism." This statement turned out to be not entirely meaningless. One does see the same stones in the foundations of despiritualized humanism and of any type of socialism: endless materialism; freedom from religion and religious responsibility, under which Communist regimes reaches the stage of anti-religious dictatorship; concentration on social structures, with a seemingly scientific approach (this is typical of the Enlightenment of the eighteenth century and of Marxism).[24]

This discussion started with the premise that schools are socialization institutions of the dominant worldview of the society. If this is true, it prompts individuals to understand the dominant worldview of the society, for this is the worldview that will permeate not only what is learned but also how it is taught. Since schools in modern societies exist for the purpose of transmitting the intellectual, social, political, and economic values of the society, schools become "conservative" institutions—preserving the status quo of the society by instilling in future generations the attitudes, values, and skills that society has deemed necessary for its overall future benefit. Since philosophies are extensions of a worldview, manifestations of the modern secular worldview should be seen in the philosophies of education that direct current educational practice. If evangelicals truly desire to use Christian schools as a means of transforming worldview, they must seriously consider how the current practices of Christian schools are directed by the leading educational philosophies of our day and how these philosophies are extensions of the predominant worldview of modernity.

THEORY AND PRACTICE

Social psychologist Kurt Lewin once wrote, "There is nothing more practical than a good theory." For most education students, a course in philosophy of education is something

23. Skinner, *Beyond Freedom and Dignity*, 206.
24. Solzhenitsyn, *A World Split Apart*, 12–13.

to be endured. It is esoteric rather than pragmatic. Yet, as Lewin suggests, good theories are practical—they explain the reasons for the things done in the classroom. While most teachers are fairly skilled in how to deliver instruction and well versed in assorted educational techniques, they often do not take much time to understand why they teach the things they teach or why they use certain methods. While teachers might claim that their practices are based on scientific evidence of what works, the study of worldview should inform them that the questions science asks are not value neutral but are driven by a particular worldview. Thus, the findings of educational psychology or sociology concerning effective practices are driven by a philosophical definition of what is effective. Ultimately, these philosophical definitions are tied to a worldview.

A thorough survey of the educational philosophies found in contemporary American schools would be far outside the boundaries of this book. Furthermore, philosophies are extensions of worldview; there can be, and often are, a number of philosophies that arise from a single worldview, and these philosophies can seemingly compete depending on what aspect of the worldview they tend to emphasize. For these reasons this examination will reduce the scope of Western educational philosophies by classifying them into two main areas—*conservative* and *progressive* philosophies. Conservative views of education tend to consider the greater needs of the society over the specific needs of the individual child although they argue that what is ultimately best for the child is preparing them to adapt to the greater needs of the society. Conservative views focus on the values of tradition and continuity, acknowledging that there is much good in the collective wisdom of the culture, and believe that students should be acculturated to that knowledge. Conservative educational philosophies seek to integrate the student into the greater knowledge, attitudes, values, and traditions of the culture. For example, E. D. Hirsch's book *Cultural Literacy* places an emphasis on the collected knowledge one must have in order to be a "good American": "Shared literate information is deliberately sustained by national systems of education in some countries because it recognizes the importance of giving their children a common basis for communications."[25] He adds that "The concept of cultural literacy helps us to make [curriculum decisions], because it places a higher value on national than on local information. We want to make our children competent to communicate with Americans throughout the land."[26] The educated student is one who has achieved mastery of a "common core" of knowledge.

The two most common conservative educational theories in American education are *perennialism* and *essentialism*. Perennialism attempts to look back through history and forward in time to shape current educational goals and practices. It seeks to celebrate the great ideas and accomplishments of Western civilization and develop a knowledge and appreciation of those ideas and ideals in the student. The ideas and accomplishments of the past serve as a means to prepare students to meet the challenges of living an effective life in the future. Perennialists are driven by four general principles that shape their approach to education. First, permanence is more real than change. The phrase, "the more

25. Hirsch, *Cultural Literacy*, 14.
26. Ibid., 25.

things change the more they stay the same" is foundational to the perennialist; while the circumstances of contemporary life may change, the goal of human beings to live as truly human throughout time remains the same. This is true because human nature remains essentially the same throughout time and location, which is perennialism's second general principle. History and geography do not change what humanity is or should be. Third, the good life—the life that is fit for human beings to live—remains essentially the same, regardless of time and place. This is true because of the fourth principle: in the end, the moral principles that should govern human behavior essentially remain the same. The study of the great ideas of the past and people's use of those great ideas to develop their cultures can reveal how students should live now and prepare them for life in the future.

Consequently, perennialists believe that all students should receive the same type of education. Mortimer Adler, one of the leading voices of American perennialism and author of *The Paideia Proposal*, expresses this sentiment by quoting John Dewey (ironically, as we shall see): "The best education for the best is the best education for all."[27] Later Adler notes, "The one-track system of public schooling that *The Paideia Proposal* advocates has the same objectives for all without exception."[28] This system of education would introduce students to the world of "permanencies": English, languages, history, mathematics, the natural sciences, the humanities, and philosophy. Students must learn to read and write, to speak and to listen. As social beings students must learn to live in community and thus develop their powers of rationality to communicate with others.

Perennialists generally fall into one of two camps—either secular or theistic perennialism. While similar in many respects, the differences between the two are nevertheless significant. The secular perennialist believes in a metaphysical world of reason; he also believes that truth can be attained through human reason. This would generally be the view of Plato, who might be considered a type of patron saint of secular perennialism. From this philosophical position, the secular perennialist would tend to view the student as a rational being in need of training. The teacher serves as the mental disciplinarian to provide this training. The curriculum would consist of those subjects that would best train the intellect and inspire the spirit (e.g., mathematics, languages, logic, the "great books"). Teaching methods would consist of those that demanded rigorous training of the intellect for the purpose of transmitting the great ideas of Western culture to the student.

The theistic perennialist also believes in a metaphysical world of reason, but sees God as the metaphysical reality behind reason. As such, education must seek to develop the reasoning powers of students to enable them to understand the natural world and develop the ability to understand God. Students, therefore, are not only rational beings but also spiritual ones. The teacher is not only a mental disciplinarian but also a spiritual leader. The curriculum seeks to introduce students not only to the permanencies of this world but also to the permanencies of the spiritual world through the study of religion and religious doctrine. The teaching methods, while similar to those of secular perennialism, seek to transmit not only the secular but also the religious accomplishments and traditions of

27. Adler, *Paideia Proposal*, 6.
28. Ibid., 15.

Western civilization. An example of theistic perennialism is Douglas Wilson's *Recovering the Lost Tools of Learning*, which is subtitled *An Approach to Distinctly Christian Education*. While conservative, the "distinctly" different aspect of Wilson's approach contrasts with the other, more prominent conservative approach to education—essentialism.

Essentialism is an educational philosophy that stresses the importance of teacher authority, both in terms of content and pedagogy, and student mastery of content. It is so named because it seeks to instill in students the essentials of academic knowledge and character. While the term was originally popularized in the 1930s, it has been the dominant approach to education in the United States since the beginning of its history. It was the rigidity of essentialist education that was the focus of John Dewey and the progressive education movement when Dewey published his 1902 *The Child and the Curriculum*. Essentialism saw a revival in the late 1950s with educational reforms that resulted from the threat of the Cold War and the Soviet launching of the Sputnik satellite and again in 1983 with the Reagan administration report, *A Nation at Risk*. More recently, the 2001 renewal of the Elementary and Secondary Education Act, more commonly known as "No Child Left Behind," reflects the same essentialist approach to schooling.

Essentialists maintain that essential or basic academic skills and knowledge should be taught to all students. The traditional academic disciplines of reading, writing, math, science, history, and literature form the foundations of the curriculum. Even in those areas normally associated with the development of creativity, such as music and art, students are required to master a basic body of information and techniques. In the essentialist classroom, students are taught to be culturally literate, that is, to possess a working knowledge of the people, events, ideas, and institutions that have shaped American society. Classroom discipline and control is emphasized as foundational to the learning process. The teacher-centered classroom is also emphasized. While student self-discipline is desirable, much of the time it is considered insufficient for student development. Because students are not equipped to know what they will need to know in the future or what knowledge is important to learn, the role of the teacher is central. For this reason, essentialists place a great deal of emphasis on the ability of a "highly qualified teacher" to bring about the desired learning outcomes in the student.

While essentialism can be seen in the current educational reforms prompted by "No Child Left Behind," public schooling is not the only area that has been influenced. A review of the scope and sequence, curriculum, and pedagogical emphasis of several Christian schooling resources, most notably A Beka Books, reflects a distinctly essentialist approach to education.

In contrast to conservative philosophies, progressive views on education are tied to the philosophical/ideological progressive movement that began in the 1870s in the United States (although many progressive principles have historical roots before this time). Progressivism developed as a response to the perceived abuses to human freedom and dignity and the constraints placed on people as a result of the excesses of the Industrial Revolution. By the late 1870s progressives began to call public attention to the problems of poverty created among the working class, particularly in urban areas, and pushed for systematic methods of social welfare and reform. Fueled by an increasing number of white upper- or middle-class women who had graduated from college, the progressive movement also saw calls for the emancipation of women in the professions and the right to vote, which eventually led to the passage of the Nineteenth Amendment in 1920. Protestant ministers, increasingly noting the need to address the growing problems of people created by industrialization and urbanization, initiated church-based responses to these problems—a theological position known as the Social Gospel—and to the progressive era of the late nineteenth and early twentieth centuries.

Progressives emphasized the importance of morality over economics, acting on the interests of individuals over the interests of large corporations. Progressives were not opposed to capitalism; in fact, most progressives were advocates of capitalism (as opposed to the socialist movements that were also quite active at this time).[29] Progressives also believed that public morality is tied to the promotion of social justice—both politically and economically. For example, the muckraker movement among American journalists, writers, and social critics (of which Sinclair Lewis's book *The Jungle* may be the most well-known example) was instrumental in exposing the abuses of both business and politics. Progressives were not limited to a single political party. Theodore Roosevelt of New York and Robert LaFollette of Wisconsin were Republican progressives while Woodrow Wilson represented the Democratic side of the progressive movement. As progressives, both parties emphasized public morality and a need to clean up the practices of both government and business. Progressives maintained that the role of government was to protect the weaker members of society against the power and interests of wealthier concerns. Toward these ends, progressives were instrumental in the passage of anti-trust legislation, child labor laws, mandatory schooling legislation, as well as food and drug protection and temperance legislation.

Progressive educators sought to prepare students to deal with the issues of a developing society, in which the rapid advances in science and technology rendered the knowledge of the past, and even of the present, of dubious use for the future. In an environment characterized by rapid change, progressives argued that what students needed most were the knowledge, skills, and dispositions that would allow them to learn on their own and adapt to changing circumstances. For progressives, the goal was to develop and apply practical knowledge and principles to the life of students now and not just to their future lives. Rather than seeing education as merely a preparation for a future life in society, a good education would be applicable now as well as later—preparing students to be good citizens and good human beings. This emphasis required that schools prepare lifelong learners, students who are not dependent on the teacher and the curriculum to structure the learning process, but create learners who are able to become aware of and define problems, to develop hypotheses and ways of testing a solution, and to evaluate the consequences of those solutions.

To progressives, people learn best from those areas that they consider most relevant to their lives. To take advantage of the intrinsic motivation students bring to learning, progressives center the curriculum on the experiences, interests, and abilities of the student.

29. Lux, *Progressive Revolution*, 156.

John Dewey, considered the father of progressive education, emphasized that education should entail the broadening of the intellect through the development of problem solving and critical thinking skills. This can be accomplished by having students actively engage in tasks, problems, or situations of interest or relevance to their daily lives. Teachers teach academic content through problem solving—observing, reasoning, reacting, researching, and actively applying relevant knowledge to a situation. Progressive education stresses the importance of active engagement of the learner in the learning process. As a result, teachers are viewed as facilitators or coaches; preparing students in such a way that enables active performance in pursuit of their own learning.

To accomplish these goals, progressives emphasize hands-on experimentation and problem solving through activities and projects. Since the situations and problems that students encounter in life rarely can be confined to one academic discipline, progressives emphasize a more integrative approach. History, economics, sociology, and geography may all be applied to social problems through the area of social studies. Science and mathematics can be applied in a multidisciplinary approach to solving real-world problems. Since human beings are social creatures and because students need to learn to interact with others in the workplace and in a political democracy with a diversity of racial, ethnic, and socio-economic groups, cooperative learning and other socially oriented approaches to instruction are emphasized.

In 1932, George Counts delivered a series of speeches, later published, which asked the question, "Do the schools dare create a new social order?"[30] As the United States—and the rest of the world—struggled with the effects of the Great Depression, President Franklin Roosevelt sought to use the resources of government through the New Deal to alleviate the effects of the depression and create conditions that would stimulate a recovery. Counts saw the United States bogged down in the social confusion caused by the Great Depression, a condition he believed to be needless and inexcusable, and solicited educators to exercise their strategic position in promoting social and cultural change. Counts believed that schools should be the social leaders, preparing the next generation to deal with the problems of society.

Counts' statement represents a second school of educational progressivism known as *social reconstructionism*. Social reconstructivists view contemporary society as facing a severe crisis stemming from its unwillingness to transform its institutions and values to meet the needs of modern life. As progressives, they believe that the problems of society are created by the immoral or unjust practices of institutions in the society that victimize people, and that these institutions must be transformed to make them more responsive to the needs of individuals. The task of schools is to engage students in a critical examination of the cultural heritage of the society, preserving those elements that have served and continue to serve people well and rejecting or reforming those elements that do not. Social reconstructivists tend to disdain conservative theories of education that call for a return to the "good old days," noting that the good old days (if they ever existed at all) are those wherein the conditions that plague society now had their beginnings and that those

---

30. Counts, *Dare the School Build a New Social Order?* 3.

who tend to promote these views have a vested stake in preserving the status quo, which serves their own best interests.

Educationally, social reconstructivists believe that schools can help students to discern the causes of social problems and begin to develop ways to help create a better world. As progressives, they believe that students will be motivated to deal with situations they find in the world around them and that teachers can use their interest to develop their analytical abilities to investigate problems. Students can engage in the task of learning the theoretical and historical causes of a problem, critically consider possible solutions, and then inquire into the knowledge base that will help them develop and implement solutions and consider the consequences. As progressives, social reconstructivists emphasize a hands-on approach to learning; unlike other progressive views, which emphasize adapting to the changes in society, social reconstructivists stress the role of schools and students as change agents in the society.

Progressive principles have never been the predominant philosophy in American education. From their inception in the 1830s, state systems of common or public schooling have primarily attempted to achieve cultural uniformity rather than diversity and to educate dutiful, not critical, citizens. Furthermore, schooling has been under constant pressure to support the ever-expanding industrial economy by establishing a competitive meritocracy and preparing workers for their vocational roles. The term *progressive* arose from a period (roughly 1890–1920) during which many Americans took a more critical look at the political and social effects of vast concentrations of corporate power and private wealth. Dewey, in particular, saw that with the decline of local community life and small-scale enterprise, young people were losing valuable opportunities to learn the arts of democratic participation, and he concluded that education would need to make up for this loss.

While sometimes viewed as less intellectually rigorous, progressives have countered that good problem solving is intellectually quite rigorous. To them, the true test of an expert is not simply that he knows more but that he also knows how to use knowledge meaningfully. The persistent charge against American schools that students don't know how to think well would demonstrate, progressives might claim, that the true sign of an educated person, the ability to think and use knowledge meaningfully, is not accomplished by more predominant conservative approaches to education. Progressives might also claim that the conservative views treat education as a noun—a thing to be gained—and use the analogy of the mind as a "bank" to deposit learning. To progressives, education can be seen as a verb—something to be done or a process to be engaged in—and they use the analogy of the learner as a "builder," someone who actively takes his tools, skills, and materials to construct something of greater value.

HOW RADICAL DO YOU WANT TO BE?

This review of the basic philosophical approaches to education was not simply to demonstrate the historical traditions of American education but also to highlight how current practices of Christian schooling are reflected in these approaches. By and large, the approach to schooling taken by most Christian schools mirrors the more conservative approaches. The question that Christian educators should begin to ask is, how radical, or distinctly biblical, ought we to be? Conservative approaches seek to preserve and promote the existing social norms and traditions of a community with the desire to promote a sense of social continuity by passing on the norms, attitudes, and values of the dominant worldview of the society. If, however, the dominant worldview of the society is a nonbiblical worldview, is it the worldview that Christian schools should desire to preserve and pass on to their students? While modernity may have certain biblical elements, its beliefs about the nature of the universe, truth, and the goals and aspirations of life are foundationally antithetical to a biblical worldview. In such a case, do conservative approaches to education, even when applied by the Christian school, inadvertently risk promoting the attitudes and values of the dominant secular worldview?

Earlier we noted that the curriculum and instructional practices of Christian schools have been closely linked with those of public schools. For many Christian educators, this linkage is uncomfortable, and some might even deny that such linkage exists. While many Christian school educators seek to offer their students an education consistent with biblical truth, or seek to integrate biblical truth into the content they teach and the behaviors they model to their students, the question remains that if a worldview affects not only what is taught but also how it is taught, does the degree of similarity between the curriculum and instructional methods of public schooling and Christian schooling give us reason to pause and critically examine our approach to schooling?

Consider the emphasis of the typical high school curriculum. The time allocated to mathematics, science, English, and social studies has direct relationship to preparing students to assume their place in the society and having an education that translates into economic utility. Why three years of mathematics and no required course in art? Why does three years of science have greater intrinsic value than three years of music? Are science and mathematics inherently more biblical than art or music? The greater emphasis on subjects such as mathematics, science, and language arts reflects their believed greater economic utility (i.e., they are content areas that more effectively prepare young people for the world of work). While I am not suggesting abandoning the sciences in favor of the arts, I am suggesting that if all cultural phenomena are the result of an underlying worldview, then the emphasis of the school curriculum is also part of that worldview, so we should critically ask what bias the current curriculum structure reflects.

The addition of Bible classes or Christian textbooks to the curriculum does not fundamentally alter the basic worldview premises upon which the curriculum is based. The Christian school can denounce the views of Darwin and evolutionary theory while still giving a bias to science over other subjects and providing science a prominent role in the curriculum, which underscores the worldview that allowed an evolutionary explanation for origins to initially develop. The scientific rationalism that led to the worship of scientism, technicism, and economism will emphasize the value of scientific knowledge and the ability to use science to create technologies for greater efficiency and control over the environment. Thus, science and technology will be guided by an economic model of progress and efficiency that will serve as arbiter for defining success, allocating resources, and determining ultimate social ends. Schooling, insofar as it is a reflection of the dominant worldview of the culture, will transmit these values to the student.

One question that needs to be asked is whether the embedded economic emphasis is fundamentally unbiblical. The answer is no—economics is an important aspect of life and a legitimate concern of people who are finite and of societies that must deal with competing desires. Economic decisions, however, are value laden, just as all areas of life are value laden; there is no value-neutral space in the universe. How individuals and societies allocate not only their wealth, but also their time, talents, resources, and abilities, is an indication of the values to which they adhere. A society that values material and economic progress, that views science and technology as the means to achieving these ends, and that sees certain political, social, and economic structures as the best ways to encourage the development of these goals can be expected to emphasize these through schooling. An economic perspective is not sinful, nor is preparation for the world of work inherently unbiblical in itself, unless these become the ultimate end of education. At that point, the economic perspective takes precedence over the biblical and constitutes a form of idolatry.

From this economic perspective, the good worker and the good person become synonymous. Interestingly, when schools engage in character education they often emphasize the traits that correspond with being a good worker. Honesty, adaptability, responsibility, and trustworthiness are all traits that any employer would covet in a worker. However, a sense of moral integrity that would cause an employee to "blow the whistle" on illegal, harmful, or unjust practices are not the qualities readily found in the society nor are they ones developed in school. The biblical emphasis on developing a good person—one that is conformed to the image of Christ—would naturally create a person who would be a good worker, but that person who also would be able to examine critically, understand, and act on conditions in the workplace and the rest of society. A biblical emphasis would seek to develop individuals who would view the confronting of sinful practices in their own lives and in the communal life of society as a moral imperative. Ultimately, the secular view of a good person as a good worker is dehumanizing, and therefore sinful; reducing one's worth to the individual's economic/material value violates the spiritual and relational wholeness of one created in the image of God.

It must also be asked if the use of a conservative curriculum model or teaching techniques leads to promoting an unbiblical worldview. Again, while it is not necessarily the case that conservative curricular or instructional decisions will cultivate the secular worldview in students, the possibility should cause us to critically examine the relationship of the curriculum and instruction techniques to the worldview that initially spawned them: Who decided what the curriculum would be? Why did they decide it should be that way? What are the goals embedded in its design? Since curriculum and instructional techniques develop over time, what values and goals drove their development? By the same token, being traditional or conservative in terms of curriculum or instructional philosophies does not necessarily make an approach to education biblical. Progressive approaches to education, while historically decried by many Christian school educators, are not inherently unbiblical; many embrace certain principles foundational to a biblical approach to education.

For example, the person and writings of John Dewey have often been vilified by proponents of Christian schooling.[31] As a philosopher, Dewey advocated positions on the nature of truth, knowledge, and value or worth that were highly influenced by a Darwinistic view of human nature and the evolution of society. All of these are fundamentally unbiblical positions, and Dewey's views on metaphysics, epistemology, and axiology generally can be dismissed. To dismiss all of his views, however, may reject many relevant aspects of his work, particularly since many of his views on learners and learning may not only be substantiated by research in human learning and cognition but, more importantly, may also be in alignment with what the Bible says about the nature of human beings and the ways they learn.

Dewey advocated for a curriculum and instructional techniques that centered on the needs and interests of the learner. He noted that when students are active, when they learn by doing, and when they see the relevance of what they are learning to the issues of their lives, they learn more, comprehend better, and process information in ways that allow them to retain and use that knowledge more effectively in the future. All of these premises have been confirmed by research in educational psychology. There is also reason to believe that all these propositions are confirmed in Scripture. For example, Daniel Estes notes that the role of teacher as facilitator and teacher as guide (analogies both attributed to John Dewey) are a prominent part of the teaching technique expressed in the book of Proverbs.[32] To dismiss these findings outright because one rejects portions of the advocate's philosophy may be to dismiss the portions of biblical truth evident in the philosophy.

Christian school educators often use the phrase "all truth is God's truth." The validity of this claim is demonstrated when they embrace the aspects of biblical truth found in those with whom they may have disagreements. To summarily dismiss those ideas because we largely dismiss the messengers may cause us to miss those pertinent concepts that would allow Christian educators to effectively develop a biblical worldview in their students. Also, in rejecting these ideas Christian educators may embrace views regarding learners and learning that may be more fundamentally unbiblical than the ones dismissed.

In closing, Christian educators must once again ask themselves the question, how radical do we want to be? Christian educators often point out that no education is value neutral, that an education is inherently a value decision. They also acknowledge that value systems are extensions of a worldview. By attempting to make the case that worldviews are communal entities, that they find their expression in the attitudes, values, and beliefs of society, we have attempted to demonstrate that the composition of schooling, both in

---

31. This view of Dewey has caused many Christian education writers to misrepresent him. For example, Edlin, in *The Cause of Christian Education*, consistently calls Dewey the "father of *modern* education" (italics mine, cf. pp. 32, 40) rather than of "progressive education" and asserts that the secularism now prominent in American public education can be traced to the influence of Dewey (cf. pp. 41–43).

32. Estes, *Hear My Son*, 127–33.

terms of what is taught and how it is taught, is an extension of the dominant worldview of the culture. Insofar as evangelicals make the claim that the secularism dominating contemporary culture is unbiblical, they should examine the contemporary practices of Christian schooling that mirror those of the dominant culture. We have also seen that worldviews can produce several philosophies and that these philosophies, often in opposition to each other, seek to achieve a similar end. The danger we risk in viewing worldviews and philosophies as synonymous is that, in rejecting one philosophical manifestation of the worldview as unbiblical, we are disposed to accept another manifestation of that worldview as more biblical. In rejecting the more progressive side of the secular worldview, we gravitate toward the more conservative side. In so doing we may actually reject portions of progressivism that are biblical and embrace aspects of conservatism that are not.

Once Christian educators become aware of and comprehend these influences, they should be motivated to critically examine the goals, objectives, and practices of Christian schooling. In so doing they may find that portions of conservative approaches to education can be kept, that some should be modified, and that others must be rejected. It also suggests the possibility that there may be aspects of progressive educational practice that can be accepted or modified. In either case, the naturalistic and economic bias of the contemporary practice of schooling must be rejected in favor of one that more accurately reflects and is true to the fundamental principles of the purpose of education contained in Scripture—purposes and practices that more accurately reflect a biblical worldview. Since a worldview, even a biblical one, can produce seemingly competing philosophies, the possibility exists of developing both conservative and progressive elements to Christian schools. Both conservative and progressive approaches, however, must seek to implement the fundamental principles of a biblical worldview as it relates to education.

Three Principles of a Biblically Based Education

5

Education: Before the Fall

God's charge to our first parents was to transform untamed nature into a social environment by cultural transformation that fits God's design.

—Richard Mouw, *When the Kings Come Marching In*

ARNIE FELT AS IF his head was swimming after the morning in-service sessions. During lunch he and a few of his colleagues discussed some of the issues that had been raised, particularly the issue that an institution, like school, could have sin embedded into its practice, even if it was a Christian school. The discussions were lively, and not without differences of opinion. Dr. Wise's arguments regarding how people create culture and the institutions within a society appealed to Arnie as a social studies teacher, and the thought that sinful people would create sinful institutions helped him not only to understand the dynamics of schooling but also to think differently about the content of his history classes. As Arnie began to contemplate the ramifications of the morning sessions, he was brought back to the issue of schooling by the discussion of his colleagues over lunch.

"Well, I think that schools should socialize young people," professed Paula Pedagogy, the fifth grade teacher. "Schools have an obligation to prepare people for society. All this talk about sin being part of institutions is a bit much. I am not sure I appreciate Wise's suggesting that there is really little difference between Christian and public schools."

Edith Erudite, veteran high school English teacher, countered, "I am not sure I agree with everything that Wise says, but some of it makes sense. I don't think he said that schools shouldn't socialize students, but that we need to be aware of the values embedded in how we socialize them. We all claim that nothing is value neutral and that everything in life has a spiritual dimension, yet we tend to treat institutions as if they were value neutral. Granted, we don't look at the people in them as value neutral, but if people create the ways that institutions operate and those people have a sin nature, then why shouldn't the practices of an institution reflect that sin nature? I must confess that I have never thought about schooling, Christian or public, in this way. It does open a Pandora's Box however—forcing us to look at our curriculum and practices in a much more critical light. I am not sure I am prepared to do that."

"It's just an academic argument," claimed Manfred Median. "I agree with Paula. If Christian schools produce better citizens, better employees, better spouses and parents, and more active and loyal church members than the public schools, then Christian schools are doing their job. We prepare students for college and give them a foundation in the Bible and doctrine. This is what the parents are paying for, and if we do this well our graduates will have an impact for Christ in the society."

Arnie listened attentively, but he was not completely convinced by his friend Manfred's argument. Like Edith, he found part of Wise's argument compelling. People do create societies and the institutions in those societies, he reasoned, and those institutions are reflections of their core spiritual condition. If people are sinners, it is quite conceivable that any society or the social institutions they create would be infused with sinful values. For Arnie, the similarity between most Christian school curriculum and pedagogy and those of the public schools, demonstrated by Wise, was a bit disconcerting. As a result, Manfred's argument, although not completely convincing, held a bit of comfort for him. And, as Edith suggested, why open Pandora's Box and critically evaluate the practices of Christian schooling? Mt. Carmel was considered a good school, parents were generally satisfied, student test scores warranted college admission for the majority, and the school ran relatively smoothly. Yet, Arnie's mind kept reflecting back to his initial observation during the first week of school. The majority of students at Mt. Carmel did not seem to reflect attitudes and values that were much different from Christian students in public schools. Arnie concluded that he was like the majority of the teachers at Mt. Carmel. He found the morning sessions compelling, even if he had not fully bought into Wise's argument. Still, he was looking forward to the afternoon sessions with the hope that they would prepare him to critically examine how he could be involved in revising his own thinking and courses to better prepare his students to think more biblically.

Dr. Wise opened the afternoon session: "Well, I hope you all had a great lunch and have come back prepared to work. After some of the conversations I had with some teachers and administrators at lunch, it seems that I have raised more questions than answers." At this statement, Arnie gave a crooked smile of agreement. "That is typical, and it is the reason that we have scheduled two days to evaluate these questions. My objective is for you to consider that assisting in the worldview transformation of your students is going to require developing a school that reflects a biblical approach to education. In raising the question—how does Mt. Carmel differ from public schools?—my intent is not to criticize what you are doing but to prepare you to examine the goals and objectives of schooling from a biblical perspective."

"Our task for the afternoon," continued Wise, "is to examine Scripture so we can begin to develop an understanding of what the goals and objectives of schooling should be from a biblical perspective. In order to understand a scriptural perspective, we are going to go back to the beginning, to the book of Genesis. I would like you to return to your discussion groups, read Genesis 1:26–31 and Genesis 2:15–17, and answer two questions. First, what do these passages tell us about human beings and the commands that God gave to humanity before the Fall? Second, what affect would these commands have on the goals and objectives of schooling? Yes, I know that these questions are a bit vague but that is for a reason. I want you all to brainstorm through the passages. Let's spend about 15 to 20 minutes examining these verses; then we will come back together to discuss what you have come up with."

Arnie and his colleagues returned to their discussion groups. As he seemed to have inherited the leadership role for the group, Arnie quickly got his colleagues to the task. "Let's each read the passages; then we can note our observations," he suggested. The group took a few moments to read the passages; then the discussion began.

"Well, the first thing I see in Genesis 1:26 is that human beings are created in the image of God," noted Byron Bunsen, the high school science teacher. "I am sure we should note that and the fact that God gave Adam and Eve rule over the animals and all the earth."

"I suppose we should also note that the image of God extends to both males and females, so that 'man' is a generic term for humanity," said Donna Dewey, the sixth grade teacher.

"We are supposed to be 'fruitful and multiply, and fill the earth, and subdue it.' That seems to be an important command," noted Rita Rookie, the new third grade teacher.

"That seems to be the only commandment that human beings have really taken to heart to fulfill," chimed in Byron. His comment brings a few laughs from other members of the group.

"That passage is a bit confusing to me," stated Barry Baroque. "I mean, I understand the 'be fruitful and multiply' part." His comment brought some good-natured joking from other members of the group. "However, I am reading from the New American Standard Bible, which says, 'and fill the earth, and subdue it' and talks about ruling over the fish and birds and all the other living creatures. I guess my confusion is with the phrase 'fill the earth.' Does it refer back to the be fruitful and multiply, in which case 'filling' would seem to refer to having lots of children and populating the planet, or does 'filling' have more to with subduing, which might be a whole different thing?"

The members of the group all checked their translations. Rita's New International Version read "be fruitful and increase in number;" the semicolon following the phrase created some discussion: "It seems that a whole new idea begins after the semicolon, so maybe filling the earth is not part of the command to be fruitful and multiply," said Rita.

Byron responded, "Well, my New King James Version also has a semicolon after multiply, but it also has a semicolon after the phrase 'fill the earth and subdue it;' which leads into a discussion about governing the earth. I am not a grammarian, but I think you use a semicolon to link independent clauses or ideas. So my question is whether 'fill the earth and subdue' goes with being fruitful or with governing the earth."

"I have the King James Version and it says 'replenish the earth, and subdue it,'" noted Donna. "I have never considered this before but 'replenish' could mean to fill with people, but it can also mean to build up or make good, so the KJV does not seem to help us answer the question."

"Well, maybe the passage in Genesis 2:15–17 will help us," suggested Arnie. "Let's look at it."

As the members of the group examined their translations, however, more confusion developed. "My NIV says 'work the earth and care for it,'" noted Rita, "although I am not sure I know what the difference would be."

"My New King James says 'tend and keep it,' which seems like the same thing to me," noted Byron.

"'Dress it and keep it' in the KJV," added Donna.

"Look at the New American Standard," said Byron. "It has 'cultivate and keep.' To cultivate something seems to imply more than just sitting around and eating fruit all day. It seems to imply that we are to do doing something to the creation and maybe what we do is part of the 'filling' referred to in Genesis 1:28."

"This is raising more questions than it answers," remarked Donna. "I must have read this passage dozens of times and never even considered that it might refer to something other than populating the earth."

"I agree," noted Byron. "I really have never considered what it means to 'rule the earth.' Does it mean that we can do what we think is good, or are there principles that should govern how we use the resources that are here?"

"I am confused by what Barry read in the New American Standard," said Rita. "What is the difference between 'cultivating' and 'keeping,' or the wording 'dressing' and 'keeping' in the King James Version? To me cultivating and dressing seems to imply that we are supposed to make things better, but if creation is perfect, how do you make it better? I mean, what is better than perfect!?"

"That is the same problem I have with the word 'subdue,'" said Arnie. "I have always thought that to 'subdue' would mean to bring under control. The texts seem to infer that the creation was wild or untamed before the Fall. How could something that is wild or untamed be 'good' as God says? To me, if God said something was 'good' I would assume he meant that it was perfect or could not be improved."

"How would Adam and Eve have known how to cultivate or keep the creation?" asked Barry. "I don't think they were created omniscient, so they would have had to learn about the creation to fulfill this command, don't you think?"

"Well, if Adam and Eve fulfilled their obligation to be fruitful and multiply, then the only option for their children would have been home schooling," remarked Byron, again bringing laughter to the group. "But seriously, it seems like Adam and Eve would have had to pass on to their children their understanding of how to cultivate and keep."

"It seems as if they would have had to teach principles of stewardship, how to properly use the creation," said Arnie as he reflected out loud, "but can you teach stewardship, and what would stewardship look like to people before they had a sin nature? I would think stewardship would have just come naturally."

Suddenly, Dr. Wise called all the groups back together to discuss their observations and deliberations. As Arnie returned to his seat, he reflected on some of the observations and comments of his fellow group members and began to formulate some questions for Dr. Wise.

To review, each society must educate its children in the knowledge, attitudes, and values of the society. In so doing they perpetuate the dominant worldview of the society.

For Christian educators operating within the dominant cultural milieu, the question of how closely the practices of the Christian school should mirror their secular counterparts is vital. Insofar as the foundational values of the dominant culture reflect a biblical worldview, it may be appropriate for the Christian school to mirror the curriculum and instructional practices of the public schools. The greater the degree of deviance from a biblical worldview found in the foundational values of the dominant worldview of the culture, however, the greater the need for Christian educators to ask the question of how radical does Christian education need to be? If the foundational values of public schooling are reflections of a secular worldview, then for Christian schools to be content to simply produce better citizens, better workers, better spouses and parents than the public schools means being content, essentially, with "beating them at their own game." Christian schools may produce moral citizens but may not necessarily produce disciples of Christ who think about society and their role in society in a fundamentally different and distinctively biblical way. Worldview transformation must involve more than producing graduates who are quantitatively superior in academic achievement or character; it must strive to produce graduates who are qualitatively different in their way of thinking and, consequently, the way they live in the world.

This qualitative difference will be reflected in the goals and objectives of schooling. For the Christian school, the goals and objectives that it should develop and convey to its students should reflect those that are biblically based and that may be distinctively different from those of the public school. These goals and objectives may not necessarily reflect changes in the content of what is taught. Students will still need to learn the skills of reading, writing, and mathematics, as well as the content of the sciences, the arts, and the humanities; however, why this curriculum is being learned should reflect the distinctiveness of an education based on biblical principles. While Christian school students should learn the content of the Bible, as well as the basics of theology, in order to enable them to think as a Christian in the world, this knowledge is not sufficient to produce dedicated disciples of Christ.

Since worldviews are communal, they are developed and reflected by proponents of that worldview as they operate in the world. Yet adherents of a worldview do not develop and reflect all aspects of a worldview with equal ability or expertise. For example, scientists develop scientific knowledge and understanding of the world; writers, musicians, and artists develop art that reflects their understanding and interpretation of the world. While the particular disciplines may be different, as adherents of the worldview their understanding and interpretation of the world should be guided by the same principles and values based in their common worldview. In a sense, this is what Christian educators often mean when they use the term *integration*—the development of ways of knowing, understanding, and operating in the world that are based on the Bible and the biblical worldview. Integration, however, also implies that the ways of knowing, understanding, and operating in the world are guided by a set of foundational principles that affect the process. While biblical educators often speak of the need to engage in integration and understand that this integration must be biblically based, there is little discussion about what these principles are and how they should direct the development of curriculum and the types of instructional strategies that would be most appropriate and effective for encouraging integration.

This section will examine three foundational principles that should guide the process of developing the goals and objectives of a biblically based education. In guiding the process of integration, these principles provide the basis for thinking about the content of each academic discipline in a way that is distinctively biblical. These principles also serve as a basis for how people should act in the world. They not only inform personal behavior but also serve as a basis for the development of a communal response to culture. As such, they reflect the understanding that worldviews are corporate entities, assisting in worldview transformation by guiding both thought and cultural creation from a biblical perspective.

The first principle, and the focus of this chapter, is that a biblically based education should develop people that will be good stewards of the creation. Stewardship refers to understanding, developing, and using the creation in ways that honor the God who created it and fulfill the expectations given by that Creator to humanity from the beginning of the creation. Next, we will examine the principle of reconciliation—how the goals and objectives of stewardship education have changed because of the introduction of sin into the world and what the biblical response of the believing community to sin's continued presence should be. The section concludes with an examination of the concept of the image of God—what it means to be created in God's image and how education should be used to develop people who are greater reflections of God's image in the world.

PRINCIPLES OF STEWARDSHIP

Chapter 3 examined the biblical cultural mandate—the idea that humans beings before the Fall were given authority or stewardship dominion over the creation. As stewards, human beings are granted executive authority to manage the creation; however, as stewards, humanity was not given autonomous authority over the creation. While human beings were granted authority by God to act on the creation, God never relinquishes his sovereign Lordship over it. Rather, God empowers human beings to exercise his authority; in other words, human beings are to manage the creation to accomplish God's purposes. As stewards, human beings are given authority to make decisions, as well as certain powers and abilities to exercise control and responsibly govern the use of creation. Also, stewards are accountable to God as the owner of the creation to demonstrate the extent to which they have accomplished the will of the Master.

The Creator God placed humanity in an environment that he called "good" and then instructed humanity to "fill the earth, and subdue it" (Gen 1:28). To fill the earth and bring it under submission are the parameters of stewardship and the standards by which God holds humanity accountable. The standards of filling and subduing are reiterated and amplified in Genesis 2:15, where we are told that God placed human beings in the Garden to "cultivate" and "keep" the creation. To "subdue" challenges the traditional understanding of creation's perfection for to subdue something is to bring it under rule or control. In light of this command, the perfection of the creation did not mean that it could not be improved upon. Rather, the perfection of the creation was that it completely fulfilled God's intended plan, a plan that included humanity's responsibility to exert authority over it. While exerting authority over the creation, humanity was not permitted to harm it (the idea of keeping) and was charged with adding value to it (the command of "cultivate"). To cultivate the creation, human beings were commissioned by God to create culture, to take the earth's resources and use them in a way that added value to the creation. This adding value or developing the resources of the creation (including human talents and abilities) would include the creation of art, music, literature, architecture, science, technology, and so forth, which would be used to fulfill the purpose of God.

The concept of stewardship and adding value to the creation is mirrored in the New Testament in Matthew 22 where Christ states that people are to love God with "all your heart, and with all your soul, and with all your mind" (verse 37) which is inextricably linked to "you shall love your neighbor as yourself" (verse 39). Proper stewardship is tied to using resources in ways that show the love of God toward others. The same idea is amplified by Matthew a few chapters later in the parable of the Talents, in which the servants who added value to the wealth of the master are praised and the servant who simply kept his talent buried so as to avoid risking loss is condemned. Several verses later Christ explains that condemnation comes to those who do not use their resources to minister to others: "Then they themselves also will answer, 'Lord, when did we see You hungry, or thirsty, or a stranger, or naked, or sick, or in prison, and did not take care of You?' Then He will answer them 'Truly I say to you, to the extent that you did not do it to one of the least of these, you did not do it to me'" (Matt 25:44–45).

This idea of adding value to the creation, which includes creating, can be seen in the culturative direction of history. Human history begins in the Garden (Gen 2:8) and ends in a glorious city (Rev 21–22). David Hegeman notes that this "basic fact of biblical history is obvious, but often overlooked because of the emphasis on redemptive history."[1] According to Hegeman, the similarities between the Garden and the glorious city are striking. Both contain a river located near the tree of life. God is in the midst of both, and in both, human beings enjoy unrestricted fellowship with God.[2] The implication of this progression in culturative history is that "from the very beginning mankind was expected to bring changes to the creation, that some sort of transformation was to take place,"[3] that the idea of cultivating was part of the mandate to humanity. Although human history does not end in a restored garden, the trees of the heavenly city (Rev 22:2) indicate that the garden was not to be abandoned, that the cultural creations of humanity were to coexist or be developed in harmony with the creation.

The cultural mandate of Genesis 1:26–31 and 2:15–17 expresses God's intention that human beings interact with the physical world in order to accomplish God's purpose. This purpose is twofold. First, human interaction with the environment is to be pursued with the purpose of bringing glory to God. Second, the will of humanity, as created in the

1. Hegeman, *Plowing in Hope*, 31.
2. Ibid., 32.
3. Ibid., 34.

image of God, is to be imposed on the creation. Commenting on the sovereignty of God as expressed in the creation, Albert Wolters writes:

> There are two ways in which God imposes his law in the cosmos, two ways in which his will is done on earth as in heaven. He does it either directly, without mediation, or indirectly, through the involvement of human responsibility. . . . In other words, God's rule of law is immediate in the nonhuman realm but mediate in culture and society. In the human realm men and women become coworkers with God; as creatures made in God's image they too have a kind of lordship over the earth, are God's viceroys in creation.[4]

Such a view of creation allows not only for human dominion in the use of the resources of the earth but also for the creation and development of social institutions to provide for orderly cooperation and to assist in the allocation and distribution of those resources to accomplish God's purpose.

Humanity engages in the process of being stewards of the creation in two ways. First, human beings engage the creation in ways that are consistent with the laws of nature—laws that God has embedded in creation's design and that bring glory to him. Part of this engagement is the discovery of the laws that God has woven into the fabric of the universe. These would include the laws of physics and the processes found in biology. The truths of the laws of nature are most familiar to the scientist, who engages in modes of inquiry designed to help discover the reality of the truths of God in nature. In considering the direct Lordship of God over the creation, however, two caveats must be noted. First, God never relinquishes his sovereignty over the creation. The natural laws that God places in the creation are always subject to intervention by the Creator when it serves his purpose to do so. Miracles are those occasions when the Creator chooses to intervene or interrupt the laws of nature to accomplish his purpose. Thus, the deist, who proposes that God created the universe and simply allows it to run according to natural law, or the materialist, who denies any divine creation or intervention and proposes a universe that is simply the byproduct of natural law, both violate this first caveat.

Engaging the creation, however, goes beyond discovery. While God never relinquishes his sovereignty over the creation, he still intends humanity to use it and imprint their image upon it. The laws of nature that humanity discovers are to be used to create that which brings glory to God. God has provided human beings the ability and has allowed human beings the freedom to exercise some control even over aspects of creation upon which God has direct authority. For example, the laws of heredity, once discovered, were manipulated by human beings to create hybrid plants or animals. Discovering the laws of electromagnetic radiation led to the creation of microwave ovens. The Genesis account of creation demonstrates that God allowed humanity to engage in and imprint its image on the creation: God "formed every beast of the field and every bird of the sky" (Gen 2:19) and then brought them to Adam to be named. God allowed Adam to name the animals as a means of granting authority over them. In so doing, Adam's dominion

---

4. Wolters, *Creation Regained*, 14.

authority is preserved, encouraged, and valued by God to the extent that God abided by the names Adam chose to use in labeling the animals.

Human beings are also commissioned by God to govern the earth in ways that will express God's will and desire for the use of the creation's resources. Indirect rule not only embraces the idea of discovering the natural laws or processes embedded in the creation, but also, as image-bearers of God, human beings can show their love and devotion to God in their inventive expressions. This is the second way that humanity engages in steward-ship over the creation—by developing ways to exercise their creativity and imagination and their organization and management of society or culture in ways that promote the advancement of the creation and support the betterment of others. Allowing for human-ity's creativity and imagination is at the heart of the command to be culture creators, expressing the standards of God through the creation of cultures and societies. As Wolters writes,

> We are not so familiar with, or feel less sure about, God's laws for culture and society, which we call *norms*. To be sure, we recognize norms for interpersonal relationships, but we are hesitant about any norms for societal institutions as such, or for some-thing so mundane as agriculture. Yet both Scripture and experience teach us that God's will must be discerned here too, that the Creator is sovereign over the state as much as he is over the animal kingdom, that he is Lord over agriculture as much as he is over energy exchanges. God's statues and ordinances are over everything, certainly not excluding the wide domain of human affairs.[5]

The idea of human beings as culture creators allows for a great deal of creativity and also for diversity and varied understandings of how to best accomplish the norms that God expects human beings to implement. The command to "be fruitful and multiply" was given to Adam before the Fall, and had there not been the Fall, human beings could have been expected to continue being faithful to that command. Over time this would have required that human beings expand beyond the boundaries of the Garden. As human be-ings migrated over the earth, they would have encountered varying geography, resources, possibly different climates, as well as variations in plant and animal life. These types of changes would have precipitated new ways of interacting with the creation and the de-velopment of new cultural forms. In each case, these groups of migrating people would have discovered new types of foods and natural resources, and would have developed new types of tools and technologies to subdue the land. Different expressions of art, music, agriculture, and animal husbandry would have been created or would have evolved as human beings sought to fulfill the obligations of stewardship in their new locations.

Accordingly, the idea of human beings as culture creators opposes the idea that there is only one way to do culture that is pleasing to God. Instead, as human beings imple-ment the general standards of God, there can be multiple forms of culture that can be honoring and pleasing to the Creator. As stewards, human beings are regents—those who govern the creation for God—rather than simply servants who fulfill specific commands or orders from God. If the commands for culture creation were specific—if humans were

5. Ibid., 15.

only permitted certain forms of art, music, agriculture, technology, etc.—then all people throughout the earth would be morally obligated to do culture the same way. Individuals and groups of people would be held accountable to conform to specific commands rather than to general principles; peoples and cultures that deviate would be guilty of sin and subject to judgment. While God does provide and require conformity to specific commands (e.g., the Ten Commandments), he allows human creativity and volition to be exercised within the limits of the general principles he provides.

For example, there are certain principles that God provides for me as an individual that are part of his will for my life. God requires that I use my gifts, talents, and time to serve him and others. As a younger man, this required making certain decisions such as whether or not I should go to college, and if so, where should I go and what should I study? Should I marry and, if so, whom? Now, without discounting the possibility that God can provide direct and specific answers to these questions, God rarely directs "go to this college" or "marry this woman." Rather, based on my willingness and desire to please God and fulfill his purposes, there were a number of possible choices or alternatives (as viewed from the human perspective) from which I could select to fulfill God's will for my life. Many of these decisions were subject to my evaluation and judgment of how I could best use the gifts and talents God had entrusted to me. As David writes, "Delight yourself in the Lord; And He will give you the desires of your heart. Commit your way to the Lord, Trust also in Him and He will do it" (Ps 37:4–5).

What is true for individuals would also seem to hold true for a society. If the desire of a people is to fulfill the general principles of subduing, filling, cultivating, and keeping the earth, then there can be a number of different ways to accomplish these goals, different ways of practicing culture that would be in alignment with God's desire and would preserve the regency of humanity that God ordains. To require identical practice would assume relatively equal geography and availability and abundance of resources, which does not exist. This inequality would place people at risk of violating the standards of God. For example, people living in the highlands would be at risk if they did not have access to the resources available to the people of the lowlands or if they developed specific technologies to live in the highlands that differed from those developed for adapting to the lowlands.

The principles of subduing, filling, cultivating, and keeping also require the development of technologies that would allow human beings to fulfill these commands, technologies that could vary in form but still accomplish the purpose and desire of God. For example, assume for a moment that the original Garden of Eden was located, as the Bible indicates, in the area between the Tigris and Euphrates Rivers (cf. Gen 2:10–15). As the human population grows, there becomes increased pressure to expand beyond the region and to cross over one of the rivers. A group of people (or an individual), cognizant of God's command to fill the earth and seeing what appears to be good land on the other side of the river, desires to cross over and settle the area. The question becomes, how do they get to the other side? There are a number of ways to cross the river: build a bridge, use a raft, build a boat, or walk along the side of the river until they discover a place where they can cross. This leads to the question of whether any of these methods is intrinsically more spiritual than the others. Is boating more spiritual than building a bridge or walking across? The answer seems to be that, given the proper desire to fulfill God's purpose and provided no irreparable damage is done to the creation, one form of crossing is not inherently more spiritual than another. God can be honored by any way chosen to cross the river, insofar as the goal is to fulfill his command.

What also should be noted is that any option would require developing knowledge and creating technologies necessary for crossing the river. For example, building a boat would require discovering and using principles of buoyancy and displacement. Building a bridge would require developing a knowledge and use of principles of geometry and structural integrity. Both might require the development of tools to implement particular designs, and so on. Even walking might produce the development of a map, which might require the development of technologies for writing or the implementation of new words or symbols to describe where to cross the river. All of these would require the creation of new learning, a knowledge base that must be shared and passed on to the next generation. In turn, subsequent generations would develop new understandings or ways of modifying and improving existing technologies. In any case, there is an added value that can now be presented back to God and can be used as capital to further advance the desires of the Master.

In a similar fashion, ways of administrating and managing human activity, particularly as human beings continued to populate and disperse over the earth, would have been developed to help organize or coordinate human action or assist in disseminating new knowledge. While individual life in the Garden was fairly isolated, communal life in the city would have been interrelated and required functional coordination. For example, many theologians have understood the role of government to be largely (or even exclusively) negative: government came only after the Fall, and its essential purpose is the restraint of evil. Others theologians, including Aquinas, Luther, and Calvin, while acknowledging the necessity of restraining evil, are critical of those who view the restraint of evil as the only function of government. Calvin, in particular, viewed government service as "the most honorable of all callings in the whole of life"—government's function among people being "no less than that of bread, water, sun and air."[6]

Ronald Sider notes that Paul specified a positive role for government before he addressed its negative function. Paul referred to government as "a minister of God to you for good" (Rom 13:4); Peter wrote that governors are sent not only to punish evil but also to praise those who do good (1 Pet 2:14). God approved and blessed the kings of Israel for leading their societies in positive activities and condemned them when they did not.[7] Further, Revelation 21:24–26 notes that government leaders (i.e., kings of the earth) in the kingdom will bring glory and honor to the nations and the earth, thus suggesting that government authority and rule has intrinsic merit apart from the effects of sin and the restraint of evil.

The absence of any reference in the Bible to government before the Fall does not necessarily mean that government, or any other institution or system of management,

---

6. Calvin, *Institutes of the Christian Religion*, 1.4.22.

7. Sider, "Justice, Human Rights, and Government," 187.

is a result of sin. First, music is not mentioned in the Bible until after the Fall (cf. Gen 4:21), but that does not suggest that music is a result of sin. Also, Sider acknowledges that if human beings were created as isolated individuals (as proposed by those who view government as a type of social contract), then the idea of government being a result of the Fall may have merit. Human beings, however, are created in the image of a triune God, a tri-unity that demonstrates mutual and loving fellowship between each of the members. As image-bearers of the triune God, humanity is made for mutual interdependence, and fulfilling their God-given role necessitates that human beings engage in cooperative tasks and loving fellowship. This requires leaders to help organize that cooperation in order to assist carrying out the mandates of dominion and stewardship in creating culture.[8]

Thus, the command to cultivate and to keep the creation not only includes the discovery and use of the natural laws God embedded in the creation, which are the focus of the natural sciences, but also provides for human beings to use their creativity and imagination to develop expressions in the arts, music, and literature. In addition, it provides for humankind to organize and manage their efforts collectively, which would include those areas traditionally associated with the social sciences. Thus, practically all areas of human endeavor have their origins in the pre-Fall commands to humanity and are subject to God's requirements to be exercised in ways that demonstrate proper stewardship dominion.

STEWARDSHIP LEARNING

The above illustrations assume that human beings did not know, as part of their initial creation, certain facts like buoyancy, displacement, geometry, or structural integrity. These academic disciplines—humanities, art and music, literature and drama—did not exist at the moment of creation. The inevitable development and evolution of systems and institutions such as economics and government to assist human beings in the organization and management of the creation can be assumed. In order to accomplish the mandates of stewardship, new concepts would have been created, and new words would have been coined to describe these new objects and ideas. Human language would have evolved from simple verbal forms (which human beings demonstrate in the earliest passages of Genesis) to written forms (visual patterns that would come to be represented graphically). These considerations raise the question of how omniscient Adam was: to what extent was Adam familiar with natural laws or principles of the social sciences or humanities? For Adam and subsequent generations of humanity to fulfill their God-given obligation to cultivate and keep the earth required the development of new knowledge and technologies—knowledge that they would not have possessed as part of the initial knowledge base given to them by God. Thus, as human beings fulfilled their God-given command to interact with the creation, they subsequently began to learn more about the creation and had to develop new ways of using their knowledge to further the purposes of the Master.

8. Ibid.

Adam's naming of the animals illustrates this point. In Genesis 2:18 God said, "It is not good for the man to be alone; I will make him a helper suitable for him." God's objective was the creation of a wife for Adam. God, however, engages in what appears to be a strange procedure to bring this about. God subjects Adam to what could be perceived as the ultimate object lesson. God brings all of the animals before Adam to be named. As Adam engages in the process of naming the animals, he realizes that while there is two of every other living creature, there is only one of him (2:20). At this point God causes Adam to fall into a sleep, takes one of Adam's ribs, and fashions the woman (2:21–22). When Adam awakes, he finds his wife, a suitable mate and helper for him, and calls her "woman." Of note, is that Adam did not possess the knowledge that he was alone and did not have a suitable helper as part of his initial created endowment. Adam's understanding of his condition was based on his ability to correctly observe various properties of the creation (in naming the animals he must note their similarities and differences) and his inductive powers of reasoning (he concludes that, unlike the animals, there is not a mate or helper suitable for him). Granted, Adam was undoubtedly a fast learner; he promptly ascertains and rightly concludes that the woman is "bone of my bones, and flesh of my flesh" (and names her as such).

These powers of observation and reasoning allowed Adam and subsequent humanity to learn about the creation while interacting with it. As early human beings interacted with the creation, their powers of observation would have yielded them much knowledge about the properties and the processes that operate in the creation. At the same time, their powers of reasoning would have allowed them to induce general principles, deduce conclusions, and invent new products or processes that would enhance the quality of the creation, adding value for the benefit of others and self and for the glory of God. Adam and subsequent humanity are endowed with the ability to engage in basic research—research driven by a natural curiosity and desire to know or understand more. Humanity also possesses the ability to engage in applied research—research designed to solve problems or invent things that improve or enhance life. For example, observing that certain substances float (and others do not) leads to conclusions about buoyancy, which could be used to make the first rafts or boats. Discovering that wind through a hollow tube or varying degrees of tautness in fibers produces a melodic sound could be used to produce piped or stringed instruments. Learning that heat applied to certain substances produces harder metals which can be shaped into tools or mixed with other metals to produce alloys could lead to early metallurgy (cf. Gen 4:20–22).

An acute sense of observation and astute powers of reasoning, however, are not sufficient to fulfill the biblical mandates of subduing, filling, cultivating, and keeping. For a person to perform the role of a steward, to govern as a regent, requires not only an understanding of the domain in which they are appointed to govern but also an imitate knowledge of the One whom the steward serves. Human beings before the Fall had an intimate fellowship with God, a fellowship characterized by God's physical presence with them in the Garden (cf. Gen 3:8). This fellowship with God allowed Adam and his wife access to understanding the desires of God; not only could they share what they had learned, but they would have had opportunity to learn appropriate and inappropriate uses of that knowledge. Knowing God would be more than simply intellectual (what God required them to do), but also affective and volitional—that God's will and delight would be theirs as well. Thus, for human beings, learning to be good stewards also requires a relationship with the One who has entrusted humanity with the responsibility of governance.

The idea that human beings are finite and that learning occurs through interaction with the environment generates certain pedagogical conditions to be considered. As finite creatures, there is no guarantee that the observations human beings make about the world are fully accurate. Human understanding about anything, even before the Fall, is not an all-or-nothing proposition; knowledge about the world develops and evolves over time. Adam's observation of fruit falling from a tree does not mean that he understood the intricacies of quantum physics or even Newton's laws of motion. Rather, continued learning would result in a greater and more sophisticated understanding of the world. Also, as finite beings who attempt to act on their knowledge of the world, they would naturally act from an incomplete understanding. This would mean that as human beings engaged in scientific inquiry and technological innovation, mistakes could occur. Those errors would inform subsequent attempts at engaging the world, providing information from which to hypothesize about why and how. Thus, learning required a type of experimental engagement with the world—developing hypotheses, implementing and testing those hypotheses, and reasoning about and evaluating the results.

Of course, engaging the world incorrectly can produce damaging consequences. In the natural world, to act on the environment in ways that are not ecologically sound can produce effects that are potentially harmful. The commands to "subdue" and to "cultivate" are active commands; they require that human beings proactively engage the world. Even so, finite creatures, acting proactively, create the potential for damaging consequences that could violate the command to care for or keep the creation. While there may be tension, there is no contradiction between these two commands. In the natural world there is a sense of balance or self-healing embedded into the mechanism of creation. Biologists have long identified this characteristic of nature with the term *homeostasis*. For example, if a farmer clears a rain forest to make room for farmland and then decides to leave the land, over time the rain forest will return, providing that the surrounding ecosystem was not sufficiently removed. God, in his wisdom, provided a healing mechanism for finite human beings who must learn from interacting with the environment and who, in the process of learning, would make inevitable mistakes. The process of homeostasis would allow human beings to proactively engage the creation in a manner that would support the command to cultivate, while providing a mechanism that, when they noticed that their actions could potentially have damaging effects, supported the command to care for the creation and do no lasting harm to it.

The motivation to learn about the creation provides the impetus for the learner to engage in actually *doing* stewardship. While human curiosity might spur some to learn about the creation for the sake of purely knowing (basic research), the initial command given to humanity, and the one that prompts humans to engage the creation is a command to *do*, to *act*, to *undertake* the process of adding value so that the fruits of that labor can be given back to the Creator for his honor and glory. This is not to suggest that basic research is somehow unbiblical—individuals cannot use knowledge that they do not possess—but to suggest that the use of knowledge is of primary importance. The results of learning about the creation and its proper use should be passed on to each subsequent generation so that they can also engage in the God-given expectation to participate in the stewardship imperative.

As children participate in the exercise of stewardship with learned adults, two types of knowledge are passed on. The first is the knowledge and skills collective humanity has learned that allow for the management of the creation. This could include the content of science, mathematics, farming, or herding. It could also include the skills of reading, writing, art, or music. As human beings continued to explore the creation and aspects of their own humanity, the disciplines of the sciences, social sciences, arts, and humanities would continue to grow and thus provide additional content and skills to be learned. This is descriptive knowledge, the knowledge of the way life is. Stewardship learning, however, would also, and more importantly, include instruction in why individuals do these things. How do the knowledge and skills of the academic disciplines further the primary goal of cultivating, keeping, subduing, and filling? Using knowledge for a specific purpose is driven by an understanding of how the world should be.

Learning how things are, the descriptive aspects of a discipline, can encourage human beings to further explore the intricacies of the creation. This could involve learning about a particular area in greater depth; observations regarding depth, symmetry, and proportion, combined with basic principles of arithmetic, would lead to the development of geometry and calculus. Once developed, these disciples could be applied in various ways, for example, in art or to architectural or engineering design.

From the perspective of stewardship, however, advances in knowledge, understanding, and application are always driven by the normative—asking, how does the conceived use of this knowledge advance the goals of stewardship? The descriptive process of learning could conceivably lead to discoveries whose application would violate the command to not harm the creation. In this case, the normative function would prevent human beings from acting upon what can be done in favor of what should be done. Proper stewardship does demand that the descriptive never drives the normative—what can be done never dictates what should be done. The ultimate goal of bringing glory and honor to God becomes the objective; it serves to motivate all learning before the Fall. Before the Fall the descriptive and normative functions of learning existed in proper balance. After the Fall, both the normative function of stewardship and its balance with the descriptive function become corrupted by the presence and influence of sin.

DEPENDENCY AND STEWARDSHIP

The reality of human finiteness and lack of omniscience before the Fall underscores in the cognitive sphere what evangelicals acknowledge is true in all other areas of human existence: human beings are dependent upon God in all aspects of life. While evangelicals note their dependence upon God for their physical and spiritual well-being (Matt 6:11; Acts 17:28; Heb 1:3), the issue of cognitive dependency is rarely considered or addressed.

While it is relatively easy to consider and define physical dependency and, theologically, to consider and define spiritual dependency, cognitive dependency is more elusive. This may be the result of a bias in Western epistemological thinking that views human beings as capable of independently knowing and understanding the world. While certain aspects of the creation can be known by humans with a relatively high level of certainty via independent observation and interaction with the environment, other aspects of knowing are almost completely dependent on God's revealing them to humans. For example, the knowledge and understanding of the principles of physics can be discovered through observation, experimental inquiry, reflection, and reasoning; however, the proper use of that knowledge can only be learned through a close relationship with the Creator. Proper stewardship requires an intimate relationship with the One to whom service is rendered, and the steward is dependent upon God to both initiate and sustain this relationship.

To be stewards of the creation, human beings must understand the desire of the Master in order to properly execute dominion. While human beings are uniquely endowed by God to discover and make sense of the world (i.e., the descriptive aspect of worldview), finiteness makes human beings less able to answer questions of what to do with that knowledge. Human beings were commissioned before the Fall to develop and keep the creation, yet developing and keeping can only be defined properly by the One who created it. As a result, finite creatures are dependent on their relationship with God to provide them the proper goals and objectives for using the creation. Without such a sense of dependence, humanity would need to seek its own answers to the questions of developing and using the creation.

A proper understanding of worldview entails both the descriptive and normative components. The normative function provides a vision that directs human activity and gives meaning to actions. When evangelicals promote the need to develop a biblical worldview, it is generally this normative aspect of worldview that is highlighted, the need to understand the proper use of one's time, energy, resources, and talents in ways that are pleasing to God. Knowledge of this vision requires an intimate and dependent relationship with the One who provides human activity with dignity and meaning. Human beings, and the societies they create, who do not acknowledge dependency on God and his vision for the creation are still in need of a normative vision to explain and direct human activity. Without acknowledging dependency on God, however, human beings must start from themselves in constructing this vision or worldview. Efforts to create such a vision for life apart from God would have failed before the Fall due to human finiteness and are doomed to failure after the Fall because of humanity's sin nature.

Finiteness creates the need for human beings to question the conclusions they develop, since being finite opens the possibility of error. Not all knowledge or understanding of the world, however, carries with it the same level or possibility of error. The more concrete the knowledge, the more logical or rational, or the closer that knowledge is to answering questions within the descriptive realm (e.g., questions regarding the physical world), the greater the probability human beings have of starting from themselves and drawing correct observations or conclusions. Inversely, the more abstract the knowledge or the closer the questions human beings ask relate to the normative realm, the greater the possibility of error and the greater the need for dependency on God to verify the conclusion.

Sinful human beings, desiring autonomy from God and seeking to deny their created dependency, will attempt to develop a new normative vision from the descriptive capabilities with which they were endowed. For example, the French philosopher René Descartes proposed the use of reason and logic.[9] Englishman John Locke sought to establish human autonomy based on knowledge gathered from experience and reflection. In either case, normative visions of the world are constructed independent of the will of God.

As noted, the more abstract the concept, that is, the further removed from the physical creation, the greater the probability of error, which increases human dependency to ensure a proper understanding. While a person can be reasonably certain regarding concepts of logic (for example, it is relatively easy to check the validity of two plus two equals four, and the answer will be true for everyone) or ideas derived from sensation. For example, human beings generally agree on such concepts as hard and soft or sweet and sour. Ideas such as beauty, justice, or truth—all of which have their source in God—leave human beings dependent on him for their proper understanding. To acknowledge the reality of such concepts, for the reality of these attributes of God are evident in the creation (Rom 1:20), without acknowledging the reality of the One whom they reflect is to force humanity to develop its own definitions of these concepts. Those definitions will be generated from the areas that human beings can know, those areas of understanding that God has empowered humanity to know (i.e., knowledge based on reason and/or sense data). By not acknowledging dependency, however, and by seeking to understand these areas from itself, humanity is destined to make mistakes, using the knowledge of what is to develop a vision of what should be, which ultimately leads them away from God (Rom 1:21–23).

Failure to acknowledge dependency on God results in humanity being forced to develop definitions from their own experiences or deductions. These definitions may come from individual reasoning or from conclusions based on observation of the world around them. For example, to say "beauty is in the eye of the beholder" denies that there is an objective or God-inspired view of beauty that can be used to evaluate the aesthetic value of anything. Denying such a God-inspired definition of beauty (e.g., one based in God's holiness as a reflection of true beauty) creates a relative aesthetic that can make a representation of even the grossest of sins beautiful if someone reasons or deems it to be.

Similarly, human beings can observe the plant and animal worlds to find a principle of natural selection that operates as a law of nature. To apply this observation of how the world works (what is) to how societies should operate (what should be), however, could lead to the development of a type of Social Darwinism, which can be used to justify chasmic gaps between rich and poor. It led John D. Rockefeller to claim that the fortune he developed through the Standard Oil Trust in the late nineteenth century was "merely

---

9. Descartes, *Meditations on First Philosophy*, 60. Descartes attempts to develop a system of knowing completely apart from dependency on God by noting that "I will suppose not a supremely good God, the source of truth, but rather an evil genius, as clever and deceitful as he is powerful, who has directed his entire effort to mislead me. I will regard the heavens, the air, the earth, colors, shapes, sounds, and all external things as nothing but the deceptive games of my dreams, with which he lays snares for my credulity."

survival of the fittest . . . the working out of the law of nature and the law of God."[10] It could also lead to the idea that those of superior intellect, imagination, or work ethic, as measured by their ability to create wealth, are "more moral" than those who cannot. As Robert Bork writes:

> In America, "the rich" are overwhelmingly people—entrepreneurs, small business-men, corporate executives, doctors, lawyers, etc.—who have gained their higher incomes through intelligence, imagination, and hard work. Any transfer of wealth from rich to poor thereby undermines the nation's moral fiber. Allow the virtuous rich to keep more of their earnings and pay less in taxes, and they'll be even more virtuous. Give the non-virtuous poor food stamps, Medicaid, and what is left of welfare, and they will fall into deeper moral torpor.[11]

Such teaching can lead to serious inconsistencies in practice between caring for the poor as a demand and extension of justice and caring for the poor simply as an extension of charity. They are the inevitable result of finite human beings, acting autonomously, to develop a normative vision of life apart from a relationship with God.

DENYING DEPENDENCY: THE PROBLEM OF "IS" AND "OUGHT"

The power that human beings have over the creation allows humanity to use the creation in ways that honor God. What brings honor to God, however, cannot be defined by human beings and can only be developed within the context of a close personal fellowship with the Creator. In Matthew 25:35–40, Christ outlines the criteria for the judgment of the nations:

> "For I was hungry, and you gave Me something to eat; I was thirsty, and you gave Me something to drink; I was a stranger, and you invited me in; naked, and you clothed Me; I was sick, and you visited Me; I was in prison, and you came to Me." Then the righteous will answer Him, "Lord, when did we see you hungry, and feed You, or thirsty, and give you something to drink? And when did we see You a stranger, and invite you in, or naked and clothe You? When did we see You sick, or in prison, and come to you?" The King will answer them, "Truly I say to you, to the extent that you did it to one of these brothers of Mine, even to the least of them, you did it to me."

The context of this passage is significant. Christ has just given the disciples the parable of the Talents, in which working for the benefit of others is said to bring him glory. In Matthew 22:36–40, the disciples learned that the greatest commandment is to love God with all their heart, soul, and mind (Luke 10:27 adds "strength," cf. Deut 6:5) and that they must also love their neighbor as themselves (cf. Lev 19:18). Jesus is the first to combine these two texts into a summary of the Law. The disciples have now learned that they must love others as an extension of their love for God and that loving God and being a faithful servant requires adding value to his investment (i.e., creation). Christ now operationally defines adding value as using the resources of creation to meet the needs of others; in so doing the actions are directed at him. Thus, the ability to know about the creation and the

---

10. Quoted in Reich, "Of Darwinism and Social Darwinism."
11. Quoted in Ibid.

creative power and control that is given to humanity is to be exercised in accordance with a particular vision that God has, which is that the resources of the creation are to be used for the betterment of others. In the course of seeking the betterment of others human beings also enhance their own lives, which is how they love their neighbor as themselves (cf. Phil 2:4; Rom 15:1–2). While the means that humans use to exercise this dominion power are within the creative realm of humanity, God defines the end or goal by providing the vision of the way things should be, the type of knowledge human beings cannot obtain starting from themselves.

While human beings, starting from themselves, can develop a rudimentary understanding of what they should not do (i.e., the law that can be seen in creation, Rom 1:18–23), or that is written in human hearts (Rom 1:24–2:16), apart from God they cannot develop a proper understanding or vision of what the world should be. This is particularly true in a fallen world where the rudimentary information or sense data used to develop such a vision carries with it the effects of the Fall. For this reason humanly developed normative visions generally fall into two major categories. The first are those visions based in observations of how the natural world works. These are utopian visions based in natural law. These theories view nature as a type of *prima facie* or first evidence or argument of what is good. From this perspective, human society would function best if it were in alignment with the way nature operates. Natural law theorists seek to ascertain the norms of human society by deriving principles of governance reflected in nature. Such a view correctly assumes that nature is an extension of the character of a perfect Creator (e.g., this would be the view of Thomas Aquinas and John Locke) but fails to adequately account for the fallenness of the world that is a result of the curse on creation in Genesis 3.

The second group of utopian theories are those that find their origin in human reason or conceptions of how the world should be. These theories note that the natural world does not guide itself by reason or intelligence, whereas human beings are separated and distinct from nature as a result of their intelligence and reason, volition and emotion. For human beings to simply conform to the laws of nature would be for human beings to deny what makes them distinctively human. While natural law cannot necessarily be violated, human reason can go beyond the demands of nature to construct visions of what should be based on the characteristics and capacities that make human beings distinct from nature. While such views correctly see human beings as distinct from nature and may even correctly conclude that there is a fallenness to nature that precludes developing universal moral maxims from nature, they fail to properly account for the fallen nature of human reason and volition, wherein the sinful nature of humanity affects what human beings will do and how they rationalize their sinful desires (Jer 17:9).

The tension between deriving principles of society from nature or from reason creates the *is-ought* problem of philosophical ethics. The problem was originally raised by the Scottish philosopher David Hume, who argued that it was impossible to develop prescriptive principles of what should be from examining the way that the world is. As Hume writes:

> In every system of morality, which I have hitherto met with, I have always remarked, that the author proceeds for some time in the ordinary ways of reasoning, and establishes the being of a God, or makes observations concerning human affairs; when of a sudden I am surprised to find, that instead of the usual copulations of propositions, *is*, and *is not*, I meet with no proposition that is not connected with an *ought*, or an *ought not*. This change is imperceptible; but is however, of the last consequence. For as this *ought*, or *ought not*, expresses some new relation or affirmation, 'tis necessary that it should be observed and explained; and at the same time that a reason should be given, for what seems altogether inconceivable, how this new relation can be a deduction from others, which are entirely different from it.[12]

A similar, yet distinct, criticism is what G. E. Moore called the *naturalistic fallacy*, a logical fallacy of reasoning creating by deriving principles of what is good from nature and what is bad from deviations from nature. Both men conclude that it is impossible to develop normative laws of morality or ethics from examining the world that is. What both Hume and Moore note is consistent with the biblical principles of knowing, that human beings are capable of understanding a great deal about what the creation is, but are dependent upon a relationship with God to know what ought to be.

When human beings attempt to develop a vision for what the world should be apart from fellowship with the Creator and when they seek to develop such a vision from their own understanding, a problem occurs. The categories, principles, generalizations, and so forth based on the nonliving world have a greater degree of certainty than those derived from living things. As the degree of complexity in the physical world increases—from nonliving to living, inanimate to animate, and from nonspiritual to spiritual—observations derived from less complex aspects of nature are less applicable and cannot be generalized to more complex organisms. Ultimately, observations made from nonspiritual entities cannot necessarily be applied to spiritual beings.

The distinction between observations made from nonliving things to living things, however, is not always clear. For example, while plants are qualitatively different from rocks, by virtue of the fact that plants are living, the types of methodologies used to come to an understanding of plants may be similar and appropriate to apply to rocks. Likewise, predictions of how rocks or plants will react under certain conditions can be made and tested in a similar fashion. While the botanist may have to account for a greater sensitivity to and diversity of environmental factors than, for example, a geologist (hence, increasing the possibility of error); this complexity appears more as a quantitative difference than a qualitative one. Since observations and predictions from the physical world render results with high degrees of certainty, and since the difference between nonliving and living entities appears only as quantitative differences of complexity, it is tempting to apply the methodology used to learn about the nonliving world to the living world.

In the case of plants, this methodology can produce a fairly high degree of certainty regarding the results. The level of certainty decreases, however, as the method is applied to animals. Since animals can have larger response repertoires than plants, which contributes to increased levels of complexity in animals, the level of predictive certainty about

---

12. Hume, *Treatise of Human Nature*, 3.1.1, p. 521.

animals goes down as the complexity of the animal goes up. The behavior of single cell animal like an amoeba is easier to predict than that of a dog, while a chimpanzee poses even greater difficulties in predicting behavior. If qualitative differences are ignored, however, and difficulties of prediction are viewed as simply quantitative (i.e., we have failed to account for all the variables due to complexity), there will continue to be a bias toward applying a methodology to the living realm that has rendered predictive and reliable results when applied to the nonliving realm. When applied to human beings, this bias renders moot the distinctively qualitative and spiritual nature of humanity in favor of a natural or biological and quantitative description.

Admittedly, the scientific method can, at times, render highly predictive results in some areas when applied to animals and even humans. For example, understanding anatomical systems and the interaction of these systems can produce highly predictive results. Since anatomical systems in animals act mechanistically, understanding the mechanism and its response to certain stimuli can produce a highly predictable and usable result. Yet, when applied to areas such as learning, reliance on the scientific method becomes problematic. While it is possible to develop techniques for training animals, the increased complexity of some animals makes the use of such techniques less than totally reliable. Interestingly, when these techniques fail to work we tend to ascribe to the animal human-like characteristics (e.g., my dog is temperamental).

There is a qualitative leap, however, from generalizing principles and techniques of learning from animals to human beings. In order to apply these principles to humans, one must conclude that human beings are nothing more than more complex animals. If this is the case, then human learning highly resembles animal learning except for the differing level of complexity. Principles developed from the study of animals can then be applied relatively easily to human beings, provided that one allows for the increased number of variables. This is the position of behavioral theories of learning, which generalize principles of human learning from experiments conducted on rats, pigeons, and monkeys. Since this position fails to acknowledge any qualitative distinction between human beings and animals, the trade-off for behaviorists is that certain aspects of humanity must be ignored in order to apply these generalities. For example, in order to increase cognition, the behaviorist must ignore or deny the spiritual aspect of a person; or, the spiritual dimension may be accounted for as a variable that affects a person's ability, capacity, and motivation to learn and can be observed and quantified. In either case the behaviorist must engage in a type of reductionism, where human beings are treated not as organic wholes but as nothing more than the sum total of their component parts. The resulting tendency is to reduce human beings to mechanistic systems from which scientific research can be used to produce predictable end results.

The example of behaviorism serves to expose a problem associated with the strict application of the scientific method to the understanding and development of techniques applied to humans (e.g., teaching strategies). To do so one must engage in a process, as described by evolutionary psychologist Steven Pinker, of *greedy reductionism*.[13] Greedy

13. Pinker, *Blank Slate*, 70.

reductionism is a process that attempts to understand or explain a phenomenon in terms of its smallest or simplest components in order to develop these ideas and techniques. To use the scientific method, the investigator must identify as many variables as possible and control all of those variables (i.e., hold them constant) so that one particular variable can be isolated and subjected to a treatment. The researcher can then note the effect of that treatment on the nonconstant or manipulated variable. By noting the treatment's effects on a particular variable, the researcher can develop techniques designed to assist in changing that variable. For example, when animals are given the prospect of a food reward, they will increase a desired response to a stimulus; if that reward is removed, then, over time, the response of the animal to that stimulus will be reduced. From observations of animal responses, behavioral psychologists have developed teaching techniques such as reinforcement and extinction to increase or reduce student behaviors. This reductionistic view of the mind is consistent with the principles of John Locke and his analogy of the mind as a *tabula rasa*, or a "blank slate."[14]

Many scientists are uncomfortable with this deterministic view of science when applied to human beings. Whereas the behavior of machines can be reduced to the inescapable laws of physics or chemistry, human beings are seen as having volition to choose their behavior. With choice comes freedom. Freedom allows human beings to have a vision about the possibilities for the future and also to believe that people can be held accountable for their actions. If, however, the only way of producing reliable information about the world is through the scientific method, a dilemma is created: a dualism must be produced that separates the mind (which cannot be observed and quantified) from the body. In this dualism, the very act of thinking supposes the existence of a mind, which humans do not want to deny, while they can doubt the existence of their bodies because they can imagine themselves as spirits that do not possess a body.[15] This is the essence of Descartes's argument when he penned his famous statement, "I think therefore, I am"; he is struggling to reconcile the dilemma of the type of reliable data that is produced by science with his desire to continue to maintain that there is something qualitatively different about human beings.

Gilbert Ryle noted Descartes's dilemma:

> When Galileo showed that his methods of scientific discovery were competent to provide a mechanical theory which should cover every occupant of space, Descartes found in himself two conflicting motives. As a man of scientific genius he could not but endorse the claims of mechanics, yet as a religious and moral man he could not accept . . . the discouraging rider to those claims, namely that human nature differs only in degree of complexity from clockwork.[16]

Ryle believed that Descartes's dilemma was prevalent among "theorists and even among laypeople," and is represented in the belief that "human bodies are in space. . . .

14. Locke, *Essay Concerning Human Understanding*, 89.
15. Pinker, *Blank Slate*, 9.
16. Ryle, *Concept of Mind*, 20.

But minds are not in space, nor are their operations subject to mechanical laws."[17] Ryle believed that the mind and space belief could not be proven, was not scientific, and named it "the dogma of the Ghost in the Machine."[18]

What results from Ryle's critique is that no fundamental distinction can be made between the brain (biological) and the mind (more spiritual). In essence, the concept of the mind is eliminated in favor of the more mechanistic understanding of the brain. While many scientists have attempted to rescue a distinction between mind and brain, such attempts only acknowledge the complexity of dealing with all the variables that make up human beings, without acknowledging any qualitative difference between human beings and other species. Ultimately, all attempts to understand human beings solely through the scientific method "biologize" the mind and seek to attempt to understand human beings, including the understanding of learning and teaching, from a scientific perspective.

Interestingly, the English philosopher Herbert Spencer believed the scientific model to be the appropriate one for the understanding of the mind over a century ago: "We must compare mental phenomenon with the phenomenon most like them. . . . The phenomenon which those of Mind resemble in the greatest degree are those of the bodily life."[19] Spencer's biologization of the mind has its roots in Darwinian evolution, and the metaphor, in the hands of behavioral psychologists, produces an understanding of the mind in which its capabilities are nothing more than the products of environmental forces over time. For this reason, behavioral psychologists sought to develop laws of learning from animals and generalize their application to human beings, who are subject to the same evolutionary forces. The biologization of the mind, however, is not the sole propriety of behaviorists. Among learning theorists, Piaget's views of cognitive development are considered diametrically opposed to behaviorism. Even so, Piaget's theories share the same biological and evolutionary bias as behaviorists. As Piaget wrote, "The psychological development that starts at birth and terminates in adulthood is comparable to organic growth . . . so mental life can be conceived as evolving toward a final form of equilibrium represented by the adult mind."[20]

As previously stated, apart from a dependency on God, human beings must develop a sense of what ought to be from their own understanding. God has endowed humanity with a unique capacity to understand what is when interacting with the creation but requires humble submission to him in order to know what ought to be. Separated from God and desiring to be autonomous from his authority, human beings are left to construct their own understanding of what ought to be from that which they know. Since humanity is not endowed with the capacity to develop an adequate vision of what ought to be, human beings must attribute a teleological effect to things found in nature. In other words, natural phenomena are explained by the use or design that they seem to fulfill.

The problem with explaining life in this way is that any attribution of value to a particular discovery in nature is done within the context of some other preexisting set of

17. Ibid., 15.
18. Ibid., 17.
19. Spencer, *Principles of Psychology*, 292–93.
20. Piaget, *The Child's Conception of the World*, 3.

values. John Searle's offers the following example: biologists can discover that the heart pumps blood through the body; however, as soon as the biologist says "the *function* of the heart is to pump blood," she goes beyond describing an intrinsic fact of the heart to precribing the normative function of the heart. This can be demonstrated by the fact that a whole vocabulary of success and failure can now be developed and applied to describing the heart. One can speak of a "malfunction" of the heart or of "heart disease"; there can be a qualitative evaluation of better versus worse hearts based on a quantitative assessment of the amount of blood being pumped. None of these assessments would be possible if the biologist only observed that a heart pumps blood.[21]

What we need to understand is that the development of a normative vision cannot be developed when human beings rely on their own understanding of what is. The mandate to be stewards of the creation requires that human beings use their talents and abilities to learn about the creation and their creativity to manage the creation for the glory of God. The stewardship mandate, however, also requires the development of a continued close fellowship between the steward and the Owner, so that the steward can manage the creation according to the desires or priorities of God. Humanity, starting from themselves, can develop a great deal of reliable knowledge regarding how the world is; but humanity, starting from themselves, cannot develop an adequate understanding of how the world should be. In the end, any such vision for life and the world apart from God will dehumanize human beings and improperly understand the purpose and use of the created world.

STEWARDSHIP KNOWING AND STEWARDSHIP DOING

Ultimately, to be a good steward requires doing. Understanding how the world works and what God wants it to be requires taking knowledge learned about the creation and acting on it to fulfill God's purpose. This relationship between knowing and doing is the reason that the commands of Genesis 1:26–31 and 2:15–17 are called the cultural mandate. The commands to "cultivate" and to "keep" require actions that will move humanity in the culturative direction of history in Scripture, from its beginnings in a garden to its fulfillment in a glorious city. Knowing what is good can never be separated from doing what is good. Such a separation is considered sin in the eyes of God (Jas 4:17).

Admittedly, there is a great deal about the world that human beings can know, and because of this, human beings are capable of doing a great many things in the world. The explosion in scientific understanding has created the ability to do what was unimaginable just a few decades ago. Even so, humanity's ability to explore the immensity and complexity of the creation is a call to humility, a call to understand that the grandeur of the creation is merely a reflection of the One who created it (cf. Job 38:1–40:5).

As a principle of Christian education, the concept of stewardship learning underscores the need for students' involvement in the process of doing God's will. To simply

---

21. This illustration and the idea that teleological effects assume a preexisting set of assumptions that allow human beings to assign function to things discovered in natures comes from Searle, *Construction of Social Reality*, 14–16.

understand the world (even if one possesses a great deal of this knowledge or understanding) and the nature and character of God (even if one possesses a great deal of this knowledge or understanding) is to violate the stewardship commandment of God given to humanity before the Fall. It is akin to knowing God with all of your heart, soul, mind, and strength but not loving your neighbor as yourself. In the mind of God, knowing him and the world he created without acting on that knowledge for the betterment of others is sin, for humanity cannot ignore the loving of others and claim to love God (cf. Matt 22:37–40; Jas 2:14–18, 26; 4:17).

Knowing and doing does not discount the idea that education can and should be a preparation for ministry. After his conversion, Paul spent several days in Damascus before preaching to the Jews (Acts 9:19–22), but then he spent several years in Arabia before presenting himself to the Jewish believers in Jerusalem (cf. Acts 9:23–28; Gal. 1:17). Yet such extended periods between learning and doing seem to be the biblical exception rather than the norm. Timothy, as he was discipled by Paul, was a coworker in his ministry and learned to be an effective minister by watching and serving with Paul. The disciples traveled with and learned from Christ, but Christ also sent them out in pairs to engage in the process of healing the sick, casting out demons, and proclaiming the good news of the gospel (Mark 6:7–13). The development of long periods of learning and preparation historically seems to be more a response to the scientific and industrial development of the culture than a representation of the biblical model of learning.

Thus, stewardship education should seek to actually engage students in applying learning to the world. Not only would such an education include transmitting knowledge about the world that previous generations had acquired, but it also would provide the challenge to students to use their talents and abilities to learn more about the world and to engage in creative discovery so that they could develop new and greater understandings of the creation. It would encourage them to develop the creative and authoritative abilities given to them by God to exercise dominion over the creation and to develop methods of managing and representing the creation in ways that respect the creative and volitional uniqueness of humanity created in the image of God. All this would be done in concert with developing a closer and more intimate fellowship with the One who is being served so that the knowledge, abilities, creativity, talents, and will would be directed to serving the One who the learner knows and loves. Finally, stewardship education would provide the opportunity to serve, not simply prepare to serve, so that the God-given desire to exercise one's abilities can find its God-given outlet in service to God.

6

Education: After the Fall

The fatality of the Fall does not consist in the fact that man was once created by God, and now, some thousands of years later, is nothing but the heir of the sin of Adam; the fatality of the Fall consists rather in the fact that every human being, in his own person, and in union with the rest of humanity, every day renews this Fall afresh, and cannot help but doing so.

—Emil Brunner, *Man in Revolt*

ARNIE BEGINS DAY TWO of the Mt. Carmel fall in-service in his usual fashion, arriving at school early. Since it is an in-service day he heads to the teachers' lounge to find coffee and to see if any other early birds have arrived. As usual, he finds his friends Manfred Median and Barry Baroque sitting and chatting. On this morning the usual coffee club is joined my Edith Erudite, the high school literature teacher. Normally, Edith uses her mornings to prepare for the day. Today, without lessons to plan or papers to grade, she joins the men in the lounge. As Arnie arrives, not surprisingly, the topic of conversation is yesterday's in-service.

"The idea of education in the Garden focusing on stewardship is a liberating idea to me," claims Barry. "I had always thought about life in the Garden as simply agricultural. As a musician though, it was difficult to think of music as something that could have had its origin after the Fall. I mean, we know there is music in heaven, so it could not be the invention of fallen man. Yet, I had a hard time understanding where the development of musical composition, instruments, and the like came from. Personally, I found yesterday's discussion refreshing."

"Well, after yesterday morning I was about to just sit quietly and grade papers for the next few days," admits Manfred. "All that talk about sin nature and institutions was a bit much for me; however, I must admit I appreciated the discussion about human nature being equipped to understand what is while still being dependent on God for understanding the should be's of life. I had never considered the idea of humans being cognitively dependent on God. Sure, we all say that human beings are dependent on God for everything, but it does seem that Christians do not understand or embrace the idea of cognitive dependence. In that respect Christians seem like everyone else: enamored by what human beings can figure out and developing our own sense of what should be. Anyway, I am willing to give Wise the benefit of the doubt—for now."

"Manfred the magnanimous," quips Edith. "I left yesterday's sessions with feelings similar to Barry's. Now I can begin to envision that there would have been poetry and literature, songs and symphonies, science and technology before the Fall. I must admit, I never considered the idea of culture creation and adding value to the earth. My whole notion of life before the Fall was one of gardening and naming animals. Suddenly, I can see where almost all the academic disciplines have their source in the pre-Fall commandment to be good stewards. I am with you Barry; suddenly, literature takes on a new meaning to me."

"What about you Arnie?" asks Barry. "What did you find interesting in the session?"

Arnie admits that he also found much in the discussions from the previous day of interest. Economics and civics can now be viewed, at least in part, as disciplines that would have existed even if there had not been a Fall. Arnie admits, however, that he still is a bit troubled. "For me, in teaching the social sciences and history, much of what I deal with is human conflict—its causes and results. While I can see the applicability of yesterday's discussion to some areas, the Fall seems to have happened pretty early in human history. I am not quite sure how it applies in a post-Fall world. Wise did promise to talk about other aspects of biblical education. I hope today's topics will address some of my concerns."

"Speaking of topics for today, it is time to go," notes Edith as the four of them get up to leave for the chapel. "You know how cranky Manfred will be if he has to sit in the front row."

While not the first to arrive, the four find places near the back. The chapel soon fills as the rest of the faculty filter in to take their places. The conversations around the room subside as Dr. Solomon welcomes the faculty and begins the day with prayer. After a few worship songs and announcements, Solomon addresses the teachers.

"Well, we seem to have had an intellectually stimulating day yesterday; many of you have expressed to me your appreciation for Dr. Wise and the topics he has addressed, even if you have not always agreed." Several teachers give knowing chuckles of laughter to this statement. "We want to encourage dialogue and a willingness to take a critical look at what we do as Christian educators, and Dr. Wise seems to have stimulated that process for a number of us. In that respect, I trust that the discussions started yesterday will continue, not only during these in-service days, but also throughout the course of the year. I am personally looking forward to the challenge that Dr. Wise will bring us today. Once again, let's welcome Dr. Wise."

"Thank you," says Wise as he comes to the front of the chapel. "Yesterday, we examined the issue of education before the Fall and concluded that preparing stewards would be a primary characteristic of education before the Fall. While the Fall takes place relatively early in human history, I tried to show that the original commands regarding stewardship were not rescinded as a result of the Fall; however, as a result of the Fall, everything changed. This morning I would like us to examine the biblical approach to education as a result of the Fall."

"To get started this morning," continues Wise, "I would like you to break into your work groups, read Genesis 3:1–24, and complete two tasks. First, determine the nature of the offer that Satan, in the form of the serpent, used to tempt Eve. Once Adam and Eve eat the fruit, the Bible records a number of consequences. Second, list as many effects of the Fall as you can find in the chapter. We will then come together as a large group to discuss your findings."

As the faculty breaks into groups, Arnie grabs more coffee from the back table. When he arrives at his group, Donna Dewey, the sixth grade teacher, already has the group on task.

"Well, the first task seems pretty easy," notes Byron Bunsen, the science teacher. "In Genesis 3:5 Satan tells Eve they will be *like* God, '*knowing* good and evil.'"

"Okay, but Wise always seems to have some little twist for us," notes Donna. "I am sure the first task can't be that simple."

"Maybe the question we should ask is how does God *know* good and evil?" says Rita Rookie.

"That's easy," chimes back Bunsen. "God is omniscient, so he would know everything."

"Wait," suggests Arnie. "Maybe Rita is asking the correct question. If the only way God knows the difference between good and evil is through his omniscience, then good and evil exist as concepts independent of God." The others try to follow Arnie's logic with an inquisitive look. "I mean, God knows good and evil because he knows everything, but, if good and evil exist independent of God, then the only way for God to be 'good' is for him to align his character and will with the concept of good."

"Which would mean that God is no longer sovereign," answers Donna, as if she is thinking out loud. "So maybe what Satan is offering is not knowledge at all."

"That would help explain Genesis 3:22," claims Barry Baroque. "God is speaking and says, 'Behold, the man has become like one of Us, knowing good and evil.' So whatever Satan offered, it seems that he was not entirely lying since God even acknowledges that Adam and Eve became like God in some way."

The group discusses several possibilities to answer the question of how God knows good and evil. Failing to come to any resolution, Donna suggests they move on to the second task. The group begins to list the effects of the Fall.

"More pain in childbirth," chimes Donna, the only mother in the group.

"Knowing they were naked," interjects Byron.

"The ground being cursed so that they had to work to eat," notes Arnie.

The group continues to make their list when Rita asks, "Why do you think Wise wants us to list the effects of the Fall?"

"Good question," notes Arnie. "We have already determined he seems to be pretty sneaky with these tasks."

"It strikes me that this is not an exhaustive list," offers Barry. "I mean, does anyone think this is a complete list of the effects of the Fall? Most of us would acknowledge that disease or debilitating injuries are a result of the Fall, yet none of those are mentioned here." Several of the group members nod their heads in agreement. "Granted, all of these are real, but maybe we should treat this as not only a piece of history but also a piece of good literature. As good literature the examples here may be categories of larger effects of the Fall."

"So, as literature," injects Rita, "when we read that the ground is cursed, it is a literary way of noting that all of the physical creation, including the animals, may suffer some effect of the Fall."

"Or, when we read that Eve's desire is for her husband and that Adam would rule over her, that it is a description of the whole range of interpersonal types of conflict," claims Arnie.

"Exactly," says Barry. "That Adam is afraid and that he experiences guilt or shame over his nakedness seems to indicate that human beings would now suffer from certain types of emotional or psychological difficulties."

"And, of course, we are all separated from God," adds Donna.

At that moment Wise calls the groups back to a general assembly. After a few minutes of commotion he begins to address the group. "Well, I trust the task was an interesting exercise for you, and in a few minutes we will review what you have discussed in your groups. First, however, I would like us to look at a quote from Francis Bacon. Bacon was an English philosopher who lived in the sixteenth and seventeenth centuries and is considered by some to be the 'father' of modern science because he developed the inductive method of scientific inquiry. Bacon professed to be a Christian, and in his book, *Novum Organum*, he wrote this about the Fall." Wise places a transparency of the following quote on the overhead projector: "Man by the fall fell at the same time from his state of innocence and from his dominion over the creation. Both of these losses, however, can even in this life be in some part repaired; the former by religion and faith, the latter by the arts and sciences."

"What do you think he meant by that statement?" asks Wise.

"Well, by religion I think he means faith in Christ," offers Edith. "Our group noted that because of the Fall, Adam and Eve led all of humanity into rebellion against God. So Christ reconciles us to God and *repairs* the innocence lost."

"Good," responds Wise. "Anyone else?"

"Science seems to deal with some of the effects of the Fall," answers Bunsen. "Our group noted that illness and disease occur as a result of the Fall, and medical research and technology can be used to address some of those effects."

"What about mathematics?" asserts Manfred Median. "I have a hard time seeing how math has been affected by the Fall."

"And hasn't science also created many problems?" interjects Greta Gadfly, the middle school social studies teacher. "Certainly science has helped deal with problems, but think of all the problems created by science—weapons of mass destruction and chemicals that lead to cancer; I think Bacon may be too optimistic about what science can do."

"Well, don't blame the mathematicians," quips Manfred. "Our discipline is pure!" His comment brings some levity to the discussion.

"Are you suggesting that mathematics is not affected by the Fall, Manfred?" questions Dana Delts, the physical education teacher. "We all thought you were a good Puritan; and now you go and deny the doctrine of total depravity."

"What if not everything has been affected by the Fall equally?" asks Edith.

Arnie starts to mull this idea over in his head. He certainly believes that everything has been affected by the Fall, but he has never considered the possibility that everything may not have been affected equally.

Wise signals the group, and the teachers respond by giving him their attention. "Some very interesting comments, and ones we will want to consider as the morning progresses, but let me ask a question. Yesterday we discussed the cultural mandate and the idea of stewardship as being a command that God gave to humanity before the Fall. How would the Fall affect the cultural mandate and the call to stewardship we see in Genesis 1 and 2? Please return to your groups for a few minutes and consider that question."

Arnie reflects on this question as he returns to his group. He knows that the Fall has affected all individuals so that the call to stewardship must also be affected by the Fall. His new understanding of the cultural mandate of Genesis 1 and 2 has caused him to realize that people live in communities with each other and that those communities form cultures. The principles of stewardship prior to the Fall would have affected the types or forms of culture that human beings would create. With the Fall, however, sinful people now live in communities with other sinful people. Obviously sin affects how people think, live, and interact with others. If that is true, Arnie thinks, it stands to reason that sin would affect both the way sinful individuals interact with the world and the types and forms of culture that they would create, but how?

As a social studies teacher, Arnie has always operated from the premise that the world was sinful and that the reason for the wars or the political, social, and ethnic struggles that he taught about in class was sin. His thinking, however, was always that wars resulted from sinful *individuals* dealing with other sinful individuals. Of course, nothing in the world is value neutral; he has always believed that. Now, however, Arnie finds himself having to consider that a cultural behavior or an institution may actually have sin embedded in it. If this is true, how is sin embedded in these behaviors or institutions? How do these cultural forms affect how people learn to think, live, and act in the world if the practices and institutions that they have grown up with reflect a sinful perspective? Before Arnie returns to his group he makes a quick trip to the coffee table at the back of the room. "Lots of questions," he says to himself. "It's going be a long morning. I think I need another cup of coffee."

God's command to cultivate and keep the Garden in Genesis 2:15 is a command to humanity to engage in stewardship dominion over the creation. In essence, God gives humanity the authority to act as regents, to govern the creation in a way that reflects the will, purposes, and goals of the Sovereign. On the other hand, humanity was not given an all-encompassing or omniscient understanding of the creation. Thus, the stewardship command entails not only learning about the creation but also passing on to future generations what has been learned, empowering them to also fulfill their God-given call to be stewards. Thus, education before the Fall would have been stewardship education— developing in each new generation the knowledge, skills, and creative dispositions to engage in the practice of biblical stewardship.

This period of innocence did not last long. Early in human history, Satan appears in the Garden to tempt and deceive Eve. Adam, choosing to follow his wife rather than the command of God, eats of the fruit, and by his action sin enters the world and affects all of humanity (Rom 5:12). The effects of the Fall are pervasive; nothing is exempt or escapes its influence. The pervasiveness of sin means that even humanity's ability to operate as stewards has been thoroughly compromised. Despite Adam's sin, God does not revoke his stewardship authority. However, now the creation is not as responsive to the actions of humanity, and its stewards are no longer willing to govern the creation for the purposes and glory of God.

This chapter will examine the effects of the Fall and their implications on a biblical approach to education. What has been the effect of Satan and the sin nature on humanity's ability to operate as stewards of the creation? As culture creators, how is the influence of the sin nature embedded into the practices of culture? How are we, as redeemed people, to view our response to the biblical command to be stewards, to be culture creators? Chapter 5 developed the idea that an education before the Fall prepared people for stewardship. Despite all the consequences of the Fall listed in Genesis 3, there is no rescinding of the stewardship command. Thus, education after the Fall must still be about stewardship, but it will be stewardship in an environment compromised and corrupted by the pervasiveness of sin. It is stewardship that must seek to implement the will, goals, and purposes of God in a way that ultimately brings glory to him, but it must seek to do so in an environment and with motives tainted by sin. An education that prepares students for this post-Fall stewardship can be characterized as the second principle of biblical education—seeking to address the effects of sin in the world through the ministry of reconciliation.

THE TEMPTATION AND THE SIN NATURE

Genesis 3 is the biblical account of the origin and initial effects of sin in the world. The opening chapters of Genesis provide the creation narrative and portray a world where humanity, represented by Adam, is in perfect harmony with God the Creator, with nature, with others (Adam's initial relationship with Eve), and with self. Humanity is given meaningful work to accomplish in the form of stewardship dominion and is to perform this work in an environment that is uniquely fitted and responsive to the action upon it. Humanity, in short, is placed by God in paradise.

The biblical narrative of sin begins with Satan, as the antagonist, in the form of a serpent, addressing Eve and calling into question the command of God (Gen 3:1) and the consequences of the command: "You surely shall not die! For God knows that in the day that you eat of it your eyes will be opened and you will be like God, knowing good and evil" (Gen 3:4–5). The account continues, noting that Eve saw the fruit as desirable to the eye and able to make one wise, so she ate of it and also gave the fruit to Adam, who ate.

With Adam's eating of the fruit, their eyes were both opened: they realized they were naked, hid themselves from each other, and made coverings of fig leaves. When they heard God walking in the Garden, they also hid themselves from him. When eventually confronted by God, Adam engages in blaming both Eve and God for his disobedience when he states, "The woman whom *You* gave to be with me, she gave me from the tree and I ate" (Gen 3:12, emphasis added). Not willing to take the blame herself, Eve then blames the serpent (Gen 3:13). God confronts and curses the serpent but delineates the effects of humanity's sin for Adam and Eve as well. In this account the biblical narrative provides the necessary starting point to answer the questions necessary for a coherent worldview. First, it accounts for the presence of evil in the world (answering the question, what is wrong?), and it also provides the first glimpse of the corollary, what can be done to remedy the problem? The first promise of the coming Redeemer is given. Addressing Satan, God says, "And I will put enmity between you and the woman, and between your offspring and hers; he [Christ] will crush your head, and you will strike his heel" (Gen 3:15 NIV). God's loving protection is seen by his casting Adam and Eve from Eden so that they cannot "take also from the tree of life, and eat it, and live forever" (Gen 3:22), an act that would have made the effects of the Fall permanent in the lives of humanity.

Before examining the effects of the Fall and their relationship to developing a biblical response to post-Fall education, the nature of Eve's temptation must be addressed. Satan says to Eve that the effect of eating the fruit would not lead to death, as God had told Adam (Gen 2:17). Satan suggests that God was denying them the advantages that could be gained from the fruit because God was essentially keeping those benefits for himself: "You will be like God, knowing good and evil." This raises the question, how does God know good and evil? In order to understand the character of the sin nature, this question must be answered for it has profound effects not only on education after the Fall but also on all aspects of human endeavor.

The simple answer would be to state that God knows good and evil because he is an all-knowing or omniscient being. His knowledge is perfect, complete, and exhaustive of all things, actual and possible, including the future actions of all free beings. While God certainly is omniscient, appealing to his omniscience does not account for his knowledge of good and evil in this context. First, in Genesis 3:22 God reflects on the Fall, noting that, "Behold, the man has become like one of Us, knowing good and evil." In this sense Satan did not lie to Eve, for his claim that they would be like God in this regard is confirmed by God himself; however, humanity did not gain omniscience as a result of the Fall. Even if that increased knowledge were limited simply to issues of morality or ethics, it is clear that humanity does not know all. Consequently, God's omniscience is insufficient to explain how God knows good and evil.

Second, to know in an objective sense is to have an understanding of something that is independent of the knower. While individuals can know from experience, they must, in some sense, have an experience that originates outside of themselves. This distinguishes knowledge from belief, which can be defined as a conviction originating from within the mind of the individual. Avoiding a major treatise in epistemology, a belief becomes true if it can substantiate the reality that exists independent or outside of the knower. For example, I may believe I can bench press five hundred pounds; however, that belief will be instantly dismissed as soon as I attempt to lift the weight. Any further claim of my strength will be either a lie or a delusion on my part. Conversely, my belief that the door is solid is verified as true as soon as I attempt to walk through it.

For God to know good and evil in this way would mean that he has an understanding or experience of good and evil independent of himself. Adam and Eve would be like God, knowing good and evil, because they now have the same type of knowledge and experience. This view of knowing, however, creates a major theological problem. For God to now be good, he must bring his character and actions into conformity with a standard of goodness that exists outside of himself. God becomes good because he is in complete conformity to the good. However, he could cease to be good if his actions or character ever stray from that standard. Such a view of God's goodness invalidates the doctrine of God's sovereignty. If God can only be good by conforming to some external standard of good, God's desire or willingness to be good is under the authority of this external standard. Even if God chooses to adopt this standard, bringing his desire or will into complete agreement so that he can only think, will, and act within this standard of the good, he still is subject to something that exists independent of himself, thus negating his sovereignty.

A viable understanding of how God "knows" good and evil must preserve the doctrine of God's sovereignty. What God understands to be good or evil must be based on something that originates entirely from *within* himself. In essence, God's "knowledge" of good and evil is not based in cognition, but in *volition*—that which God wills as good becomes the good. In this sense, God "knows" good and evil because he determines or defines what good and evil will be. What God desires is good, and that which God does not desire is evil. Thus, good and evil are now subject to his sovereign will; his volition is not, and never can be, subject to anything. Understanding God's "knowledge" of good and evil as volition also preserves the perfect goodness of God. Since the good is what God desires or wills, God can never fail to be good since he cannot act outside of what he wills to do.

Since "knowing" good and evil is *volition*, Adam and Eve can be like God in their knowledge of good and evil because they now possess the ability to choose for themselves right from wrong. As a result of the Fall, human beings now claim the sovereign right to define good and evil for themselves. In addition, fallen humanity now defines the good in terms of self-interest—what will be good for oneself, rather than the interests of God and others. Conversely, evil becomes that which is not in one's best interest. Human will and desire for sovereignty replace God's sovereignty and will in defining good and evil. In essence, the character of the sin nature is to desire the sovereign right to define all the terms or control all the definitions of good and evil. Humanity's rebellion against God stems from its desire to possess and implement this corrupted perspective.

It is worth noting that Satan used the same desire to tempt Eve that caused him to fall. Many theologians maintain that Isaiah 14:12–15 is a narrative account of the fall of Lucifer. Ezekiel 28:12–15 describes what many believe to be Satan or Lucifer before his fall. He was positioned among the highest of the created beings, with access to the very throne of God. Because of his beauty, pride corrupted his reasoning (Ezek 28:17). Lucifer's own reasoning is recorded in Isaiah 14:12–14:

> How you have fallen from heaven,
> O star of the morning, son of the dawn!
> You have been cut down to the earth,
> You who have weakened the nations!
> But you said in your heart,
> "I will ascend to heaven;

> I will raise my throne above the stars of God,
> And I will sit on the mount of the assembly
> In the recesses of the north.
> I will ascend above the heights of the clouds;
> I will make myself like the Most High."

Satan desired God's sovereignty and this desire caused him to be cast from heaven. This same desire is what Satan used to tempt humanity, causing their banishment from the Garden. Like Satan, as a result of the Fall, human beings now desire to be like the Most High; they desire to raise their own thrones above God's and desire their own sense of good apart from God.

THE EFFECTS OF THE FALL

By eating the fruit from the tree of the knowledge of good and evil, Adam and Eve disobeyed the command and will of God. While Satan may not have lied to Eve in telling her that they would be like God, able to determine for themselves good and evil, he did lie by claiming that they would not die. David Smith notes that the effects of the Fall produced symptoms of death that were disastrous, immediate, and long-term. The most significant effect was to damage the relationship that human beings enjoyed with God. With the introduction of sin, the intimacy that humanity had with the Creator was replaced with estrangement. In addition, sin created a gap between what God intended human beings to be and what they had now become.[1] Sin also led to humanity's alienation from self, from others, and from all of the natural creation—all relationships that God intended humanity to experience as harmonious. As a result, sin always has two effects. Each sin represents a transgression against the will of God and, simultaneously, an affront to the image of God in humanity. Bernard Ramm notes that when a person sins, that sin represents a statement of human autonomy or independence against the sovereign authority and law of God. At the same time, each sin represents an affront to the image of God since the effect of sin is directed against either another person, the sinner himself, or the creation that humanity has been entrusted to govern.[2]

The penultimate effect of the Fall was that humanity immediately became estranged from God. With the Fall, human beings became "children of wrath" (Eph 2:3). In Romans 1:18 through 3:19, Paul sets out to prove that all humanity is accountable to God because of sin and concludes that, in relation to the Law, "every mouth may be closed [i.e., with absolutely no defense] and all the world may become accountable to God." Sinners are considered lost and wandering toward their destruction. This concept is seen in the three parables of lostness (sheep, coin and son) of Luke 15. Sinners are born into a state of lostness and, as a result, wander from the purpose and will of God. As Ramm notes, "To be lost is to be lost to God, to oneself, to others, and to the kingdom of God and its purposes."[3] As the parable of the Prodigal Son shows, this lostness results in willful sin.

---

1. D. L. Smith, *With Willful Intent*, 402.

2. Ramm, *Offense to Reason*, 110.

3. Ibid., 112.

Ultimately, sin produces spiritual death (Eph 2:1–3) a death that results in being separated from God for all eternity. The unredeemed or unregenerate of humanity are cast into the lake of fire along with Satan and his angels (Rev 20:10–15). This "second death" or banishment to the torments of hell (Rev 20:14) is a result of the death in Genesis 3. Sin results in spiritual death (Rom 6:23; 7:10–11; 8:6; Eph 2:1–3) and the birth of a sin nature results in an inability on the part of humanity to experience positive spiritual communication or communion generated from within themselves toward God, rendering human beings insensitive to any positive spiritual realities apart from the work of God.

While the spiritual consequences of sin cannot be diminished, educationally the result of the Fall produces alienation from other aspects of the created order. Ramm describes this alienation as a "pathological situation" in which "one part of the psyche is out of touch with another part."[4] To be spiritually alienated is to be separated from that which was previously in one's best interest: those conditions that existed before the Fall when human beings experienced their true humanity through loving God and seeking his glory through loving and serving others. Fallen human beings, by acting in ways that seek to pursue individual interest apart from service to God and others, now act in ways contrary to their best interest. The effects of alienation extend to humanity's relationships with God, as well as with self, others, and nature. James Garrett uses the term *alienation* as synonymous with enmity against God,[5] and Paul Tillich makes the term interchangeable with "estrangement."[6] Alienation is an imbalance within oneself, a loss of self, which leads to estrangement or lostness with others. Os Guinness refers to human alienation as fourfold: theological, sociological, ecological, and psychological.[7]

Theological alienation or the separation of humanity from God is not only seen in humanity's spiritual condition but is also demonstrated in the Genesis account by humanity's act of hiding from God after being confronted by their sin (Gen 3:8–10) and by Adam and Eve's expulsion from the Garden so that they could not eat from the tree of life (Gen 3:24).

Sociological alienation, or the separation of humanity from others, is the second type of alienation. After their sin, Adam's and Eve's "eyes were opened," and they realized their own nakedness, causing them embarrassment and shame (Gen 3:7). Adam's attempt to blame both Eve and God (Gen 3:12) is indicative of both Adam's estrangement from Eve and from God. Conflict in human relationship is described when Eve is told that her desire will be for her husband (i.e., seeking his position of authority or dominion) and that he will not want to relinquish it: "and he shall rule over you" (Gen 3:16). After the Fall come examples of other conflicts, beginning with Cain and Abel (Gen 4:4–8). While not all alienation leads to hostile attitudes or actions, it remains true that all human relationships since the Fall, whether between individuals or with the community or society, are characterized by some level of estrangement or conflict. As Ramm writes:

4. Ibid., 126.
5. Garrett, *Systematic Theology*, 1:310–11.
6. Tillich, *Systematic Theology*, 2:44.
7. Guinness, *Dust of Death*, 25–28.

> Labor is alienated from management; parents are alienated from children and children from parents; husbands are alienated from wives and wives from husbands; pupils may feel alienated from the school system; young people feel alienated from the establishment; citizens feel alienated from bureaucratic government; voters feel alienated from the political process; elderly people feel alienated from the mainstream of community life; minority and racial groups feel alienated from the dominant community. All of this historically would be called effects of sin but today is masked under the concept of alienation.[8]

In the modern world the industrial revolution and modern industrialization have produced forces that increase alienation. The effect of sin in this area has caused the disintegration of the traditional family and social groups and has produced a type of individualism that leads to loneliness. The individual's relationship to large government, large economies, and large bureaucracies is seen as impersonal or dehumanizing. This alienation from others undermines the sense of community and mutual interdependence that human beings were intended to have with others before the Fall.

Ecological alienation, or the distancing of humanity from nature, is the third result of the Fall. As a result of Adam's sin, God proclaims, "cursed is the ground because of you; in toil you shall eat of it all the days of your life" (Gen 3:17). A creation made to respond to humanity is now less responsive; it does not yield as easily to human action upon it. In addition, the creation now suffers under the weight of humanity's imperial desire to determine how it will be used. The commands to cultivate and to keep are now redefined, not from God's perspective but from that of sinful humanity who now desire to use the creation for their own benefit. The creation no longer is considered something to be cherished, nurtured, and responsibly developed, but it becomes a tool for meeting the fallen objectives of humanity. Consequently, human actions have had environmental effects, while technological innovations have unintended consequences for human health and safety. Human beings have created weapons capable of destroying all life on the planet, and many species of fish and animals have been hunted or polluted into extinction.

Finally, sin results in psychological alienation, the fracturing of the person from self. With the Fall, human beings begin to suffer psychological difficulties. For example, there now exist shame and vulnerability (Gen 3:7), guilt and fear (Gen 3:10), and frustration (Gen 3:19). Sin results in a sense of existential lostness; human beings experience a lack of direction, a lack of purpose, or a sense of apathy. Consequently, some people turn to alcohol, drugs, or sex to reconstruct themselves or to fill the spiritual void created by the loss of stewardship purpose. Others are driven to success, achievement, and accomplishment apart from the will of God. Some seek power over others or the environment, while others feel powerless. As a result, the Fall produces a humanity that Paul characterizes in this way:

> And just as they did not see fit to acknowledge God any longer, God gave them over to a depraved mind, to do those things which are not proper, being filled with all unrighteousness, wickedness, greed, evil; full of envy, murder, strife, deceit, malice; they are gossips, slanderers, haters of God, insolent, arrogant, boastful, inventors

8. Ramm, *Offense to Reason*, 127.

of evil, disobedient to parents, without understanding, untrustworthy, unloving, unmerciful; and although they know the ordinances of God, that those who practice such things are worthy of death, they not only do the same, but also give hearty approval to those who practice them. (Rom 1:28–32)

Although the Fall left humanity in a depraved state, human responsibility for stewardship over the creation was not revoked. Human beings are still required by God to cultivate and to keep, to administer the creation for his glory and to promote his will. Yet, because of their depraved condition, human beings no longer seek after or desire to know the will of God. They now seek to define the good or proper uses of the creation from their depraved perspective, a perspective that seeks to maximize their own sense of sovereignty and benefit. What human beings can learn and how they act upon the creation are now governed by a sense of should that is of their own defining. Starting from themselves, humanity is incapable of developing a sense of how the creation should be used so that it brings glory to God. Proper stewardship requires an intimate knowledge of the Owner and an understanding of what it is that will bring glory to him. This intimacy and dependence was a necessary component of humanity's relationship to God before the Fall. After the Fall, human beings no longer seek to know the will of God and pursue that which they believe to be good in their own eyes (Judg 21:25). In addition to humanity's desire to sovereignly use the creation for their own benefit, Satan also desires to lay claim to the earth and to rule over it (Matt 4:8–9). The effects of sin in the world, specifically how the influence of Satan and the post-Fall desires of human beings to define good and evil, are reflected in the development and influence of culture.

SATANIC INFLUENCE: THE PRINCE OF THE POWER OF THE AIR

The Apostle Paul acknowledges that all human beings are subject to the power and pervasive influence of sin, not only internally as a result of their own sin nature but also through the influence of Satan and culture. Commenting to the believers in the church at Ephesus, the Apostle notes, "You were dead in your trespasses and sins, in which you formerly walked according to the course of this world, according to the prince of the power of the air, of the spirit that is now working in the sons of disobedience" (Eph 2:1–2). As "sons of disobedience," human beings cultivate a life that indulges the "desires of the flesh, and of the mind" (Eph 2:3). Paul identifies Satan as an active agent working through the fallen nature of humanity to develop ways for human beings to indulge their sinful desires. This indulgence of body and mind can be fulfilled with the content of culture, which human beings are still responsible to create. That is, as stewards, human beings are called to be culture creators, yet as sinners, human beings can only create culture that is an extension of their fallen nature. Paul acknowledges that the "sons of disobedience" do not pursue the gratification of the flesh autonomously, but they are influenced by Satan as an active agent who seeks to reign over this world as the "prince of the power of the air."

All of creation has been affected by the Fall, so the world that human beings now inhabit and seek to govern as stewards is not the world into which God initially placed them. For this reason, the creation suffers and waits for the day of redemption (cf. Rom 8:18–22). Also, because of the sin nature, human beings now seek to govern and use the creation according to their own definitions of what is good or their own visions of what the world should be. These definitions no longer align with the desires and glory of God; instead, they are definitions designed to fulfill the desires of and to bring glory to human beings. The condition of being spiritually "dead in your trespasses and sins" and the desire to indulge the "desires of the flesh, and of the mind" are often characterized by theologians as the doctrine of total depravity.

The doctrine of total depravity, traditionally understood, asserts that the Fall did not render human beings as sinful as they could be but that the effects of sin are profound and corrupt every aspect of human nature and humanity's relationship with God. The results of this corruption not only adversely affect humanity's relationship with God but also influence every aspect of humanity's being. As Ramm notes, "Paul comments on the theme of Total Depravity in [Romans] 3:13–18 by using the metaphor of the human body, to say that sin (1) penetrates every part of the psyche so that the whole self participates in sin, and (2) it very profoundly affects the human psyche. Sins may be inspired not only by pleasurable passions, but by the reason and the spirit."[9]

In regard to culture creation, Smith notes, the effects of sin and the depraved nature of humanity are equally profound. The power of depravity is so great that corrupted human nature becomes insufficient to know or seek the Creator.[10] Since stewardship is predicated not only on knowing about the creation but also on knowing the desires and will of the Creator, one ramification of the doctrine of total depravity is that human beings no longer desire the will of God. Also, even if human beings would desire to know the will of God, the sin nature now renders them incapable of knowing God or his will. Commenting on the idea of human depravity, the early church father Athanasius wrote, "[they] so wholly rejected God, and so darkened their soul, as not merely to forget their idea of God, but to fashion for themselves one intervention after another. . . . And, in a word, everything was full of irreligion and lawlessness, and God alone . . . was unknown, albeit He had not hidden Himself out of men's sight."[11]

The fashioning of "one intervention after another," to keep God out of sight, as suggested by Athanasius, is a process in which Satan is an active participant. As the "prince of the power of the air," Satan has a vested interest in maintaining his authority by working in the hearts and minds of human beings who have been given stewardship authority over God's creation. For example, during Christ's temptation by Satan, Jesus does not refute Satan's authority to offer all of the kingdoms of the world to him if he will bow down and worship the Devil (cf. Matt 4:8–10). Later, Jesus affirmed the power and authority of Satan by referring to him as "the ruler of this world" (John 12:31). In his first epistle, the apostle John instructs believers "not to love the world nor the things in the world. If anyone loves the world, the love of the Father is not in him" (1 John 2:15). By addressing "the world" separately and distinguishing it from "the things of the world," John notes that "the world" is more than and different from the things contained in the creation itself. The "world" is an organized system of beliefs, attitudes, values, agendas, and so on that is directed by Satan, who seeks to nullify

9. Ibid., 126.

10. D. L. Smith, *With Willful Intent*, 25.

11. Athanasius, "On the Incarnation of the Logos," 11.4.42.

God and act in opposition to him. For this reason John notes that believers are in God (or have their allegiance with God) and in opposition to a world system that is under the power of Satan (cf. 1 John 5:19). James writes that believers are to be "unstained by the world" and that "friendship with the world is hostility toward God" (cf. Jas 1:27; 4:4).

The doctrines of the Fall and total depravity are relevant to the goals of education since they relate to the biblical teachings of humanity's responsibility to be culture creators and stewards. Almost all academic disciplines find their source in the original commands to cultivate and to keep; fulfilling these commands requires that human beings learn as much as they can not only about the creation but also about the Creator whom they are to serve. As a result of human depravity, however, the creation is no longer governed according to God's definition of good but according to definitions constructed by fallen human nature. In one sense human beings were created to be independent, endowed by God with spirit and reason, creativeness and thought, so that humanity could learn and act on the creation. At the same time, as the Swiss theologian Emil Brunner notes, human beings were created as dependent on God, not only for life and breath, but also for vision and purpose.[12] He continues, "Man does not sin like Satan himself, purely out of defiance and rebellion. He is led astray by sin. Evil forces were already there before him; man is not great enough to discover sin and introduce it into the world. But man is led astray in such a way that once desire is aroused, it militates against confidence in God.[13] As Martin Luther once wrote, "In the devil there is far greater enmity against God . . . than there is in man."[14]

Satan capitalizes on created humanity's dependence for vision and purpose. He uses human dependence to question God's adequacy and to instill doubt into the mind. Through sin, human beings become separated from God. Once separated, Satan works in their hearts and minds to guide them toward their own demise. Brunner notes, "Humanity: the battlefield of demons; the human spirit: the arsenal of the instruments for the destruction of life. How impotent is human reason in construction, how almighty in destruction."[15] While human beings can be influenced by Satan to work toward their own alienation and destruction, it is through the created human desire to develop culture that Satan works in opposition to God to construct "the world"—the organized system of beliefs, attitude, values, agendas. The development of culture is fundamentally rational. It is a construction and work of the human mind as it seeks, individually and corporately, to fulfill the stewardship commands of God. When schooling is seen as fundamentally the development of a rational approach to the world, the basis for a biblical approach to schooling is tied to culture creation. While the development of culture may be rational, the motives for developing culture can only be understood as an extension of a faith perspective. The power that creates culture is rational; the direction of that culture is spiritual. As the secular historian Oswald Spengler wrote, "Religion, whatever it may be, is the soul of all human culture; and where it dies, there culture declines into mere civilization and technique."[16]

12. Brunner, *Man in Revolt*, 130.

13. Ibid., 131.

14. Cited in Ibid., 131.

15. Ibid., 184.

16. Spengler, *Decline of the West*, 1:174.

While all of culture can be understood from a faith perspective, not all of culture shares this faith component equally. The effects of the Fall can be identified as a fissure between God and humanity, humanity and nature, humanity and others, and also humanity and self; however, not all of these fissures are experienced uniformly. They are not equally represented in the scriptural context of "the world." Human beings, as spiritual beings, can only understand themselves in relationship to God, a relationship that is quintessentially spiritual. Those aspects of creation that are not extensions of the image of God in humanity can more easily be understood through reason alone. For example, knowledge of the process of photosynthesis is the same for a Christian botanist as it would be for a nonbeliever. The processes of algebra, calculus, or trigonometry are the same for the non-Christian mathematician as they are for the redeemed. While there may be significant differences in the application of these truths, driven by faith assumptions about the world, there is little difference in the understanding of Christians and non-Christians with regard to the basic principles of these disciplines. Other aspects of life, though, require a greater sense of spiritual life and sensitivity in order to be more fully grasped. For example, what constitutes a beautiful piece of poetry, art, music, or literature is fundamentally driven by different faith assumptions about the world. Beauty can be defined by and operate quite differently for the believer as compared to the unbeliever. In these areas a greater spiritual reliance is necessary for gaining understanding; reliance on reason alone will lead to error. As Brunner notes:

> The 'higher' we ascend in this scale, the nearer we come to the sphere of that which is connected with the personal being of God and of man, which can no longer be perceived by reason but only by faith, the more we shall see that the self-sufficient reason is a source of error. . . . in practice the reason is continually exceeding its rights in sinful arrogance and forgetfulness of God, and, as the creator of culture, in particular, it makes itself and its creations into idols.[17]

As Satan seeks to work in the lives of unbelievers, the relationship of those areas that can be known more completely through reason and those areas that require a greater closeness to God become significant. Satan seeks to destroy humanity because human beings bear the image of his enemy God and because humanity is the special object of God's grace and redemption (1 Pet 5:8). While Satan is limited in his powers to destroy life (cf. Job 2:6), his ultimate goal is to maintain the breach between humanity and God and to preserve the destruction that is an inevitable consequence of humanity's fallen state. As a finite or limited being, Satan experiences similar types of restrictions regarding the use of time, energy, and resources as other limited beings. For example, as a finite being, I have only so many hours in the day that I can use to be productive, I can be in only one place at one time, and I have limited resources at my disposal. As a result, I have to set goals and priorities and then allocate my time, energy, and resources in such a way as to accomplish those goals.

Satan, as a limited being, must also set goals and prioritize them while allocating his time, energy, and resources (including how to use and direct other fallen angels) to accomplish those goals. Since Satan's goal is ultimately to keep humanity from forming

17. Brunner, *Man in Revolt*, 248.

a relationship with God, those areas that are more dependent or proximate to the God-humanity relationship are more subject to the corrupting influence of Satan than those areas that are more concrete or less influenced by a spiritual understanding. In terms of the academic disciplines, those areas that reflect a greater connection to the God-humanity relationship would be more susceptible to the corrupting influences of Satan than those further from that relationship. As Brunner writes;

> The more closely we are concerned with the centre, with man's personal relationship with God and man's personal being, the greater will be the influence of unbelief upon the higher life of the mind and spirit. The further we move away from this central point the less evident does it become, and it is therefore still more difficult to recognize it. If a person studies anatomy or physics it will be impossible to tell from his scientific work, pure and simple, whether he is a Christian or an unbeliever. But his faith or his unbelief will come out very clearly in his way of thought and life as man. The more that knowledge has to do with the world as world, the further it is removed from the sphere of sin, and therefore the more "neutral" it becomes.[18]

The idea that those academic disciplines that are closer to the God-humanity relationship are more corrupted and, as a result, are in greater need of attention in integration can be seen in figure 2:

Figure 2:

Hierarchy of Academic Disciplines and Need for Biblical Integration

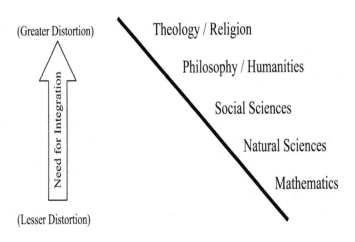

Adapted from Emil Brunner, Man in Revolt: A Christian Anthropology (Philadelphia: Westminster Press, 1979).

As Christian educators who diligently seek to engage ourselves and our students in the process of integrating faith, learning, and life, the relationship of academic content

18. Ibid., 255.

to the corrupting influence of sin and Satan is critical. Since sin creates disintegration in a discipline, the greater the influence of sin, the more pressing the need for integration in that discipline. Thus theology, as an academic discipline that most closely reflects the relationship between God and humanity, is a discipline in which we should expect to encounter the most corruption or disintegration. Satan would have a highly vested interest in corrupting theology so that the true "signal" of God's relationship to humanity would be lost among false beliefs or static "noise." For this reason, a plethora of religions, sects, and theological variations exist, making the truth of God more difficult to find among the many competing views. Similarly, the humanities (e.g., philosophy, literature, and the arts)—as reflections of God to humanity, humanity to humanity, or humanity to self—are subject to a high degree of corruption. The social sciences, reflections of the humanity's relationship to others or self—may show slightly less corruption. Some areas, such as pure mathematics or the natural sciences, may demonstrate little effect of corruption.

For example, while the issue of origins is of critical importance and advocates of creationism or intelligent design would differ significantly from evolutionists in their views on origins, for the vast majority of material taught in the biological sciences, there is little difference between a biblical and nonbiblical approach. In contrast, there would be profound theological and philosophical differences that would permeate all the assumptions and content in a course on psychology, literature, or history. Thus, Christian literature teachers may find the task of integration more daunting, requiring greater care and diligence, than the task of teaching chemistry, which may explain why some areas of the curriculum do not lend themselves as easily to the process of integration as others. Apart from teaching that "God is a God of order," there may be little need for integration in mathematics, but integration may be the focus of the curriculum for the humanities and social studies.

THE INFLUENCE OF HUMAN DEPRAVITY

While Satan works to guide the creation of a world system that is opposed to God and is condemned by Scripture, the presence of sin and the sin nature radically alters humanity's relationship to the creation and the performance of his stewardship responsibilities. The four alienating effects of sin dehumanize human beings, tarnishing the image of God that they were intended to be. In addition, the effect of sin is the desire on the part of human beings to seek to rob God of the glory intended for him (i.e., attempting to make God less than God) and to dehumanize others (i.e., robbing others of God's image that is intrinsically a part of who they are). These effects radically alter the way human beings operate in and on the world that God commissioned them to govern.

In regard to the stewardship command and its consequences on education, R. Scott Rodin notes that the entrance of sin into the world created four effects.[19] First, Adam and Eve's rebellion against God cost them their fellowship with God; they lost the very relationship for which they were created. As a result, humanity lost its reason for being. While God commissioned human beings to be stewards of the creation, that stewardship

19. These four effects are addressed in greater detail in Rodin, "Stewardship," 270–72.

was an extension of humanity's intimate fellowship with God. Since stewardship is predicated on working toward the goals of the Master, the loss of intimacy with God leaves humanity wayward. Since intimacy with God was the reason for which humanity was created, the introduction of sin cost human beings they very reason for their existence. The consequence of this separation is that Adam attempts to hide from God and avoid his presence.

Second, having lost their fellowship and reason for being, Rodin notes, humanity seeks to replace that loss with the desire to create, acquire, or take by force those things that would recreate purpose and meaning in life. In so doing, "life taking replaced life giving."[20] Self-interest becomes the reason for living. Human beings, who autonomously define what motives and actions are right or just, now compete with God for sovereignty and, as a result, the actions associated with words like *dominion, rule,* and *subdue* are now stripped of their grace content, being redefined in a more human-centered fashion.

Third, sin radically altered human beings' relationships to one another. In the Garden Adam and Eve were lords and servants. Lordship, or stewardship dominion, meant the opportunity to care for others and the creation, as God cares for all of creation. It was a call to be caretakers, nurturers, providers, and enablers, those who empower others to do the same. Lordship or stewardship requires an others-orientation. In this respect, Adam and Eve were created in such a way that they could not conceive of themselves apart from their relationship to God and their relationship to each other. Adam could not be fully human apart from God or apart from Eve. Adam could not be a servant if there was no one to serve, a caretaker if there was no one to care for. Because of the Fall human beings now seek to define themselves starting from themselves. The creatures who were created for fellowship now find themselves in isolation. Human beings are now forced to seek meaning and significance not as servants but in terms of self and self-understanding. Self-definition can take on the form of power, dominance, pursuit of personal pleasure or happiness, and self-actualization or gratification. Rodin continues, "By grasping the chance to be like God, the creature changed from being the 'servant of the Lord' to being the 'Lord over servants.'"[21] Karl Barth notes, "Wanting to act the Lord in relation to God, man will desire and grasp lordship over other men, and on the same presupposition, other men will meet him with the same desiring and grasping."[22]

Finally, human fallenness shifts the understanding and perspective from being a steward of creation to being an owner. In defiance to the God who gives all things freely, human beings become takers, usurpers of that which does not actually belong to them, and covet that which can never actually or ultimately be owned. The things of this world, entrusted to humanity by God to be administered as proxy-owners, are now claimed by fallen humanity as its own, and the resulting added value directed toward self-benefit.

Because of sin human beings no longer seek to create culture from the perspective of their relationship to God or servanthood to others. Rather, human beings now seek to

20. Ibid., 271.
21. Ibid., 272.
22. Karl Barth, *Church Dogmatics,* IV/1.

create culture that will normalize the sin nature, making desired human sovereignty and self-fulfillment, the autonomous ownership and use of resources, and the pursuit of power, dominance, pleasure, and self-actualization a reality. Under the influence of Satan, sinful humanity creates sinful cultures and develops cultural forms and norms with sin embedded into their very fabric. The essential characteristics of the sin nature permeate the culture-creation process. As a result, human beings cannot create culture that will bring honor and glory to God or seek to care, nurture, provide, and enable others. Nonetheless, because the stewardship mandate was not revoked with the Fall, God expects humanity to bring glory to him by serving others and will judge them by his unwavering standards of holiness and righteousness and his desired goals in the governance of creation.

Since the Fall, sinners have created culture. The Bible suggests that the domestication of animals and farming (Gen 4:2) and the development of music, musical instruments (4:21), and metallurgy (4:22) were created after the Fall. Yet the effects of embedded sin can be seen in both the form and the function of what is created. That is, a cultural tool (form) is designed to accomplish a specific purpose (function), and there are implicit values embedded in both. The result is that nothing is value neutral. For example, I can use a cultural tool like a computer (form) that is designed to allow me to access, process, and transmit information or data quickly, efficiently, and cost effectively (function). In using this cultural tool, however, I am also being socialized into the implicit values that underscore the technology and its development—in this case the emphasis on data or information, on communication as propositional rather than relational, and on speed, precision, and efficiency as important social values. Thus, the computer becomes obsolete or, in a moral sense bad, when it no longer performs its functions as quickly and efficiently as a newer model. The fact that I become impatient with my old computer (based on my knowledge of the efficiency of new computers) and that I covet one of these new computers indicates the success the culture has had in instilling these values in me.

While not all the forms of culture or the products of a culture are entirely sinful—in total opposition and contrary to the design and created order of God—insofar as they are created by sinful human beings they bear the mark of the fallen humanity who created them. Thus sin, to some degree, is embedded in the forms and functions of culture that humans create. Nevertheless, human beings retain some semblance of the image of God and, therefore, construct some aspects of culture that are in agreement with the will and desire of God. For this reason, sinful humans are able to do things that are, at some level, good. Sinful people can still engage in practices that are caring, nurturing, and enabling and can provide for the needs of others. They are less apt, however, to do so than they were before the Fall and often do these things from a sense of self-gratification rather than total concern for others.

In addition, as they construct culture, human beings cannot ignore those laws and processes of reality that God has embedded in the creation. Just as there are physical or natural laws that human beings must take into account when creating certain cultural artifacts (e.g., the principles of physics must be incorporated in the design and building of a bridge), the spiritual aspects of human beings must also be taken into account when developing socio-cultural institutions. Thus, all cultures have forms and functions to facilitate family and community life. To ignore these aspects of creation would be to engage in practices that would be doomed from the start. Since all cultures, however, are infused with sin and exhibit the corrupting influence of the sin nature, they contain the seeds of their own eventual demise.

One ramification of embedded sin is that a person can be affected by the sin embedded in the culture while not actively engaging in the sin itself. For example, the sin of racism can be institutionalized, so that racism becomes a normal or accepted practice of the culture. In apartheid South Africa, if a person was born into the dominant white minority, they inherited certain opportunities and cultural power at the expense of those who were born into the subordinate black majority. Opportunities for education, employment, political office, and so forth were reserved and allocated, in large part, based on race. A white person in South Africa would experience these benefits whether one was an active racist or not. Conversely, a black person would experience the negative effects of this practice, whether they actively engaged in race hate or not. The accepted working of the society was based on a sinful practice, one group seeking to preserve power, pleasure, and dominance by controlling or making servants of another group of people. By allowing the practice of the society to go unchallenged, the sinful practice became the social norm, which allowed a white person to engage in a type of "passive racism,"[23] where the racist practice of the society was so ingrained in the fabric of the society that it became normal and, therefore, self-perpetuating by the dominant group.

EMBEDDED DEPRAVITY: MODERNISM

In chapter 4 we discussed the rise of scientific rationalism and its eventual development into the secular worldview of modernism. As a vision for life, modernity embraces three "gods": scientism (a belief in science), technicism (belief in the power of technology), and economism, or a belief that life is essentially material and economic in nature. While there is much discussion regarding the emergence of a postmodern worldview in contemporary America, postmodernism still serves more as a critique of modernity rather than the dominant worldview of the society.[24] As a worldview, modernism can be characterized by four principles that distinguish it from the premodern way of looking at the world. John Dewey, in *Reconstruction in Philosophy*, outlined these principles. First, modernity is no longer preoccupied with the supernatural world of religion but finds "delight in natural science, natural activity, and natural intercourse." Second, the premodern or medieval emphasis on religion and the authority of the church is replaced with the "growing belief in the power of individual minds, guided by methods of observation, experiment and reflection, to attain the truths needed for the guidance of life." Third, the modern world is guided by a belief in the inevitability of progress, so that "the future rather than the past dominates the imagination. The Golden Age lies ahead of us not behind us." Coupled

---

23. For a fuller explanation of the difference between active and passive forms of racism see Tatum, *"Why Are All the Black Kids Sitting Together in the Cafeteria?"* 11.

24. Anderson, *Reality Isn't What It Used to Be*, 3. Also see Walsh and Middleton, *Transforming Vision*, 132.

with the belief in the inevitability of progress is the belief that human beings, through intelligence, effort, and courage, can shape their own fate. Finally, the "patient and experimental study of nature," that is, the process of scientific inquiry, will "[bear] fruit in inventions which control nature and subdue her forces to social use," ultimately leading to progress.[25]

The spiritual nature of worldviews means that its normative vision of what life should be guides the development of culture. Seeking autonomy from God, sinful humanity must embrace a new vision, an alternative worldview, to guide and direct the culture-creation enterprise. The vision will become embedded in the forms and functions of cultural life. Modernity, with economism as its "golden head," seeks to replace the responsibility of stewardship governance with the delusion of individual autonomy and absolute ownership of creation. Scientific reason is employed to normalize self-interest and the autonomous use of resources. As Walsh and Middleton write,

> Western capitalism has its religious roots in discovering natural laws. Both Jean-Jacques Rousseau and Adam Smith believed that the first and most important law governing human existence is that of self-preservation or self-interest. Smith argued that as long as people obeyed the law of self-interest and rationally attempted to advance their own economic interests, society would flourish and economic prosperity for all would abound. Somehow the self-interested activity of autonomous individuals, concerned for their own gain and not for the public interest, would be led by an "invisible hand" to promote an end which would be beneficial to the whole society. Economic life in the marketplace has its own laws, Smith argued, and if left unfettered by religious or government regulations it will automatically act in the best interest of the society as a whole.[26]

This normative vision for culture becomes embedded in all social institutions, including the forms and functions of school. Science is employed to discover the ways in which human beings think and process information. Form these discoveries educators develop instructional methodologies or technologies designated to help students learn with greater efficiency. Highly qualified teachers are those who not only know their content area well but also possess a sufficient repertoire of educational techniques and understand the science of teaching sufficiently to increase student learning—all of which are measured by other educational technologies: standardized achievement tests for students, *Praxis* exams for teachers, and so forth.

What, however, is the goal of increased student learning? Since the 1980s, the number one priority of schooling has become the educating of future workers, which will increase the economic development of the nation, a priority that has displaced the more traditional goal of schooling to educate a moral and democratic citizenry. The 1983 report *A Nation at Risk* claims that

> The world is indeed one global village. We live among determined, well-educated, and strongly motivated competitors. We compete with them for international standing and markets, not only with products but also ideas of our laboratories

25. Dewey, *Reconstruction in Philosophy*, 47–49.
26. Walsh and Middleton, *Transforming Vision*, 136–37.

and neighborhood workshops. America's position in the world may once have been reasonably secure with only a few exceptionally trained men and women. It is no more. . . . Knowledge, learning, information, and skilled intelligence are the new raw materials of international commerce. . . . Learning is the indispensable investment required for success in the "information age" we are entering.[27]

The report went on to cite that America's loss in economic competitiveness to nations like Japan and West Germany was due to a "rising tide of mediocrity" that characterized American public education. Subsequent reform strategies, whether they be the Educate American Act (*Goals 2000*) of George H. W. Bush and William Clinton, *No Child Left Behind* by George W. Bush, or President Obama's Race to the Top initiative all emphasize increasing America's economic competitiveness. The Educate America Act made the promise that "By the year 2000, United States' students will be first in the world in mathematics and science achievement."[28] Why mathematics and science? Why not art and music? Seemingly, mathematics and science have greater economic utility than music or art. President George W. Bush, in the forward to *No Child Left Behind*, writes, "In a constantly changing world that is demanding increasingly complex skills from its workforce, children are literally being left behind."[29]

While science, technology, and economics are not inherently evil or sinful, it is the belief that science, technology, and economics determine how the world is and how the world should be that violates the principles of God. Science, technology, economics, or any other academic discipline is appropriate only when used to serve the interests of stewardship. When separated from the purposes of glorifying God and serving others, these disciplines become tools of normalizing and institutionalizing the sin nature. In a society where the guiding principles and vision of the dominant worldview are actively, yet often unperceptively, hostile to God, Christian educators must seek to reinstitute the principles of stewardship that underscore the initial commandment to learn about and develop the creation, all for the glory of God. The need to reinstitute the principles of stewardship and to instruct students regarding their application in a sin-saturated world underscores the second principle of biblical education—the principle of engaging in the ministry of reconciliation.

THE PRINCIPLE OF SHALOM AND THE MINISTRY OF RECONCILIATION

In the film *Grand Canyon*, actor Kevin Kline plays a Los Angeles attorney who, in the opening scene, driving home one evening, leaves the main highway to take a series of side streets. Eventually he finds himself in area of town that is less than safe, where his expensive Lexus breaks down. He calls for a tow truck to provide him assistance, and while he waits, members of a street gang approach him and begin to threaten both him and his car. In the nick of time the tow truck driver, Simon (played by Danny Glover), arrives and begins to hook up the disabled vehicle. His activity brings protests from the gang

---

27. National Commission on Excellence in Education, *A Nation at Risk*, 1–2.
28. Paris, *Leadership Model for Planning and Implementing Change for School-to-Work Transition*, 22.
29. Bush, "Foreword," 1.

members, who see Simon's activity as interrupting their own. At this point Simon takes the leader of the gang members off the side and tells him, "Man, the world ain't supposed to work like this. Maybe you don't know that, but this ain't the way it's supposed to be. I'm supposed to be able to do my job without askin' you if I can. And that dude is supposed to be able to wait with his car without you rippin' him off. Everything's supposed to be different than what it is here."[30]

The world that people experience today is not the one that God created. The doctrines of the Fall and of total depravity declare that the world God created has been marred by the introduction of sin and that sin has permeated all of the creation. Despite the attempts of human beings to normalize sin and the sin nature, the world "ain't the way it's supposed to be." As Cornelius Plantinga notes, most people (Christians included) view sin as simply the spoiler of creation. Sin mars the creation, and the talents, abilities, and creative powers of sinners are often used in ways that further befoul the creation and that promote their own sense of power, dominion, and self-gratification. Beyond stewardship, redeemed people are given the added responsibility of addressing the effects of sin in the world, in essence, to attempt to redeem the world from the consequences of sin and return it to a state of shalom, the way things ought to be.[31] Resistance to this responsibility to redeem the world, failure to confront and deal with the effects of sin, especially for believers who have been called to be a holy people, is also an effect of the Fall.[32]

The prophetic literature of Scripture not only condemns the sin of Israel and speaks of judgment upon the nations of the Earth for their violations of the laws of God, but also includes visions of a future time when God, nature, and all of humanity will be reconciled into a world characterized by justice, fulfillment, and delight. During this time, nations will be at peace and the weapons of war destroyed (Isa 2:2–4); it will be a time when "the wolf will dwell with the lamb" and "the nursing child will play by the hole of the cobra" (Isa 11:1–9). It is a period when justice will bring economic prosperity, as well as domestic security and tranquility (Isa 32:14–20); when work is again fulfilling, productive, and no one lacks for food or the necessary resources of life (Joel 2:24–29). The Hebrew prophets refer to this weaving together of God's righteousness with nature and humanity as *shalom*—the period "in which natural needs are satisfied and natural gifts fruitfully employed, a state of affairs that inspires joyful wonder as its Creator and Savior opens doors and welcomes the creatures in whom he delights."[33] Shalom is, in other words, "the way things ought to be."

Christ is the Prince of Peace (Isa 9:6) or the Prince of Shalom. He is the One who restores humanity to its intended state of fellowship with God. Believers are now at peace with God (Rom 5:1). Christ restores them to fellowship with God, to the peace of God that allows them to be reconciled in their hearts and minds to God and, therefore, to one another (Phil 4:7). Christ is the source of peace, so that human beings can be reconciled to each other. Paul can write that in Christ "there is neither Jew nor Greek [racial distinc-

30. *Grand Canyon* [DVD].

31. Plantinga, *Not the Way It's Supposed to Be*, 10.

32. Ibid., 8.

33. Wolterstorff, *Until Justice and Peace Embrace*, 72.

tions], there is neither slave nor free man [social class distinctions], there is neither male nor female [gender distinctions]; for you are all one in Christ Jesus" (Gal 3:28). On the anticipated basis of Christ's work, the prophets wrote of the time when all of nature would be restored to fellowship with humanity, and the creation eagerly waits for the day of this redemption (Rom 8:22). Christ is the One who brings all of creation back into line with God's original intent. God so values humanity's relationship to himself and the creation that he was willing to sacrifice his own Son to redeem it. In this respect, some theologians have spoken of salvation as "re-creation,"[34] with Christ being the One who restores all things to the way they are supposed to be.

The principle of shalom has profound implications for Christian living and, as such, a biblical approach to education. As Wolters states,

> The practical implications of that intention [i.e., redemption] are legion. Marriage should not be avoided by Christians but sanctified. Emotions shouldn't be repressed but purified. Sexuality is not simply to be shunned, but redeemed. Politics should not be declared off-limits, but reformed. Art ought not to be pronounced worldly, but claimed for Christ. Business must no longer be relegated to the secular world, but it must be made to conform again to God-honoring standards. Every sector of human life yields examples.
>
> In a very significant sense this restoration means that salvation does not bring anything new. Redemption is not a matter of an addition of a spiritual or super-natural dimension to creaturely life that was lacking before; rather it is a matter of bringing new life and vitality to what was there all along. It is true enough, of course, that the whole drama of salvation brings elements into the picture that were not part of God's creational design. . . . At the bottom, the only thing redemption adds that is not included in the creation is the remedy for sin, and that remedy is brought in solely for the purpose of recovering a sinless creation. . . . Grace does not bring a gift added on top of nature; rather, grace *restores* nature, making it whole once more.[35]

Second Corinthians 5:19 reads, "God was in Christ reconciling the world to Himself." While this passage most specifically applies to the spiritual reconciliation of humanity to God through Christ, the principle of shalom indicates that "the world" is not simply the subset of believers who are in the world but that the reconciliation process of God through Christ affects all things. Thus, Paul could write that Christ "is the Savior of all men, especially of believers." (1 Tim 4:10). Sin invokes the judgment and wrath of God, yet "He causes His sun to rise on the evil and the good, and sends rain on the righteous and the unrighteous" (Matt 5:45) and the judgment of sin is delayed and has been pur-chased because of the promise of the reconciling work of Christ (cf. Gen 3:15, 21). This reconciling work extends not only to the breach between God and humanity but also to all the effects of sin, so that, in Christ, human beings can be reconciled not only to God but also to themselves, others, and eventually even to nature. Since God is in the process of reconciling all things to himself, Paul writes that "whether, then, you eat or drink or whatever you do, do all to the glory of God" (1 Cor 10:31).

34. Wolters, *Creation Regained*, 58.

35. Ibid., 58–59.

While Christ is in the process of reconciling the world to himself, believers are to be "ambassadors for Christ" (i.e., representing the One engaged in the process of reconciliation). Ambassadors represent the will or interests of the one who sends them. For believers, the world (a system of beliefs, attitudes, values, and agendas that are governed by Satan and are hostile to the things of God) is an alien nation to which they have been called to represent Christ. As ambassadors, believers are to call into question the way things are and to represent the will of the Owner-Creator as to the way things should be. In this sense, the call to be ambassadors is a call to demonstrate God's intended design, his shalom, to the world.

Believers are also given the "ministry of reconciliation" (2 Cor 5:18, 20). To minister is to actively engage in a purpose; in this case, the function is reconciliation. As a minister, the believer not only represents the will of the Owner-Creator, but also actively engages in the process of reconciliation. The ramification of reconciliation for believers is that the church, as the body of Christ, should not only proclaim the truth of God but also actively engage in doing God's will. While the process of reconciling people back to God through Christ is paramount, and believers diminish the truth and power of the gospel if they fail to fully emphasize this point, it is also true that to ignore the entirety of the gospel and the responsibility of believers to be engaged in the reconciliation process, is to make the gospel anthro-centric. If the gospel is viewed as only the process of reconciling humanity to God, the full message of the gospel is lost—a loss that has tremendous ramifications for a biblical approach to education.

The terms *ambassador* and *minister* relate back to the original intentions of stewardship found in Genesis 1–2. To be ambassadors requires a relationship with and an understanding of the One who sends them (i.e., they must be citizens of the country that they represent). To be a minister requires believers to perform the function of the One who commissions or ordains them. The original call to stewardship required an intimate relationship with God, so that the steward would know what would bring glory to him, but stewardship also entailed the responsibility to actively engage or work the creation: to add value and do no harm. Fallen humanity, shackled by the sin nature and directed by the influence of Satan, cannot perform the requirements of the pre-Fall mandate to be stewards of the creation; but redeemed humanity, now possessing a new nature and no longer enslaved by the power of Satan, can once again, through the power of the Holy Spirit, engage the world as stewards according to the way God had originally intended.

Christ's earthly ministry provides insight into the significance of humanity's stewardship responsibilities. Christ did not involve himself in social issues as part of his earthly ministry. After feeding the five thousand, the Gospel of John reports that "Jesus, perceiving that [the crowd] were intending to come and take Him by force to make Him king, withdrew again to the mountain by Himself alone" (John 6:15). Before Pilate, Jesus did not deny his kingship but stated that his kingdom was not of this world (John 18:33–27). While Christ was more than capable of acting in a way that would have brought shalom to this world, until he establishes his kingdom in this world, the privilege and responsibility of governing and acting on this world belongs primarily to humanity. God so respects the stewardship responsibility given to humanity that, rather than minimize it by usurping humanity's authority, Christ elevates it by restoring human beings to their proper relationship with God so that they can more fully accomplish their given role.

Understanding the believers' role and restored ability to engage in reconciliation stewardship allows a biblical approach to education to avoid two extremes. The first is the tendency to minimize Christian engagement in the world. Essentially, this view disengages believers from social or cultural involvement based on the idea that that there is "no need to polish the brass if the ship is sinking." That is, since the world is ultimately going to be destroyed and replaced with a new heaven and earth, there is little need to engage in culture creation or restoration. From this perspective, the most important role for believers, individually and corporately, is to "get as many people into the lifeboats as possible," or evangelize them to accept the salvation message of Christ. Certainly evangelism is critical, and to be labeled an "evangelical" essentially means that engaging in evangelism is the individual's and church's defining trait. The lifeboat perspective, however, provides little incentive to engage the world, particularly the academic world, other than as a survival technique. Vocations, other than the calling to ministry, become simply ways of sustaining life and helping to finance evangelistic activities.

Ultimately, such a view creates a dualism between those vocations that are full-time Christian ministries, and those that are not, rendering those vocations outside this definition as less important or prestigious in the kingdom. Similarly, understanding principles of biblical integration are useful only to the extent that they protect the person from the corrupting influences of the sciences and humanities. The academic disciplines are not viewed as areas needing redemption for their own merit, since they are viewed as having little eternal value. Consequently, the academic world and the vocations that stem from them cannot be a source of joy nor provide a sense of satisfaction, or be areas of true calling, since they serve only as a means to achieve the greater end of evangelism. Academics provide the content and training for work, to support family, church, and other ministries but have little intrinsic value of their own. The stewardship reconciliation view, while not minimizing the critical importance of evangelism, views the proper exercise of stewardship as having tremendous eternal value. Since the goal of biblical stewardship is to add value to the creation in ways that glorify God, reconciling the arts and sciences in ways that reflect the glory of the Creator has value for the kingdom—value that is eternal and imperishable (Matt 6:19–21).

The reconciliation approach to stewardship also serves as means of avoiding triumphalism, the belief that the church will succeed in fully transforming society and culture. While the reconciliation view prevents Christians from abandoning the world as a lost cause and retreating to small enclaves of like-minded believers, it also prevents them from believing that all the world can be redeemed or that a biblically based way of thinking and behaving in the world can be imposed upon unregenerate people. Commenting on the role of believers in relationship to these two views, Cornelius Plantinga writes,

> As a matter of fact, Christians have been put in a solid position where the reform of culture is concerned: we have been invited to live beyond triumphalism and despair, spending ourselves for a cause that we firmly believe will win in the end. So, on the one hand, we don't need to take responsibility for trying to fix everything. The

earth is the Lord's, and he will save it. On the other hand, we may take responsibility for contributing what we uniquely *have* to contribute to the kingdom, joining with many others from across the world who are striving to be faithful, to add the work of their hands and minds to the eventual triumph of God.[36]

RECONCILIATION STEWARDSHIP

A biblical approach to education is to prepare students to engage in the practice of stewardship for the responsible dominion of the creation. After the Fall this view of stewardship expands to include the reconciliation of all things to Christ. The church, as the body of Christ, serves to represent Christ to this world to implement the work of reconciliation. As ambassadors, believers represent Christ, and as ministers, they are responsible for doing the work of reconciliation. The most critical, and most obvious, work of the church is to engage in the reconciliation of humanity back to God. For evangelicals this is the primary reason for ministry and a major function of the church; evangelizing is guiding people to make a profession of faith, revealing to them how they can have a committed relationship to Christ. Stewardship after the Fall, however, also obligates the church to demonstrate the supremacy of Christ in all areas of life: that Christ is Lord of all things and that the relevance of the gospel is not a future event but has implications for how life is to be lived now.

While the church is the body of Christ and the God-ordained collective for preparing people for the work of ministry, the current practice of most churches does not provide for nor include specific training in a biblical approach to the arts and sciences or to a biblical consideration of the academic disciplines and their relationship to the vocations. A belief that everything corrupted needs to be redeemed and that believers are to be the ministers of this reconciliation compels believers to address the corrupting influences of sin wherever it is found. As Plantinga writes,

> Wherever life has been corrupted, it needs to be reformed. Accordingly, a prime citizen of the kingdom will typically be a reformed-minded citizen, looking for ways to address some of the deformities in human life and culture. As you know, reform happens in many ways. It may occur when a nation gets shamed into seeing its injustice (think of civil rights legislation) or its carelessness (think of new building codes that require wheelchair accessibility). It may occur when the conscientious efforts of good people in business, medicine, law, labor, education, and elsewhere gain sufficient momentum so as to make positive differences in those fields.[37]

For the church, as a body of believers, performing the role of a reformed-minded citizen will require the development of renewed ways of thinking and informed integration of the truths of the Bible. It will also require knowledge and evaluation of academic content that allows for responsible dominion. Without such a perspective, a nonbiblical approach to these areas of life will fill the vacuum and dominate the thinking of believers in ways that will not be consistent with the biblical call to stewardship. Economics,

36. Plantinga, *Engaging God's World*, 119–20.
37. Ibid., 117–18.

educational life, law and politics, ecological practices, and so on will all continue whether or not a biblical approach informs their practice. Communal life requires that these areas be addressed, and if they are not adequately addressed by a biblical worldview, another worldview must fill the vacuum and inform cultural thinking and practice. Believers, living in the world as ambassadors and ministers, can either demonstrate the relevance of the biblical message to these areas of life or default to the thinking and practices of unbelievers, who must also address these necessary concerns of life but can only do so from the perspective of the sin nature. The biblical perspective calls for the glorifying of God through the loving nurturance of others. It is a perspective that places the individual above things, values the welfare of people over profits, and seeks to minimize or eradicate the negative effects of the Fall wherever they are found, knowing that doing good toward others is like doing good to Christ himself.

The realities of a post-Fall world create conditions that even unbelievers are compelled to address for cultural life to exist. Still possessing the image of God, unbelievers will often engage in practices that demonstrate the loving nurturance of others, even if their actions have no eternal or redeeming value. Reformed theologians, such as Louis Berkhof, have referred to this tendency on the part of unbelievers as *common grace*, those "general operations of the Holy Spirit whereby He, without renewing the heart, exercises such a moral influence on man through His general or special revelation, that sin is restrained, or is maintained in social life, and civil righteousness is promoted."[38] Donald McCleod maintains that common grace not only provides for the restraint of sin but is also the means by which the Holy Spirit enables unregenerate individuals to perform civil good.[39] For example, when Jonas Salk used his talents and gifts to develop a vaccine to combat polio, he performed an act that restrained evil (by eradicating the post-Fall disease of polio and its effects). Although Salk never made a profession of faith in Christ, his discovery helped to breach the Fall's gap between humanity and nature. While the church does not necessarily deal with issues of science, mathematics, art, history, or literature, the Christian school and university represent agents of the church where such issues can be addressed and biblical responses developed that not only influence responsible dominion in believers but also promote the exercise of common grace in the society at large. The church, on the other hand, can cultivate a cultural theology that assists believers in understanding stewardship reconciliation as a God-given obligation.

IMPLICATIONS FOR CHRISTIAN EDUCATION

The principles of stewardship and reconciliation have tremendous utility to help educators fulfill two of the primary distinctions of a biblically based education—the integration of faith to learning and the application of that learning to living in the world. *Integration* is a term that Christian educators seem to brandish about but often have difficulty putting into operational practice, frequently minimizing the true power of a biblically integrative curriculum to inform practice. When biblical integration is seen as little more than the

---

38. Berkhof, *Manual of Christian Doctrine*, 224.

39. McCleod, *Behold Your God*, 121.

attaching of a proof text to principles taught in science, social studies, or literature or the using of Bible-based examples to provide homework exercises for students to perform, the power of integration becomes trivialized and, as such, may be seen as unimportant or inconsequential to students. Kenneth Gangel addressed the concern when he wrote,

> One of our continuing problems is that we are able to talk about the integration of faith and learning better than we can practice it. Indeed, in some quarters it almost becomes a symbol, a shibboleth to be uttered but not demonstrated. Invariably it is a rallying cry which will bring nods of approval from the faithful among multiplied hundreds of teachers in Christian classrooms at all levels of education as they continue to grope for evasive implementation of the ideal."[40]

While Gangel seeks to provide principles that will guide the process of integration for the educator, these principles seem to lack an operational quality and, thus, may not be terribly useful for the development of day-to-day integrative lesson or unit planning.

The principles of stewardship and reconciliation provide the educator with a means to operationalize the process of integration at the curriculum, unit, and lesson level. Acknowledging that some areas of the curriculum will require greater attention and effort to biblically integrate than others, stewardship and reconciliation provide an operational framework to assist the educator in engaging in the process. Several examples might be helpful in demonstrating the utility of this idea. The first is a framework for developing a whole course perspective. For example, few Christian schools engage the study of psychology, and yet, given the particular development, needs, and concerns of adolescents, they tend to have relatively high interest in this subject area. Psychology, as a legitimate field of study, was abandoned by evangelicals for a greater part of the twentieth century, most notably as a result of the work of Sigmund Freud and psychoanalytic theory, the evolutionary bias of behavioral psychology, and the self-focus perspective of humanistic psychology. Since Christianity, however, has always been concerned with understanding human nature, Christian psychology would seem to have been a natural area of concern and study for believers. The initial reluctance of evangelicals to embrace the emerging discipline of psychology, as well as its failure to confront those nonbiblical interpretations of humanity, constituted a breach of responsibility by the church at that time.

Nonetheless, the discipline of psychology can provide a number of observations and explanations regarding human behavior that are not addressed specifically by the Bible. For example, when human beings engage in various defense mechanisms for coping with anxiety (e.g., denial, projection, rationalization, etc.), these behaviors can adversely affect their relationship with themselves, others, and with God. The existence of anxiety and anxiety-producing stressors can all be related back to the separations experienced as a result of the Fall. The Christian psychology teacher could contrast these types of abnormalities resulting from the Fall with a view of normality based on pre-Fall relationships that humanity was intended to have with God and with others. Christian teachers can examine how psychology relates, both positively and negatively, to how individuals understand and define self, relate to others, and relate to God. How these relationships are

---

40. Gangel, "Integrating Faith and Learning," 29–30.

defined biblically and psychologically can be compared and contrasted. Psychology can be used to inform learners about the nature of the deceitfulness of the human mind or "heart" as a result of the Fall. It can be used to describe the characteristics of some of the most severe mental illnesses and the more common and relatively less dramatic forms of psychological maladjustment. It can inform them about the type of need experienced by human beings with fallen natures, and a sin-based view of normality can be contrasted with a biblically based view of humanity. All of these areas make psychology an interesting and legitimate discipline for evangelical engagement.

A second example is drawn from the humanities—specifically looking at areas of art and music. For most evangelical young people, the idea that "beauty is in the eye of the beholder," is axiomatic; thus, issues of the relative merits of art, music, and potentially even the intrinsic value of other people can be defined subjectively, with the individual being the arbiter of what constitutes beauty. Such a view would discount the idea of an objective standard of beauty that can be known, substituting the notion that the standard of beauty resides with and within the individual. Stewardship and reconciliation could be used to demonstrate that, prior to the Fall, art that would have been considered beautiful would have reflected the holiness of God and elevated the human spirit to consider and pursue God or accomplish his will. Music that stirs the heart and the mind can be used to help students consider how they reflect the image of God in their lives. Art that inspires individuals to better themselves, pursue the godly betterment of others, or appreciate the creation (even in its fallen state) would become part of a biblical definition of beautiful art.

In contrast, after the Fall, human beings sought to develop their own definitions of right and wrong, good and evil, beautiful and ugly, and did so from the self-centeredness of their sinful nature. As a result, art can be used to manipulate others or pursue a personal agenda. Art can be used to encourage erotic behavior, dehumanize others, or elevate the self above God, others, or the creation. Ultimately, such art not only disvalues God, others, and the creation, but because it is not based in a proper understanding of God, it will also, ultimately, dehumanize the artist as well. The tragic lives of sensitive individuals who created art that ultimately dehumanized them, whether Beethoven or Kurt Cobain, Poe or Hemingway, can be examined in view of how sin affected their creativity and how their individual views of beauty sabotaged their relationships with God, others, nature, and themselves.

Since learning has its basis in stewardship, integration must be more than simply aligning academic content to the Bible or sound doctrine. Proper integration will also prepare people to be stewards, and reconciliation requires integration to focus on stewardship in a sinful world. Biblical integration prepares individuals to fulfill their God-given responsibility to be stewards and culture-creators, in their own lives as well as collectively with members of communities. Curriculum integration demands application, and without application, a biblical approach to the academic disciplines is rendered simply a way of knowing, not a way of living. The spirit of the relationship between knowing and doing in integration is captured by James Beane:

> Curriculum integration centers the curriculum on life itself rather than on the mastery of fragmented information within the boundaries of subject areas. It is rooted in a view of learning as the continuous integration of new knowledge and experience so as to deepen and broaden our understanding of ourselves and our world. Its focus is on life as it is lived now rather than on preparation for some later life or later level of schooling. It serves the young people for whom the curriculum is intended rather than the specialized interests of adults. It concerns the active construction of meanings rather than the passive assimilation of others' meanings.[41]

The principles of stewardship and reconciliation can serve as integration points for developing a biblical sensitivity and an application of the knowledge and skills learned in school. While the process of curriculum integration should be focused on an examination of how sin has adversely affected humanity's relationship with God, and subsequent relationships to others, nature, and the self, integration should also encourage the asking of questions concerning how believers should be operating in the world to counter these effects. Also, as Beane suggests, integration should be current, with a focus on "life as it is lived now," and should involve "the active construction of meanings." The expectations of stewardship were given to all human beings, and the call to be ministers of reconciliation to all believers. While acknowledging that younger students or people who are novices in terms of the knowledge, skills, and abilities in a discipline cannot function as more experienced teachers or peers, youth and inexperience do not excuse a person from engaging their biblical responsibilities. Rather, youth and inexperience are a call to the community of faith to provide the mentoring required to empower others to engage in the functions that God has required (Titus 2:1–8). To constantly provide knowledge and skills consistent with the biblical teachings of stewardship and reconciliation without providing opportunities to exercise those newfound abilities can relegate learning to irrelevance and may even constitute a type of biblical-educational malpractice (cf. Jas 4:17).

The school can promote and develop the application of stewardship and reconciliation on two levels. At the personal level, students can be encouraged to understand themselves, the talents, skills, abilities, and gifts that have been provided to them by God, and their use toward the purposes of stewardship and reconciliation. While students need to be exposed to biblical thinking and encouraged to think biblically regarding a wide range of academic areas, God's requirements for them to be faithful in those areas will differ according to how he has sovereignly created and nurtured them. Drawing from Paul's teaching regarding spiritual gifts, there are a variety of gifts and a variety of ministries—all of which come from God (1 Cor 12:4–5). These gifts and ministries are given by the Holy Spirit for the common good (1 Cor 12:7). The purpose of these gifts and ministries is to promote the will of Christ with the church, a unity stemming from diversity. Paul notes that the church constitutes many members but one body (1 Cor 12:12, 20); if all members had the same gifts, where would the body be (1 Cor 12:19)? The diversity of gifts within the body is so that the church can more effectively pursue the purposes for its existence. For this reason, no member of the body should view his or her gifts as unimportant (1 Cor 12:21), and no other member of the body can look at others and view their gifts as

---

41. Beane, "Curriculum Integration and the Disciplines of Knowledge," 622.

unimportant or unnecessary (1 Cor 12:22–25). Similarly, students need to develop an appreciation for all aspects of the academic disciplines (which are the focal purpose of school) and for those people who have been especially gifted by God. They also need to develop an understanding of how God has equipped them to pursue the call of steward-ship and reconciliation in their own lives.

Interestingly, there is no call in Scripture to discover one's spiritual gift. While Paul speaks of "earnestly desiring the greater gifts" (1 Cor 12:31), searching for one's gift is never commanded in Scripture. For every spiritual gift mentioned, however, there is also a call for all believers to be active in that area. For example, while some people are specifically given the gift of evangelism and others the gift of teaching, all believers are expected to be engaged in evangelism and teaching (Matt 28:19–20). While some people specifically have the gifts of hospitality or helping, this does not dismiss all believers from similarly being hospitable and helping others (1 Cor 12:28). Giftedness, as a biblical con-cept, does not include a type of division of labor, whereby certain aspects of discipleship are foregone in favor of those more gifted. Rather, the teaching of Scripture is that as individual believers engage in the process of routine faithfulness (i.e., practicing all of the requirements to which God has called them), those areas in which God has specifically gifted them will be manifest in terms of interest, effectiveness, or motivation in ministry. Applying this principle to schooling, stewardship and reconciliation will require that all students develop an understanding, appreciation, and working knowledge of all of the academic disciplines. Routine stewardship and reconciliation will require knowledge of mathematics, science, social sciences, and humanities. While engaging in these areas, stu-dents will also discover those areas in which God has particularly gifted them. Just as with spiritual gifts, where understanding of God's gifting come from engaging in ministry, so, too, a person's understanding of the academic talents and abilities will come from engag-ing in those processes as good stewards and ministers of reconciliation.

The ideas of stewardship and reconciliation can also be used to facilitate the devel-opment of and transformation toward a biblical worldview in students. The premise of section 1 of this book is that worldviews are communal and that individuals are social-ized into a particular worldview by other, more experienced adherents of that worldview. For example, children come to learn about the predominant worldview of the culture through interaction with parents, other adults, institutions of the culture (e.g., school, media, church, etc.), or peers. Since the initial development of worldviews is communal and interactive, the transformation of a worldview will also be communal and interactive. While philosophies are both individual and rationally held, worldviews are faith concep-tions that are maintained corporately and influence how people live in relationship to one another. While philosophies stem from worldviews, there are fundamental differ-ences between the two. Those fundamental differences must be taken into account when considering how to engage in the worldview transformation of students. The danger of understanding worldviews as synonymous with philosophies is that techniques designed to address the rational and analytical nature of philosophies will be used in an attempt to transform worldview. Given the essential differences between worldviews and philoso-phies, such techniques will be relatively ineffective in changing worldview.

By engaging students in the types of activities that are designed to promote the development of stewardship and reconciliation, they can also be engaged in processes that allow for the transformation of worldview. Christian schools or universities, as institutions that serve the church, can engage the surrounding community in ways that promote the principles of stewardship and reconciliation. Science classes that study the effects of pollution not only can engage in learning science content, but also can frame that content within a context of reviewing how humanity's actions have had negative influences on the environment. Students can examine the detrimental effects of sin on both the creation and human beings. Since humanity's physical well-being depends on the environment, these effects of sin need to be addressed as an act of reconciliation. Stewardship concerns can be addressed by examining how such knowledge of environmental conservation can be implemented in the local community. The school might then serve as a community resource implementing a biblical perspective or empowering the church to do so. For example, the school might help to develop ideas for or participate in river clean-up projects or recycling programs. Such projects would encourage a greater understanding of ecosystems (e.g., with river clean up) or the various properties of different types of recycled products (e.g., the chemical compositions of papers and plastics and the biodegradable properties of each).

In the above example, not only are students potentially learning a great deal of academic content and framing that content in terms of principles that encourage biblical integration of faith and learning to life, but they are also engaging in a process of worldview transformation. In the process of working with teachers who not only engage students in academic content but also encourage and guide them to think about that content in the context of real-world problems, students begin to see the world from a more biblical perspective. Engaging in river clean up and gaining a firsthand understanding of the effects of pollution on an ecosystem can help create a greater sensitivity to the environment and cause students to begin to see the physical world as God sees it. Engaging in recycling can help students view resource use more responsibly and cause them to see the effects of resource use in a consumer culture (which can facilitate discussions about integrating science and economics, as well as relating both of these to biblical principles of stewardship and reconciliation).

In addition, by working with teachers and other experienced adults who can mentor them in understanding and acting on the world in more biblical ways, students working with others on actual tasks will develop an appreciation of all the talents and abilities that people can contribute to the overall success of a project. For example, students who may not possess a great deal of analytical ability or high levels of content knowledge in a particular discipline may have skills and knowledge from other areas that they can contribute to the success of a project—skills and abilities that are necessary and may be lacking in others. Working as a team, students can begin to appreciate the diversity of knowledge and abilities necessary for success, and they may develop an understanding of unity through diversity that exemplifies Paul's description in 1 Corinthians 12.

The natural sciences are not the only areas in which the Christian school can engage in service learning that helps support student participation in stewardship. The Christian school can encourage the development of art and music programs that move beyond the realm of being curriculum "specials" to being fully vested and required aspects of the curriculum. The late Christian philosopher and theologian Francis Schaeffer noted that

> As evangelical Christians, we have tended to relegate art to the very fringe of life. The rest of human life we feel is more important. Despite our constant talk about the Lordship of Christ, we have narrowed its scope to a very small area of reality. We have misunderstood the concept of the Lordship of Christ over the whole of man and the whole of the universe and have not taken to us the riches that the Bible gives us for ourselves, for our lives, and for our culture.[42]

Given the prominence of art (including film), literature, and, particularly, music in youth culture, student involvement in the creation of artistic work and guided analysis of the art of others tends to generate high levels of interest among students. Christian schools could encourage community concerts for local musical talent (not just those of student groups) or create galleries where the art work of students and local artists can be displayed and shown. Student analysis of art, film, and music could be posted and displayed with these works in a way that demonstrates a biblical understanding of what is beautiful and which aspects may depict falleness in particular works of art. The prominence that the Christian school provides for the arts should reflect the high view of the arts and music that is part of God's revelation to humanity in the Bible.

In the social sciences students can engage in serving the broader community in a number of ways. Students can be involved in established ministries such as Habitat for Humanity, the YMCA, or other types of community-based help or relief agencies. The Christian school could help to establish tutoring ministries, with high school students providing support to the community by helping students prepare to pass proficiency exams or providing general homework support. As is the case with the natural sciences, student and class participation in various ministries might provide experiences that could be analyzed from the perspectives of the social sciences. Building houses with Habitat for Humanity might lead to discussions of homelessness in America (sociology) or the effects of federal, state, and local economic policies or business decisions on employment and unemployment (government and economics). The antecedent events that have contributed to the contemporary manifestations of problems in society can be examined (history).

Certainly a community-based approach to the social sciences would not suffice as the whole of the curriculum. For example, it would be difficult and require a great deal of creativity to provide students with a sufficient background in world history using such an approach. A more active approach to teaching the social sciences, however, would require that Christian educators and curriculum developers consider an approach to the social sciences that is less discipline specific (i.e., dealing with history, sociology, economics, government, etc., in relative isolation) and more integrative and indicative of the way students genuinely experience the social sciences in the community at large. Such an approach would also allow for a consideration of a biblical approach to the social sciences from a more holistic and more experientially authentic perspective.

---

42. Schaeffer, "Art and the Bible," in *Complete Works*, 2.375.

The premise throughout this section has been that human beings are responsible to develop and engage culture for the glory of God and the betterment of others. That human beings should be involved in these types of endeavors was part of the biblical mandate before the Fall and continues as a human responsibility after the Fall. What this chapter has attempted to demonstrate is that a biblical approach to schooling would reinforce these biblical principles of stewardship and reconciliation: stewardship, because God demands that humanity govern the creation for his honor and glory as steward-regents; reconciliation, because the effects of the Fall on human beings and on the creation create conditions that must now be addressed if human beings are to fulfill their stewardship requirements. In this way the principles of stewardship and reconciliation become biblical principles that give purpose and direction to schooling. They can be a means of demonstrating the value of all aspects of the curriculum and of providing teachers and administrators with overarching principles for biblical integration of both the curriculum and instructional methodologies.

Acting as stewards and as ministers of reconciliation in the world, however, is predicated on students' understanding of their standing as beings created in the image of God and on teachers' understanding of their role as facilitators who help to cultivate the development of that image in their students. While Christian schools can encourage students to become stewards in a post-Fall world, students will not be able to fulfill their biblical calling individually, or as members of the larger Christian community, unless they understand what it means to be created in the image of God. They must comprehend that this relationship refers not only to their individual status but also to the obligation that being in God's image has in their relationships to others. The next chapter will examine the third foundational principle for developing a biblically based approach to education—schooling that encourages the development of the image of God in students.

7

The Image of God and Education

Thou awakest us to delight in Thy praise; for Thou madest us for Thyself, and our heart is restless, until it repose in Thee.

—Augustine, *Confessions*

As the morning session draws to a close the room is abuzz with the teachers' discussion of the biblical ramifications discussed in the workshops. In wrapping up the morning session, Dr. Wise has teachers share in smaller groups, and then with the faculty as a whole, what they have learned over the last day and a half. Many of the teachers share their insights regarding the pre-Fall concept of stewardship, the meaning of the post-Fall idea of reconciliation, and the way these principles can assist them in the process of biblical integration. As several teachers share, almost all are attentive, and several teachers nod their heads in agreement and encouragement. Most will later share with colleagues that they have found the presentations and discussions informative and enlightening.

"I want to thank those of you who shared your comments regarding our session this morning," says Dr. Wise. "I trust that in viewing post-Fall education as a process of reconciliation, you can find a biblical mandate for involvement and integration in each of the academic disciplines you teach. In a few moments Dr. Solomon will dismiss you for lunch, but before he does, I would like to give you a little assignment for discussion. In order to facilitate our afternoon session, please discuss these two questions with the people at your table. First, what does it mean when the Bible says that human beings are created in the image of God? Second, how does living in a sinful world threaten that image? When we return from lunch I will ask you to share points from your discussions as the basis for beginning our final session."

Dr. Solomon informs the teachers that lunch has been provided by the school board in the cafeteria. "On each table," he informs the teachers, "are placards with your names on them. Please find your table quickly so that lunch can be served and you can begin your discussions."

The teachers adjourn from the chapel to the cafeteria where Arnie is certain the teachers have been assigned seating to maximize the intermingling of teachers between grade levels and subject areas. The administration has a fixation on cross-pollination, thinks Arnie, as he recalls his friend Manfred Median's slightly cynical description of the mixing process. To Arnie's surprise he finds he is placed with his friends Manfred, Barry Baroque, and Byron Bunsen. "So much for cross-pollination, Manfred," says Arnie as he joins his friends and they share remarks on how the administration always seems to keep them off balance.

After their meal, the conversation turns to the discussion questions posed by Dr. Wise. "I believe that the image of God has much to do with human beings being rational, intelligent creatures," starts Manfred. "It is the essence of Isaiah 1:18, where God says 'Come now, and let us reason together.' God would only say that to a being who is intelligent and reasonable. I think it is our rationality and moral awareness that shows our connection to God."

"Well, let's not forget the aesthetic," chimes Barry. "I fully agree that humans are rational and moral, but they are so much more. They are creative and artistic. They pursue beauty and the spiritual or mystical dimensions of life. Humans can love. They create art that attempts to express that love. They seek a relationship with God and with others, which also is expressed in many artistic forms. These relationships seem to be the reason that many unbelievers acknowledge that human beings have a soul that differentiates humans from the animals."

"I think you're both right," notes Byron. "My son just finished a unit in his sophomore Bible class. We were discussing it at dinner, and he noted that the curriculum defines the *image* of God in three ways—mind, will, and emotion. It seems that Manfred's response tends to capture the first two of those while Barry's response is encapsulates the idea of emotion. It may be a bit concise, but I think, as a definition, it captures the essence of our being created in the image of God."

"It can't be that simple," notes Arnie. "All of your definitions are certainly correct, however, all day yesterday and during our morning session, Wise has been emphasizing the importance of community and culture and its role in education. Your definitions all focus on the individual. Even Byron, who speaks about our human need for relationships, tends to address this characteristic as an individual one. I suspect that Wise would like us to consider the idea of the image of God, not so much from a psychological perspective, if I can use that term, but from a sociological one. How is being created in the image of God tied to our necessity for relationships others? Even the Genesis account notes the communal aspect of God when it reads 'Let *Us* make man in our image.'"

"Maybe 'Us' is the point of the second question," reasons Barry. "When Wise asked us to define how a sinful world threatens the image of God, maybe he wants us to examine the relationship of living in a sinful culture and how that affects our understanding of what it means to be created in the image of God. We have noted that worldviews are normative; they tell us what the world should be like and who we think we should be. Well, wouldn't a fallen worldview provide me with an image of who human beings are that is not only incorrect individually, or psychologically as Arnie said, but also sociologically? Wouldn't the Fall produce not only alienation from myself, but also produce alienation in my relationship with others? And, what if the church largely ignored the idea of the image of God being relational? Could we expect to see some of the same effects of communal alienation even within the church?"

"It is funny that you should mention people feeling alienated and the church," says Byron. "As a deacon, our pastor has us read certain books that he thinks are important for us as leaders of the church, and we discuss these as part of our leadership meetings. Recently, we have been reading a book on creating a sense of true community in our churches. The author notes that many people in our society feel a sense of alienation and lack of belonging, so they will often come to church to find a sense of community. Unfortunately, he notes that people frequently don't find the connectedness they desire in church because a true sense of community is often missing there as well. The reason, he believes, is that church, like the culture, emphasizes individualism and consumerism rather than a set of common beliefs and a sense of purpose necessary for true community. Even the practice of meeting in small groups, common in many churches, does not provide community because people come to those groups with individual expectations rather than a commitment to a set of common beliefs and purposes."[1]

"Well, I can agree that individualism and consumerism are prevalent in our churches and that it represents a threat to community and, consequently, the image of God," continues Arnie. "Just look at our students. They are constantly striving to buy the latest fashion, to 'get the look,' and to be noticed by the group. It seems that to be noticed, they have to find a way to stand out from the crowd, compete with others for attention. Rather than being acknowledged for who they are, they tend to turn themselves into 'objects,' just like the products they see, which compete with other products to be noticed and desired. Just think of the number of times fashion standards have been an issue of faculty discussion. Recall two years ago when issues regarding students and dress code were so intense that the administration seriously considered implementing school uniforms? The real irony is that, in their quest to be individuals, students allow advertisers to define what being in style entails. Certainly advertising tells individuals who they should be. Maybe it is the desire to sustain markets and advertising that constitutes a threat to community."

"Arnie!—you almost sound like a Marxist," jokingly chides Manfred.

"Well, it certainly affects our students' perceptions of how much money they think they must have or how much they believe they will need to earn to be successful," notes Byron. "Granted, some of our students aspire to Christian service-oriented professions like pastor, missionary, or Christian school teacher. Yet, all of us over the years have had students tell us that they didn't think they could earn enough money in those professions. Still, not all of this loss of motivation can be blamed on people desiring more. All of us know that it is increasingly difficult to make ends meet. All of our wives work. We all feel the need to take on extracurricular activities such as coaching or directing plays or clubs to make extra money. We all take some type of job in the summer. Don't these financial pressures detract from the time we have for our families and the time necessary to cultivate community in our churches?"

---

1. Frazee, *Connecting Church*. The reference here is a brief encapsulation of Frazee's premise in chapter 1, "The Problem of Individualism."

"Well—I would expect Barry to sound like a Marxist," says Manfred, throwing up his arms in mock frustration, "but now you are sounding like one also, Byron."

"What about how people seem to interact more with machines than people these days," injects Byron, in a discussion that is now more characteristic of a brainstorming session. "Look at our students—they spend an exorbitant amount of time with computers, text messaging, social networking, chat rooms, video games, and TV. It seems like people interact more with machines than they do with people. The other day I saw a couple, and the girl was chatting casually to her friend on a cell phone while the guy just sat there waiting for her to finish. She interacts electronically with someone several miles away, all the while knowing he will be there when she needs him to be there. In a sense he represented a secondary relationship and the cell phone was primary. Also, how many of our students seem addicted to those online virtual gaming worlds where thousands of people can participate at the same time? It just struck me, maybe we are starting to treat people as machines—devices that we manipulate and control for our own betterment. These attitudes would seem to threaten community and our understanding of the image of God in others."

"And machines become obsolete and are disposable," adds Barry. "When a newer model becomes available that we think will serve us better, we are apt dispose of the older version in favor of a newer one. I think you're right, Byron; maybe as a culture we are starting to treat others more like machines. Thinking of people like machines would certainly allow people to view others as disposable. I recently read a Barna Group study stating that one in three marriages in the United States end in divorce, and that this rate is virtually identical for those who claim to be born-again Christians. The study even noted that of those born-again Christians who have divorced, nearly 80 percent will divorce and remarry.[2] Granted, I don't think we literally treat people like machines, but if we increasingly interact with objects we can manipulate, wouldn't our expectations for interacting with people be affected?"

"Okay, I have been resisting your arguments, but you guys are starting to make some sense to me," admits Manfred grudgingly. "Years ago I helped implement the addition of advanced placement courses here at Mt. Carmel. I have also advocated for and sponsored our National Honor Society chapter here at school. I believe these have been great additions to our school, and we all have to admit they have been a drawing point for a number of prospective parents who were considering sending their students to our school. I also think these additions have been a real benefit to the students who have successfully participated in these programs. The AP courses have provided college preparation and credit and have afforded a rigorous academic challenge. They also have equipped those students with the type of competitive advantage that they will need to be successful in college. Adding these courses, however, has meant almost creating a high school within a high school: students in the AP classes are removed from regular interaction with other students. Granted, this segregation is true of all forms of academic tracking. We track for the perceived benefit of the individual student, but now I am wondering if there is not some sort of trade-off to the sense of community? These tracks seem to create academic division within the school. If I had to do it over again, I am sure that I would still press for

---

2. The Barna Group. "Marriage and Divorce Statistics."

an honors' track; however, this discussion has given me a moment to pause and consider the cost of this trade-off."

"Remember the definition of the sin nature that Wise gave us this morning?" recalls Arnie. "He noted that our sin nature seeks to define what is right by our own desires, like the verse at the end of the book of Judges where 'everyone did what was right in his own eyes.' In essence, we want to control all the definitions. Could it be that by promoting and cultivating such a high level of individualism, we are inadvertently encouraging and fostering the sin nature?"

"Don't go there," says Byron. "I am still struggling with Wise's statement that Christian schools don't seem to look or act much different from public schools. Except for Bible classes and chapels, our curriculum is very much like that of the public schools, and our teaching methods are not all that different either. I always thought the Christian school approached the curriculum and used instructional methodologies that were similar to those found in public schooling but from a biblical perspective. That is, they took the curriculum and instructional methods and infused them with biblical values. That idea, however, would require a belief that the structure of the curriculum and the forms of instruction are value neutral and that the secular content could be voided and a biblical perspective imposed. If what Wise suggests is true, that the curriculum and instructional methodologies are not value neutral, then we have a problem. Since nothing is value neutral, the curriculum and these instructional methodologies were created from a value system or worldview that may not be biblical at all. Now you are suggesting that, if the structures of the curriculum and the forms of instruction we use have values embedded in them that are hostile to biblical values, we may actually be encouraging the sin nature. This idea is really hard for me to accept."

"What's the alternative?" asks Manfred. "Education is about the individual, and learning is individual learning. Even if you use cooperative learning techniques, the bottom line is that individuals are the ones who learn. Anything else is some type of communalism."

"Arnie did not say we are cultivating the sin nature," injects Barry, coming to the defense of his friend. "But consider what we have learned over the last two days and from earlier this year. If sin is embedded in the culture, and the sin nature essentially desires autonomy, not only from God but also from others, wouldn't it be natural to expect cultures that are progressively more fallen to become less communal? And, in the process, try to normalize that lack of community?"

"Now you really do sound like a communist," says Manfred. "Your argument would defend primitive communal cultures and communist societies as less fallen than our capitalistic democracy."

"Let me defend Barry," responds Arnie. "Remember Wise said that the modern secular worldview worships scientism, technicism, and economism. The key here may not be communism or capitalism, but the alienation that results from reducing the world to economic factors. I mean, the curriculum and instructional methodologies we use were primarily developed by unbelievers, and unbelievers often seek to normalize the sin nature. If Wise is right, then sin always has the effect of devaluing or dehumanizing people.

If the curriculum and instructional methodologies we use were designed to help promote the development of *economic* beings, our use of those techniques could be inadvertently devaluing our students. Not that we see our students as less than human, but our curriculum and instructional techniques would not serve to promote or develop the image of God in them."

"Well, now we are back to where we started," observes Manfred. "What makes a person valuable and how do we define the image of God? Wise has a lot of explaining to do this afternoon. I see that we are being called back to the meetings. I think our group has generated lots of questions for him to answer."

As the teachers return to the chapel for the afternoon sessions, Arnie reflects on Manfred's last comment. He asked a good question, he thinks. How does one define the image of God? Given what we have just discussed in terms of curriculum and instruction, it would seem that the answer to Manfred's question could have serious ramifications for how we think about curriculum and instructional methods. Also, how does the Bible define the idea of the image of God? There are references to characteristics of God that are shared by human beings—things like mind, will, creativity, and emotion. Yet there are also references that speak of the relational qualities of God that are shared by human beings. Have we, as Western individualists, been guilty of imposing a particular view of humanity, one that tends to focus on the personal attributes rather than a more relational or communal definition when we interpret this idea from Scripture? This may be a very interesting afternoon.

In his 1968 book, *Escape from Reason*, evangelical philosopher Francis Schaeffer outlines the development of Western philosophical thinking from the time of Thomas Aquinas in the thirteenth century. Schaeffer notes that the development of Enlightenment thinking can be traced, in part, to Aquinas and his belief that humanity's will, but not his reason or capacity to reason, has been affected by sin and the Fall. Over the course of history, this medieval view in the trustworthiness of human reason influenced the thinkers of the European Enlightenment so that, by the eighteenth century, it was believed that reason could be the ultimate authority for establishing truth. Over time this belief in reason pushed aside a belief in God and established the authority and autonomy of rational humanity. Such faith in reason and humanity's ability and authority to determine what was ultimately true lead Friedrich Nietzsche to claim,

> God is dead. God remains dead. And we have killed him. How shall we, murderers of all murderers, console ourselves? That which was the holiest and mightiest of all that the world has yet possessed has bled to death under our knives. Who will wipe this blood off us? With what water could we purify ourselves? What festivals of atonement, what sacred games shall we need to invent? Is not the greatness of this deed too great for us? Must we not ourselves become gods simply to be worthy of it?[3]

Being created in the image of God, however, means that humanity's desire to "kill God" in order to promote autonomy though reason ultimately leads to a death of humanity as well. Humanity's intrinsic worth, historically secure in the biblical truth of their re-

---

3. Nietzsche, *Gay Science*, 181.

flection of God's image, is lost; humanity now becomes defined through science, through nature, and through rationality. The result is that by the mid-twentieth century the loss of humanity's intrinsic worth and its subsequent devaluation were demonstrated to the world by the Nazis during the Holocaust and by the millions of victims of political repression in the Soviet Union under Joseph Stalin.

Karol Jozef Wojtyle (later to become Pope John Paul II) was raised in Poland when his nation suffered the abuses of both the Nazis and the Soviet communists. Reflecting upon early experiences, and in light of his theological and philosophical training, he became convinced that the fundamental crises of Europe and the West were the result of the normalization of false ideas in the West regarding the nature of humanity. As John Paul II wrote,

> The evil of our times consists in the first place in a kind of degradation, indeed in a pulverization of the fundamental uniqueness of each human person. This evil is even much more of a metaphysical order than of the moral order. To this disintegration planned at time by atheistic ideologies, we must oppose, rather than sterile polemics, a kind of "recapitulation" of the inviolable mystery of the person.[4]

To the late pope, the incredible scientific, technological, and economic progress of the West was coupled with a moral and spiritual regress that had devastating effects for modern humanity.

This devaluation and disintegration of the image of God is not limited to the fascist regimes of the mid-twentieth century or even atheistic communism. John Paul II understood that Western individualism and selfish capitalism could lead to the same moral and spiritual problems as the atheistic systems of fascism and communism. Francis Schaeffer, in his book *How Should We Then Live?*, notes that the effects of a moral and spiritual regress would also be experienced in the democracies of Western Europe and the United States. He observed that societies that historically had abandoned a belief in moral absolutes in favor of an atheistic view of the world, specifically those nations controlled by the former Soviet Union, gravitated toward greater state control. In these situations the economic needs of the collective (i.e., the state) superseded the intrinsic dignity of individuals as spiritual beings. Although Western democracies secured civil liberties for their citizens based on the moral absolutes and belief in the dignity of humanity expressed in the Bible and the Judeo-Christian tradition, the devaluation and loss of inherent human dignity resulted when the biblical view of people as inherently spiritual and moral beings was replaced with a secular definition reducing human worth to economic and material factors. Schaeffer predicted that once people had come to accept this view of humanity, they would be willing to limit, suspend, or sacrifice their personal liberties to a government that would promise to preserve the "personal peace and affluence" of the population.[5] Among those conditions that would cause people in the West to "accept a manipulative, authoritarian government," would be economic breakdowns, shortages of natural resources, and terrorism.[6]

---

4. Lubac, *At the Service of the Church*, 174.

5. Schaeffer, *How Should We Then Live?* in *Complete Works*, 5:227.

6. Ibid., 5:245–52.

Pope John Paul II understood that the loss of human dignity he observed was not an ethical problem but a metaphysical one. It was not that Nazism, communism, or the materialistic democracies of the West were acting unethically; in essence, they were ethically consistent with their metaphysical understanding of what human beings are. If human beings are defined simply as glorified animals, if they simply are higher levels of evolution than the rest of the material world, if there is no soul and no eternality to their being, if their worth is not based in an absolute and transcendent authority, then there is no intrinsic human dignity that needs to be considered. We are left with a situation in which social and legal ethics are decided by power, not principle, and in which a powerful state—whether dictatorship or democratically elected—gains the power to define what is right and wrong.

John Paul II also understood that the church would need to reestablish a definition of humanity that recovered the biblical sense of inherent human dignity and worth. The pope called for a return to a theological description of humanity, a metaphysical definition that would confront the materialistic, scientific, and economic definitions of humanity that had arisen in contemporary societies. In essence, it was the responsibility of the church to rearticulate an overall theistic vision of life, one in which the dignity of humanity is based in their spiritual dimension rather than their natural one. What the pope stressed was a reassertion and cultural permeation of a Christian humanism that would counter the secular humanism that had evolved and overtaken Western culture.

John Paul II based his theological definition of humanity on three fundamental convictions. First, all human beings are characterized as beings who are engaged in the search for truth.[7] This search for truth, however, must be characterized by the use of reason that is governed by faith. Second, human cultures are the result of particular philosophies and religious commitments. How people think about the world and themselves influences how they live. Explaining the importance of culture to the development of a person's sense of humanity, Catholic theologian Richard John Neuhaus explains, "this Pope is convinced that culture is the most important. How people try to make sense of the world, how they define the good life, how they inculcate the moral visions by which they would live—this is the stuff of culture."[8] For John Paul II, a sin-developed culture is the root cause of the human condition. These two assumptions lead to the pope's final conviction: given the power of culture to shape human thought and history, the church's view of humanity must permeate culture in order to transform it.

In essence, only a biblically based understanding of humanity as beings created and representing the image of God can restore culture to the place where all individuals are viewed as having true worth and value. Without such a transformation, culture will continue to define human beings in ways that reduce their true worth—definitions controlled by those with the greatest cultural power and vested interest in those definitions. Any definition of humanity that is not based in a biblical definition is, from the perspective of a biblical worldview, ultimately dehumanizing. These nonbiblical definitions, because they

---

7. John Paul II, *Fides et Ratio*, 43.
8. Neuhaus, "Foreword," 14.

are either incomplete or bear the vestiges of sin, reduce human beings to less than God intended them to be. Schools, as institutions of the larger society, are places where these dehumanizing visions can permeate the curriculum and instructional approaches to education. This chapter will briefly examine the development of these dehumanizing visions of humanity and how they are manifested in current educational practice. As educators interested in developing a biblical worldview in our students, biblicists must embrace the challenge to develop and model a biblically based definition of humanity that will allow students to see themselves, and others, with the worth and dignity that God places in human beings created in his image.

TWO VIEWS OF HUMANITY

The biblical view of humanity is based on an understanding that human beings are a reflection of the likeness of their Creator—they display the image of God. As theologian Emil Brunner writes,

> Man, in contrast to the rest of creation, has not merely been created by God and through God, but in and for God. . . . Hence he can and should understand himself in God alone. Just as it is said of no other creatures "let us make," so also it is said of no other that it has been created "after His likeness" or "in His image." What does this mean? The whole Christian doctrine of man hangs upon the interpretation of this expression.[9]

Brunner notes that one of the first comprehensive definitions of humanity was developed by the first-century church father Irenaeus, a definition that would dominate Christendom for 1300 years. Irenaeus proposed that the biblical definition of humanity is comprised of three elements. The first he called the *image of God*, consisting of humanity's freedom to perform as stewards and their capacity to exhibit reason and rationality (the *humanum*). The second is the *likeness of God*, which comprises the will and the ability to act with self-determination on nature. Third is the *justitia originalis*, or the state of original innocence or sinlessness that allowed for spiritual communion between humanity and God. For Irenaeus, with the entry of sin into the world the *justitia originalis* was lost, and the likeness of God was consumed by the presence of sin, so that now humanity's will is shaped by nature; however, the image of God (i.e., the *humanum*), his ability to act as stewards and operate from reason, was retained.

With the Protestant Reformation many Reformers confronted an error in Irenaeus's definition that had been reformulated and subsequently elevated to the official doctrine of the Roman Catholic Church through the work of Thomas Aquinas. To Irenaeus and Aquinas, while humanity's state of sinless innocence and will to act in a manner glorifying to God had been lost in the Fall, his ability to think and reason had not. To them, post-Fall humanity was capable of demonstrating, through proper training and education, the pre-Fall rational abilities that God had originally intended. In contrast, Reformational emphasis on the total depravity of humanity meant that not only was innocence lost and the will corrupted as a result of the Fall but that reason was also corrupted, so that the

---

9. Brunner, *Man in Revolt*, 92.

reason of humanity, like the will, was oriented to serve one's own self-interest. Rather than separating reason from the sin nature, as suggested in the theology of Irenaeus and Aquinas, the Reformers stated that reason was subject to and a tool of the sin nature. While the Reformers stressed the totally depravity of humanity, they also emphasized that the image of God was not lost in this depravity. Just as God continues to recognize human beings as created in his image, the *humanum* is not completely lost, so that even human beings in their sinful state remain capable of recognizing that they are different from the animals.[10]

The result of sin, according to the Reformers, is that the image of God in humanity is marred but not lost. As spiritual beings, humans are and can never be reduced to the state of animals, which lack eternality. The spiritual death that results from sin is the loss of humanity's ability to initiate spiritual activity that is pleasing to God. As a result, sin condemns eternal humanity to hell. This is the qualitative result of sin—from spiritual life to spiritual death while still maintaining eternality. This qualitative aspect of spiritual death is passed on to all of Adam's progeny. The results of sin, however, are not simply qualitative, but can also be quantitative. While all human beings are born sinners, some may sin more than others. Engaging in sin causes a continued marring of the image in God, so that human beings exhibit less of what God intended them to be. Sinful human beings retain possession of the ability to think and reason, they exhibit a moral sense, can express spiritual longings, and retain the capacity to feel and demonstrate love, and so on (Matt 7:11). Although retained, these human capacities are affected by the Fall and the sin nature. Created in God and for God, sinful humanity now desires to serve its own self-interests. Consequently, sin dehumanizes or renders the image of God marred, resulting in a lesser reflection of himself in humanity than the Creator intended.

Thus, a Reformational view of humanity maintains that human beings were created as perfect reflections of the image of God. Human beings retain this image of God all of their lives; it separates them qualitatively from the rest of creation. While still retaining the image of God, all humanity since the Fall experiences the effects of total depravity— not that human beings are as bad or sinful as they can possibly be, but rather that every aspect of their being has been affected by the sin. For this reason sinful humanity can still think and act as moral beings, yet think and behave in ways that are neither motivated by or pleasing to God (Isa 64:6; Matt 7:21–23), instead following the leading of their fallen nature to engage in greater sin (Rom 1:28–32). Thus, the qualitative marring of the image of God can be compounded by the quantitative engagement of humanity in the practice of sin, further marring the already distorted image of God. Foundational to the Reformational view is that human beings are not as God created them, that the humanity seen and experienced today is a fallen humanity, not one exhibiting the characteristics intended by God prior to the Fall. As a result, human beings are in need of reconciliation, and it is Christ who comes to restore the image of God in fallen humanity. Thus, post-Fall humanity is abnormal, and a proper understanding of what is good for human beings or for the creation that they were created to govern cannot be derived apart from

10. Ibid., 94–95.

the gospel message of reconciliation in Christ and the restoration of the image of God in humankind.

The Reformational view of a marred, abnormal image of God in need of divine restoration is contrasted by a second view of humanity that has profoundly affected Western thought. This alternative view preceded the Christian era by four centuries, and its influence can be seen in the formulation of the image of God by Irenaeus and Aquinas. It is the anthropology of Aristotle (384–322 BC), the Greek philosopher who was among the first, and arguably the most influential, to develop a comprehensive view of humanity in the Western world. Of his influence Brunner wrote,

> Aristotle must have been the first to undertake to bring together all of the particular knowledge of man into a systematic order, and to present from one central point of view an interpretation of man. His attempt has had incalculable influence upon the whole of Western thought. The Aristotelian anthropology has been part of the supporting structure of European history. This immense influence should not be regarded as due to an unusual depth of thought, but to the fact that in him—in a way which has never been repeated—philosophical, scientific and psychological thought was combined with the non-reflective knowledge and understanding of the ordinary, non-philosophical and non-scientific human being.[11]

Aristotle's influential views on the nature of humanity come primarily from his ethical theories. In his major ethical work, *The Nicomachean Ethics*, Aristotle attempts to understand the nature of virtue and what it is that makes a human being good. Foundational to Aristotle's thinking, and in contrast to the Reformational view, is that Aristotle assumes human nature as normal, that is, what he views in humanity is how human beings have essentially been in antiquity past and will continue to be in the future. Thus, as Aristotle attempts to define what constitutes a virtuous person, he does so by trying to normalize the abnormal, where changing the quantitative behavior of sinful humanity becomes the standard for virtuous behavior. It is from this perspective that Aristotle seeks to answer the question, What makes a good person good? What is it that differentiates human beings from the rest of living things? Aristotle concludes that all living things seek to sustain themselves physically, that is, they have a "nutritive soul," and that humans and animals are separated from plants by a sense of awareness (i.e., they possess a "perceptive soul"). What separates human beings from all other creatures, however, is the ability to think rationally (the *anima rationalis*), and thus virtue consists in the development of the rational capacity of human beings to choose that which is virtuous.[12] In essence, for Aristotle, it is the ability to reason and to act rationally that makes one human. For this reason Aristotle could write, "For men are good in but one way, but bad in many," and virtue only comes from cultivating the ability to be governed by rational choice, which would allow a person to pursue the virtuous mean.[13]

While Aristotle emphasizes the role of reason and individual choice in the pursuit of virtue, he also explains that the pursuit of virtue leads to proper living in community. For

11. Ibid., 26.

12. Aristotle, *Nicomachean Ethics* 1.13, pp. 24–27.

13. Ibid. 2.6, pp. 38–39.

Aristotle, the cultivation of reason is foundational to both an individual's ethical behavior and his theories of politics, wherein "the State" becomes an association of people with a view of a good or noble purpose.[14] The chief purpose of the State in education, or the "end of political science," is "making the citizens to be of a certain character, viz. good and capable of noble acts."[15] To be human is to make rational choices and to act in accordance to those choices. Thus, to cultivate reason is to cultivate a person's humanity. The more rational a person is the more "human," and humane, the person becomes. Virtue is characterized by reason, while ignorance and the passions control vice; consequently, the well-trained and informed mind will choose rationally that which is virtuous. The Aristotelian view can be seen in the public service spots on NBC television where a celebrity spokesperson provides several seconds of wisdom and closes with the tag line "The More You Know," which assumes that the human failure to act virtuously is the result of a lack of knowledge. Moreover, the chief purpose of education, from an Aristotelian perspective, would be the cultivation of knowledge and reason above all other attributes, for in so doing people will become more human.

While the influence of Aristotle can be seen in contemporary society—from the goals of education to public service spots on television—his ethical theory is foundationally based on a premise that is theologically false. Aristotle assumes that the world he observes is normal and good, and he seeks to derive ethical principles from that which operates well in the world. In this sense Aristotle is guilty of what is called the naturalistic fallacy, or belief that what is natural is good. Aristotle fails to acknowledge that the world is fallen and that sin has affected every aspect of nature. Rather than seeing human reason as bearing the effects of the Fall, he assumes that reason is intact and that human will is subject to reason rather than reason being a tool of the will.

By falling victim to the naturalistic fallacy, Aristotle, and later Irenaeus and Aquinas, introduced errors in the understanding of humanity that have affected Western thought to the present day. Through the influence of Aristotle, the nature of humanity in Western thought has been defined philosophically rather than theologically. Like a golf shot— where a small error in the swing at impact can affect the trajectory of the ball, and that mistake becomes exacerbated the farther the ball travels—so too Aristotle and Aquinas's error, as it has traveled through time, has had tremendous consequences for the understanding of the nature of humanity for Western culture. As Francis Schaeffer writes, "In Aquinas's view the will of man was fallen, but the intellect was not. From this incomplete view of the biblical Fall flowed subsequent difficulties. Out of this, as time passed, man's intellect was seen as autonomous."[16]

As a result of the Aristotelian and Thomistic view of humanity's unfallen capacity for reason, reason becomes deified; it becomes an idol to be pursued. Unaffected by sin, the development and perfecting of reason allows the individual to determine that which is good, and the capacity for reason provides individuals the ability to morally operate

---

14. Aristotle, *Politics* 1.1, p. 25.

15. Aristotle, *Nicomachean Ethics* 1.9, p. 18.

16. Schaeffer, *Escape from Reason*, in *Complete Works*, 1:211.

apart from divine revelation. Since it is now the capacity to think rationally that marks the individual's true humanity, the development of the *anima rationalis* also leads to the development and elevation of the autonomous individual. The more individuals know, the more rational they become, allowing them to exist with a greater degree of autonomy. Education, through the development of the *anima rationalis*, also becomes the process of developing the autonomous individual. It cultivates the belief that the more students know, the more capable they become of pursuing their own hopes and dreams, aspirations and desires. It is the cultivation of the belief that human beings, apart from communion with God, possess the ability to determine what is good. Scripture portrays this belief as the essence of the sin nature. It is the lie that Satan used to tempt Eve (Gen 3:5), the reason Adam and Eve were expelled from the Garden of Eden (Gen 3:22–24), and the reason that chaos reigned in Israel during the time of the Judges (Judg 21:25).

It was this view of unfallen reason that the Protestant Reformers sought to correct in their formulations of the image of God. Luther understood that allowing the image of God to be defined by supposedly unfallen human capabilities, particularly reason, would ultimately allow for even Satan to possess the image of God: "If the *Imago* consists in that power of the soul (in the *anima rationalis*) then it would follow that Satan too would be formed according to the image of God, since in him these natural qualities are far stronger."[17] What the Reformers sought to do was to understand humanity theologically rather than philosophically; as spiritual beings created in the image of God, human beings can only be understood in reference to the One whose image they were created to reflect. As a spiritual being, God lives in communion with the other members of the Trinity (cf. Gen 1:26), consequently the image of God in human beings cannot be understood apart from the human being's relationship with God and with others who also bear God's image (cf. Matt 22:37–40). To attempt to understand humanity apart from God or the person's relationship to others is to further dehumanize humanity.

The cultivation of the autonomous individual as the ideal of society or the goal of education becomes, in reality, the dehumanization of the individual. The result of autonomous human reason is the creation of an intellectual narcissism that allow individuals to define themselves and operate from their own power and ability to distinguish that which is right, and education (through the cultivation of students' knowledge and reason) empowers individuals toward this moral end.

THE PSYCHOLOGIZING OF HUMANITY

The first thing said about human beings in the Bible is that their relation to God is like that of a picture to its model. Humankind must first of all be defined theologically; only then may the philosopher, the psychologist, and the biologist make their statements. The fact of what man is does not merely raise a human question, but is a "theological" concern; he is not to be understood in himself nor from that reason which is in him. He can be understood only in light of that which stands "over against" him, the Word of his Creator.[18]

---

17. Luther, quoted in Brunner, *Man in Revolt*, 507.

18. Brunner, *Man in Revolt*, 102.

The consequence of the Aristotelian error, embraced and promoted by Aquinas, that traveled through history to influence the proponents of the European Enlightenment and modernity was that Western thinkers increasingly sought to define humanity not from a theological perspective but from a philosophical one. Over time, this departure to the philosophical led to humans' eventually defining themselves first psychologically and later biologically. The deification of reason, by the time of the Enlightenment in the eighteenth century, led to the glorification of science as the method by which human beings could ascertain truth. Schaeffer notes that the Aquinian belief in reason as unaffected by the Fall created a dualism between grace (the things of God, heavenly things, and the spiritual nature of humanity) and nature (the created order, the physical universe, and the physical nature of humanity).[19] Over time, because a belief in unfallen human reason (nature) assumed that human beings could arrive at truth apart from a relationship with God (grace), nature eventually overwhelmed or consumed grace so that anthropological questions, questions of the nature of human beings and human interactions, are no longer considered theologically.

Even so, human beings are fundamentally spiritual beings, possessing characteristics of the image of God that cannot be explained via natural causes. Even Aristotle understood that there was an inner quality to humanity that could not be explained physically; he used the term *soul* to describe it. Once removed from theology, human beings are now left to describe the spiritual aspects of humanity using the tools of philosophy and science. For example, human beings have the capacity to feel and express love because they reflect the image of God who also feels and expresses love. Separated from a theological base, human beings now must explain the origin of these human capacities from a philosophical or psychological perspective. In essence, this is what Sigmund Freud attempted to do by formulating his concept of *libido*—the instinctual desire for sex. By reducing the capacity to love to that of the desire for sex, Freud conceives this spiritual quality of humanity in philosophical and psychological terms.

Even Freud's attempt to describe the spiritual quality of personality from a philosophical/psychological perspective, however, was not considered scientific enough for some thinkers. The libido, as an instinctual drive, is biological, but Freud's description of the personality in psychological terms was not considered empirically verifiable, and, as such, could not be considered true science. Humanity sought to understand itself scientifically in terms of the physical world and biology. In order to understand humanity scientifically, however, requires that those attributes that one desires to comprehend must be identified, isolated, and subjected to empirical testing and manipulation. The complexity of human beings could be understood, or so it was believed, by reducing the complex to the simple. Combined with the Western propensity to exalt the individual over the communal, the desire to understand humanity scientifically led to the development of psychology as a separate academic discipline apart from philosophy.[20]

19. Schaeffer, *The God Who Is There*, in *Complete Works*, 1:63.

20. In the late eighteenth century many philosophers saw this evolution as desirable. The German philosopher Immanuel Kant believed that philosophy needed a science to verify the speculations of philosophy. As Kant wrote, "It is, indeed, the common fate of human reason to complete its speculative structures as

In general, the evolution of psychology as an independent field of study tended to develop in two separate yet not necessarily discrete approaches. The first can be characterized as *psychology from philosophy*—where the scientific method of psychology first attempted to verify, and later to develop, psychological constructs or ways of understanding human personality. For example, philosophical inquiry might conclude that human beings tend to think in terms of space and time, cause and effect; they have memory and operate from motives. Initially, early psychologists would apply the scientific method to construct experiments to verify and demonstrate or disprove the validity of these psychological ideas that were constructed from philosophy. Over time, such experiments produced results that were later identified and labeled as psychological constructs, that is, philosophical labels for phenomenon without corresponding biological structures. Thus, Swiss psychologist Jean Piaget concluded through his research that human beings possessed mental schemes that would change in notable ways through the processes of assimilation and accommodation. In addition, memory theorists empirically verified the existence of constructs such as long-term and working memory, which have distinct characteristics and operate in different ways. This branch of psychology generally developed in Continental Europe in the late nineteenth to the mid-twentieth centuries.

The second branch of psychology can be characterized as *psychology from biology*—where scientists attempt to demonstrate that aspects of human psychology are manifestations of human biology. For example, the current emphasis in education on brain-based learning is an attempt to take the findings of neuroscience and apply them to teaching and learning. The attempt to identify and label learning problems as psychological disorders that have their basis in biochemical or neurological abnormalities is a manifestation of this branch of psychology. The recent emphasis on gender differences in learning is based on the argument that there are distinct biological differences between male and female brains that create distinctive learning styles and differences.[21] This branch of psychology generally developed in Great Britain and the United States in the late nineteenth through mid-twentieth centuries.

Two important caveats need to be stated. First, while these two branches of psychology have different points of origin, the two are not discretely independent. Historian Lawrence Cremin notes that what most influenced educational development in the twentieth century was the "idea of an objective psychological theory firmly rooted in evolutionary biology."[22] As these two branches of psychology merged, the more scientifically oriented biological model became increasingly predominant over the philosophical. An example of this can be seen in the best-selling book by Harvard psychologist Steven Pinker, *The Blank Slate*, where he argues that the philosophical understanding of human nature must give way to the discoveries of anatomy, neuroscience, and evolutionary biology.

---

speedily as may be, and only afterwards to enquire whether the foundations are reliable." *Critique of Pure Reason*, 47.

21. Two excellent examples of this perspective are Gurian and Stevens, *Mind of Boys*, and Sommers, *War against Boys*.

22. Egan, *Getting It Wrong from the Beginning*, 97.

Second, to note the development of a psychological conception of humanity apart from the theological view is not to deny the validity and utility of some of the findings of psychological research. Even after the Fall, human beings still possess a tremendous ability to ascertain how the world is while continuing to be dependent on God to understand what ought to be. Of course, when interpreting the results of psychological research, these abilities need not be distinct. People's understanding of what ought to be affects this perspective when interpreting the results of their experimentation. Even when cautioned by this understanding, however, Christians can use the findings of psychological research to enhance the educational process. For example, an understanding of the differences between working memory and long-term memory, which helps to explain how things are processed and stored in each, can greatly inform the instructional processes for teachers. To deny the validity of certain learning problems as having either neurological or biochemical origins because many biologists maintain an evolutionary perspective can have grave consequences for the students that educators seek to assist.

At the same time, the process of using science to psychologize the mind or to biologize human nature comes at a grave cost to a moral and spiritual understanding of humanity. To reduce humanity to a set of physical and psychological attributes is to lose the wholeness that is part of its spiritual nature. The result is that human beings become glorified animals. Their God-given nobility to live in relationship with God and to work for the betterment of others is denied. Humanity is dehumanized and made less than God intended it to be. This loss of human nobility is most easily observed in the psychological theory of behaviorism.

Behavioral psychologists seek to explain learning in terms of environmental factors. Unlike other types of psychology that attempt to explain behavior in reference to internal states or structure, behaviorists generally demonstrate the link between some environmental stimulus and the response of an organism to that stimulus. While different versions of behaviorism account for the link between the stimulus and the response differently, for behaviorists the stimulus-response link serves as a type of lowest common denominator for behavior. Thus, all behavior can be accounted for by these stimulus-response links. Because behaviorists attempt to explain all behavior in terms of environmental factors apart from internal states in the organism, behaviorists claim that behavior can be explained scientifically, that the scientific method can be used to construct experiments that empirically test the relationship between a stimulus and a response.

Behavioral psychology operates on the philosophical principle of determinism—that all events (including human behavior) are caused by prior events. The determinist believes in a material-causal world, where spiritual forces either do not exist or are of no consequence. As a result, one of the principle consequences of determinism is that human beings do not possess free will. As creatures that simply respond to environmental stimuli, they are passive until the environment acts upon them, and their responses can be accounted for in terms of the consequences of those responses. As a result, human beings cease to be personal beings. Human beings, like all other things that exist in a material universe, are the result of the interaction between the forces of time, energy, matter, and probability (or chance)—the impersonal factors that constitute all reality.

Given this commonality, human beings are not intrinsically different from animals in terms of responding to environmental stimuli. Human beings, because they have larger brains and, thus, presumably possess more intelligence (a problematic term for many behaviorists because of its vague nature), also possess the ability to respond to stimuli faster and with greater complexity. These responses, however, are different from animals only in quantity or complexity; they are not uniquely human. Consequently, the same dynamics that explain animal learning can be used to explain human learning, which helps account for why behaviorists have applied the results of experiments using rats, pigeons, and monkeys to human learning. John Watson, a pioneer in the development of behavioral psychology notes, "the behaviorist, in his effort to get a unitary scheme of animal response, recognizes no dividing line between man and brute."[23] Watson goes on to note, "the behavior of man and the behavior of animals must be considered on the same plane; as being equally essential to the understanding of behavior."[24] The belief that human beings are intrinsically different; that they possess inherent honor, freedom, and dignity, is dismissed by behaviorists. Behavioral psychologist and philosopher B. F. Skinner, in his treatise *Beyond Freedom and Dignity*, writes,

> In the scientific picture a person is a member of a species shaped by evolutionary contingencies of survival, displaying behavioral processes which bring him under the control of the environment in which he lives, and largely under the control of the social environment which he and millions of others like him have constructed and maintained during the evolution of the culture. The direction of the controlling relation is reversed: a person does not act upon the world, the world acts upon him.[25]

The denial of human will leads to a view of human beings as passive entities that can, and should, be manipulated for the social good. Since there is nothing intrinsically valuable in being human, there can be no violation of human freedom or dignity in this manipulation. The passivity and malleability of human beings is expressed in the most famous quote attributed to John Watson: "Give me a dozen healthy infants, well informed, and my own specified world to bring them up in and I'll guarantee to take anyone at random and train him to become any type of specialist I might select—doctor, lawyer, artist, merchant-chief; and yes, even beggar-man and thief, regardless of his talents, penchants, tendencies, abilities, vocations, and race of his ancestors."[26] As Skinner wrote, "[the human being] does not engage in moral struggle, and therefore has no chance to be a moral hero or credited with inner virtues. But our task is not to encourage moral struggle or to build or demonstrate moral virtues. . . .[Those who believe in moral virtues] have formulated the task in such a way that they cannot accept the fact that all control is exerted by the environment and proceed to the design of a better environment rather than of better men."[27]

23. Watson, "Psychology as the Behaviorist Views It," 158.

24. Ibid., 175.

25. Skinner, *Beyond Freedom and Dignity*, 201–2.

26. Watson, *Behaviorism*, 104.

27. Skinner, *Beyond Freedom and Dignity*, 76–77.

Skinner advocated the manipulation of the stimulus-response link through the use of reinforcement (a process he called operant conditioning) to create a world where people were not good but where they "behaved well."[28] As an approach to education, behaviorism advocates that teachers are to modify student learning in highly structured environments, most commonly known as direct instruction, where defined learning objectives are pursued in an orderly and systematic fashion. A student is said to have mastered these objectives when they can demonstrate competence at a predetermined level.

Despite the many critics of behaviorism and its loss of influence as a psychological theory, behaviorism nonetheless has substantial influence in American education.[29] In many respects the educational initiative *No Child Left Behind* has many principles of behavioral psychology embedded in it. Stating that all students will be able to demonstrate proficiency in basic academic subject areas because they have been taught by a "highly qualified teacher" who possesses competent knowledge and skills in scientific-based methods of instruction and a broad knowledge of the content-area subjects assumes the passivity and malleability of students. The persistence of behavioral approaches to education may lie in a belief in the science of behavior, a science based in biology and the physics of anatomy.[30] Reducing behavior and learning to biology and physics preserves the trust in science and the legitimacy of the scientific method and of human reason to determine truth.

The belief in human reason and the scientific method as means to determine truth has lead to the biologizing of the human mind. Throughout much of the history of Western philosophy, a distinction has been made between the mind (as the state of intelligence), consciousness, and reason in the person (which were viewed as aspects of the person's soul), and the physical body. This dualism between mind and body can be seen in the works of Plato and Aristotle, but was also reintroduced in Western philosophical thought in the works of the French philosopher René Descartes. From his perspective, the brain, which is physical and therefore part of the body, was different and distinct from the mind, which was part of the human soul. Having a soul distinguished humans from all other organisms, resulting in the belief that only human beings had a mind and a brain. The advent of evolutionary biology, however, also helped produce the field of evolutionary psychology, in which learning is viewed as the adaptation of the brain to the environment. By viewing learning as simply biological—for example the development and changing of neural patterns and synapse connections in the brain—the concept of a distinctive human mind as differentiated from an organic brain is obliterated. Philosopher Gilbert Ryle disparagingly referred to the belief of a mind distinctive from biology and the brain as the myth of "the Ghost in the Machine." He notes that "the dogma of the Ghost in the Machine . . . maintains that there exists both bodies and minds [and] . . . these and other analogous conjunctions are absurd," and thus he argues that such a myth needs to

---

28. Ibid., 66–67.

29. Many of the criticisms of behaviorism in education, as well as summations of its major critics, can be found in two books by Kohn. Of note are the books *Punished by Rewards* and *The Schools Our Children Deserve*.

30. Skinner, *Beyond Freedom and Dignity*, 175.

be abandoned.[31] Psychologist Steven Pinker, echoing the sentiments of both Skinner and Ryle, notes that to maintain a belief in such false ideas as the "ghost in the machine" is actually to deny true humanity because such beliefs are opposed to true human nature, and recent scientific discoveries cast such beliefs into doubt.[32]

While behavioral psychology openly equates the development of mind as synonymous with changes in the biological brain, so that human distinctiveness is inherently lost, a similar loss occurred in cognitive psychology. In the cognitive development theory of Piaget, often viewed as diametrically opposed to the findings and applications of behaviorism, the mind is comparable to biological growth: "The psychological development that starts at birth and terminates in adulthood is compared to organic growth. . . . Just as the body evolves towards a relatively stable level . . . so mental life can be conceived as evolving toward a final form of equilibrium represented by the adult mind."[33] The relationship of biology to cognitive development can be seen in the fact that Piaget often referred to his theory as that of genetic psychology or genetic epistemology. As a result, Piaget advocated for a type of education in which teaching would be subordinated to the natural process of cognitive development that was part of biological maturation.[34] When schools failed to teach in accordance with these developmental patterns, Piaget contented that "It is not the child that should be blamed . . . but the school, unaware as it is of the use it could make of the child's spontaneous development, which it should reinforce by adequate methods instead of inhibiting as it often does."[35]

The result of either a behavioral or Piagetian approach to the psychology of learning is that the mind is viewed as synonymous with the brain so that the mind becomes a byproduct of nature. The mind, which from the time of Aristotle was viewed as the quintessential essence of humanness, becomes a product of the evolutionary processes, so that even this human distinctive is lost. The idea of human beings as unique from the rest of the earthly creation because they bear the image of God—an image based in the spiritual, the personal, and the relational because God is spirit, personal, and relational—is consumed by the evolutionary and impersonal forces of time, energy, matter, and probability. Twentieth-century psychology, whether in the form of behaviorism or cognitivism, inherits the notion of progress that is part of evolutionary biology, which has its roots in the notion of the inevitability of human progress that comes from the worldview of secular modernity. Evolutionary biology states that organisms advance from simple to more complex. In behaviorist learning this is seen in Bloom's taxonomy: knowledge leads to comprehension, comprehension to application, and so on, until the process finally terminates in the ability to engage in evaluation. In Piagetian terms, cognitive development is the process of growth from a concrete to a more abstract understanding of the world.

To summarize, the Aristotelian belief in reason as the defining characteristic of human beings over time led to an emphasis on the individual and personal autonomy that

31. Ryle, *Concept of Mind*, 22.

32. Pinker, *Blank Slate*, 13.

33. Piaget, *Child's Conception of the World*, 3.

34. Piaget, "Piaget's Theory," 716.

35. Piaget, *Comments on Vygotsky's Critical Remarks*, 11.

continues to permeate Western culture. In addition, the elevation of reason, when combined with an unwavering belief in science as the only method for discovering truth, led to the loss of the human distinctiveness of the soul as biology subsumed it as subject to the physical body. Consequently, by the late twentieth century, humanity had come to be understood as essentially experience within the limits of biology. Such an understanding of human nature has profound effects on teaching and education. For the purpose of this study three are of note.

The first is that experience alone does not determine who a person is or who that person will become. While experience is very powerful and its importance and cannot be discounted, two people can share a great many experiences and still differ in how they think or act. For this reason earlier chapters have noted the effect of experience on the development of an individual's worldview, but they have also noted that a number of different philosophies can come from the same worldview. Experience is a powerful factor in forming and shaping a person's goals, attitudes, values, and expectations—the criteria from which a person interprets experience. The interpretation of similar experiences helps to explain how people from the same region, country, or culture can share the same worldview. Experiences alone, however, are not enough to determine goals, attitudes, values, expectations, thus helping to account for the variations of philosophies within a particular worldview.

Behaviorist learning theories fail to take these variations into proper account, noting that variations in behavior, even among people with highly similar experiential backgrounds, can be accounted for by slight variations in the experience or slightly different ways that an individual's responses to those stimuli were reinforced. In either case, the individual learner remains passive in the learning process, and increased learning can be manipulated by others through greater control and enrichment of the environment. Constructivist learning theories stem from a more biblical view in this regard, for these theories claim that a person's goals, attitudes, values, and expectations are a significant part of learning and must be considered in the instructional process—a conclusion that makes learners far more active and in control of their own learning.[36]

In fairness, those theories that emphasize the connection of biology to learning note that the effects of experience must by understood within the parameters of biology. For example, a Piagetian would object to a behaviorist view of learning by explaining that control and enrichment of the environment cannot achieve certain educational ends. Educators cannot control and enrich an environment to the extent that five-years-olds can learn calculus; for in most people certain biological constraints on brain growth development limit this process. Other cognitive theorists explain that there are certain biological limits to the speed and ability a person has for processing, encoding, and storing information in memory.

Yet both behaviorial and biological perspectives are guilty of denying a biblical view of humanity and replacing it with one that is ultimately dehumanizing. The behaviorist view perpetuates the belief that a human being enters the world as a blank slate and that

36. Roso, "Constructivism in the Classroom," 43.

environment and experience serve as nearly the sole determinants of who the person is and will become. The neurological or brain-based perspectives note that genetic and biological endowments are critical to explaining or accounting for learners and learning. These two perspectives form the basis for the nature versus nurture debate that is part of educational psychology. While noting that experience is significant and a consideration of biological factors is critical in understanding human beings and the learning process, they are not fundamental. The biblical understanding of the image of God notes that human beings are not simply the product of their environment (nurture), nor can they be understood simply in terms of biology (nature). Being in the image of God means that human beings are born with spiritual aspects to their personhood that must be considered in the learning process to engage in education biblically. That human beings were created to love and have fellowship with God, to live with and love others in a community relationship, and to serve as steward-regents of the creation (all of which are responsibilities of humanity even in a post-Fall world) are aspects of biblical personhood that must be taken into account when developing a biblical approach to education.

Second, the elevation of reason combined with the belief in the inevitably of human progress has led to a view of education and development that defines maturity in terms of growth from inferior to a superior. Of course, inferior and superior are value-laden terms that place an emphasis on what is considered important and, at the same time, discount that which is secondary or of minimal concern. The emphasis of contemporary education is the development of reason and the acquisition of academic content to fuel the engine of reason. While reason is not to be discounted, current educational practice mirrors an Aristotelian emphasis on reason and minimizes a biblical emphasis on the soul and the heart. It is no accident that the Bible consistently describes the heart, not the head, as the essence or center of the person. Brunner notes that "The human being who is most fully developed in mind and spirit, that is, a real *person*, will also be most full of soul. The soul can only become complete as 'heart,' that is, in the totality of personal being."[37]

For Christian educators the assumption seems to be, at least in terms of practice, that the development of heart is a byproduct of the Christian schooling experience rather than an aspect that needs to be actively cultivated. However, developing the spiritual nature of the individual can only be cultivated through discipline, and discipline must be an active and engaged process. Again noting Brunner:

> The spiritual value of our life is always reached through limitation. Thinking is limitation of the infinite possibilities of mere imagination; willing is limitation of the infinite possibilities of desire; artistic creation is a limitation of selection; it is the process of elimination. Spirit means discipline: logical discipline, aesthetic discipline, ethical discipline. The highest discipline is that of belonging to God. Here all self-will is taken away from man, and in this alone he becomes a truly spiritual, genuine personality. This is the kind of freedom which God gives to man; in this alone does he make him really human. *Deo servire libertas.*[38]

37. Brunner, *Man in Revolt*, 372.
38. Ibid., 267.

Spiritual education can never be achieved simply as a byproduct of an emphasis on the development of reason; it must be actively cultivated through the practice of reason and the arts and in the ethical use of knowledge. *Deo servire libertas*—in service to God there is liberty—means that there must be a trade-off, where some of the pursuit of reason and content must be sacrificed to provide for direct and focused discipline in such areas as the graphic and performance arts and the ethical use of knowledge and aesthetics in service to God through service to others.

Finally, an emphasis on reason places the educational focus almost exclusively on the individual, which accounts for why almost all undergraduate teacher education programs require a course in educational psychology rather than in sociology. The emphasis on the individual must be augmented with a stronger emphasis on a theological understanding of community, how being in the image of God means reflecting that image to others. Descartes's famous *cogito ergo sum* ("I think, therefore, I am"), where reason becomes the essence of being, is apostasy. Human self-consciousness is spiritual (theological) because human beings are spiritual. The "I" in which Descartes and other philosophers begin is like the "I" of God, an autonomous and independent entity (Exod 3:14). As a result, the emphasis on reason as the quintessential essence of humanity leads to self-deification.

This emphasis on reason at the expense of other aspects of humanity creates a divided personality, which severs our responsibility to serve others from love. Obligation and desire are placed in opposition to one another. This is not only seen in humanity's relationship to God, where human beings are no longer in proper relationship with him, but also in relationship to others. Love, no longer understood as a responsibility, becomes possessive. Individuals now seek to use others or things in ways that bring enjoyment to themselves. A biblical approach to education would seek to reunite reason with the other aspects of humanity that are theologically defined and, in the process, restore a biblical view of love that is expressed in obligation and service to others.

HOMO ECONOMUS

The modernist reduction of humanity as essentially biological conforms to its belief in a reality that is exclusively material. Such a reality leaves no room or credence for the spiritual. In a universe that is material, an emphasis on social factors such as community and relationships eventually gives way to the prominence of the individual and self-interest. The binding obligation of covenant in relationships succumbs to the personal interest of contract. Aristotle asked, "Do men live, *the* good, or what is good *for them*?"[39] In an impersonal universe, where the concept of a transcendent good is eliminated, individuals are left with only the option of pursuing what is believed to be good *for* them.

Living in a universe where the reality *of* life is understood in terms of the material results in a consistent vision *for* life that can only be understood from the material as well. In such a universe, many unbelievers still seek to maintain a romantic vision of the personal. For example, humanistic psychologists emphasize the need for self-actualization; yet, in a world that has been reduced to the material, where the spiritual is denied or relegated

39. Aristotle, *Nicomachean Ethics* 8.2, p. 194.

to an afterlife, the spiritual purposes of life are replaced by the material. Personal peace and material affluence become the dominant vision for what life should be. As a result, the pursuit and accumulation of wealth and the sense of identity and security that wealth can bring serve to define the quest for who people should be. Spiritual man gives way to material man; human beings are economic creatures who must be adapted to conform to a solely material world. Theologian Walter Wink notes, "Our economic system appears to be wholly secular, but it bears the marks of a priestly religion,"[40] to which Brian Walsh and J. Richard Middleton remark, "It is priestly because it mediates our worldly salvation, the good life of increasing material prosperity and well-being. This is the definitive modern version of the utopia which we are progressing, the promised land of wealth and economic security."[41]

"Worldly salvation" comes by conforming to the image of the savior. In an economic world, this demands the creation of *homo economus*—the economic man—that can function well in and serves the demands of the system. The properly conformed economic man performs two equally vital functions for the preservation and growth of an economic world. The first is that *homo economus* must be a consumer, made comfortable with answers to the worldview questions of "who we are" and "who we should be" that are given in terms of the things owned and the image these things allow individuals to portray. The chief tool of this socialization in contemporary society is advertising. Media critic Jean Kilbourne notes that

> Advertising sells products but it also sells a great deal more than that. It sells images, it sells concepts of love and sexuality, of romance, of success; and perhaps, above all, of normalcy. To a very great extent it tells us who we are and who we should be.... In addition to selling products advertising teaches all of us, above all, to be consumers. It teaches us that happiness can be bought. That there are instant solutions to life's complex problems; and that products can meet our deepest human needs.[42]

Historically, by the early twentieth century, the use of science and technology as tools of economic development led to a situation where the major concern for economic growth was not that not enough goods were produced, but that not enough goods were consumed. By the 1920s mass production technology, typified by Henry Ford's assembly line system for producing automobiles, had extended to a great many industries. Mass production made these industries more efficient and production less expensive, so mass production and the distribution of goods were viewed as necessary for economic survival. In 1924 department store magnate Edward Filene noted that "competition will compel us to 'Fordize' American business and industry."[43] Sociologist Stuart Ewen observed that a system of mass production created a problem for American business: "The mechanism of mass production could not function unless markets became more dynamic, growing horizontally (nationally), vertically (into social classes not previously among the consumers)

---

40. Wink, "Unmasking the Powers," 14.
41. Walsh, and Middleton, *Transforming Vision*, 139.
42. *The Ad and the Ego* [DVD].
43. Filene, cited in Ewen, *Captains of Consciousness*, 24.

and ideologically. Now men and women had to be habituated to respond to the demands of the productive machinery."[44]

The result of the increased capacity of industry to mass produce goods was that advertising moved from a means of informing people about the existence of goods and services to an industry dedicated to the manufacturing of consumers who would respond to the production needs of industry. As Ewen notes,

> The production line had insured the efficient creation of vast quantities of consumer goods; now ad men spoke of their product as "business insurance" for profitable and efficient distribution of these goods. While line management tended to the process of goods production, social management (advertisers) hoped to make the cultural milieu of capitalism as efficient as line management had made production. Their task was couched in terms of a secular religion for which the advertisers sought adherents. Calvin Coolidge applauded this new clericism, noted that "advertising ministers to the spiritual side of trade."[45]

In the documentary *The Ad and the Ego*, Kilbourne, Ewen, and sociologists Sut Jhally, Bernard McGrane, and Richard Polley observe that the effect of advertising cannot be understood in terms of a single ad at one time, but that advertising's power comes from creating a media environment that is pervasive and provides consistent messages in terms of who people should be. They note that the average American is exposed to over 1500 ads each day, with the effects being, in Kilbourn's words, "cumulative and unconscious."[46] Advertising creates a view of the world that is taken for granted as normal because consistent messages of who people are and who they should be are presented in multiple media all the time, creating an environment where alternative views of normalcy are silenced. Ewen challenges the viewer to ask questions regarding the impact of living in an advertising-infused environment in terms of how advertising shapes human understandings of the world, of power, and of the self.[47] Jhally notes that an advertising-infused world is not normal, that it is constructed, raising the question of who constructed it and for what purpose. Jhally concludes, "if you want to understand modern society, advertising is the best place to look."[48]

As a system of worldview education, advertising provides human beings with the means and standards to evaluate who they are and who they should be. Such an evaluation inevitably creates a tension or gap between the person's self-perception of who one is and the vision of who society says one should be. The modernist worldview, like all worldviews, must provide the means by which the individual and the society can decrease this gap. The message of advertising is that the conflict is resolved by placing self in competition with the constructed images of life that appear in the ads—the people, lifestyles, and standards of material normalcy presented. A subtext in all advertising is that people

---

44. Ewen, *Captains of Consciousness*, 24–25.

45. Ibid., 32–33.

46. *The Ad and the Ego* [DVD].

47. Ibid.

48. Ibid.

do not meet the standard of who they should be, and then it offers the world of material goods as the means of "salvation."

Bernard McGrane notes that advertising is the opposite of therapy, which is designed to create a sense of inner peace. Advertising is designed to generate an inner sense of conflict.[49] While McGrane does not advocate a biblical position in his critique of advertising, his assessment demonstrates the sin of idolatry, where human beings attempt to pursue spiritual peace in ways contrary to God's design. As a result of comparing self to the objectified visions of people portrayed in ads and striving to become like the people portrayed, human beings engage in the process of self-objectification. Such a process exacts a spiritual cost by replacing God's design for human fulfillment through worshipping him and service to others with the belief that humanity can only be achieved through the consumption of goods and services.

Walsh and Middleton call a belief in *economism* a "god of the age." It is an idol that provides the message "consume and see that this god is good."[50] Idolatry, as does all sin, dehumanizes human beings. Sin causes people to focus on the self: to define both God-given needs and self-generated desires in terms of what is pleasing to themselves and to pursue ways of meeting needs and desires in ways that are contrary to the will of God. As a system of idolatry, the dehumanizing effects of economism will be experienced by all who are influenced by the system, whether they are consciously engaged in it directly or not. As a vehicle of economism, the effects of advertising dehumanize to some degree all individuals who exist in that environment, attempting to create an understanding of the self and others that is contrary to the intended image of God in humanity. For example, advertising often uses a woman's body as an object for the selling of products. To promote consumption, advertising corrupts a God-created human desire (sex) and uses the female body to link that desire to a product. In this sense the technique is consistent with Pavlovian psychology, which seeks to create new reflex responses (in this case purchasing a product) from an existing one (in this case the desire to achieve sexual gratification).

Apart from the objectification and exploitation of women who model, however, the advertisement can have dehumanizing consequence for both the men and women who are subjected to it. For women, the use of models to exemplify a particular version of femininity creates a standard that permeates the culture and creates conditions under which young women must now define themselves as women based on this standard of physical perfection. A particular look is created, in terms of body image, hair style, complexion, wardrobe, and so forth, and women are expected to conform if they wish to be desired and accepted. As young women internalize this vision, as the predominant vision of femininity they are exposed to as they grow up in the culture, the process of comparing themselves to the vision often generates anxiety, self-criticism, and doubt. As a result, women are socialized to pursue a particular look through the consumption of various products and services and are made to feel like failures if they do not achieve it. Choosing to disengage from such a system is rarely an option for women because of the pervasive-

---

49. Ibid.

50. Walsh and Middleton, *Transforming Vision*, 138.

ness of this definition of femininity that dominates advertising and the culture. Women who attempt not to conform to this definition of femininity experience tremendous social consequences that increase the likelihood of conformity.

For men, the vision of physical perfection embodied in advertising provides the standard from which they also form their conceptions of femininity. As the standard, men now evaluate women as more or less feminine, better or worse, desirable or less so, on the basis of how well a woman conforms to this objectified standard. While women are made to feel less adequate if they do not conform to the standard, men are also made to feel less masculine if they do not have a relationship with a woman, or cannot attract a woman, who conforms to this standard. In either case, it is not the direct engagement of sin by the individual that creates the dehumanizing effect, but rather their immersion in a system that makes objectified or dehumanized versions of people the accepted or normal definition. Such a system of dehumanization can create attitudes and values that make an individual more likely to participate in direct sin (a criticism of contemporary culture that many evangelicals have made for years). To focus only on the sins in which people engage rather than the system that makes such sin more probable, however, is to be blind to the pervasiveness of sin and the deviation from God's definition of normal that saturates the culture.

The second demand that *homo economus* must fulfill in an economic world is that of producer. The effective "producer man" is both skillful and efficient, using his skills and time to their maximum economic potential. In classic economics, the factors of economic production, or those things necessary for economic activity, have long been identified as resources (land), investment capital, labor, and management skill or entrepreneurship. Historically, it was understood that if a nation wanted to stimulate economic development, it would need to increase or develop at least one (and optimally all) of these factors. Often development was understood in terms of increasing or getting more of a particular factor. Thus, nations would vie for more territory or access to natural resources or would invest in technologies to make their existing workforce more efficient. The rise of mercantilism in the eighteenth century and increased colonialism and imperialism in the nineteenth and twentieth centuries were attempts by nations (primarily the economically developed nations of Europe) to supply the home nation with sufficient quantities of resources, capital (usually gold or silver), and labor that could be used by entrepreneurs to stimulate economic growth and development in the home country.

With the decline of mercantilism, colonialism, and imperialism in the years following World War I, economists started to increase their interest in the factor of labor and its role in economic growth and development. Initially this interest focused on the increased use of technology as the means of making labor more efficient. After World War II and the devastation of Europe, many economists were less than optimistic about the time it would take for Europe to recover economically, noting that the rebuilding of the infrastructure and industrial capabilities of the affected nations would take time. The Marshall Plan instituted by President Harry Truman was an attempt by the United States to promote the development of these economies (particularly in West Germany) through the investment of capital. What amazed many economists was that within twenty years West Germany was not only able to restore its domestic economy, but its Gross Domestic Product had once again reached the point of competing internationally with the United States. In Japan, particularly during the years of the Korean War, the United States invested large amounts of capital with a similar effect: Japan's economy soon recovered to the point that it also became an international competitor with the United States.

The development of these economies was assisted by the United States' investment dollars, but the speed at which these nations recovered was generally unforeseen by economists. Economist Theodore Schultz argued that this underestimation of recovery was a failure by economists to realize the importance of the human factor in production. As Schultz wrote,

> The toll from the bombing was all too visible in the factories laid flat, the railroad yards, bridges, and harbors wrecked, and the cities in ruin. Structures, equipment, and inventories were all heaps of rubble. Not so visible, yet large, was the toll from wartime depletion of the physical plant that escaped destruction by bombs. Economists were called upon to assess the implications of these wartime losses for recovery. In retrospect, it is clear that [we] overestimated the prospective retarding effects of these losses. . . . We fell into this error, I am convinced, because we did not have a concept of *all* capital and, therefore, failed to take account of human capital and the important part that it plays on production in a modern economy.[51]

By the mid-1950s, economists began to consider the effects of human capital on economic production and the steps government and industry could take to increase it. Whereas (in the late eighteenth and nineteenth centuries) economists saw little economic utility for public investments in schooling, by the mid-twentieth century, human capital theorists saw government investment in schooling, as well as in public health and nutrition, as a means of increasing a nation's economic potential. Consequently, a nation's failure to invest in these would have serious economic consequences.[52] While the initial increase in federal involvement and funding for education during the Eisenhower administration was based on national security concerns, human capital theorists were instrumental in developing arguments in support of Lyndon Johnson's *War on Poverty* in the 1960s, which led to large increases in federal spending for education, health care, and compensatory programs through the Economic Opportunity Act of 1964 and the Elementary and Secondary Education Act of 1965.[53]

By the early 1980s, education and economic competitiveness had become inextricably linked. The Reagan administration, in its 1983 report *A Nation at Risk*, blamed the decline in American economic competitiveness (particularly with Japan and West Germany) on public education and declared that its remedy both educationally and economically was improving academic standards.[54] President George H. W. Bush's 1991 *Goals 2000* proposal and President Clinton's 1994 Educate American Act both linked United

---

51. Schultz, "Investment in Human Capital," 7.

52. DeYoung, *Economics and American Education*, 91.

53. Spring, *Sorting Machine*, 186–92.

54. Tyack, and Cuban, *Tinkering toward Utopia*, 34.

States' success in a global economy to the state of America's schools.[55] As a result, from the mid-1950s to the present, children increasingly have come to be viewed as a national economic resource.

Human capital theorists argued that increasing the public investment in education, so as to teach the technical skills and content needed for economic success, would enhance worker productivity. An increased emphasis on mathematics and science achievement, as well as on developing skills in the areas of computer literacy, would make American students more productive and competitive in a global economy. The increased academic standards promoted in the 2001 *No Child Left Behind* legislation and more recently President Obama's Race to the Top initiative demonstrate bipartisan agreement on the use of schools as the agents for providing the manpower needed to promote increased economic productivity. Since the mid-1950s, and increasingly since the 1980s, the structure of the curriculum and the means of teaching and assessment have been oriented to the development of human beings who are more economically productive.

A belief in schooling as a tool of economic development represents more a faith in economism as a utopian view of society than an economic reality. Critics of human capital theory note that increased academic standards and attainments do not necessarily improve worker productivity but do produce "educational inflation." Economist Thomas Green notes that the inflation of educational credentials has decreased the value of a high school diploma and a college degree to the point that a diploma (and increasingly a degree) no longer improves a person's economic position but must be attained merely to survive.[56] David Labaree notes that human capital theory has led to an educational system in which student focus on learning is minimized and the acquisition of the proper educational "credentials" (e.g., courses, degrees, or test scores) needed for social mobility becomes the focus.[57]

In addition, critics note that there is little correlation evidence to suggest that using schools as tools of economic productivity enhances national economic competitiveness. During the economic boom of the 1950s, many educational critics wrote of the deplorable state of public education. For example, the banner year in criticism (1953) saw the publication of titles such as *Educational Wastelands*, *Quackery in the Public Schools*, and *Let's Talk Sense about Our Schools*. Similarly, the economic boom of the late 1990s was also met with criticisms of schooling and called for curriculum reforms and accountability. In neither case were succeeding periods of economic prosperity experienced by the United States attributed to the success of American teachers or schools for providing trained labor.

Even so, the dogmatic conviction of a relationship between schooling and economic productivity becomes deaf to evidence to the contrary. For example, even as the Reagan administration was pointing to a decline in academic standards as the reason for a U.S. decline in global competitiveness, the *National Assessment of Educational Progress* (NAEP) demonstrated that instead of a decline, the years 1970–1980 actually revealed student achievement slowly rising. Historian Carl Kaestle observed that "Not only is it

55. Spring, *American Education*, 13.

56. DeYoung, *Economics and American Education*, 127–28.

57. Labaree, *How to Succeed in School without Really Learning*, 1–13.

not true that there has been a great decline [in student achievement] since that time, but it is also true that we are educating a much wider proportion of our population now than in the 1950s."[58]

As noted in chapter 4, the overall heath and robustness of a culture is dependent upon a shared vision of what constitutes the good life. This vision provides the vantage point from which members of the culture can determine where they are (both individually and as a society) and forms the basis for developing a means of arriving at where they believe they should be. In order to survive and thrive, the worldview must be sustained by and reinforced in the members of the culture, while new members must be socialized to accept the vision as the norm. The mechanisms of advertising and the use of education to create human capital, in large degree, are the means by which a society dedicated to a belief in economism sustains and propagates its vision.

Clearly, however, any worldview that departs from a biblical vision of life must attempt to normalize sin and the sin nature. This process of normalization brings with it dehumanizing consequences. Advertising produces effects that tend to objectify human beings and thus render them as less than what God intended. Education designed for the purpose of producing good workers must ultimately emphasize those traits and abilities viewed as having economic utility at the expense of other traits or abilities. As a result, mathematics and science take precedence over art and music in a curriculum that must reflect this priority. In a global, information- and service-based economy, instructional techniques that develop tolerance and cooperation must be pursued. While the material world and economics are important aspects of human life, to elevate economic activity to the aspiration and goal of human existence is to inevitably reduce humanity to the position of objects. Once reduced, humanity, like any object, is subject to manipulation by anyone who has the power and will to do so.

THE IMAGE OF GOD: PSYCHOLOGICAL AND SOCIOLOGICAL

The necessity of a normative vision, one that defines how the world should be, is essential to any worldview. Sinful humanity, rejecting its dependency on God, seeks to affirm its autonomy by constructing its own normative vision. That vision will not only define the ideal for the whole of society but for the individual as well. While the cultivation of the self can take many forms, historically, in the West, the primary means of accomplishing this goal has been through the development of autonomous reason. As a result, Western societies have generally placed primary emphasis on the individual. In the social sciences, one of the chief questions regarding the best approach to studying social phenomenon (i.e., the factors that contribute to individual and collective social behavior) involves the debate between individualists and holists. Individualists contend that social phenomena can best be understood as aggregates of individual interactions in society. This belief causes individualists to emphasize the study of the individual person, believing the proper understanding of the person will lead to a proper understanding of social occurrences. Social historian W. H. Dray notes that holists (or collectivists), contend that social

58. Quoted in Bernard and Mondale, *School*, 186.

phenomena can be studied as autonomous events, and that group interactions display characteristics unique from those displayed by a single individual.[59] While holists have made significant contributions to the understanding of humanity, Western societies have generally displayed a bias toward individualism.

This bias toward individualism and its emphasis on the individual as the basis for interpreting social phenomenon has influenced the perception of most Christians when asked to define the image of God. When most evangelicals consider how they are created in the image of God, they generally state those characteristics that are also a part of the personality of God. In essence, they tend to answer the question by noting, "I am like God because I possess _____." Frequently, the blank is filled by things such as intellect, reason, will, emotion, or love. When asked to define love, which is relational, many respond with something roughly akin to "God is love so we also can love." This ability to love, rather than actually engaging in loving relationships with others, is considered paramount; so when questioned regarding whether not loving actually denies the image of God in an individual, most believers find it difficult to answer.

While not to deny the validity of understanding the image of God in individual or psychological terms, the relational character of God that is instilled in humanity demands expanding the definition to include a more communal or sociological component. As a triune being, God is God in union with the other members of the Godhead. While each member of the Godhead may have distinctive roles (e.g., each member plays a different function in the process of salvation), yet in all areas—whether in God's creation of the universe by his Word and Spirit or the Spirit's making one a child of the Father and member of Christ's body—they act in concert. For human beings, as image-bearers of God, to fully comprehend their divine reflection, they must understand this relational characteristic.

The "fruits of the Spirit" identified in Galatians 5:22–23 are relational characteristics; they are dispositions exhibited in believers as they interact with God and others. God's created intent for human beings was that they would live in obligatory relations, where human beings would willingly seek the glory of both God and others over their own interests. With the Fall, this desire was reversed. Since the Fall, human beings seek autonomy from God to rule their own lives, while also seeking to impose their will on others for their own benefit. The fruits of the Spirit indicate the character of God in his relationship to humanity and reflect God's expectation for how redeemed people are to live and respond in their relationships with others. The "fruits" reveal not only the relational character of God but also God's intended design for true humanity—a state that all human beings enjoyed before the Fall. Thus, an individual not only possesses the *ability* to love, because God is love, but *must* love in order to be truly human. Not to love, while acknowledging that humanity has the potential, is ultimately dehumanizing, for failure to exhibit the relational characteristics of God to others is sin (cf. Jas 4:17).

The characteristics of the "fruits" are those of the Holy Spirit—the member of the Trinity who is content to bring glory to the other members without receiving glory in

---

59. Dray, "Holism and Individualism in History and Social Science," 53.

return. Christ's intent was to redeem human beings so that they could once again realize what had been lost, in essence stolen by Satan in the Garden—their true humanity (cf. John 10:10). As a result, the redeemed of God are able to experience the intended life of God, life more abundant. Christ exhibits this character in his divinity and his perfect humanity when he "lays down His life for the sheep" (John 10:11) so that human beings can experience God's intended glory for them. At the same time, in seeking the glory of humanity through his own sacrifice, Christ received glory (cf. John 17:4–5).

In contrast to living in obligation and service to others is a life of selfishness and self-glorification. This life is forbidden by God, as seen in the first two declarations of the law in the Ten Commandments. Exodus 20:3–6 says:

> You shall have no other gods before Me. You shall not make for yourself an idol, or any likeness of what is in heaven above or earth beneath or in the water under the earth. You shall not worship them or serve them; for I, the Lord your God, am a jealous God, visiting the iniquity of the fathers on the children, on the third and fourth generations of those who hate Me, but showing lovingkindness to thousands, to those who love Me and *keep My commandments*. (emphasis added)

In attempting to understand humanity's relationship to the image of God, a couple of points in the first two commandments are worth noting. First, the injunction to have no other gods is a return to the pre-Fall state when God was the focal point of human existence. Adam and Eve understood who they were, and they were to experience all they could be in fellowship and service to God as stewards, in seeking to know God and govern the creation for his glory. God understood that human beings, in their sin nature, would seek to supplant him with gods of their own devising. The fact that no other gods exist means that the worship of any other god would ultimately detract from what human beings were created to do—to have fellowship and render glory to the one true God.

Second, humanity was commanded not to make any carved or "graven" image of these gods. As expressions of these false gods, an image distracts from the true God. As an expression of the true God, any image is inherently limiting: an attempt to force God into a box of human devising. In this sense, an idol can also serve to impose a human definition on who God should be, which is also a manifestation of humanity's sinful desire to define absolutes of right and wrong—including who God should be. Finally, God ends this passage by stating that he shows lovingkindness to those who love him and keep his commandments. Before giving the rest of the Decalogue to Moses, God treats these first two commandments as a type of summary. From this point on, the majority of the books of Moses are an amplification of the Law. The keystone of the first two commandments resembles the summary of the Law given in Matthew 22:37–40, where Jesus notes that on loving God and others "depend the whole Law and the Prophets."

The question then is, how do the first two commandments of the Decalogue relate to Jesus's summation of the Law in Matthew 22? Jesus's command to love God with all of one's heart, soul, and mind (Luke 10:27 adds "strength" when recording this teaching) comes from Deuteronomy 6:5 and is part of Moses's review of the Law with the children of Israel before they entered the Promised Land. The relationship of Jesus's command to Moses's is easily made—to love God with all of one's being is the positive statement of

God's prohibition to place nothing before him. If individuals love God with every aspect of their being, they cannot have any other gods before the Lord. However, the relationship to the second commandment is more problematic—how is loving others as yourself (i.e., seeking the good of others like you now seek your own good) a positive reiteration of the second commandment? The answer may become clearer by first answering another question: can one violate the injunction regarding graven images without violating the commandment to have no other gods before the Lord? Normally, when considering the sin of idolatry, we focus on the creation of a false god of which people make a graven representation. In this situation, both the first commandment and the second commandment are violated. In addition, evangelicals commonly understand that anything that dominates a person's thoughts, motivations, or actions can represent a "false god" or idol, even if there is no graven representation of it. Thus, the love and pursuit of money constitutes idolatry, as would being consumed by success or status, the pursuit of pleasure, or any other goal of life that is not directed toward service to God. In these situations, the first commandment is violated while, technically, the second commandment is not.

The question, however, is can one violate the injunction against graven images without having another god? In Exodus 32:1–4 the Israelites demand that Aaron make them a god. After melting gold into the form of a golden calf, Aaron declares, "This is your god, O Israel, who brought you up from the land of Egypt." Aaron well understood that it was Jehovah God who had performed the miracles that led to Israel's freedom from Egyptian captivity, so his declaration of the golden calf as God can be seen as a violation of the second commandment while still maintaining that there is no other god but Jehovah. As stated before, God forbids the practice of making concrete representations of him, for such images are inherently limiting and display the sin nature's desire to control God by defining who he is to be. This explanation, however, still does not answer how the injunction against graven images is positively reiterated by Jesus in the command to love others. To answer this question, the prohibition against graven images must be considered in relation to the teaching that human beings are in the image of God.

As finite and cognitively limited beings, humans often need concrete representations of abstract concepts. This is certainly true of children, as any elementary teacher can easily attest, but it is also true of adults who lack a foundational understanding of a concept. Generally, a person's ability to understand an abstract concept is predicated upon having a concrete or real-world representation from which to relate. God as spirit, with spirit constituting an abstract concept, makes the understanding of God difficult for finite and cognitively limited humanity. Understanding humanity's limited ability to comprehend him, God graciously provides object lessons to human beings (a technique God used on other occasions, cf. Gen 2:18–24) in order to facilitate their understanding of him—those object lessons being his image-bearers, namely, each other.

While not denying that graven images allow human beings, in their sin nature, to impose a limiting definition on God (that which we define we also control), graven images also serve to alleviate human beings of their responsibility to live as the representation or image of God before others. Pre-Fall humanity was created to glorify God, and this is best accomplished in relationship to others. To love God with all of one's heart, soul, mind, and strength means also seeking the good of others as an expression of that love. In this way human beings can understand God through his reflection in others. When Jesus claims, "He who has seen Me has seen the Father" (John 14:9), he makes a statement that not only affirms his divinity but also his perfect humanity.

Without exhaustively developing the idea, Jesus often ascribes characteristics of himself to those who are redeemed. Jesus claims sonship with God (Mark 14:61–62) and calls his disciples "sons of God" (Matt 5:9). Paul also uses the principle of sonship to describe the believers' relationship to God (cf. Gal 3:26). Jesus claims to be the "light of the world" (John 8:12), a role that he also assigns to his followers (Matt 5:14). Paul claims that Jesus is the "image of the invisible God" (Col 3:15), just as Genesis claims all humanity is created in the image of God. In his infinite perfection and completeness, God does not require that his image-bearers reflect his likeness back to him; however, God does require human beings to reflect his likeness to those who require a reflection to comprehend him. Thus, human beings are obligated to God to demonstrate him before others. However, human beings, in their sinful condition, refuse to live in service obligation to God or others. As a result, sinful humanity makes graven images to alleviate their responsibility to live in such a way toward God that also obligates them to others. In essence, graven images allow sinful humanity to say, "Look at that image to understand God so you don't have to look at me."

For years psychologists have explained a child's development and understanding of God in anthropomorphic forms, ascribing to God the characteristics of either a parent or a superhuman in the sky.[60] Robert Coles notes that psychoanalytic psychologists have long tried to substantiate Freud's claim that "God really *is* the father,"[61] while Erik Erikson contended that a child's first experiences of helpless dependence on seemingly powerful and omnipotent parents predisposes the child to think about God in terms similar to the parents.[62] James Fowler, in his theory of faith development, claims that young children (ages 3–7) are intuitive-predictive, meaning they ascribe to the beliefs of their parents and then envision spiritual beings (like angels and God) from concrete representations (like parents or characters in stories).[63] Piaget proposed that a child's inability to think abstractly causes him or her to blend persona such as God with fantasies (e.g., Santa Claus) but also with concrete representations in the world (like parents or other adults).[64]

Similarly, the Bible notes a human need for a physical representation of God. Jesus came in human form so that humanity could behold the glory of the Father (John 1:14–15). Jesus introduces the ministry of the Holy Spirit to convict the world of sin and instruct the believer in righteousness by noting that he was returning to the Father so that the disciples would no longer be able see him (John 16:8–10). Jesus also notes that the ultimate apologetic of the reality of who he is would be that his disciples would demonstrate love one to another (John 13:35). While children—or adults—are not dependent solely

60. Richert and Barrett, "Do You See What I See?" 283.

61. Coles, *Spiritual Life of Children*, 340–41n.2.

62. Erikson, *Childhood and Society*, 250.

63. Fowler, *Stages of Faith*, 132–33.

64. Piaget, *Moral Judgment of the Child*, 56–58.

on human representation to be able to understand the person of God, such a witness is powerful in the development of a human understanding of who God is.

Biblically, human beings are not defined, nor can they experience the fullness of their humanity, through material attainments or by individual criterion that are generated from the self. Rather, human beings, while intrinsically valuable as image-bearers of God, experience this value in terms of their relationships. In Genesis 1 and 2, Adam and Eve experience perfect communion with God, themselves, each other, and the rest of the created order. This perfect communion is characterized by their living to glorify God by living in obligation for the glorification of each other. With the Fall, all of these relationships are severed, so that humanity now seeks to live in obligation to and for the glorification of self. With the Fall, sinful humanity denounces its obligations to God and to others and now seeks to serve its own desires. As a result, human beings are dehumanized, becoming less than God intended them to be, and are in need of restoration if they are once again to experience the abundant life God created and intended humanity to enjoy.

CHRISTIANITY: THE TRUE HUMANISM

The emphasis of this discussion is that Adam and Eve were never more human than when they were in the Garden before the Fall. The relationships they experienced—with God, each other, themselves, and the rest of the created order—reflected God's intent for them when he declared that everything he created was good. As a result, Adam and Eve, as image-bearers of the Creator, were able to experience the relational harmony that characterizes the Trinity. The relational harmony of the Creator is characterized by the Father glorifying the Son, the Son glorifying the Father, and the Holy Spirit's contentedness to glorify the other members of the Godhead without seeking his own glorification. Just as God experiences his ontological unity in relation to the other members of the Godhead, Adam and Eve experience their ontological or essential humanity in relationship to each other and to God. They were joined to each other, one flesh, both naked but not ashamed (Gen 2:24–25).

For this reason a proper understanding of the Trinity is critical for the development of a proper understanding of the image of God in humanity. The triune nature of God places an emphasis on his relational character. His unity is fundamentally tied to the kinship demonstrated by the three members of the Godhead. The image of God is not defined simply by those aspects of God that are shared by human beings individually, such as God having intellect, emotion, and will, but also, and more importantly, by his relational attributes. Theologically, when defining the nature and character of God, two sets of attributes are commonly identified. The noncommunicable attributes are those which God preserves exclusively for himself. These would include sovereignty as well as the attributes of omniscience, omnipotence, and omnipresence. In Scripture, whenever believers are commanded to demonstrate Christlike character, the expectation of God is not that individuals demonstrate these noncommunicable traits. Rather, Scripture commands believers to demonstrate the communicable attributes of God, such as those characterized as the "fruits of the Spirit" in Galatians 5:22–23. These "fruits" deal with aspects of humanity's relationship with God and with others; they are attributes of the believer that are identified or defined in comparison to Christ and empowered by the Holy Spirit. Thus, the development of God-esteem, or the cultivation of the image of God in individuals, must be tied to an understanding of the relational character of God.

With the Fall, their eyes were opened, the unity that they had experienced was broken so that they realized that they were naked and covered themselves (Gen 3:7). At the sound of God in the Garden, they hid from his presence (Gen 3:8). The subsequent narrative of Genesis 3 records that, as a result of the Fall, Adam and Eve were separated from all that they were previously created to experience and enjoy. As a result, Adam, and all of subsequent humanity, is dehumanized, becoming less than God had intended. While an affront to God, sin also has the effect of dehumanizing the person who engages in it. God, in creating humanity to enjoy fellowship with him, provided humanity with the greatest gift that he could give, namely himself, and supplied guidelines for how humanity can experience that gift. Sin steals the bliss that human beings were meant to enjoy, because it robs the very essence of their being. Sin objectifies the individual; as a result, the sinner now seeks to objectify others. Because of sin, sinners now think in dehumanizing ways, engaging in a process that further dehumanizes them even if their thoughts and motives are never acted upon. Lust makes a person guilty of adultery; anger and contempt for others bring the same condemnation as committing murder (Matt 5:21–28).

In supplying the moral Law, God provides humanity with parameters designed for human benefit. First, the Law demonstrates how human beings can experience all that God intended them to be. In addition, because sinful human beings cannot fulfill the requirements of the Law, the Law demonstrates their need of a Savior. Sinful individuals, in delusion, believe they experience life, yet the Law shows their true condition—spiritual death. The delusion of sin comes to light in the Law, showing the need to be restored or made "normal" again though Christ (cf. Rom 7:7–12; 8:1–3).

As a result of Christ's redemptive work, Christianity is the only true humanism, the only way human beings can experience all that they are capable of being. Through Christ there is no condemnation, and in Christ the process of reconciliation, the process of shalom, is pursued on humanity's behalf. Through Christ humanity is now reconciled to God, and progressively to others, to self, and to the natural creation. Through the indwelling power of the Holy Spirit, human beings are now able to once again experience what humanity was meant to be, to pursue a pre-Fall Adamic state, where they can once again live for the glory of God by pursuing the glory of others.

Relationally, believers become conduits of God's grace to others. God uses human beings as his ministers to demonstrate his grace, his mercy, and his presence in the world. In Christ the believer is justified, he is declared righteous and returned to positional innocence before God. At the same time, the life of discipleship is also a call to pursue righteousness, to pursue a life of consecration or sanctification, so that the believer can be a "living sacrifice," able to pursue the good and acceptable and perfect will of God (Rom 12:1–2). That perfect will consists of once again engaging in the practice of glorifying God through the glorification of others; as the apostle Paul writes, love "does not seek its own" (1 Cor 13:5). Sin tarnishes the image of God. In a sense, sin clogs the spiritual conduit so that the free flow of God's provision to others is restricted in the believer, since grace cannot freely flow through one committed to the glorification of self. In addition, sin can also pollute the expressions of grace that come from human beings one to another. Yet, since human beings are created for God, and empowered by the Holy Spirit to pursue the selfless glorification of others, ultimately acting as a conduit for the benefit of others serves to bring the greatest joy and benefit to the self. As John Piper writes, "The deepest and most enduring happiness is found in God. Not from God, but in God. The happiness we find in God reaches its consummation when it is shared with others in the manifold ways of love."[65]

IMPLICATIONS FOR A BIBLICALLY BASED EDUCATION

Previous chapters noted that a biblically based education would prepare students to fulfill the cultural mandate that God gave to Adam before the Fall and never revoked as a result of the sin. The cultural mandate was characterized as God's command to humanity to cultivate and keep, or to add value and do no harm. Human beings were to learn about the world in order to expand their understanding and create modes of expression that would serve as a means for the development of culture. Because of the Fall, the effects of sin now corrupt these cultural expressions so that God's original intent that human beings would serve as his steward-regents is now compromised. Humanity now serves the glorification of self rather than of God. Thus, a biblically based education in a post-Fall world is designed to prepare people to reengage the creation according to the intended principles of God. It is an education that equips young people to engage in the ministry of reconciliation so that they are once again prepared to act as the stewards God intended them to be.

With an understanding of the image of God, Christian educators can now understand the full purpose and intent of a biblically based education. While the process of education is often seen as a socializing or humanizing endeavor, only through a relationship with Christ can human beings experience all that they were intended to be, which is the ultimate goal of humanism. A biblically based education will prepare students to engage in the process of understanding and the development of culture for the reason that God intended—the glorification of God through service to others. In a world that experiences the dehumanizing effects of the Fall, a proper understanding of the image of God provides the foundation for developing a curriculum and instructional practices that not only allow for confronting the forces that seek to dehumanize the student but also provide the focus of reconciliation—the glorification of God through service to others. Once again, only in this process will students learn to experience all that God intends for them. As a result, a proper understanding of the image of God provides several principles that should inform the development and practice of a biblically based education.

First, a biblically based education will not succumb to the temptation—so prevalent in Western educational practice—to deify reason; but it will prepare students to use their minds to respond to the Word of God. The truly human person is one who responds to

---

65. Piper, *Desiring God*, 23.

God and to others in love. Humanity, like God, is spiritual. While reason is part of humanity's shared character with God, it is not the quintessential characteristic that defines humanity. A biblically based education restores knowledge and reason to their proper place, as *one* aspect of humanity but not *the* aspect of humanity. Knowledge and reason are to be cultivated, and are to be cultivated in a manner that promotes high standards and academic excellence, but they are to be understood as tools for service to others. Reason and knowledge are tempered by issues of the heart so that the arts and humanities are as critical to a biblically based education as are mathematics and the sciences. A curriculum that unduly emphasizes the development of reason at the expense of the heart needs to be evaluated in light of its ability to help students develop a proper biblical perspective on reason's sensitivity and subservience to the needs of others.

Second, a biblically based education is centered on the Word and the Word incarnate—Jesus Christ. An emphasis on the Scripture is necessary to avoid falling prey to the definitions of humanity that dominate the culture: definitions based in philosophy, psychology, biology, or economics. Humanity must be defined theologically, and when so defined, this definition should have ramifications for what is taught and how it is taught. Any other definition of humanity is, in the end, dehumanizing or reductive and, educationally, will cultivate a person ill prepared to assume the responsibilities and experience the joys that God intends for his children. The model of the well-educated student is Jesus Christ, who demonstrates the characteristics of perfect humility and submission to the will of the Father by giving himself for others. This characteristic is displayed by Christ not simply in his death but also throughout his life. He used his powers to heal the sick, restore the disabled, feed the hungry, comfort the distressed, and teach those in ignorance—all in a manner that pointed to their need and glorified the Father. The cultivation of a biblical worldview will produce a mind like Christ, who did nothing from selfish ambition or personal interest, but "although He existed in the form of God did not regard equality with God a thing to be grasped, but emptied Himself, taking the form of a bond-servant, and being made in the likeness of men" (Phil 2:2–7).

Next, such an education is progressive—it trains people to be life-learners who are both dependent on God and dependent on others whom he sends into their lives to help educate and edify them. While the concept of life-learning or training people to become lifelong learners is not a distinctively biblical idea (most philosophies of education embrace this as a goal), the biblical application of the principle is different from its secular counterparts. Secularly, the concept of lifelong learning, as an extension of the development of reason, is to produce people who can independently engage in their own learning. It is the development of the "renaissance person," a person of broad intellectual interests who is equipped to pursue those interests in a manner that brings personal satisfaction. Such a person may engage in learning with others, and even submit themselves to the teaching of others as necessary, but in the end, the secular concept of lifelong learning is inherently individualistic—the goal is personal development, economic flexibility, or personal satisfaction. Biblically, lifelong learning is others oriented. First, it acknowledges that, while human beings are well equipped by God to comprehend what is, they will remain in constant dependence and reliance on God to understand what should be.

To "hunger and thirst for righteousness" (Matt 5:6) is a state of constant hungering and thirsting, and only in this state does God promise to satisfy. Being "filled" with the Holy Spirit is a command to be constantly and continually filled, and the ability to serve God and live in proper relation to others is dependent on this persistent filling.

Educationally and practically, lifelong learning is manifest in two ways. It begins with an understanding that individuals have been empowered by God with gifts, talents, and abilities for the edification of others. Biblically motivated lifelong learners are those who place themselves in submission to the authority and teaching of those gifted by God to develop themselves for greater service. At times, this may result in the believer submitting to the authority of unbelievers. While this submission is never a relinquishing of God's moral authority in the life of the believer, God has graced unbelievers with talents and abilities that provide them opportunity to instruct believers in ways that prepare the believer for greater service to God and others. Further, a biblical perspective on lifelong learning understands that the talents, gifts, and abilities given to a believer are for the benefit of others. Thus, while all believers are to be in submission to those empowered to contribute to their edification, they also understand that they have the responsibility to contribute to the edification of others and that these two responsibilities may coexist. Thus, while learning, students can also be encouraged to teach—either peers or students younger than themselves—and in so doing demonstrate sensitivity to how the ones they teach contribute to their own edification. Teachers can model lifelong learning to students by engaging in joint enterprises or projects in which teachers demonstrate leadership but also submission when students possess greater skills or knowledge, allowing students to demonstrate leadership for a time.

Fourth, the student's relationship to God and others is the goal of education. The goal of most contemporary educational practice is to equip the student to pursue a life that is personally fulfilling, with personal fulfillment generally viewed as economic. Thus, an emphasis on the acquisition of knowledge and reason is not for their own sake but for their ability to enable individuals to attain those things they desire (e.g., wealth, power, status). This relationship of knowledge as a tool of acquisition is well understood by students, who often demonstrate no interest or desire to learn those things that are not on the test or have little utility in terms of passing a course or gaining the desired degree. In contrast, an education that promotes the development of the image of God is others oriented: the purpose of acquiring knowledge and skills is for the glory of God and the betterment of others. In addition, to be others oriented is not voluntary; it is an obligation and responsibility owed to others. To the secularist, education can empower students to pursue the betterment of others, if they so choose, understanding that this pursuit is ultimately defined by students as being in their best interest. To the biblicist, an education does obligate. To the person "who has been given much, much will be required; and to whom they entrusted much, of him they will ask all the more" (Luke 12:48). The biblicist understands when that the students pursue the interests of others, their own humanity is realized, and so an obligation to others *is* in the student's best interest.

In summary, an education that encourages the development of the image of God is one that encourages the exhibition of that image to others. Human beings *are* the image of God; they are not in preparation to be so. While the process of sanctification allows the believer to demonstrate a clearer reflection of that image than that of the carnal saint or the unbeliever, all human beings reflect God's image. While preparation is important, and while preparation for service cannot be discounted, to require that students simply prepare while providing them little opportunity to exercise their call as stewards and ministers of reconciliation is to risk rendering students docile and to promote intellectual and spiritual passivity. The call of the educated Christian is to servant leadership. It is a call to do the Word of God and not simply to know it. Like all active knowledge, it can only be learned through engagement and practice, through the process of apprenticeship. Jesus instructed the disciples, but then he sent them out to minister to the people and then to return to engage in further learning for further service (cf. Mark 6:7–13; Luke 9:1–10).

While restrictions and parameters may need to be placed on service so that the student learns all that is necessary to fully serve, to train a person to be a reflection of God and to acquire knowledge and skills for service but not provide for their practice is theological and educational malpractice. Theologically, it forestalls service and communicates the message that ministry and service are always in the future, not an expectation in the here and now. Educationally, since service is predicated on having sufficient knowledge, service can be forestalled indefinitely since there is always more to learn. Such practice not only violates Christ's example in the preparation of the disciples, but violates pedagogical principles for the training of apprentices, which focuses on the cyclical pattern of observing and learning from the master, practicing what has been learned, being critiqued by the master, which leads to further learning, observation, and practice. The apprenticeship model is the biblical model for lifelong learning, with Christ as the Master whom believers watch, from whom believers learn and practice, and by whom they are critiqued and instructed to a greater ability to serve.

Finally, a biblically based approach to education acknowledges that all education is apprenticeship education, that all education is driven by the goal of developing students who will be active agents or ambassadors of Christ in the culture. Individuals do not learn to acquire the ability to engage in stewardship, but to fulfill the biblical command to be stewards. Similarly, in a post-Fall world, the believer does not learn integration simply for the intellectual practice of aligning faith and learning, but for the practice of life, engaging the effects of sin and transforming the culture for Christ. The principles of stewardship and reconciliation are understood in light of service to others being valuable because those ministered to are in the image of God. Thus, community and the ethical use of knowledge are the goals of an education that is biblical. Ultimately, the biblical worldview is one that restores humanity to all that God intended, and the process of worldview transformation can only be engaged from an understanding of who human beings are and God's desire for who they should be. As image-bearers, created to glorify God through service to others, worldview transformation can only be accomplished through the students' learning to use knowledge for the benefit of others. To engage in the process of worldview transformation in any other way is to risk creating theology students but not disciples, people who know the Word but don't do the Word. In the end, despite what individuals may believe, such an education does not serve to glorify God.

SECTION THREE

Developing a Transformative Education Environment

8

Three Views of Christian Schooling

As Christian we are not only to know the right worldview . . . but consciously to act upon that worldview so as to influence society in all its parts and facets across the whole spectrum of life, as much as we can to the extent of our individual and collective ability.

—Francis A. Schaeffer, *How Should We Then Live?*

Several weeks have passed since the Mt. Carmel winter in-service sessions. Arnie continues to mull over the ideas about worldview learned in both the August and winter sessions. He finds himself slowly trying to incorporate the principles that Dr. Wise presented into the preparation and teaching of his courses. In his history classes, Arnie uses the concept of humanity's separation from others to explain conflicts between groups and nations. Often class discussions focus on power, the ways nations or groups of people use it and try to retain it, and on how those without power try to gain it. In his senior civics classes Arnie incorporates the principles of responsible stewardship, engaging his students in the consequences of sin, the practice of reconciliation, and the enhancement and development of the image of God in people as the means of evaluating government actions as biblically honoring and responsible. While realizing that he has a long way to go in fully understanding and implementing these ideas, Arnie believes that he is beginning to engage in the process of biblical integration in ways that are more meaningful for him and make greater sense to his students.

Still, there are facets of Dr. Wise's teaching from those in-service sessions that still trouble him. Ideas presented in August continue to occupy Arnie's thoughts. As a social studies teacher, Arnie is intrigued by the idea that worldviews always relate to culture and serve to explain and guide how individuals and societies act in the world. Arnie has always believed that it was part of his responsibility as a Christian school teacher to prepare his students to be able to evaluate culture from a Christian perspective. "If Wise is correct," Arnie reasons, "then simply preparing my students to *understand* the world biblically is not enough. They must also be able to *act* biblically in the world." This realization, however, has become problematic for Arnie, since he has come to realize that many groups of devout believers view culture and a biblical respond to it in fundamentally different ways. Arnie recalls the conversation between his friends Manfred Median and Barry Baroque back in October when they strongly disagreed about issues in the local election. Arnie sees how these two men, both keenly biblical thinkers, differ significantly in their responses to culture.

The issue is crystallized for Arnie one morning in early March. Sitting in the teachers' lounge before school, Arnie is writing college recommendation letters for students. It is a task that Arnie enjoys, giving him opportunity to reflect on how the Lord has worked in a student's life during his or her time at Mt. Carmel. He prepares to write a letter for Danielle Diligent, an outstanding student, who has expressed her desire to teach high school social studies. Arnie thinks back to previous conversations with Danielle, recalling her openness to being called to teach in either a Christian or public school. He is surprised to see Danielle's application to Keswick College, a Christian school with a fine reputation for preparing teachers, but a program that is not nationally or state accredited and does not lead to a state teaching license. She must have concluded that God wants her to teach in a Christian school, reasons Arnie, and begins to write the letter.

As he does, Arnie finds himself thinking back to his days as a student at Whitefield University, comparing its teacher education program to that of Reformation Christian College, where Dr. Wise teaches. As a student at Whitefield, Arnie received a strong biblically based, liberal arts education. His professors encouraged, and often required, that he demonstrate the ability to integrate his understanding of history with biblical principles. Since becoming a teacher, he has had the opportunity to have several student teachers from Reformation Christian College. He has always been impressed with their preparation—knowledge of their content areas, understanding of the Bible, and use of various methods of teaching. While Arnie holds all three institutions in high regard, it strikes him as unusual that both Whitefield and Reformation have programs that are state or nationally accredited and lead to a state teaching license, while Keswick does not.

As Arnie finishes Danielle's letter and mulls over the differences between the three colleges, he is joined by his friends Manfred and Barry. Each pours himself a cup of coffee and makes his way over to the table where Arnie is sitting. Manfred picks up the letter Arnie has just finished for Danielle and begins to read it.

"Danielle is certainly a good student and a fine young woman," comments Manfred. "She will make a fine teacher. I am also glad to see that she is going to Keswick—my alma mater I might add," he states proudly.

"Keswick," says Barry in mock surprise and chiding Manfred. "Does anyone from Mt. Carmel still go there? I would think between all of their rules and Manfred's reputation that our students wouldn't even consider Keswick."

"Keswick is a great school," admits Arnie, "and I am glad to see that Danielle has chosen to go to a Christian university for teacher preparation. I was sitting here thinking about just that. At one point Danielle mentioned to me that she might be interested in teaching in a public school, and yet Keswick's program does not lead to a state teaching license. Maybe she has discerned that God is calling her to Christian schooling. I went to Whitefield, and we have several teachers and student teachers from Reformation

Christian. Many of them teach in Christian schools, but their programs also lead to state certification. I was just wondering why Keswick's program does not."

Manfred comes to the defense of his alma mater. "Keswick is a great school. Sure they have a lot of rules, but the rules are designed to help students learn the importance of developing a disciplined Christian life. A Keswick education provides a person with a strong sense of God holiness and the importance of personal piety. Personally, I experienced tremendous growth in my faith and developed a strong commitment to ministry while there. To answer your question Arnie," Manfred continues, "Keswick does not offer a state-approved teacher education program by design. Keswick is committed to Christian schooling and wants to prepare teachers to be leaders in the Christian school movement. If you believe that a Christian school is the best place for a young person to be educated, why prepare teachers for an inferior environment, especially one that is hostile to our biblical values? I recall several of my professors noting that seeking state approval would mean that the Keswick program would be required to conform to requirements that would compromise their biblical standards. So, Keswick's position is one of conviction."

"The idea of institutional conviction makes sense," says Arnie. "I just think it is interesting that when I attended Whitefield, there was a strong desire to ensure that students had the option of teaching in Christian or public schools. Reformation Christian's students seem to indicate the same thing. At both schools the emphasis is on the student's personal conviction and preparing young people to pursue God's calling to them in either public or Christian schools."

"I went to Woolman College," chimes in Barry, "which has a fine liberal arts tradition. I really believe I received a strong, biblically centered education while I was there. What I find interesting, in light of this conversation, is that my professors at Woolman rarely encouraged us to consider teaching in a Christian school. It was not that they were anti–Christian schooling; rather, the message was that Christian teachers were needed in the public schools to work toward their transformation. Like Manfred's experience at Keswick, at Woolman we were strongly encouraged to develop our faith, but the message was that faith always had social consequences."

As Barry finishes his statement the early bell rings signaling the beginning of the school day. All three men get up, wishing each other a good day, and head to their respective classrooms. As Arnie walks to class, he finds himself thinking. He and his friends all received, in his opinion, fine educations from three strong Christian institutions of higher education. All three schools are academically solid and biblically committed. The doctrinal statements of all three schools uphold the fundamental tenets of evangelical Christianity. He could agree to any of the three in good conscience and with conviction. Yet, in considering the three schools, Arnie notes certain differences that have a tremendous impact on institutional emphasis and practice. Arnie finds himself considering Dr. Wise's observations from earlier in the year—that worldviews always deal with culture and that a number of philosophies can come from the same worldview. These schools certainly respond to culture differently, thinks Arnie. But how can they hold such differences in their response to cultural issues while having almost identical doctrinal statements? Do these represent differing worldviews? This seems unlikely to Arnie, but possible. Or, he continues, are these different philosophies or ideologies that lead to different cultural responses?

As he considers these questions, Arnie begins to think about the educational conse-quences of the three positions. Would the curriculum of a school change depending on which philosophy was implemented? What might be the ramifications for instructional methods or desired learning outcomes? Would each view lead to a different definition of a well-educated student? The social studies teacher in Arnie begins to wonder whether each may have certain advantages and disadvantages. There must be some trade-offs, he reasons. What does each approach gain as a benefit, and give up as part of its approach?

VARIETIES OF THE BIBLICAL WORLDVIEW

As previously stated, there are fundamental differences between worldviews and philoso-phies. Worldviews are psychic-founded and, consequently, as members of a group are socialized into the culture they develop perceptual frameworks or ways of understanding that are similar to other members of the culture. More importantly, the process of world-view development means that members of a culture develop a normative vision, a vision for life, similar to other members of the culture. The use of the lens analogy by many worldview thinkers underscores the perception-based idea of worldview. Consequently, changing a worldview requires a new vision, a new way of comprehending the world, that calls into question the values of the dominant culture.

Philosophies, on the other hand, are more individual understandings of the world that are both analytically founded and analytically qualified. That is, a well-developed philosophy should be based in reason, and a better philosophy is one that is considered more logical or rational. While there is a connection between how one thinks about life and how one should act, the relationship of philosophy to behavior is more tenuous. For example a single person can hold a "philosophy" of marriage (and even give counseling from that perspective) while never having to live that philosophy on a daily basis.

The bridge between worldviews and philosophies are world conceptualizations. These consist of the normative mythos or cultural vision and the ideologies that seek to implement the vision into daily life. Unlike philosophies, which often require a greater level of rational sophistication to develop and defend, ideologies allow the members of a group to align themselves, by faith, to certain philosophies that are advocated by the proponents of the ideology. In this sense world conceptualizations are faith-founded—based on a vision that allows its adherents to make sense of what *is* from the conceptual reference to what *should be*. In this way world conceptualization in general and ideologies in particular are more conscious articulations of the worldview. Just as a worldview can give rise to many distinct philosophies, a number of different ideologies can manifest themselves from the same worldview.

The bridge effect of ideologies between worldview and philosophies works in both directions. Like worldviews, ideologies generally are more holistic and applicable to how people live in the world than philosophies. In that sense, ideologies have a cultural re-sponse component that informs its adherents' interpretations and responses to the world. The vision of the world articulated by an ideology is faith-founded and taken to be true even if the individual adherent of the ideology cannot articulate a reasonable or logically coherent defense. Also, ideologies tend to be more communal than philosophies. The adherents of an ideology tend to identify themselves with a particular group, and some part of their definition of self is tied to this communal identification. That identification may be all encompassing (as we generally consider it to be if one claims to be a Christian or a Muslim) or more specific (as when a person claims a particular political affiliation).

Ideologies, however, like philosophies are analytically qualified. While people tend to identify with an ideology (or ideological community) on faith, that faith is predicated in the belief that the ideology is rational and coherent, even if they are not particularly able to articulate and defend all aspects of the ideology. Because belief in the ideology is based on its reasonableness, however, individuals may be willing to change their ideological orientation when confronted by arguments that appear more convincing than those of their initial ideology. Oftentimes this change requires individuals to separate from their identification with one group and align themselves with members of another group. For this reason people claim to be Republicans or Methodists but could change their ideological affiliation to Democrat or Baptist. While these changes are individual, they are not the type of analytically founded changes of philosophers; rather, they are identifications with a new community or group. Thus, a change in ideology requires the individual to place one's faith in the validity of another set of arguments (taken on faith) believing that those arguments constitute a better or more coherent explanation for the world.

Similar to philosophies, ideologies also are less holistic then a worldview. Several ideologies can come from the same normative vision of the worldview. For example, Americans often speak of the "American Dream," and this concept influences much of the thinking and social purpose of both individuals and the society. This vision can encourage the development of such character traits as independence, autonomy, self-sufficiency, fairness, equality, empathy, and compassion. The mythos can produce characteristics that may, in practice, seem contradictory. Thus, some members of the culture will align themselves with an ideology that tends to emphasize certain attributes (e.g., independence, autonomy, and self-reliance) while others will align themselves with a competing ideology (one that may emphasize fairness, equality, empathy, and compassion). While each group will claim that it values all the traits of the worldview vision, human finiteness leads one group to place greater priority on one set of traits while minimizing the other set. As a result, members of one group may charge that the other group, for example, lacks empathy (a charge denied by members of the accused group), while the accused group may counter that the members of the first group encourage dependency (because they do not appear to emphasize self-reliance), a charge the second group will deny. What results are different ideological groups accentuating certain aspects of the worldview while minimizing others. Since worldviews always lead to behavioral actions, these differences can result in members of differing ideological groups understanding and responding to culture in ways that may appear competing, while still maintaining that they are advocates of a particular worldview.

Proponents of the biblical worldview are not immune from the conflict of competing ideologies. A biblical worldview is holistic and provides a comprehensive set of principles regarding how the world is and how it should be. It leads to a type of mythos that will encourage the development of character and behavioral traits that, while not contradictory, can be difficult for finite individuals or groups to harmonize. As a result, different ideological types develop as adherents of the biblical worldview; one group will emphasize one set of character and behavioral traits, while another group will congregate around others. Since these variations lead to particular cultural responses, there can be within the biblical worldview a number of different responses to culture, which the adherents of that ideological group claim to be *the* biblical response to culture, with adherents of another biblical ideology making a similar claim.

To this point the discussion of the biblical worldview has focused on a singular notion—that is, *the* biblical worldview. While holistic and comprehensive, when entrusted to finite individuals, a worldview is subject to this ideological splintering effect even when the effects of the sin nature or theological error are not considered. That is, devout people acting in good faith can develop various responses to culture and still be adherents of the biblical worldview. Even the most cursory study of those who claim to be evangelicals will reveal differences in their views and responses to culture. These variations can create dramatic differences in how members of a group view the issue of worldview change, the purpose and practice of Christian schooling, and the Christian school's approach to worldview transformation.

The variety of Christian responses to culture is the focus of the 1951 book by H. Richard Niebuhr entitled *Christ and Culture*. Niebuhr's book examines, both in historical and contemporary terms, the responses of varied Christian groups to the demands of living in the world as followers of Christ. Niebuhr proposed that these responses can range from those who seek to emphasize opposition between Christ and culture to those who see a fundamental agreement between Christ and culture.[1] Between these extremes lie a number of varying responses to culture. Niebuhr contends that these responses can be identified as five types that share certain characteristics. While a full explanation of all Niebuhr's types are outside the scope of this discussion (e.g., Niebuhr identifies types that correspond more closely with the theological positions of Roman Catholicism, Eastern Orthodoxy, and theologically liberal Protestant traditions), three of his types correspond to what can be considered evangelical responses to culture. This chapter will focus on these three types. Also, Niebuhr is quick to note that no type is exhaustive or emphasizes all aspects of the Christian message equally. As Niebuhr writes, "Christ as the living Lord is answering the question [of Christianity and civilization] in the totality of history and life in a fashion which transcends the wisdom of all his interpreters yet employs their partial insights and necessary conflicts."[2] As a result, Niebuhr avoids making any claim to the superiority of one type over the others, noting that "the giving of such an answer by any finite mind, to which any measure of limited and little faith has been granted, would be an act of usurpation of the Lordship of Christ which at the same time would involve doing violence to the liberty of Christian men and to the unconcluded history of the church in culture."[3]

---

1. Niebuhr, *Christ and Culture*, 40–41.
2. Ibid., 2.
3. Ibid., 232.

Christ against Culture (Type I)

From the perspective of *Christ against Culture*, Christ is the sole authority over the Christian and not simply the highest of all authorities. Consequently, the call to follow Christ is a call to reject any allegiance or loyalty to culture. It is a radical response, encompassing an all-or-nothing choice, where "if anyone loves the world, the love of the Father is not in him" (1 John 2:15b). Salvation and sanctification require a retreat, as much as possible, from culture, and this retreat includes separation from the influences of art, music, and other aspects of popular culture, as well as from certain academic disciplines (e.g., psychology, sociology, and worldly philosophy). This separation may also include distance from areas such as politics or military service. The language of the Type I position often speaks of following Christ at all costs, forsaking the world, renouncing earthly pleasures and influences. It is a language that encourages the believer to take up one's cross and count all other things as loss for the sake of Christ.

The adherent to the Christ against culture ideology maintains that Satan is the "prince of the power of the air" (Eph 2:2), the ruler of this world until Christ returns to dethrone him. Allowing the influence and authority of Satan in one's life, through living according to the dictates of culture, is to submit to him as authority. Since culture is polluted by the influence of Satan, the more individuals live congruently with the culture, the more they are subjected to the corrupting influences of the world. Formerly "children of darkness," believers are commanded to walk as "children of Light" (Eph 5:8). Believers are not to participate in "the unfruitful deeds of darkness, but instead even expose them" (Eph 5:11), where "exposing" is to live in radical separation from them. Type I proponents maintain that the Christian life is a call to holiness, to be perfect as the heavenly Father is perfect (cf. Matt 5:48; 1 Pet 1:16). Culture is invariably and antagonistically anti-Christian, and the influence of culture is seductive, so that only through radical separation from the culture can the disciple hope to develop this holiness. The call to holiness, however, is not simply a call to personal piety but also a call that involves engaging in the communal life of the church. As a result, the proper response to culture is to separate from it in favor of aligning with other members of a consecrated community.

The result, as a cultural response, is an attempt to separate from the world and its influences in favor of adherence to social groups and institutions that reflect a similar commitment to holiness. The desire to remain separate from the world combined with the communal nature of humanity leads to the creation of Christian communities—institutions inhabited by Christians and for Christian—that serve to buffer the disciple from the negative influences of the world. These communities, ideally, are extensions of the church and can include institutions such as Christian schools, Christian service and social agencies, and Christian retirement communities. As a cultural response, it can also include the development of genres of music or art that focus exclusively on "Christian" themes (i.e., themes that deal almost exclusively with the believer's relationship to God). The development of these distinctive Christian genres reflect the Type I belief that music and art have been corrupted by the world and must be returned to a spiritual/moral base. The Type I response to culture can also include the development of Christian social or business networks through which believers identify and seek to socialize or do business with others of like faith and practice.

The Christ against culture position can be identified by the phrase "separation for holiness." It is an ideology dedicated to the development of holiness or personal piety as the ultimate goal of the Christian life. As Richard Foster characterizes the holiness tradition, it is "an ever deeper formation of the inner personality so as to reflect the glory and goodness of God."[4] Each individual believer is part of the committed "bride of Christ" who is commanded to be faithful and to ready herself for Christ the bridegroom (cf. 2 Cor 11:2; Rev 19:7). This desire to be found faithful, combined with a strong emphasis on the church as the bride of Christ, leads to an emphasis on a church that lives distinctively and separate from the world. It also leads to a strong sense of community, in which the other members of the church help to train, provide examples, and reinforce the rules of behavior, so that individual believers can fulfill their personal commitment to the purity of the church as a whole.

While the emphasis on rules and behavior may be viewed negatively by those outside of the tradition, the Type I adherent understands that separation to God and from the world calls for behaviors that reflect the desire to cultivate a purity of heart. For the mature believer, virtuous living is the behavioral extension that reflects the transformed character of the heart. Character as reflected by godly behavior, however, must be developed. Thus, a lifestyle that is disciplined and structured behaviorally is designed to cultivate maturity in the believer. It is the process of crucifying the sin nature (Rom 6:6) so that the nature of Christ can rule in the life of the believer. Even Paul acknowledged that spiritual maturity is an arduous process involving a struggle in living for Christ (Rom 7:15–25), so the Type I adherent understands that a disciplined lifestyle provides the parameters for living in a way that is glorifying to Christ and ultimately contributes to the believer's edification and sanctification. In essence, disciplined behavior changes the heart so that it ultimately can become a reflection of the heart.

This relationship of behavior to character leads to what Foster describes as a "tough-minded, down-to-earth, practical understanding"[5] of growing in the grace and knowledge of Christ (2 Pet 3:18). The Bible is viewed as the *sole* authority for faith and practice, so that knowledge and memorization of Scripture is emphasized as a means to help cultivate the spiritual person and avoid sin (cf. Ps 119:11). The body, mind, and spirit are trained through the spiritual disciplines of prayer, Bible reading and study, meditation on the Word, as well as private and corporate worship. These activities are designed to allow believers to present themselves as a "living sacrifice" before God (Rom 12:1). This disciplined lifestyle lends itself well to military analogies for the Christian life, with the mission of bringing more people into the kingdom of heaven, thus creating a strong evangelistic emphasis among Type I adherents.

As with all ideological manifestations of a worldview, since they are incomplete because of human finiteness, certain shortcomings or weaknesses may also become ap-

---

4. Foster, *Streams of Living Water*, 85.

5. Ibid., 88.

parent. The strengths of the Type I position can lead to potential dangers in practice. The first of these dangers is that the either-or, Christ or the world, orientation can lead to a congregation of believers that develops a passive or hostile isolation from the general community it seeks to evangelize. Isolationism is often perceived by the general community and places the congregation in juxtaposition to the people whom it seeks to evangelize. Consequently, although there is a strong desire by the church to evangelize the community, its isolation from the community limits its contacts. Thus, Type I churches have historically resorted to evangelistic techniques such as evangelistic crusades, "cold call" evangelism (e.g., tract ministries, door-to-door evangelism), or electronic media.

Another danger lies in the combination of the staunch separation of local congregations and its emphasis on certain spiritual disciplines and behavioral conformity to develop the Christian life with the need for all ideologies to have strong defenders of faith (i.e., people who serve as "philosophers" for the position). These factors can lead to two phenomena. The first is a congregation that expects a high level of behavioral conformity by its members. In essence, to be accepted as part of the faith community, the individual must conform to the behavioral standards of the congregation. This is particularly true when the behaviors of the individual are seen as worldly compared to the standards of the congregation, which are viewed as godly. This may lead to the second phenomenon, the rise of strong pastor-leaders who are able to articulate and command behavioral conformity to the standards of the congregation. Often these behavioral standards are defined by the pastor-leader, who serves to develop the analytical base and defend the ideological position of the congregation.

Finally, Foster notes that the holiness tradition, which corresponds closely to the cultural position of the Christ against culture ideology, is subject to three "pitfalls." The first is a tendency to degenerate into legalism, where the "center of attention is turned away from the heart and onto externals of one sort or another."[6] In essence, the behavioral standards of the congregation are no longer evidence *of* Christian character but *are* Christian character. This subtlety can lead to the second pitfall: viewing the performance of certain behaviors as earning merit or standing before God. That is, living in conformity to the rules of the congregation grants the individual a sense of special favor or psychological satisfaction that may not be based on the work of the Holy Spirit. The third potential pitfall is "perfectionism," a belief that if the behavior standards are maintained, then it is the believer who attained them.[7] This belief undermines the sufficiency in Christ and dependency on the Holy Spirit for development of the Christian life. The inevitable corollary is that failure to conform to the behavioral standards of the congregation indicates a lack of discipline and failure to develop Christian character; thus, the individual believes he must now work harder (e.g., read the Bible or pray more) in order to conform to what is defined as the normal Christian life.

The Type I emphasis on holiness and personal piety align with the teaching of Scripture and are proper extensions of the biblical worldview, providing its adherents

6. Ibid., 91.
7. Ibid., 93.

both a vision and means of preparation for interpreting and acting in the world. As a finite manifestation of the biblical worldview, however, the Christ against culture ideology is susceptible to two criticisms. First, the approach is guilty of a limited, and arguably naive, view of culture. The Type I response views culture as something from which a person or congregation can separate. It views culture as something "out there" when compared to the practices of the church, which are "in here." While certain aspects of culture can be renounced, for example, music and art, aspects of commercial culture, and even certain institutions, these practices make the Type I response subcultural rather than acultural. Since culture permeates one's language and ways of thinking, it penetrates the church from within, as much as its adherents try to insulate themselves from those effects from without. Seeing culture as only negative and separable from the experience of the individual, the Type I response fails to account for how worldviews, and the ideologies that stem from them, are psychic or perceptually founded. They do not consider that isolation from certain aspects of the culture does not remove the person from the aspects of culture that were part of their initial orientation to the world and that continue to affect their descriptive and normative conceptualizations of the world.

Second, while the Christ against culture ideology responds well to the separation of humanity from God that results from the Fall, it minimizes or ignores the responsibility of believers individually and the church corporately to respond to the Fall's horizontal effects. Niebuhr is critical of the Type I response on this account, noting a tendency to divide the world into material and spiritual dimensions.[8] Ultimately, in order to be consistent in their position, the logic of the Type I response requires a Christ who himself is separate from culture. Such a position denies the incarnate humanity of Christ, who lived culturally as a Jew and who condemned spiritual separatism in the parable of the Good Samaritan (cf. Luke 10:25–37). As a human being Christ sought to live not only spiritually in a proper relationship with the Father but also culturally in proper relationship with the world around him, and he instructed his disciples to do the same as a dimension of their spirituality (Matt 25:34–40).

Christ and Culture in Paradox (Type IV)

For many Christians, attempting to disengage from culture is not only practically impossible, but also theologically shortsighted. To some, the position of the Christ against culture response—that all of culture is corrupt, negative, and in opposition to God—is to deny the blessings of a creation that God declared to be "very good" (Gen 1:31). While the effects of sin are total, so that everything in the world has been affected by sin, this does not negate the fact that God made the world to be enjoyed (Ps 104:14–15). As a result of sin, though, there is a tendency on the part of humanity to abuse the good gifts of God. For this reason Paul tells the Corinthian believers that "all things are lawful for me, but not all things are profitable. All things are lawful to me, but I will not be mastered by anything" (1 Cor 6:12).

---

8. Niebuhr, *Christ and Culture*, 81.

Theologian Greg Johnson notes that, for Paul, to enjoy the creation while not misusing or abusing its pleasures was to engage in "godly joy."[9] Similarly, Jesus enjoyed the creation to the point that his critics accused him of being a drunk and a glutton (Matt 11:19). Even in a fallen world, God's goodness and gracious character are extended to all humanity and human beings, through the creativity and ingenuity provided to them by God, can create to enhance the pleasure of creation and minimize the pain of living in a fallen world. For the believer to utilize and enjoy these creations is neither sinful nor to be avoided, as long as those things do not detract from giving glory to God or retard the development of godly character.

This approach to culture encapsulates Niebuhr's second evangelical position, labeled *Christ and Culture in Paradox* (Type IV). To the proponent of Type IV, the world and its cultures are radically corrupted by the effects of sin and the Fall, so that the depravity of humanity affects all aspects of culture. Despite the totality of sin's effects, however, humanity and culture have not been abandoned by God. Institutions have been ordained and established on earth to restrain the encroachment of evil and to allow individuals to pursue righteousness without being besieged by the fallen tendencies of sinful humanity. The sin of humanity is countered by the grace of God; a grace that not only deals with humanity's spiritual condition but also regulates the temporal life. The sinful tendency of humanity is the glorification of self, so Niebuhr notes that even the ordained authority of God is used as an instrument of sin, "yet as coming from God and heard from His lips it is a means of grace."[10] As ordained by God, earthly authorities are to be obeyed. As established by God, they are to be recognized as having his authority, and to oppose them is to oppose God himself (Rom 13:2). The recognition of sinful humanity graciously empowered by God to preserve order and prevent chaos leads the believer to the inevitable conclusion that both Christ and temporal authorities are to be recognized and obeyed, while acknowledging that, because of sin, those authorities may become contradictory or opposite each other. As Niebuhr writes,

> In these the duality and inescapable authority of both Christ and culture are recognized, but the opposition between them is also accepted. To those who answer the question in this way it appears that Christians throughout life are subject to the tension that accompanies obedience to two authorities who do not agree yet must both be obeyed. . . . God requires obedience to the institutions of society and loyalty to its members as well as obedience to a Christ who sits in judgment on that society. Hence man is seen as subject to two moralities, and as a citizen of two worlds that are not only discontinuous with each other but largely opposed. In the *polarity* and *tension* of Christ and culture life must be lived precariously and sinfully in the hope of a justification which lies beyond history.[11]

As a result of the tension created by the competing authorities of Christ and culture, there is a tendency on the part of the believer to create a dualism between the claims of Christ and the legitimate authority of the world, authorities that cannot be reconciled into

9. Johnson, *The World according to God*, 90.

10. Niebuhr, *Christ and Culture*, 157.

11. Ibid., 42–43.

any lasting synthesis. These competing claims create a tightrope for the believer to walk—obeying the claims of the world where legitimate and disavowing the claims of temporal authorities when they attempt to supersede the authority of Christ. Where the ordained institutions of the world make legitimate demands on believers that are not opposed to the revealed commands of God, these demands are to be obeyed. For example, both Jesus and Paul imply that the state has the authority to institute and collect taxes, and command believers to be faithful in the paying of their taxes (cf. Matt 17:24–27, Rom 13:7);.

However, the authority of Christ always supplants the claims of the world. If the government were to require or endorse practices contrary to the revealed will of God, it becomes the responsibility of each believer to oppose and work to change those unbiblical decrees. As a result, in reference to the theology of Paul, Niebuhr notes, "political authorities were recognized as divinely instituted, and obedience to their laws was required as a Christian duty; yet believers were not to make use of the law courts in pressing claims against each other. Economic institutions, including slavery, were regarded with indifference or taken for granted. Only religious institutions and customs of non-Christians were completely rejected."[12] The difficulty for the believer is that one must constantly evaluate the claims of the world against the claims of the superior authority of Christ, or as Peter notes, "we must obey God rather than men" (Acts 5:29).

This tension between Christ and culture is negotiated by Type IV advocates through the emphasis and development of three vital concepts: discernment, grace, and integration. First, the mature saint is one who has cultivated a sense of *discernment*, the ability to comprehend the competing claims of both authorities and recognize when God is calling the believer to live within the boundaries of culture or to oppose those boundaries as contrary to the commands of God. Discernment provides the believer the ability to understand, like Paul, which things are lawful but not profitable (1 Cor 10:23) and to act in culture accordingly. As a result, discernment precedes engagement with culture; the Christian must first ascertain whether a particular aspect of culture is biblically permissible and can be enjoyed or whether it must be rejected as being in opposition to the will of God.

Discernment, as a hallmark of the mature believer, produces two characteristics of Type IV evangelicalism. One is a pragmatic view of culture. Since discernment precedes engagement, the Christian response to culture is primarily reactive; one must first discern that which is and then determine whether it is appropriate for engagement by believer. This evaluation is usually conducted using the standard of whether the practice is sinful and, if not, whether engaging in the practice aids or hinders the spiritual development of the believer or other believers. For example, a book or film may not be freely enjoyed until a believer determines that it does not contain sin or cause the believer to be hindered spiritually. Anecdotally, some believers report experiencing guilt over finding themselves enjoying a book or film before a proper discernment or evaluation of its spiritual worth has been determined. As a result, art and other aspects of culture may lose much of their aesthetic value, creating a tension between the spiritual and the aesthetic. Discernment,

---

12. Ibid., 164.

as a cognitive act of spiritual utility, must analyze and evaluate culture intellectually and spiritually. Francis Schaeffer addressed the potential for aesthetic loss when he wrote that "a work of art has value in itself. For some this principle may seem too obvious to mention, but for many Christians it is unthinkable. And yet if we miss this point, we miss the very essence of art. Art is not something we can merely analyze or value for its intellectual content. It is something to be enjoyed."[13]

Discernment also leads to an emphasis on individual autonomy. Niebuhr notes that since discernment is intellectual and evaluative it leads to an emphasis on the individual Christian as a "dynamic, dialectical thinker." Citing the theology of Martin Luther as a quintessential Type IV thinker, Niebuhr writes, "the freedom of the Christian man [becomes] autonomy in all the special spheres of culture."[14] As a result, rather than being separate from culture, the Christian is free to study and engage in culture. Niebuhr notes, however, that participation may require that the rules to be followed in culture engagement be independent of church law or ecclesiastical authority.[15] The primary considerations for the Christian are whether a certain cultural pursuit or career engagement demonstrates a love for God and a desire to serve others. Using this criterion, Luther excluded certain religious or vocational pursuits. For example, Luther was critical of monastic life, since it did not meet the criteria of serving others. Niebuhr also notes that Luther believed a Christian could pursue a career in areas such as commerce, politics, and even the military, since these careers were consistent with the social institutions ordained by God and could be used as a means of obeying God and serving others. Since these pursuits were not under the auspices of ecclesiastical authority, "a Christian [is] not only free to work in culture, but free to choose those methods which were called for, in order that the objective good with which he was concerned in his work might be achieved."[16]

This emphasis on discernment and individual autonomy leads to a perspective on worldview transformation that is more individual than communal and where worldviews are treated similar to philosophies. The result is a more rational or analytic approach to worldview transformation; the individual believer is logically persuaded to commit to the theological tenets and subsequent behavioral outcomes of the faith.

Second, Type IV Christianity places great emphasis on the concept of grace or living graciously with fellow disciples. Theologically, the Christian is liberated from the requirement of works as a means to salvation (Eph 2:8–9), so believers are said to have a liberty that transcends the demands of the Law (cf. Rom 6:15; Gal 5:13; 1 Pet 2:16). The freedom from the Law provided by Christ is not a license for the believer to engage the sinful desires of the flesh but rather to follow the desires of righteousness and live a life of holiness (Rom 6:22). This liberty, combined with the concept of discernment, leads to a view of Christianity that pictures followers of Christ as ones who walk alone with Christ, being part of the community of faith but without fully considering their relationship to the community. Practically understood, as disciples engage in the process of "[working] out

13. Schaeffer, *Art and the Bible*, in *Complete Works*, 2:393–94.

14. Niebuhr, *Christ and Culture*, 179.

15. Ibid., 174.

16. Ibid., 175.

[their] own salvation with fear and trembling" (Phil 2:12–13), those things not specifically forbidden in Scripture are permissible. As Paul notes, because of differing maturity levels or previous experiences, some believers might choose to engage in practices that others would not for fear that doing so would not be spiritually profitable and may even be sinful. Paul notes this situation in 1 Corinthians 8 when discussing the controversy surrounding the eating of meat that had been sacrificed to idols; Paul claims he is free to eat such meat as long as in so doing he does not cause another to stumble.

Consequently, as believers exercise their liberty in Christ and operate individually in the world in correspondence to their level of biblical discernment, the potential exists for conflict as individuals or groups within the church disagree over what is permissible or spiritually profitable. Grace provides the social cohesion necessary to maintain unity in the midst of liberty and discernment diversity. Living graciously with fellow believers means that those ways of thinking or standards of conduct that are not biblically forbidden should not cause division among individuals in the community of faith. In essence, insofar as a believer does not violate the commands of Scripture, no other believer or group of believers can impose their way of thinking or standards of conduct on another. To live graciously is to permit individuals within the community to work out their own salvation, while providing the spiritual guidance that will allow them to engage in their individual walk for the glory of God. The idea of grace is summarized in this statement by Augustine: "In essentials unity, in doubt [or nonessential] questions liberty, in all things charity."[17]

Finally, Type IV Christianity, possibly to a greater degree than its evangelical counterparts, must confront the need for all believers to engage in the process of integrating faith, learning, and living. For adherents of the Type I perspective many of the issues regarding cultural engagement are clear—things either conform to the will and authority of Christ or they do not. For the proponent of the Type V or *Christ the Transformer of Culture* position (which will be examined next), all issues are biblical issues, and certain principles should guide the collective response of the church in those areas. For the Type IV adherent, both Christ and culture constitute legitimate authorities, which are to be obeyed. The difficulty for the believer is that these authorities, because of sin, can achieve no lasting harmony or balance since the tendency of sinful humanity is to use culture to usurp the authority of God. As discussed earlier, this tension is the impetus for emphasizing and developing discernment as a hallmark of spiritual maturity.

This tension can also lead to the creation of dualisms—the relegating of some aspects of life to the authority of Christ and others to the authority of culture. Since the believer is commanded, however, to engage all aspects of life for the glory of God, the existence of dualisms is unacceptable and requires developing a synthesis between Christ and culture authority. For the educated believer, the process of bringing synthesis to issues of Christ and culture is the process of integration. Integration extends discernment in that integration requires the believer to understand both the content and principles of biblical Christianity as well as the content and principles of various academic content areas,

---

17. Augustine, cited in Foster, *Streams of Living Water*, 229.

bringing these together in a way that allows the disciple of Christ to live for the glory of God. For example, noting that the Bible is not a textbook for areas such as business, communications, or criminal justice, an integrationist would seek to delineate the biblical principles that should direct a person who engages in professions such as advertising, video production, or law enforcement.

As a result, the Type IV position may be more pragmatic than either of its evangelical counterparts. The Type I adherents maintain the view that culture is inherently evil and cannot be redeemed. Thus, for the believer, the only faithful response is to withdraw from it. As will be shown, the Type V, *Christ the Transformer of Culture* adherents possess an idealism that allows them to maintain that culture, while corrupted by sin, has not been abandoned by God and can ultimately be restored to the way God intended it to be. For the Type IV advocates, the reality that the structure of society can be legitimate and obedience to it ordained by God combined with the understanding that this authority can also be sinful and dynamic requires a response for how the believer is to live in the world under such authority. As Niebuhr explains,

> The dualist, however, is setting forth the ethics of action, of God's action, man's and the wicked powers'. Such an ethics cannot consist of laws and virtues nicely arranged in opposition to vices, but must be suggested and adumbrated; for living action can only be suggested and indicated. It is an ethics of freedom not in the sense of liberty from law, but in the sense of creative action in response to action upon man.[18]

While the Type IV position lends itself to a certain type of cultural reform, with the believer seeking to bring all aspects of life under the authority of Christ, it is a reform that is generally individual and reactive. Reform is individual in that the cause of evil in the world is sin and the secular authorities ordained by God are created to restrain evil while allowing a righteous person to participate in that which is good. As a result, the Type IV proponent believes that if individuals sin less and engage in right actions, then social reform (although tenuous) is temporarily possible. The reform is also reactive in that the believer must first evaluate the rules or actions of culture, determining whether their demands are permissible, before submitting to them. As a result, the Type IV position leads to social conservatism, described by Niebuhr as "a logical consequence of the tendency to think of law, state, and other institutions as restraining forces, dykes against sin, preventers of anarchy, rather than as positive agencies through which men in social union render positive service to neighbors advancing toward true life."[19]

The Type IV position of Niebuhr corresponds to the *evangelical* tradition described by Richard Foster in his book *Streams of Living Water*. It is a tradition whose great themes include the faithful proclamation of the gospel, the centrality of Scripture as repository of the truth, and an emphasis on the faithful interpretation of Scripture by the community of faith.[20] These three themes, Foster contends, provide the two great strengths of the evangelical tradition. The first is emphasis on conversion that leads to the practice of

18. Niebuhr, *Christ and Culture*, 186.

19. Ibid., 188.

20. Foster, *Streams of Living Water*, 219.

evangelism, missionary activity, and the call to "make disciples of all the nations . . . teaching them to observe all things" (Matt 28:19–20). It is the call to experience converting grace that leads, as Foster describes, to "the existential call to commitment; evangelical witnesses give us a clear theology of salvation. It is a doctrine of *sola gratia*, grace alone. It is a doctrine of *sola fide*, faith alone. It is a doctrine of *solus Christus*, Christ alone."[21]

The evangelical tradition's second great strength is a commitment to the authority and fidelity of Scripture as the source of truth and guide to faithful living. The centrality of Scripture in the life of the believer leads to a strong emphasis on doctrine and faithful interpretation of the Bible. Moral action is founded on proper understanding. For evangelicals, Foster notes, the desire is to "think as rightly about God as finite human beings [are able to think]. We do seek to love God with all our minds. We do endeavor to rightly divide the word of truth. This is our intention."[22]

While acknowledging the strengths of the evangelical tradition, Foster notes three "potential perils" that can cause distortions in the tradition. The first is a tendency to "fixate on peripheral and nonessential matters," a danger that emerges when "out of proper concern for truth and sound doctrine, people are unable to distinguish matters of primary importance from matters of secondary importance."[23] This tendency can lead to a second peril—a sectarian mentality, where issues of secondary importance are raised to the level of primary importance so that the unity of the community of faith is threatened or undermined.

Finally, the tension between Christ and culture can lead to a limited view of salvation. This limited view of salvation can be manifested in two ways. The first view of salvation focuses primarily on the individual and neglects the call of the gospel to areas such as social responsibility and communal involvement. That is, evangelism becomes solely the process of getting a person into heaven and loses sight of the call of commitment to every aspect of life that is to be the character of the true disciple of Christ. This tendency can lead to the phenomenon of "cheap grace," a view of salvation as a way of avoiding hell without extending the gospel to all areas of the believer's life. This individual orientation leads to a second problem, a failure to extend the good news of the gospel beyond the individual to encompass both communal and institutional life. As Foster notes, "Christ came to break the shackles of both personal sin and social sin. The salvation that is in Jesus Christ impacts all levels of human existence: personal, social, institutional."[24]

Christ the Transformer of Culture (Type V)

The pervasiveness of sin in the world means that sin's effects permeate all human activity. The result of sin in the world is that sinful humanity seeks, ultimately, to glorify the self—to satisfy one's own desires and to use others as a means of gratifying one's passions. This pursuit to fulfill the desire for sovereignty, over God and over others, is not simply

21. Ibid., 225.
22. Ibid., 227–28.
23. Ibid., 228.
24. Ibid., 230.

demonstrated in a person's individual relationships, but is also performed on the stage of culture. The pursuit of the tools of power and autonomy, the vehicles used to promote self-sovereignty, can be seen in relations between persons, genders, races, and social classes. It is evident both in the relationships between individuals and between nations and cultures. For the Type IV proponent, the pervasiveness of sin means that the relationship between Christ and culture is always in a tenuous balance, one that can never be resolved in a lasting and positive synthesis. Sinful human beings create cultures that reflect and allow them to exercise the proclivities of their sin nature. This understanding leads to a pessimistic view of culture. While not desiring to abandon culture, as the advocates of Type I propose, the Type IV adherent seeks to integrate his faith with culture, all the while understanding that the power of sin means the ultimate deterioration of culture.

For other Christians, the pervasiveness of sin does not lead to a pessimistic attitude or response to culture. God is sovereign, and his call to humanity to be stewards and to create culture was not rescinded with the Fall. While all aspects of creation are qualitatively affected by the Fall, it is still the creation that God declared good. These aspects of creation maintain their inherent goodness but are now perverted, affected by the power and presence of sin in human beings and the ways they choose to use the creation. Evil is not the antithesis of the good but the corruption of creation by fallen individuals who pursue their own interests apart from the intended design of God (cf. Rom 1:23). Redeemed people, however, operating in the world and developing culture in obedience to the mandates of stewardship and the principles of Scripture can reform and begin the process of reconciling the creation and culture in ways that reflect the will and character of God.

This is the perspective of the "conversionists," the Type V or *Christ the Transformer of Culture* position. The conversionist believes that the death of Christ not only atones for the sin and guilt of rebellious humanity but is also the basis for the redemption of all of creation. That "creation was subjected to futility" because of sin and "will be set free from its slavery to corruption into the freedom of the glory of the children of God" (Rom 8:20–21) is the result of the death and resurrection of Christ. The "new creation" of humanity in Christ leads to a new interaction with culture. Old things are "passed away" and "new things have come" (2 Cor 5:17). This transformation of the believer is the basis for the "ministry of reconciliation" (2 Cor 5:18), a ministry that involves not only the reconciling of others to God but also the reconciling back to God of all things affected by the presence and power of sin. As Niebuhr writes, "The effect of the conversionist's theory of culture in his positive thought about creation is considerable. He finds room for affirmative and ordered responses on the part of created man to the creative, ordering work of God."[25] This creative work can even be performed by unredeemed humanity, albeit unknowingly or unwillingly, as they conform to God's creative order and the organization of society. As Christians appropriate the whole of the gospel to every aspect of their lives, both individually and corporately, and seek to fulfill their commission as stewards and agents of reconciliation, they infuse the culture with the principles of truth, love, and justice that are part of the created order and God's desire for the organization of society. The cumulative effect is to engage and influence the culture in a way that reconciles it back to God.

25. Niebuhr, *Christ and Culture*, 192.

Thus, rather than the Type I retreat from culture or reacting to those aspects of culture that are deemed unbiblical (as advocated by Type IV dualist), conversionists engage culture; they are proactive, knowing that all of creation and culture is affected by sin and all aspects of life require a biblical response. Type V proponents believe that the pre-Fall mandate of stewardship and the post-Fall commands to reconciliation cannot be fulfilled through isolation from the culture nor from a belief that some forms of perverted culture are appropriate for engagement without some reversal of the effects of sin. As Niebuhr explains, while the soul is not redeemed through culture, the "Christian life is a transformed mode of cultural existence" that leads to a "hope for the conversion of the whole of humanity in all its cultural life."[26]

For Niebuhr, the proponents of the Type V position include such notable believers as Augustine, Calvin, and Jonathan Edwards. For Augustine, the structures and values of culture are not value neutral; the sinfulness of humanity resulted in the embedding of sin in the very structures of society that humanity created: "There is nothing so social by nature, so unsocial by its corruption, as this race . . . although bound together by a certain fellowship of our common nature, it is yet for the most part divided against itself, and the strongest oppress the others, because all follow after their own interests and lusts."[27] The result was that humanity's sinful nature led to the development of a corrupt culture that serves to increasingly corrupt human behavior. Calvin, like Augustine, emphasized the sinful depravity of humanity, but noted that human beings' vocations (which he expressed in the idea of "calling") could be pursued as expressions of their faith, love, and desire to glorify God. Niebuhr interprets Calvin to say that the structures of society used to guide human interaction were not simply for the restraint of evil but could be used to promote the common welfare.[28] Niebuhr goes on to note that the eighteenth-century American Puritan Jonathan Edwards shared Calvin's beliefs, not only regarding sin and salvation but also regarding calling, and believed that the regeneration of human beings led them to act for the regeneration of culture.[29]

The result is a type of Christianity that deals with all aspects of individual, social, and cultural life. Type V proponents do not limit their involvement in culture to such issues as abortion or gay marriage, but see all issues as moral issues. Federal fiscal and budgetary policies are moral issues ("where your treasure is, there your heart will also be" (Matt 6:21), as are issues of poverty, health care for those in need, prison reform, environmental policy, and corporate ethics. While Christians are often forced to react to abuses in these areas, the advocates of Type V also propose that believers take more proactive approaches to all aspects of life. Also, since the call of Christ is viewed as both a call to reconciliation back to God and a call to community, Type V advocates emphasize community and a more communal response to issues of culture than their more individualistic Type IV counterparts.

---

26. Ibid., 206.

27. Augustine, *City of God* 26.26.

28. Niebuhr, *Christ and Culture*, 217.

29. Ibid., 219–20.

Niebuhr's Christ the transformer of culture position aligns with what Richard Foster identifies as the *social justice* tradition. It is a tradition that, Foster notes, emphasizes the need for a right ordering of society—that right or just relationships in society lead to right living, that what is "good" and "required" is "to do justice, to love mercy, and to walk humbly with your God" (Mic 6:8). It is a tradition that seeks to reconcile people separated as a result of sin by race, gender, social class, or nationality, first in the church (Gal 3:28) but also as an expression of love to those outside of the church. The social justice tradition seeks a bridge between personal ethics and social ethics—areas viewed as frequently disconnected. For example, the social justice proponent would note that it is inconsistent for the disciple of Christ to read the Bible and advocate truth while supporting social structures or institutions that perpetuate injustice.[30] As students of the truth of God, believers are charged with the task of providing what theologian Walter Brueggemann calls a "prophetic ministry," which seeks "to nurture, nourish and evoke a consciousness and perception alternative to the consciousness and perception of the dominant culture around us."[31]

Like each of the previous traditions or types examined, the Type V perspective is subject to certain weaknesses as well.[32] First, and possibly the greatest, is the tendency for issues of social justice to become ends unto themselves. As evangelicals the first commission is to evangelize—to preach the gospel so that people can be brought into the kingdom of God—and engaging in social justice is a means of loving others in a way that demonstrates the validity and authenticity of the gospel. Because of the great temporal needs of people in society, however, the demands for caring and promoting justice can consume a great deal of energy. As a result, the immediacy of the temporal tends to take predominance over the primacy of the eternal. Second, because the social justice tradition operates on the level of both action and lifestyle, there is a tendency for those involved in issues of social concern to be judgmental of those who are not. The social justice tradition is susceptible to creating a type of legalism or critical spirit toward those who do not share their convictions. This may explain why loving mercy and walking humbly with God are precursors to doing justice in Micah 6:8. Finally, as with other traditions, the social justice tradition can become too closely aligned with a particular political party or agenda. While faith is political—in that politics, like faith, involves questions of values and action—faith cannot be co-opted to a particular agenda or political party. Jim Wallis, in his book *God's Politics*, addresses the tendency of people of faith to align too closely with particular agendas or political parties by nothing that "God is not a Republican . . . or a Democrat."[33]

---

30. Foster, *Streams of Living Water*, 176–78.

31. Brueggemann, *Prophetic Imagination*, 3.

32. See Foster, *Streams of Living Water*, 179–81, for his descriptions of these "potential perils." The brief depiction provided here is taken, in part, as a summation of his description.

33. Wallis, *God's Politics*, xiv.

THE CASE FOR THE TYPE V SCHOOL

Christian philosopher Francis Schaefer notes, Christians are called to combat or "resist the spirit of the world," but they must also understand that "the world-spirit does not always take the same form." If the Christian is to effectively fulfill Christ's commission, he must understand and address the "the spirit of the world *in the form it takes it takes in his own generation.*"[34] Schaeffer goes on to challenge the church with the words of Martin Luther:

> If I profess with the loudest voice and clearest exposition every portion of the truth of God except precisely that little portion which the world and the devil are at that moment attacking, I am not confessing Christ, however boldly I may be professing Christ. Where the battle rages, there the loyalty of the soldier is proved, and to be steady on all battlefields besides, is merely flight and disgrace if he flinches at that point.[35]

Changes in response can take time, the transitions are never easy, and they may even be resisted by those who, for reasons of conviction and experience, believe they are "boldly professing Christ" even as Satan has changed the battle lines of the culture. To prepare the student to evaluate and respond to the world biblically, that is, to develop a biblical worldview, requires not only an understanding of the world as it currently is but also an understanding of the cultural forces that have shaped the students' current understanding of who they are and who they should be. Failure on the part of the church or the Christian school to adequately address this challenge is to promote a perspective of worldview transformation and biblical integration that is other worldly, disconnected, simply academic—and irrelevant. The vibrancy of the Christian school to accomplish its mission of worldview transformation is fundamentally tied to its ability to change its curriculum and instructional methods to meet the changing demands of the culture in ways that preserve and emphasize the relevance of biblical truth.

In the last several years a number of evangelical writers have cited the growth and influence of postmodernism and its accompanying cultural relativism on Christian young people.[36] Some have treated this culture shift as almost wholly negative, while others view the development of postmodern culture as an irreversible reality, noting that its emergence has rendered young people more sensitive to certain aspects of the gospel. Regardless, both sides view the cultural shift as one creating social conditions that require an evangelical response. The erosion of a belief in absolutes of any type (and certainly biblical authority falls into this category) has helped create a generation that views experience and relevance as the barometers of what is true. The influence of postmodern thinking has helped create a generation of young people who desire to make a difference in the world yet who are increasingly suspicious of institutional authority. The postmodern influence also has

34. Schaeffer, *The God Who Is There*, in *Complete Works*, 1:11.

35. Luther, cited in Schaeffer, *The God Who Is There*, in *Complete Works*, 1:11.

36. For a more extensive treatment of the influence of postmodern philosophy and cultural relativism on young people, see Barna, *Real Teens*; Erickson, *Postmodern World*; and McDowell and Hostetler, *Beyond Belief to Convictions*.

contributed to a lack of identity and sense of purpose so that young people seem drawn to adults who lead genuine, caring, and consistent lives that can help provide them direction.

For Christian educators to facilitate worldview transformation in their students, they must understand the cultural environment for which they are preparing students, but must also realize that this is the cultural environment from which their students come. Failure to change the curriculum and methods of schooling in favor of clinging to some perceived golden age of Christian education may produce well-educated students but fail to produce the desired type of biblical thinkers.

The process of evangelism may serve as an example to illustrate this point. The Type I and Type IV approaches to evangelism focus almost exclusively on the God-person relationship: sin has created a breach in the relationship between God and humanity, one that can only be reconciled by the atoning work of Christ. Being restored to God requires understanding one's depth of sin and guilt before God, the sufficiency of Christ as the remedy for sin and its penalty, and the acceptance of Christ as the only means by which a person can achieve reconciliation and eternal life. As a result, the process of evangelism involves bringing people to a realization of their sinful state before God and the necessity of repentance and acceptance of Christ as their Savior. This process, however, is predicated on an assumption that people share a similar vocabulary and perspective from which to engage these propositional truths. For example, the terms *sin*, *heaven*, and *hell* must have shared meaning. The authority of the Bible as true and a willingness to recognize its legitimacy (which also involves rejecting the claims of other religions) must be sustained. The acceptance of the exclusive claim of Christ when he states, "I am the way, and the truth, and the life; no one comes to the Father but through Me" (John 14:10) and its subsequent rejection of all other means of salvation, both religious and secular, must be maintained.

Currently, however, the relativism of a postmodern and post-Christian culture makes such exclusive claims of truth seem increasingly untenable, not just to unbelievers but also to many young people who claim to be believers or who come from Christian backgrounds. George Barna, in his study entitled "What Church Kids Believe," notes that 46 percent of Christian young people either agreed or were unsure of the statement "It does not matter what religious faith you follow because all faiths teach similar lessons." Fifty-one percent either agreed or were not sure of the statement "The devil or Satan is not a living being but is a symbol of evil." The statement that "All good people, whether or not they consider Jesus Christ to be their Savior, will live in heaven after they die" was accepted or expressed as unsure from 31 percent of the respondents.[37] While maintaining the biblical truth on which this approach to evangelism is founded, Gaede notes that to share biblical truth as *the* truth is increasingly difficulty in culture that discounts absolutes and elevates tolerance as the highest virtue.[38]

A Type V approach to evangelism, while still maintaining the foundational truths of the gospel message, may be more suited to evangelize individuals who have grown up in a postmodern and post-Christian culture. While the message of the gospel is the reconciliation of humanity back to God, it is also the good news that God is in the process of re-

37. Barna, cited in McDowell and Hostetler, *Right from Wrong*, 18.
38. Gaede, *When Tolerance Is No Virtue*, 23.

storing *shalom* or peace to a world that has been ravaged by the effects of sin. In addition to the alienation that sin creates between themselves and God, human beings now find themselves alienated from others, from nature, and even from themselves. As Christians seek to demonstrate the relevance of the gospel message in all of these areas of life—for example, in dealing with issues stemming from the effects of sin on personal and social relationships, in working for environmental stewardship, or in providing compassionate care for those who are physically, emotionally, or socially distressed—unbelievers begin to question the believers' motivation. This leads to sharing about the restored relationship between humanity and God, which is made possible by Jesus Christ. In a postmodern and post-Christian age, when the validity of propositional truth has been displaced by an emphasis on experience and integrity, where what people do is more important than what they say, the value of living a genuine Christian life may be the greatest witness.

The example of evangelism underscores the value that young people who have grown up in a postmodern and post-Christian culture place on experience and authenticity. The erosion of belief in absolutes means that propositional truth or a trust in creeds or doctrines becomes meaningless to them, and the validity of anything can only be established through experience. In such an environment, the validity of Christianity can only be substantiated through the experience that young people have with those who claim to be Christians. When young people experience inconsistencies, detect hypocrisy, or fail to see the relevance of Christianity for themselves (other than a means of avoiding hell and attaining heaven), their response is to generally reject the truth of the gospel due to lack of experience with the gospel.

When Jesus states, "By this all men will know that you are My disciples, if you have love for one another" (John 13:35), he substantiates that the experiences of unbelievers with the lives of believers is a legitimate test for the authenticity of the gospel. Nicolas Wolterstorff notes that acts of worship and acts of justice and compassion are linked with authentic Christianity, both in the Old and New Testaments (cf. Isa 11:11–17, 27; Amos 5:21–24; Mic 6:8; Matt 5:6, 10; Jas 2:14–17). To practice one without the other is to engage in a false worship. As Wolterstorff writes, "Worship acceptable to God, authentic worship, is the worship of a pure heart. And the only pure heart is the heart of a person who has genuinely struggled to embody God's justice and righteousness in the world and genuinely repented of ever doing so only halfheartedly."[39] A Christianity that focuses solely on the vertical, whether in worship or the process of reconciling others to God, without also focusing on the horizontal relevance of the gospel in the world is one that seem insincere or irrelevant to many influenced by postmodern culture. Increasingly, it appears that a Type V approach may be more equipped to demonstrate the relevance of Christianity to a world that deems creed credible only through authentic experience.

Niebuhr labeled the Type V tradition "conversionist"—a type of Christianity that believes "culture is under God's sovereign rule, and that Christians must carry on cultural work in obedience to the Lord."[40] More than the other evangelical traditions, the conver-

---

39. Wolterstorff, "Justice as a Condition of Authentic Liturgy," 21.

40. Niebuhr, *Christ and Culture*, 191.

sionist approach provides for a more thorough integration of faith, learning, and living in the world. It does so by rejecting the idea that believers must separate from culture (as in Type I) or the Type IV emphasis to discern their appropriate (and potentially paradoxical) relationship with a fallen world. It affirms that human beings were created for cultural activity and sees godly involvement in all aspects of culture as the fulfillment of that mandate. Gordon Spykman summarizes this aspect of the conversionist approach:

> Confessing redemption as the restoration of creation (the Reformational worldview) stood for the sovereignty of God over all, and held that the saving work of Jesus Christ liberates the Christian community for obedient discipleship and responsible stewardship in every aspect of life. Scripture reopens the doors to every corner of God's creation. Christian liberty is a gift of God in Jesus Christ, a freedom which is to be exercised in holiness. Such holy freedom impels Christians to reclaim every sphere of life for the King—home, school, church, state, college, university, labor, commerce, politics, science, art, journalism, and all the rest.[41]

The conversionist tradition advocates the development of a Christian culture that stands in opposition to and influences the dominant non-Christian culture. Unlike the oppositional view of culture (Type I) or the paradoxical relationship to culture (Type IV), the conversionist tradition does not call for the development of a Christian counterculture. Rather, it seeks to influence the culture for Christ, transforming it, as much as possible, to conform to the will of God here on earth. While many conversionists may seek to help usher in the kingdom of God here on Earth, it should be noted that the conversionist approach does not need to be tied to any particular eschatology. To live faithful to the calling of God on earth serves as evidence of the authenticity, power, and authority of Jesus Christ to change lives, even if this action brings few cultural results. As such, it is a means of being a living gospel before a watching world. The process of opposing and influencing the dominant non-Christian culture requires the ability to think biblically, to apply the principles of biblical stewardship, reconciliation, and the image of God in ways that expose and contradict the inconsistencies of a culture based in unbelief. To do so, the conversionist approach requires a level of sophisticated content-area knowledge and biblical thinking, which Christian educators seek as they facilitate integration and transform worldview in their students.

Authentic worship that is based in the practice of justice and righteousness, as Wolterstorff suggests, is based on three Old Testament principles. These three principles, in part, form the basis for thinking and acting biblically from the conversionist perspective. The first is the Hebrew word *mishpat* or "justice"—the idea of morality and righteousness beyond legal authority or retribution. It is the word used by the prophet in Amos 5:24 and upon which Wolterstorff comments, "When God, speaking through Amos, said 'Let justice roll down like a mighty river,' the meaning is not 'May prisons multiply and police forces expand.' God does not mean, 'may criminals writhe as they receive their just desserts.'"[42] In contrast, it is a sense of justice that is connected with righteousness to the

---

41. Spykman, cited in Holwerda, *Exploring the Heritage of John Calvin*, 166.
42. Wolterstorff, "Justice as a Condition of Authentic Liturgy," 8.

extent that biblical scholar Volkmar Herntrich viewed the terms as nearly synonymous.[43] It is the word for justice that is applied to the treatment of widows, orphans, and aliens (Deut 10:18), as well as to those oppressed (Ps 103:6). Governing authorities are commanded to execute this form of justice and are condemned by God when they do not (cf. Isa 10:1–2; Mic 3:1–3). The principle of *mishpat* justice was foundational to the caring for the poor (Isa 58:5–7) and the redistribution of land during the Year of Jubilee (Lev 25:8–13).

The second principle is *hesed*, which is often translated as "compassion" or "lovingkindness." It is the character of God that is reflected in Psalm 103:17 when the psalmist writes, "But the lovingkindness of the Lord is from everlasting to everlasting." It is also the standard of behavior that God required of the Israelites in Hosea 6:6 when he commands, "I delight in loyalty [*hesed*] rather than sacrifice." The principle of *hesed* is the basis for the practice of gleaning (Lev 19:9–20) and was applied to the restrictions on lenders securing collateral and charging interest in borrowing (Deut 24:12, 17). The principle of *hesed* not only applied to the treatment of others but was also extended to the treatment of animals (Exod 23:17) and to the land (Lev 25:5); thus, the practice of *hesed* was to be applied to all of creation. These two principles are woven together by the prophet Micah when he writes, "And what does the Lord require of you but to do justice [*mishpat*] and to love kindness [*hesed*] and to walk humbly with your God" (Mic 6:8).

The final principle is that of *shalom*—"peace"—or the way God intended things to be. *Shalom* is wholeness, unity, or universal delight. Jesus as the "Prince of Peace" (Isa 9:6–7) is the one that restores *shalom*, the One that returns all of creation to God's original intent. The prophet Isaiah proclaims the Prince of Peace as the One who will rule in righteousness and fairness (Isa 11:4) but also as the One who restores creation to the point where the lion will lie down with the lamb, the lion will eat grass like the ox, and the young child can play near the hole of a cobra (cf. Isa 11:6–9). As Foster writes, "Economically and socially, the vision of shalom means a caring and a consideration for all peoples. The greed of the rich is tempered by need of the poor. Justice, harmony and equipoise prevail. Under the reign of God's shalom the poor are no longer oppressed, because ravaging greed no longer rules."[44] These three principles all find expression in Psalm 85:10, "Lovingkindness [*hesed*] and truth have met together; Righteousness [*mishpat*] and peace [*shalom*] have kissed each other."

These three Old Testament principles also find expression in the New Testament. Christ twice condemned the worship of the Pharisees because their lives did not evidence the lovingkindness of *hesed* (Matt 9:13; 12:7). In Matthew 23:23 they are condemned for their acts of righteous tithing while neglecting justice, mercy, and faithfulness to those in need. It is on the basis of these types of behaviors that Jesus condemns the Pharisees (by quoting Isaiah) as those who "honor me with their lips, but their heart is far from Me" (Matt. 15:8) and that Jesus commands his disciples to leave their offerings at alter and be reconciled to their brothers before returning to worship (Matt 5:23–24). Similarly, the

---

43. Herntrich, cited in Foster, *Streams of Living Water*, 168.
44. Foster, *Streams of Living Water*, 171.

principle of *agape* love detailed by Paul in 1 Corinthians 13:4–7, and which he calls the more excellent way (1 Cor 12:31), is a New Testament manifestation of the principles of compassion, justice, and peace. It is from the basis of *agape* that Paul seeks to rectify many of the problems in the Corinthian church. In the book of Ephesians, Paul uses the principle of *agape* as the basis for unity in church (4:1–16) and harmony between husbands and wives (5:22–33), parents and children (6:1–4), and slaves and masters (6:5–9). It is critical to note that all of these relationships are based on a life of genuine and authentic *agape* love empowered by the Holy Spirit (Eph 5:1–2; 18–21).

While each of the three types of evangelicalism examined in this chapter has particular strengths and accompanying weaknesses, the biblical principles of *shalom, hesed,* and *mishpat* seem to be particularly well suited to address the need of making the gospel relevant to young people within the church and to those outside the church—those who increasingly deny the reality of absolute truth. As previously mentioned, these three principles are foundational to the Type V conversionist response to culture. In chapter 3 the concepts of freewill individualism, relationalism, and antistructuralism were presented as characteristics of evangelical thinking. Given the discussion on evangelical types, these tend to be more characteristics of Type I and IV thinking. While Type V conversionists share the characteristics of freewill individualism and relationalism with their evangelical brothers and sisters, conversionists tend to be more open to structural explanations and to responses that address the manifestations and effects of sin in the world. Rather than simply encouraging people to sin less as a remedy for the effects of sin in the world (which would be the typical approach of an antistructuralist), the structuralist sees the effects of sin as woven into the very social structures, institutions, and cultural life of the society. Thus, it is naive to simply ask people to stop sinning as a means of eliminating sin. In a society where a growing number of people reject the validity of propositional creeds in favor of pragmatic and authentic living, the power of the gospel to inform and affect the practice of life in the world becomes an increasingly powerful apologetic.

The Type I antipathy and limited engagement with culture fails this apologetic test. Their response acknowledges that social structures are corrupt and bear the effects of the Fall and sin, but they also believe that any attempt to reform or change them is short-sighted, futile, and detrimental to the church's mission of saving souls. Consequently this lack of engagement with the culture provides the incentive to create a type of Christian subculture that serves as a structural system that allows believers to survive and thrive in a hostile world. As a result, the Type I response to government is that it should serve as a restraint of evil rather than a structural entity to promote righteousness or *mishpat.* In a similar fashion, the antagonism and hostility toward, or the rejection of the social and cultural structures in the society means that the Type I response is unable to utilize these as vehicles for the promotion of *mishpat.*

While it would be wrong to say that the Type I response is not loving or caring, its separation from the culture makes it increasingly difficult to be involved with unbelievers to demonstrate *hesed.* Also, the content-oriented approach to the gospel (presenting the salvation message and asking people to acquire, assent, and then personally apply the truth of the gospel) often fails to resonate with young people, both believers and unbelievers, who increasingly judge the validity of truth in terms of its practicality or applicability—both personally and communally—to the whole of life. For *hesed* to be meaningful, however, it must be practiced, and it can only be practiced as the disciple engages with those who are most in need of love, caring, and kindness—whether inside or outside the church.

The separation approach to culture practiced by advocates of the Type I position makes it difficult to practice the principles of *mishpat*, *hesed*, and *shalom* in the world and, thus, to integrate these into the process of Christian schooling. Arguably, the Type I advocate might even question or deny the legitimacy of these concepts to the practice of Christian schooling. Failure to do so, however, can create a false dichotomy between the individual believer and culture, supposing that culture is something that can be separated from and failing to acknowledge the extent to which culture has been formative in the development of worldview in students. To simply separate from culture fails to address the formative effects of the nonbiblical worldview on students and creates conditions where the pervasive effects of sin on culture are not noticed and, therefore, ignored.

In a similar fashion, the Type IV, *Christ and Culture in Paradox*, response also suffers from weaknesses in the application of *mishpat*, *hesed*, and *shalom*. Unlike the Type I response, where a negative evaluation of an aspect of culture is a clarion to avoidance, the Type IV advocate must determine whether a particular aspect of culture can be changed or reintegrated into conformity for the glory of God. As an aspect of *mishpat*, the dualist may seek to bring aspects of culture into submission to the gospel if, in fact, they are determined to be redeemable aspects of culture. The individual orientation of the Type IV response, however, means that such determinations are generally personal, and that the active agent is the individual believer acting solely or in concert with others who have made a similar assessment. The individual orientation to the determination of the problem also tends to lend itself to an antistructural approach to dealing with the problem. That is, if individual orientation and action is the source of the problem, the solution is facilitated through proper discernment and integrated action. The result is that the Type IV response fails to properly consider the structural effects of sin: injustice is simply the result of individual sin, so the solution to injustice is persuading people to see the error of their sinful thoughts and actions and respond in repentance.

Such a response leads to an individual and voluntary response to *mishpat*, where the practice of righteousness is viewed as the charitable responses of individuals rather than dealing with structural injustices and the inequalities that result from these structural practices. Thus, the Type IV advocate shares a view of *mishpat* with their Type I brethren that focuses on government or other social structures as restrainers of evil rather than as a vehicle that can be used to promote the public good.

The Type IV dualist also places a strong emphasis on the acquisition of content knowledge of the gospel, which can inadvertently discourage the type of integration that properly displays the biblical principle of *hesed*. While the Type IV approach encourages ministry, it tends to do so through the individual who engages in acts of love or kindness rather than promoting a more systemic and communal approach. The Type IV emphasis on volunteerism is an expression of *hesed* in that people are encouraged to reach out to others in need in real and loving ways. However, as an expression of charity and compassion it fails to capture all that is required by biblical *hesed*.

By failing to address unjust social conditions that create inequalities, the dualist approach may inadvertently communicate to those whom it seeks to love the message that the conditions in which they find themselves are largely of their own creation and that they can overcome their circumstances by being more like the dualist. The combined "blame the victim" and a "pull yourself up by your own bootstraps" message, because it fails to realize or acknowledge the effects of sin that are not of the victim's own device, can leave those served feeling resentful or used by the dualist as a means to salve their conscience. Also, it can leave the dualist wondering why the ones served do not change and act more like the dualist to overcome their difficulties or he may feel resentful at the lack of appreciation displayed by those he has attempted to help. In either case, the concept of empowerment that is part of *agape* love and a *mishpat* approach to lovingkindness is not fully appropriated by the Type IV response.

Ultimately, the Type IV response leads to a disconnection between the principles of *mishpat* and *shalom*. Like the Type I response, evangelism from the Type IV perspective tends to focus, almost exclusively, on the vertical relationship between God and humanity. While less antagonistic and isolationist regarding the horizontal, the dualist often experiences difficulty in applying the gospel to the horizontal aspects of life. It is this difficulty that helps account for the major emphasis on discernment and integration from Type IV advocates. In practice, integration may make the connection from the gospel (faith) to academic content (learning), but the application of learning to life is much more difficult. The reason for this may be, in part, that teachers can develop lesson plans that actively seek to integrate faith with learning, while the individual and voluntary nature of the Type IV approach means that the application of learning to life is entrusted to students whose status as novices, in terms of both spiritual and life maturity, makes proper integration questionable. Without some type of apprenticeship guidance, where the application of faith and learning is demonstrated and applied to life, students are ill prepared to engage in the type of integration necessary to properly engage in worldview transformation. The result is a type of secularized Christianity with little demarcation between the biblical and unbelieving response to certain aspects of culture, a situation that can render believers as practical atheists in their reaction to the world.

On the other hand, the Type V conversionist approach to culture provides certain strengths in responding to culture that can help facilitate worldview transformation in students. In terms of *mishpat*, the conversionist understands that the total depravity of humanity resulting from the Fall affects not only all aspects of the individual but also extends to the cultures and social institutions that they create. Similarly, redeemed people, who live in accordance with their restored vertical relationship with God, will seek to implement righteousness and justice in their horizontal relationship with the world. The conversionist understands that while Christ reconciles individuals to God, he also grafts them into a communal body so that the horizontal implementation of righteousness and justice is not simply an individual and voluntary response but also a communal mandate for the followers of Christ. The *mishpat* of Scripture is the restoration of the standards of righteous justice in providing all human beings that to which they are entitled as image-bearers of God. This *mishpat* may extend to acts of charity that deal with the temporal effects of sin, but it must also address those systemic aspects of structure that assist in the perpetuation of injustice. The conversionist understands that the denial of justice is always the result of sin, either on the part of the individual or corporately and systemically, and that the practice of *mishpat* requires believers to both learn about and engage in the restoration of biblical justice.

The principle of *hesed* is one that extends from attitude to practice; it is a call for all believers to engage in the exercise of reflecting the image of God to others through acts of love and kindness. To love God means that one loves others; unbelievers understand who Christ is and the authenticity of his gospel message through the actions of his disciples in the world. Providing for the practice of *hesed* not only gives students an opportunity to reflect who they truly are as believers but also provides for others to see God through them. While the practice of *hesed* can be done individually, it must also be engaged in corporately and communally. The church is a community of believers that is described by singular terms such as vine (John 15), body (1 Cor 12), and bride (Eph 5). The Christian school that engages in the communal practice of *hesed* not only teaches young believers what being a Christian is but also provides the opportunity to experience who they are intended to be in Christ.

As a result, *shalom* is now a biblical principle that extends not only to the believer's relationship with God but also to all aspects of life. The peace procured by Christ between God and humanity is a model of the peace that the believer seeks to bring into her practice with the world. Just as Christ restores humanity to the place that God intended before sin affected the relationship, the church's practice of *shalom* in the world seeks to demonstrate God's intent for individuals to live in stewardship and harmony with others, the creation, and the self. It is the opportunity to show the relevance of the gospel to all aspects of life. It also constitutes learning that has a purpose—the demonstration of the relevance and reality of the power of God as a means not simply to attain life after this one but also to live life in this world abundantly. It provides students with a practical reason to learn and restores the pre-Fall idea of education for stewardship while addressing the post-Fall necessity of education to attend to the effects of sin in the world.

A TRANSFORMATIVE SCHOOL

The transformation and development of a biblical worldview in students must acknowledge the cultural forces that have shaped their current worldview, as well as utilize both curriculum and instructional approaches that will facilitate worldview change. Failure to acknowledge the affects of the current culture on student thinking and attempts to encourage them to think biblically apart from their cultural foundation risk creating a dualistic or disconnected approach to worldview transformation.

It is important to acknowledge that while the goal may be worldview transformation, the changing of the content or character of thought to align with the values and attitudes of God, the process is a developmental one. As a developmental process, the movement is from where the students are to the place where they need to be. The term *transformation* may best characterize the final objective, but *development* is the approach that must be used to foster movement toward the goal. This development can only be accomplished by acknowledging the starting point of the learner and then using content and techniques that are both biblical and pragmatic to move the student toward the final goal. Failure to think developmentally risks the possibility of creating parallel ways of thinking, where certain issues and aspects of life have been discussed and a biblical perspective provided but where students are ill equipped to develop their own biblically aligned responses to the issues they face after leaving school.

The creation of a transformative Christian school, one that can encourage and support the development of a biblical worldview in the current cultural context, requires the restoration of two biblical concepts that have been diminished in American education. The first is to reestablish the importance of *community* in contrast to the individualism that is a primary value of American culture and is promoted in the culture of schooling. Since a major purpose of schooling in modern societies is to prepare people for economic life, not only must certain content be acquired for success but so also must certain attitudes and values be developed. In a market-based economy, two of these attitudes are individualism and competition, and American schooling has become particularly adroit at developing both of these values. Individualism as a value simply means that one person's success can be pursued and is independent of another's influence. Competition means that achieving the goal requires performing better than others. While Americans may promote the idea that everyone is a winner, the economic reality of scarcity means that, in the end, there can only be a handful of winners with others relegated to "also ran" status. Donovan Graham expresses the consequences of these values in schooling:

> Competition is widely used as a motivating device for classroom learning. Although this practice seems intuitively valuable and acceptable, it is unfortunately harmful for most students. For each winner, here are usually 25 to 30 losers. The vast majority of students are likely to experience discouragement and failure, Using competition to motivate people (1) inspires only people who think they can win, (2) discourages and disillusions people who do not think they can win, and (3) often leads to a breakdown of morality when winning becomes so important that any means of winning is acceptable (Combs 1979). One person's success depends on another's failure (Campolo 1980).[45]

Individualism and competition represent strong economic values that may need to be rethought in light of the biblical teachings of community and cooperation. Certainly the Holy Spirit empowers individuals with gifts, and the Lord entrusts individuals with certain talents, abilities, resources, and opportunities for which they are to exercise stewardship. A proper understanding of *shalom, mishpat,* and *hesed* from the Old Testament combined with the New Testament emphasis on *agape* love will focus on the role and development of cooperation and community in the use of spiritual gifts. The body life of the church cannot be maintained when certain members believe that they can achieve spiritual goals apart from others (1 Cor 12:12–25) or when people pursue their own goals

45. Graham, *Teaching Redemptively*, 167.

and do not actively seek the interests of others (Phil 2:3–4). While it may be tempting, particularly for American evangelicals, to try to balance the opposites of individualism and community or competition and cooperation, in the end it is an attempt to "serve two masters," where one is relegated to the place of lesser prominence and the winning value dominates the school culture.

Second, the transformative school will move from an analogy of education that emphasizes the acquisition or "banking" of knowledge to encourage a model of apprenticeship or "building." Modern schooling is designed around a model of education that defines knowledge scientifically, that is, knowledge can be quantified and measured. The current emphasis on proficiency testing and meeting minimum competency standards demonstrates this particular bias. One can measure proficiency by establishing what needs to be known and then quantitatively assessing whether the student has acquired the information or skills. In essence, proficiency and beyond is established by those who have acquired more information or skills or who perform better on these quantitative assessments. Combined with the values of individualism and competition, the banking analogy allows people who are either naturally talented or who have cultivated certain learning styles to perform better in school than those who possess different talents or skill sets. Psychologist Howard Gardner argues that not all students learn the same way and that all people are born with a particular set of strengths or intelligences. While all students are capable of learning through the intelligences that Gardner proposes, he also notes that the structure of the institution and the values embedded in the institution allow those with certain strengths to flourish more readily while others find themselves constantly struggling because their natural intellectual strengths are at odds with those valued by the institution.[46] The scientific and banking approaches to schooling tend to favor those students who possess greater linguistic or logical-mathematical intelligence while devaluing those who possess such abilities as interpersonal, musical, or bodily-kinesthetic intelligences.

This is not to debase the need for standards or criticize those who advocate that certain levels of proficiency must be attained by students. A scientific view of learning, where acquisition or the banking of knowledge becomes the analogy for an educated student, however, means that certain talents and abilities that God has sovereignly bestowed on some for the purposes of promoting the kingdom are not valued or properly encouraged within the Christian school. As Doug Blomberg writes,

> Scientific knowledge is only one special way of knowing amongst others; it is not the archetype of knowledge, to which all other ways of knowing must aspire, but of which they always fall short. Other ways of knowing are not unscientific; as if they inadequately meet the scientific canons: they are non-scientific, and must be judged according to other norms.[47]

The apprenticeship or building analogy acknowledges that not all types of knowledge can be assessed in quantitative terms. For example, I may learn to be so technically

46. Gardner, *Unschooled Mind*, 12–19.
47. Blomberg, *No Icing on the Cake*, 53.

sound on the piano that I can play the piece flawlessly. If, however, one hears me play and compares my performance with a gifted pianist, the differences will be readily apparent, even if no objective standard or rubric can be developed to assess the differences between us. The scientific standard, in this case, is simply insufficient to adequately evaluate this difference, and yet the difference is significant if one values the aesthetic beauty of a well-played piece of music. As Albert Greene writes,

> The goal of the Christian school is also the exploration of creation, but it also approaches the creation in a different way. While it presents the so-called "facts" that science uncovered, it sees them as revealing God and providing channels of service and communion with Him. In this sort of exploration, the important thing is to identify the gifts a student has and to help the student use them in exploring. Gifts, as the Bible indicates, come in many varieties. These are intellectual gifts, artistic gifts, social gifts, gifts of persuasion and influence, gifts of helping, and many others. Each one opens up a different aspect of creation and so leads to an appreciation of another side of the Creator. It is important that the Christian school be aware of these differences and provide for each student ways to explore the creation that match his or her gifts.[48]

Combined with the goals of cooperation and community, students must be encouraged to use their gifts and to embrace the gifts and talents of others in seeking a common purpose—the promotion of the kingdom of God. As fellow believers, students are engaged in the processes of stewardship, reconciliation, and the promotion of the image of God in others alongside their more skilled and mature brothers and sisters in Christ—their teachers. By working cooperatively, by recognizing and seeking to develop and utilize all the abilities of students, as well as fostering the development of those areas that are not as strong but still necessary for the individual student to develop, the contributions of each student can be more clearly appreciated. As Greene concludes, "humility, that foundational element of the Christian life, is thereby encouraged, and the mutual support that all need is more readily available."[49]

One of the primary goals of almost all Christian schools is the integration of biblical faith with academic content and then seeking to make this integration applicable to life. The examination of the various evangelical traditions in resolving the tension between Christ and life in a fallen world has shown that the separatist approach of Type I or the dualistic approach of Type IV creates problems for integration that can, in the current cultural context, be more readily addressed by the Type V approach. The conversionist approach of Type V, with its focus on developing stewardship, engaging in reconciliation, and promoting the image of God, seeks to address the totality of the problem of sin in the vertical relationship to God, but its emphasis on *mishpat* and *hesed* also seeks to restore a horizontal relationship of *shalom* in the church's engagement with the world. By seeking to restore the creation to the place God intended, believers must now think and act. As a result, the conversionist approach to Christian schooling seeks to have students experience their true humanity, to truly reflect the image of God in themselves, which serves as

48. Greene, *Reclaiming the Future of Christian Education*, 173–74.
49. Ibid., 174.

the ultimate integration. All areas of life are given practical relevance; academic content is no longer separated from righteous or obedient living.

Stronks and Blomberg use the analogy of a game to describe schooling. "Games, like schools," they contend, "are serious business. One has to play the game as if it were real life."[50] The rules of the game help to define what will or will not be acceptable in achieving a particular goal. While coaches and players may develop unique individual or team strategies to win the game, what constitutes a win is defined by the rules of the game itself. The question is, what is the real "game" that the safe haven of school is preparing students to play? The structure of schooling at the high school level for most Christian schools is a college preparatory curriculum, that is, the rules of the game are designed to define a "win" as adequate preparation for higher education. The successful elementary and middle school or junior high is one that prepares students successfully for the game of high school. While a laudable goal, the rules of the game encourage a skill set that promotes sitting passively and absorbing information. It rewards those who can most efficiently acquire the greatest amount of information in the shortest amount of time and recall this information with an occasional requirement of rudimentary analysis, synthesis, or evaluation—all skills necessary for a successful undergraduate college experience.

In contrast, the game of life requires people to experience, discern, and act. It requires people to order life and respond to circumstances (both proactively and reactively) in ways that correspond to the values of the Bible and the commands of Christ to his followers. If Christian schooling is simply a preparation for higher education, then the rules of the game may be well suited to produce this result. If the goal of Christian schooling, however, is truly the integration of faith and learning with an application to life, then the curriculum and instructional methodologies that constitute the rules of the game must reflect this definition of a win. Again, the use of an apprenticeship model, where the master and student interact and are involved in a common purpose and operating from a common set of values will better facilitate worldview development in the current cultural context than the linear teacher-directed and content-oriented approach to integration.

The transformative approach to schooling emphasizes the role of biblical Christianity and the part of the individual disciple to cultivate the values of the kingdom of God in the world. The similes of salt and light used by Jesus in Matthew 5:13–16 compare with the stewardship commands to cultivate and keep given to Adam in Genesis 2:15. In both cases, the good works produced are designed to glorify God in heaven. Just as Adam was incapable of fulfilling his stewardship responsibilities without someone to direct his good works toward (and thus "it is not good that the man should be alone," Gen 2:18), so disciples of Christ must act in ways that demonstrate good works horizontally; they must practice *shalom* in the world. What historian George Marsden has called "The Great Reversal"—the withdrawal of many evangelical and fundamental Christians from promoting the public welfare starting in the early twentieth century—must be accompanied by a second reversal where, in the words of Charles Finney, "the promotion of the public

---

50. Stronks and Blomberg, *A Vision with a Task*, 194.

and private order and happiness is one of the indispensable means of doing good and saving souls."[51]

The type of transformative school proposed here also provides for the creation of the type of community necessary to facilitate worldview development. As the school acts as a community to support and encourage the development of a biblical worldview, it underscores the distinction between a worldview and philosophy. As suggested in chapter 2, twentieth-century evangelicals have traditionally made little distinction between the two concepts, in practice treating these as synonymous terms. The analytically founded and analytically qualified nature of a philosophy, when seen as synonymous with a worldview, meant that the changing of worldview, like the changing of a philosophy, would be both individual and cognitive. That is, to change the worldview of a person required a better argument, or a more convincing apologetic, demonstrating the logical superiority of the biblical position to a secular or nonbiblical argument. For this reason, books like Josh McDowell's *Evidence that Demands a Verdict* have often been used as a text for teaching worldview issues. The individual and rational nature of philosophy corresponds well with the individual orientation of the Type IV position or the Type I idea of a separate community that trains the individual for righteous living in the world. As a result, Christian schools whose origins and practice correspond more closely to the Type I and IV approaches tend to address worldview transformation in this more individual, rational, and apologetic style.

Worldviews, however, are not synonymous with philosophies and cannot be effectively changed if the fundamental distinctions between them are not addressed. Worldviews are pre-theoretically and psychically founded. They act as filters to interpret the world, to attach significance to the particulars of life. They function as a lens that allows individuals to see the world from a particular perspective. In short, worldviews help individuals to make sense of how the world is and guide motivations and actions by providing a vision of how the world should be. The foundation of a person's worldview is laid early in the life of the individual by the values of the culture, the society, the community, and the interpersonal relationships into which the child is born. As individuals learn the tools of their social world (e.g., the language, technology, mannerisms, behavior patterns, etc.), they are also acculturated with the values of that society. The power of a worldview is the faith that a society places in a particular vision of the world, an ideal that is embedded in its social mores and institutions, which comes to influence the thinking and motivation for actions of individuals and is reinforced collectively by the members of the society. To transform worldview is to replace the faith vision of the surrounding culture with a new faith vision, one that is applied and practiced in every aspect of life and is reinforced by a community of like-minded and like-motivated individuals acting in their relationship to God and with each other. The Christian school, under the authority and direction of the larger community of the church, can serve as a vital institution for the development and application of the biblical values of stewardship, reconciliation, and

---

51. Charles G. Finney, cited in Marsden, *Fundamentalism and American Culture*, 87.

the image of God to the content of the academic disciplines to the relevant concerns of individual and communal life.

This approach does not negate a rational approach to worldview change but seeks to make the connection between intellectual understanding and righteous and obedient living. The phrase "we do not know who discovered water but it was not likely to have been a fish" (attributed to Marshall McLuhan) communicates the idea that the effects of an environment, including a social one, are hard to perceive when one is immersed in it. The apologetic approach to worldview transformation has been designed, essentially, to get the individual "fish" to see the water. While acknowledging that fish may need to learn to swim differently in the water, current Christian schooling attempts to orient or integrate them without acknowledging that most fish swim in schools.

The process of learning to live faithfully and obediently in a complex society requires the modeling, nurturance, and reinforcement of a community that seeks to train its members to embrace its vision but also to be contributing members. The apprenticeship model of the transformative school allows teachers and students, as fellow members of the community, to contribute to and reinforce each other toward the common goal of the edification of the body. As fellow believers, gifted for the purpose of edifying the church, Christian students are given the biblical responsibility of using those gifts for the glory of God and the strengthening of others. Teachers, who as adults are both spiritually and intellectually more mature, are given the responsibility of developing and nurturing those gifts and talents in students. The biblical model is not one-directional. Young believers, while recognizing their spiritual, social, emotional, and intellectual immaturity, are given the same commands of obedience as their more mature teachers. To those given much, much will be required; and to those proven faithful, much more will be entrusted (cf. Luke 12:48; Matt 25:29). The apprenticeship model of Christian schooling provides a basis for worldview development and change by creating the type of community where stewardship, reconciliation, and the promotion of the image of God are the values that discern how the world is and provide the basis for evaluation and motivating action to put into practice what God intended.

9

Common Grace and Education

*The church of Jesus Christ is the only society on earth that exists entirely
for the benefit of its nonmembers.*

—William Temple

ARNIE WALKED THE HALLWAY toward to his classroom. Like most teachers, he mentally
rehearsed the agenda for the day. He inventoried the materials he had ready, concluding there were no last-minute details that needed his attention. Arnie typically made
sure he had things ready for the next day before leaving school in the afternoon. This
ritual was one that he practiced for his own self-assurance. Rarely did he miss details.

As Arnie walked the hallway, he noticed Barry Baroque standing in the doorway of
Manfred's classroom. Manfred served as the faculty representative on the board of Mt.
Carmel Christian School. "Oh, yes, the board had a meeting last night," thought Arnie.
"Barry must be trying to get the details of the meeting." Assured that he had his day
prepared, and also curious as to the discussions of the board, Arnie decided to join the
conversation. Greeting his two colleagues, he sat in one of the student desks and asked
Manfred how the meeting had gone last night. Manfred quickly tried to summarize the
discussion to that point.

"You recall that the state legislature approved the use of vouchers for private religious
schools in selected districts last summer," started Manfred. "Well, it turns out that Mt.
Carmel is within the voucher borders. A number of families in the area have inquired
about enrolling their students here next year. The problem we discussed is that a number
of the families asking to use vouchers come from unchurched backgrounds. Many of the
board members are positive about taking vouchers, but that discussion led one member
to ask whether Mt. Carmel was prepared to take students from non-Christian homes."

"What was the board's reaction to that statement?" asked Barry.

"That set off a big discussion," answered Manfred. "It really came down to two
views—split almost directly down the middle. Half of the board was opposed to the idea.
One member of that group said he thought that Christian schooling was only for believers
and that students from nonbelieving homes would change the atmosphere in the school
negatively. The other half noted that admitting some unbelieving students to the school

would provide an evangelistic ministry. That group pointed out that admitting a limited number of students would not have a significant negative effect on the culture of the school and that the opportunity to impact those students and their families for eternity was worth the effort."

"Wow, sounds like yesterday's meeting was pretty lively," commented Arnie.

"You bet," answered Manfred. "Usually those things are pretty dull and uneventful. Last night, however, I think we could have sold tickets."

"I have to ask," injected Barry. "The member who noted that Christian schooling should only be for Christians—did he provide any reasons for his belief? His statement has caused me to wonder whether or not unbelievers could benefit from the type of education we offer here at Mt. Carmel."

"If you had asked me that in August, I would have told you, yes," stated Manfred. "I mean, if the curriculum and our presentation as teachers is biblically solid, then our students would be receiving a biblically integrated Christian education. This would be true regardless of whether the students are believers or not. Since our in-services on worldview, however, I am beginning to question that idea. If the ministry of the Holy Spirit is, as we say, critical to the process of guiding believers into all truth, then maybe unbelievers cannot benefit from a biblically based education. If transformation really is a work of the Spirit, then we can't really expect unbelievers to benefit much from what we are trying to do in changing a student's worldview."

"Are you suggesting that transformation is critical to the process of integration? That is a pretty student-centered response, Manfred," teased Barry. "But doesn't your first statement really capture what most of us have tended to believe here for years? I mean, generally we have been taught that if we present strong academic content and that if we, as teachers, take the time to integrate that content with Scripture, then our students are receiving a *Christian* education? We have long focused on curriculum and teacher presentation. Now you want to go and make the student, and their Christian experience, the center of the integration process."

"I know, I can't believe I am even saying it," laughed Manfred. "Those worldview transformation in-services, however, have made me begin to realize that I have tended to remove the Holy Spirit from the process. We talk about using only Christian curriculum and the responsibility of the teacher to be diligent in integrating biblical truth with what we are teaching. Yet, without the Spirit working in the heart of the student, any worldview change seems impossible."

"Let me play the gadfly," responded Arnie. "The problem with what you just said is that suddenly truth is only true for believers. Yes, the Holy Spirit is the source of sanctification in the life of the believer, and that would include the transformation of their worldview. But we also say that the truth of the Bible is *true truth* and that it is as true for the unbeliever who rejects it as it is for the believer who accepts it. Even Dr. Wise made this point in the in-services. The stewardship mandate was issued to all humanity and was not revoked as a result of the Fall. So unbelievers remain responsible before God for how they use that which has been entrusted to them. Just the other day in U.S. history class, we talked about Jonas Salk, the inventor of the polio vaccine. I asked the class why polio was present in the world, and they all agreed it was a result of the Fall. I then noted that, as far as we can tell, Dr. Salk was not a believer. I asked the class if his discovery of the polio vaccine helped eliminate an effect of the Fall? They had to agree that, to some extent, it did, but they still had a hard time with the idea that an unbeliever could be engaged in reconciliation."

"Okay, Mr. Gadfly," rejoined Manfred. "Are you suggesting that the principles of Christian education are just as applicable to unbelievers as believers? I mean, if you are, I can just go back to my old way of doing things and drop the quasi-guilt I feel about not being student-centered enough." Laughing, Manfred added, "It is just too depressing."

"And here I thought you were getting a heart," said Barry, winking at Manfred.

"To answer your question," continued Arnie. "Yes, I do think the principles of stewardship, reconciliation, and image of God are just as applicable to unbelievers as believers. As his disciples, believers should engage these principles in ways that seek to glorify God. Unbelievers, too, can receive an education consistent with these biblical perspectives. They can learn to live their lives more consistent with biblical truth—and because it is true, their lives may well be better as a result. We have to be careful to make sure they realize that their works will not merit salvation. It may just be that by understanding what it means to be fully human that they come to understand the inconsistency of their lives and are drawn to Christ."

"You know, sometimes unbelievers live in ways that are much more righteous than many Christians," noted Barry. "Philosophers throughout history have seen education as a means of teaching all people how to live good lives. If Christianity is truly a life more abundant on this earth and not simply in heaven, then I think Arnie has a point. Unbelievers can be taught to live better lives from a biblical perspective. Still, Manfred's point is well taken. The Holy Spirit must count for something, so how do we avoid teaching people to act biblically in the world and still note that those actions don't merit salvation?"

"I'm not sure," responded Arnie. "Yet our in-services during the year have caused me to think that if Christianity is true, then it has to apply to every aspect of life. Also, if it is objectively true, then its truth is not limited to believers. In addition, the purpose of an education is, as you say, Barry, to *live* the good life. As a result, simply teaching the concepts of biblical truth, without actually engaging students in the process of stewardship and reconciliation, constitutes an incomplete Christian education. The truth of the Bible demands obedience and its truths apply to all of humanity. While obedience through works will not result in salvation, there can be benefits gleaned from being obedient to God. So maybe all people can benefit from a Christian education."

WHAT IS CHRISTIAN ABOUT A CHRISTIAN EDUCATION?

The question of what constitutes a Christian education is not an easy one to answer. Not unlike the more general question, What is a good education?, the starting assumptions one brings frame the discussion and generally lead toward particular conclusions. Discussions on the nature of education, Christian or otherwise, are predicated on certain beliefs about what the student should be like as a result of being educated. While the field of educational philosophy is filled with a great number of answers to this fundamental question, those formulations tend to fall into two general categories. Those categories not only apply to answering the general question of education but also have directed the discussion about the nature of a quality Christian education.

The first answer is that education is the acquisition of content knowledge—what is taught by the teacher and retained by the student constitutes an education. Certainly this approach can be seen in the current emphasis on standards and proficiency testing to ensure the attainment of content at a particular grade level. Applied to Christian education, this approach defines a good education as one in which the student learns the content of the academic disciplines and also learns how those disciplines are grounded in or can be viewed from the perspective of the Bible. In this approach, the development of a sound Christian education will focus on the curriculum and curriculum development in which teachers present content aligned with Scripture so that students can receive concepts and principles that are biblically integrated. As with its more general counterpart, this type of Christian education relies primarily on some standard outcome, usually through the display of a critical learning skill by which students demonstrate that they have acquired the desired mastery.

This view of a good education is based in the banking analogy—a good education is defined by the quality and quantity of that which is deposited in the minds of students. This view makes certain assumptions about students that tend to drive the educational process. From this perspective, students are generally considered passive. The minds of students are regarded as blank slates to be written on or filled by the teacher. What students bring to the education process is largely insignificant. Since students are novice learners, any incidental knowledge they have previously obtained can be regarded as a potential obstacle to the more expert-like knowledge possessed by their teachers or contained in the curriculum. Given that the source of knowing is outside students and that learning constitutes the acquisition of good content, the consequence for Christian education is that believers and unbelievers alike can be given biblically based content with relative effectiveness. This consequence is particularly cogent when the desired outcome of education is focused more on knowing than doing. Granted, there is a belief among most Christian educators that the Holy Spirit will take the content of the curriculum (or curriculum-based instructional processes) and work in the lives of believers to implement that content in the practice of their faith. Generally, this outcome of education is secondary or is pursued in conjunction with the acquisition of content.

The second answer to what constitutes a good education focuses on the construction process. In this approach, changes in student thinking and subsequent actions are the goals of a good education. From this perspective, student knowledge must be demonstrated in action, and action must be applied to the process of life. This approach is represented by the building analogy—content knowledge represents the raw materials from which students build something. In this approach, however, the goals of education must also include a focus on the acquisition of certain skills so that content can be used in ways determined by students (builders). Since the emphasis is on skill development as well as content acquisition, the practice of the knowledge learned (i.e., the application of content) represents a primary outcome to be pursued. In this approach to education, Christian educators would make a concerted effort to ensure that students not only understand academic content but also apply the principles of faith to learning and life.

The constructive view of education assumes a more active role on the part of students. As a result, what students bring to the education process is highly significant. Who the students are, their motives, talents, and desires, what perspectives they bring, what prior knowledge and experiences they have—these must be considered since all this forms the foundation upon which they will build and the direction in which learning will go. Granted, not all of these experiences are positive. For example, students may possess misinformation that needs to be corrected or have negative motivations or desires that need to be altered. These factors must be actively and consciously addressed rather than assuming that good content will simply eliminate incorrect knowledge or improper desires. Unlike the more teacher- and curriculum-centered content acquisition approach, the constructive approach is primarily student-oriented, emphasizing meaningful learning and connection to prior knowledge.

Since the constructive approach places a substantive role on students and the elements they bring to the educational process, for Christian education, the fact that the students are believers, those in whom the Holy Spirit dwells, is highly significant. Acknowledging the active work of the Spirit in the lives of students should mean that a transformative Christian education can only occur in the lives of believers. In this respect, the goals and outcomes desired by most Christian educators in the lives of their students can only occur if the Holy Spirit is actively a part of the constructive process. To assume otherwise, that is, to take the more passive view of students that is generally done by the teacher- or curriculum-centered approach, is to engage in Christian education in a manner that practically ignores the importance of the Holy Spirit in the objective of content acquisition. While acknowledging that the Holy Spirit will take the content that students know and transform them in light of the truth of that knowledge, most Christian education tends to operate in a manner that generally ignores the presence and the work of the Spirit in the lives of students.

While both perspectives or analogies communicate significant aspects of the teaching/learning process, both are flawed in that they tend to borrow from a more secular and psychologically based approach to education rather than from a distinctively biblical one. From the biblical perspective, the process of learning is never focused simply on the individual but rather on the role of the individual within the larger context of the faith community. Coming to faith is the process of being grafted into the vine that is Christ (John 15:1), and apart from drawing strength from the Vine, the believer can do nothing (John 15:5). Similarly, while loving Christ is symbolized in the vine analogy, loving others is symbolized in the body relationship where Christ serves as the head (Rom 12:4–8). In this analogy, the apostle Paul notes that the purpose of the spiritual gifts is not for edifying the individual but for believers to use their abilities to strengthen and develop others. Thus, any approach to Christian education that fails to place the goals and objectives of that education within the larger context of the believers' obligations to the body of Christ is a Christianized adaptation of a more secular perspective—a response that will inevitably have negative consequences for the practice of worldview transformation.

Because the role of community is so prominent in the lives of believers, the discipleship metaphor must assume a significant place in the development of a biblical approach to education. For Christians, the idea of discipleship carries with it two foundational assumptions. First, the person has had a transformative experience of redemption. The result of this experience is that the Holy Spirit indwells the believer. Consequently, the Holy Spirit guides the believer to truth (John 16:13). Second, because it is the desire of the Holy Spirit to glorify Christ (John 16:14), the Spirit prompts the believer toward conformity to the image of Christ. The desire to be disciples of Christ means that believers place themselves under the authority of Christ and the Holy Spirit, who leads believers to conform to the image of the Lord. Submission is required on the part of believers, first to Christ, then to the leading of the Holy Spirit, and finally to those placed in authority over them by God, those who can help the disciple achieve the desired goal.

The foundations of discipleship indicate that, while content is important, the heart or motivation of students is the key to achieve the ends of a biblically based education. For this reason Paul instructed believers not to grieve or quench the work of the Holy Spirit in their lives (cf. Eph 4:30; 1 Thess 5:19). Research into student learning reflects this biblical principle. Commenting on research into the learning process, educators Robert Marzano and Debra Pickering note, "attitudes and perceptions color our every experience. They are the filter through which all learning occurs."[1] They also note that these factors are more predictive of classroom success than factors external to the student, such as quantity or quality of classroom instruction.[2] Interestingly, those factors that contribute most significantly to positive attitudes and perceptions in students are a sense of acceptance by teacher and peers (community), physical comfort and order in the classroom, and learning tasks that are significant or have value. The Christian life is a communal experience directed at the significant task of glorifying Christ through loving God and others. Since the Christian life is a communal experience, the goal of biblically based discipleship, of which worldview transformation is an integral part, is to prepare believers to function effectively as part of the community. For this reason, Christian education cannot be approached as content to be deposited by the teacher or possessed by the student. Rather, discipleship demands that the purpose of receiving content is so that it can be made active and be directed toward engagement with others for their betterment and to the glory of God.

These goals are often expressed by Christian educators. The frustration for nearly every teacher comes when students do not show a motivation to think or live as disciples of Christ. Unable (or unwilling) to change student motivations, the focus of the educational endeavor shifts from the learner to those factors that are more easily controlled by the teacher and the school. What often results is that the process of Christian education becomes centered on content. As a result the curriculum becomes a major consideration, including how the content is biblically integrated (either by the curriculum itself or the teachers using it). In turn, this often leads Christian schools to concentrate their efforts on curriculum, or more specifically textbook adoption (whether the text is from a Christian

---

1. Marzano and Pickering, *Dimensions of Learning*, 3.
2. Ibid., 20.

or secular publisher), level of course content (AP or college track being more desirable), and teacher development (particularly in biblical integration). While these are all significant variables, to focus on these to the near exclusion of those more student-centered goals can result in schools and teachers who believe they are engaging in Christian education when their students demonstrate an appropriate acquisition of factual or head-knowledge without ever demonstrating the application of that knowledge to life. As a result, Christian teachers may note that students' thinking and actions do not significantly differ from their unbelieving peers or that the values they espouse do not reflect a qualitatively different view of the world than the dominant worldview of the society.

While each believer becomes a Christian individually through the saving work of Christ, individuals only experience and fully function as Christians within the church, which is the body of Christ. Apart from the context of community—regardless of content strength, masterful presentation, or biblical integration—Christian education will become dead orthodoxy. While it may be intellectually stimulating, without finding meaning within community, it will fail to encourage effective stewardship, engagement in reconciliation, or the promotion of the image of God in others. At best, it will prompt a response in students that inspires them to act individually, outside of the context in which learning takes place and apart from those who are responsible to disciple them. This can lead to engagement in activities independent of the support and encouragement of the faith community. Such actions also risk being fundamentally unbiblical by viewing the practice of stewardship and reconciliation outside of the context of the church. Since the Holy Spirit provides gifts to believers for work within the body of Christ, which is the church (1 Cor 12:11), to engage in the ministry outside of community is to risk doing so apart from the power of the Holy Spirit—done through an individual's own power or might (cf. Zech 4:6).

The idea that only Spirit-filled believers can engage in a student-centered approach to Christian education does not mean that students cannot be transformed by strong content or effective teaching. Also, recognizing the indwelling ministry of the Holy Spirit does not mean that Christian educators leave students to develop their own understanding of academic content or its application. The command to make disciples conveys the idea of shaping students, working with the Holy Spirit to use the content of the curriculum and instructional expertise to develop Christ-likeness in students. Insofar as the desire to be Christ-like is the desire of the disciple/student, Christian education is the processes of helping the student achieve his or her goal. The importance of student goals, where motivation determines not only the amount of content that is learned but the ends to which it will be applied, will often create dissonance for Christian educators. It should call into question the belief that significant Christian education has occurred when the attitudes and values and the goals and aspirations of Christian students do not vary significantly from nonbelieving peers.

Such comparisons cannot be made in the abstract. For example, one specific group of Christian students cannot be compared to all public school students in general. Rather, the question that should be addressed is whether the attitudes, aspirations, goals, and values of a group of students in terms of how they define themselves now and who they think they should be in the future differ significantly and biblically from their unbelieving peers who are similar in terms socio-economic class, geography, race, and so forth. In addition, any focus on curricular content and integration must take into consideration the use of instructional methodologies that will encourage and develop a more communal experience. When changes in instructional methodology are essentially absent from consideration, the emphasis of improvement will remain focused on bolstering curriculum content and improving teacher integration. While adopted with the best of intentions, these approaches to education are not value neutral. Prompted by a desire to legitimize this approach, Christian educators accommodate these two elements, attempting to make them biblical. In the process, they inadvertently adopt the values of individual empowerment that dominate secular philosophy and educational psychology rather than develop a uniquely biblical approach to Christian education designed to foster discipleship and communal responsibility. As a result, the emphasis of Christian education becomes more an emphasis on "education" rather than on "Christian."

HUMAN COMMONALITY AND COMMON GRACE

To be a Christian is to undergo a change in which individuals begin to progressively experience their true humanity. When Jesus noted that he had come that "they may have life, and have it abundantly" (John 10:10b), the word "abundant" is a quantitative term, assuming that those who experience the life Jesus brings will have more of what they already have. The abundance that Jesus promised is not simply the extension of life into eternity, but must be understood in light of the first part of the verse, where Jesus notes that "the thief comes only to steal and kill and destroy." Sin (or sin personified in Satan) takes or steals humanity from life; sin makes human beings less than they were intended by God to be. This theft of humanity eventually leads to death.

Too often the promise of the abundant life is seen only in reference to salvation and eternity, being divorced from the restoration of the quality of life that God intended for human beings before the Fall. The life Jesus brings not only extends present life into eternity but also restores that which was lost in humanity as a result of sin. It is a life of restoration and repair. This quantitative change assumes a qualitative or transformational change, an experience that Jesus describes as being born again (John 3:3). The qualitative change, though, can occur with the believer experiencing little of the abundance of life that Christ describes. Paul reminds the Corinthian believers that they are brothers but notes that they are living not like Christians but as unbelievers (1 Cor 3:1). Later in the book, Paul desires to teach them a more excellent way to live (1 Cor 12:31). Theologically, the abundant life promised by Jesus is not simply one of justification—where the believer now has the guarantee of eternal life—but also involves sanctification or experiencing the perfect humanity that is found in the person of Christ. This abundance requires the transformation of justification (being born again) and also the active engagement of the believer to experience this abundance.

The quantitative term of abundance indicates that Christians can experience more of their humanity than unbelievers, those from whom the thief continues to steal and destroy their humanity. The destructive aspects of the verse ("the thief comes only to steal and kill and destroy") focus on the qualitative difference between believers and unbelievers—believers are spiritually alive while unbelievers remain spiritually dead—yet the verse communicates much more. Believers can have restored to them that which was stolen as a result of sin. The abundant life is not simply one that is eternal; it is a life that is fuller and richer, more purposeful and rewarding, demonstrating contentment and peace. The humanity lost as a result of sin can once again be realized. This meaning has the potential to be lost if salvation remains the exclusive focus of the verse.

Currently the focus of instruction is often on individual or group differences. The postmodern spirit of the age emphasizes diversity and the idea that the values and vision of one group cannot be imposed unilaterally on another. Since all systems of value and all visions for how the world should be (known to postmoderns as *metanarratives*) are considered morally equal, no one group has the right to impose its values or beliefs on another without its consent. Contemporary Christians can be guilty of a similar spirit when they emphasize the qualitative difference between the believer and the unbeliever that fails to also account for the common humanity, or the image of God, that is reflected in both. This is not to undermine the importance of the qualitative transformation of being born again. To be an evangelical means that one places a particular emphasis on leading people into the qualitative transformational experience of salvation. Evangelicals, however, have also been entrusted with the best metanarrative, a superior vision for life and a set of values that are applicable and that work for the betterment of all.

The biblical metanarrative is the story of Christ and the way redemption and reconciliation of all things bring glory to him. The Bible portrays Christ as both Savior and Creator of the world, with his position as Creator allowing him to also serve as Savior (John 1:29). This is John's point in his Gospel when he notes that Christ was from the beginning (the Word) and that all things came into being because of Christ (John 1:1–3). As Creator and Sovereign, Christ's Lordship exists and remains over every aspect of life. His Lordship is not exclusive to the church or to those things that have been identified as "Christian." Because sin attempts to steal from God what belongs to him, including the image of God reflected in all humanity, the biblical metanarrative can appear to be limited to those individuals or aspects of life deemed "Christian," yet there is not a non-Christian world that has been relinquished to Satan or to fallen humanity. Describing the biblical metanarrative, the Reformed theologian and writer Herman Bavinck wrote, "The essence of the Christian religion consists in this, that the creation of the Father, devastated by sin, is restored in the death of the Son of God, and recreated by the Holy Spirit into a kingdom of God."[3] Much of the richness of Christianity, Bavinck believed, was lost if the focus remained exclusively on the salvation of the individual.

God reveals his metanarrative of redemption and the glorification of Christ in two ways. The first is through Scripture and, ultimately, in the incarnation of Christ. He is the good news to a world that was created perfect and complete but which has been corrupted by sin. To human beings, image-bearers of God, he is the good news of restoration from the dehumanizing processes of sin—the destruction of a relationship with God and the

---

3. Bavinck, *Reformed Dogmatics*, 3:17.

theft of their full humanity. The Bible is the message of what theologians refer to as *special revelation* or *saving grace*—God's mercy and grace to humanity who, because of sin, are under condemnation. As the story of grace, of the transformation from being "children of wrath" to being members of the family of God (Eph 2:1–22), the Bible serves as a special message of faith and practice to those who have been redeemed.

The metanarrative of God is also revealed, however, in the creation itself and in history. It is the general work of God toward humanity in which Christ is not made specifically known. Creation and history convey the message of God's intent toward all humanity so that all are without excuse (Rom 1:18–20). Paul notes in Romans 2:14–15 that "the work of the Law" of God is written even on the hearts of unbelievers and that their relationship to the Law will be evident in their minds (conscience) and the way they act in the world. The biblical metanarrative conveyed through creation and history is often referred to by theologians as the *general revelation* of God. Like special revelation, where the message of saving grace accompanies the description and condemnation of sin, the metanarrative revealed through creation and history contains a corresponding story. The condemnation resulting from sin revealed through general revelation has its own corresponding message, what Reformed theologians often refer to as *common grace*.

In Reformed theology, common grace is distinctive from special grace. Common grace is that which is extended to all humanity but does not necessarily lead to salvation. Even so, because of the redemptive work of Christ, common grace is a manifestation of the salvation process. As Lewis Berkhof writes,

> When we speak of "common grace" we have in mind, either those general operations of the Holy Spirit whereby He, without renewing the heart, exercises such a moral influence on man through His general or special revelation, that sin is restrained, order is maintained in social life, and civil righteousness is promoted; or, those general blessings, such as rain and sunshine, food and drink, clothing and shelter, which God imparts to all men indiscriminately where and in what measure it seems good to Him.[4]

Though a theological distinction can be made between general and special revelation, both are part of the revelation of God whereby humanity can know about him. Similarly, while there is a clear difference in the purpose of saving and common grace, both are manifestations of God's grace to humanity. As such, it is essential to consider both as part of the same biblical metanarrative—the glorification of Christ. The Dutch scholar Abraham Kuyper notes that saving grace assumes the existence of common grace, for without the restraint of sin and evil, no one would be alive to receive special or saving grace.[5] To limit special grace to individual salvation, however, is to engage in a type of anthro-centrism whereby the message of salvation restricts the full extent of the glorification of Christ. The gospel message is Christ reconciling all things to himself (2 Cor 5:18), and Christians are a type of "first fruits" of that reconciliation process (cf. Jas 1:18 niv). It is a reconciliation process that not only restores the breached relationship between God and humanity but also repairs all the consequences of sin resulting from the Fall.

---

4. Berkhof, "Common Grace."

5. Kuyper, "Common Grace," in *A Centennial Reader*, 169.

When the glorification of Christ, rather than simply the salvation of humanity, becomes the central emphasis, saving grace and common grace can be viewed as two aspects of the same grand story. It is also a story in which Christians—as members of the body of Christ, as ministers of reconciliation, as first fruits of all he created—are allowed to play a significant role in the demonstration of that process to the world. As redeemed people, Christians are the embodiment of Christ, who is engaged in the reconciliation of all creation. It is a creation over which Christ remains as sovereign, so Christians are to demonstrate his Lordship and sovereignty over every aspect of life (Col 1:16–23).

Christ, as the reconciler of all things, recreates human beings spiritually. Through Christ, God makes the spiritually dead person to become alive (Eph 2:5). He also, however, recreates the world that bears the effects of sin, just as human beings bear the effects of sin. Just as the Bible speaks of the new birth and the new man (John 3:1–3; Eph 2:15), it also speaks of a new heaven and a new earth (cf. 2 Pet 3:13; Rev 21:1). Human beings not only exhibit the effects of sin in the severed relationship between themselves and God, others, nature, and self, but they also continue to demonstrate or reflect these effects through their willful engagement in sin. The sinful effects of humanity are borne by the creation, which also reflects these effects in its actions (e.g., natural disasters, development of harmful viruses, etc.). Since the actions of human beings create the negative effects of sin in the world, the actions of human beings can also assist in reducing and possibly eliminating of some of these effects. Christ comes to deal not only with the spiritual or invisible results of sin in humanity but also with the visible effects of sin that are manifested in the natural and social world (Col 1:16). For this reason, believers are called to do good works, not to earn salvation but to demonstrate their acknowledgement of the sovereignty and Lordship of Christ over all creation and their desire to glorify God (Eph 2:8–10).

Failure to grasp the glorification of Christ as the grand narrative of the Bible can result in a Christianity that is applied only to the saving of souls or to spiritual concerns and not to the visible aspects of all of creation. It represents a failure on the part of the church to acknowledge Christ as the Lord of all things. The result is that certain aspects of life (e.g., personal behavior, the church, evangelism, the Christian school) are considered "Christian" since they are directly linked to those things perceived as spiritual. All other aspects of life, however, become relegated to another sphere of influence, another lordship, because they do not specifically address the issues of salvation or personal sanctification. Granted, few believers would admit to such a drastic distinction, and the language of evangelicalism acknowledges the Lordship of Christ over all things. Still, a limited view of the gospel results in linking the concerns of the visible world to an invisible one that focuses only on personal salvation and sanctification. The result is a type of biblical integration that is selfish or self-focused. The focus becomes how the individual Christian or the faith community can live morally in the world and avoid the negative influences of sin that threaten their relationship with Christ. The offensive nature of Christ and the church to overcome the power of sin in the world becomes defensive; rather than overpowering the gates of hell, the church attempts to bunker down to withstand the siege (cf. Matt 16:18). This limited view of the gospel creates a false dichotomy that leaves Christians little impetus to change the world and, instead, seeks only to avoid its negative effects.

A result of this false dichotomy is a type of anti-intellectualism, or what historian Mark Noll has labeled "the scandal of the evangelical thinking . . . often resulting from a way of pursuing knowledge that does not accord with Christianity."[6] Failing to extend the gospel message beyond justification and sanctification, failing to embrace the concept of common grace, has left contemporary evangelicals with little impetus to promote a wholly biblical approach to academic, professional, or socio-cultural life. Consequently, there has been little development of a uniquely biblical approach to the arts, economics and commerce, government, and so forth that promotes the glory of God by addressing sin and its influence both on individuals and on the institutions and practice of the society. While evangelicals continue to promote biblical integration, the focus on withstanding the attack of the world produces an understanding of integration that is more defensive than offensive. In essence, biblical integration becomes a type of coping mechanism to buffer Christians from the effects of the world rather than a holistic vision for life that promotes cultural transformation.

The doctrine of common grace also strengthens the biblical idea that all human beings are image-bearers of God. It reinforces the idea that all of humanity has been entrusted by God with the responsibility of stewardship and that this task was not revoked as a result of the Fall. The communal nature of believers established in the church is not unique to the redeemed; all human beings were created to live and work with others in community. While social harmony is corrupted by sinful individuals seeking their own advantage with little regard to the interests of the group, the idea of innate human commonality implies a mutual dependency that would have influenced cultural development before the Fall. This commonality and mutual dependency would have led to systems of governance, economic practices, patterns in music and art, means of education, and other aspects of culture that would have promoted stewardship and work for the common good. God, even before the Fall, would have taken delight in high human development that enhanced social bonds, which led to humanity bringing glory to him through seeking the betterment of others.

Although the destructive nature of sin means that the fundamental demands of stewardship cannot be fully practiced in the post-Fall world, God does not revoke the stewardship mandate but extends it by obligating humanity to reconcile the divisions created by sin and its effects. Given the sin nature, any degree of human obedience to this command is predicated on the extension of common grace by God. Without the extension of common grace, human beings would be subject to the destructive consequences of sin. In essence, human beings, as children of Satan (cf. John 8:44), would seek to engage in the very processes of their father, the thief of John 10:10, who seeks to steal, kill, and destroy. The result would be behaviors, both individually and culturally, that would be divisive and destructive—to individuals, to nature, and to others. That human beings can, at times, even in their unbelieving state, engage in acts of self-sacrifice, create works of art that inspire, uplift, or assist, or establish laws or social institutions that are nobler than

---

6. Noll, *The Scandal of the Evangelical Mind*, 12.

the collective tendencies of their sin natures are evidences of God's extension of common grace to humanity.

Kuyper notes that the enrichment of the visible world (exterior) in a fallen world sheds light on the poverty of the spiritual nature of humanity (interior) apart from Christ. He writes,

> Enrichment of the *exterior* life will go hand in hand with the impoverishment of the *interior*. The common grace that affects the human heart, human relations, and public practices will ever diminish, and only the other operation, the one that enriches and gratifies the human mind and senses will proceed to its culmination.[7]

Common grace provides an understanding of the human heart, human relations, and the human spirit that serves as a lead to evangelism. Human beings seem to have nobility yet are given to selfishness, wickedness, and savagery that produces a type of mental, emotional, and spiritual dissonance, which can serve to highlight the impoverishment of the human spirit—a condition that can only be addressed through Christ. The Bible also notes that the good works of believers toward others serve as a means of judgment, showing unbelievers their failure before the standards of God (cf. Prov 25:21–22; Rom 12:20). Operating in the external world, however, requires that individuals have a proper perspective about it: that the world is fallen and not as God intended. In other words, the actions taken in the world proceed from an understanding that the reality commonly experienced by human beings is not normal from God's perspective; instead, it is abnormal and needs repair. As a result, the concept of common grace, and all biblically based education, is predicated on cultivating an abnormalist view of the world and learning how an educated person should live in such a world.

NORMALISTS AND ABNORMALISTS

Christian theology historically has been based on the view that God created a world that he deemed as good (Gen 1:31), but that this goodness was corrupted by the introduction of sin—an event theologically known as the Fall. This historical event corrupted every aspect of human spiritual, moral, emotional, social, psychological, and physical being, but it also affected every aspect of the nonhuman creation as well. As a result, the experiences human beings have of the world externally, as well as the ways that they understand it internally, are not as God intended. Human beings understand and respond to these external experiences as not bad (i.e., the opposite of good) since the creation still maintains some of its original splendor. In truth, all aspects of creation have been corrupted so that they no longer retain all of the divine magnificence that was part of the original evaluation noted in Genesis 1:31. This theological reckoning of the world, known as the abnormalist view, renders the conclusion that all of the creation, both the human and the nonhuman, are abnormal and needs restoration.

Applied to education, the abnormalist view means that students must come to understand that the world in which they live is not the world God created. This view of education should affect not only what and how students should learn but also govern how an educated

7. Kuyper, "Common Grace," in *A Centennial Reader*, 181–82 (italics in original).

person should live in the world. The idea that Christ is glorified through the redemption and reconciliation of all things to himself is the process of reconciliation—taking that which has become broken (abnormal) and restoring it back to its normal state—the one that God originally intended. Philosopher Nicholas Wolterstorff states this case:

> The fact that Christianity is a soteriological religion presupposes that there is, in its judgment, something that we and the cosmos need saving from. It presupposes that there is something amiss in our situation. Things are not right as they are; they are not as they ought to be. Things are, in that way, abnormal. And the Christian believes that an abnormal remedy is required if we are to be saved from this abnormal situation.[8]

Christian learning, therefore, is different from secular learning. Secularists, because they deny the reality of the Fall, are normalists, assuming that the world is the way it has always been. As a result, any way of understanding the world on this assumption will be guilty of committing what philosopher G. E. Moore labeled the naturalistic fallacy—the application of an ethical standard of good to those things that exist in nature.[9] As the West moved from a religious to a material worldview, a process that started with the Enlightenment in seventeenth-century Europe, the dominant perspective of the culture was centered on the natural or material world. As a result, the naturalistic perspective has come to serve as the norm, the one that people growing up in Western cultures are socialized to accept as true. It is from this dominant perspective that individuals make assumptions about not only how the world is but also how the world should be. In Western cultures, based in the Enlightenment's emphasis on human free will, reason, and science, individuals and societies can create the world they desire by exercising their reason and scientific methodology to understand and corporately construct how they believe the world should be. Since education in Western societies, both formal and informal, assumes the fallen world to be normal, it reinforces these Enlightenment concepts in students and teaches them to adjust appropriately. The result is an education that is schizophrenic, an adjustment to live in a world that is not real. Insofar as Christian education also seeks to prepare young people to adjust to culture in a way that accepts the world as normal or to simply avoid the negative influence of a fallen world, it also adopts an approach to education that is normalist. This is not a transformation of the mind that enables the believer to live out God's will in the world.

8. Wolterstorff, "Abraham Kuyper on Christian Learning," 215–16.
9. Moore, *Principia Ethica*, 12.

Figure Three:
Biblical / Secular Thinking Continuum

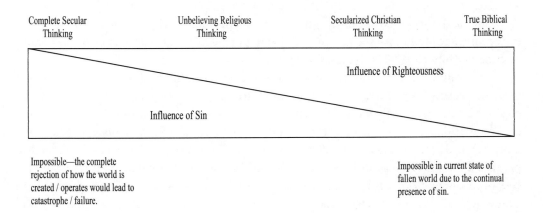

| Complete Secular Thinking | Unbelieving Religious Thinking | Secularized Christian Thinking | True Biblical Thinking |

Influence of Righteousness

Influence of Sin

Impossible—the complete rejection of how the world is created / operates would lead to catastrophe / failure.

Impossible in current state of fallen world due to the continual presence of sin.

Generally Christian education seeks to counter the negative effects of secular thinking by cultivating biblical thinking in the mind of the believer. Often these attempts are labeled worldview transformation, biblical integration, or Christian critical thinking. While laudable, this goal can be problematic, creating an either-or distinction that is blinded to other possibilities, which can be detrimental to biblical thinking. Rather than viewing secular thinking and biblical thinking as an either-or proposition, it is helpful to see them as ends of a continuum. The Fall did not render the world the opposite of God's intent (i.e., from good to bad); rather it corrupted the good, rendering it less than God intended. As figure 3 demonstrates, *Complete Secular Thinking*, thinking that completely rejects anything biblical, including the physical and socio-moral realities inherent in the creation by God, would be impossible. No individual or culture could pursue such an agenda without failure for they would have to reject even the natural law that is embedded in the created order. Conversely, *True Biblical Thinking*, completely and harmoniously aligned with the teaching of Scripture and the will of God, is also a theological impossibility, due to the presence of sin in the believer and in the world, until Christ establishes his kingdom.

Between these extremes lay a number of possible alternatives based upon the degree to which sin and righteous are accommodated. What can result is thinking that is religious (i.e., theistic) where the existence of God or gods is acknowledged and where life must be lived in a way that appeases or will secure divine favor. What can also result is a type of *Secularized Christian Thinking*, which acknowledges the truth of the Bible but fails to appropriate those truths in a transformative way. In practice such a view promotes an adjustment agenda for Christian education. Its goal is to prepare students to withstand the negative effects of the world. It is called secularized because such thinking produces a type of deism, where the reality of God is acknowledged but his sovereign power and Lordship are effectively denied. Secularized Christian thinking is an extension of the normalist perspective in that it fails to acknowledge the transformative power of God to be glorified in processes of reconciliation other than bringing people to God through individual salvation in Christ. Failing to account for these intermediate positions creates a danger to biblical education in that any perspective to the right of *Unbelieving Religious Thinking* can be accepted as biblical and, therefore, proper. This leaves those who have unknowingly adopted more secularized Christian perspectives with little impetus to change or consider biblical alternatives to their positions.

True biblical thinking fully appropriates the abnormalist position, not only seeking to understand the spiritual, moral, emotional, social, psychological, and physical effects of sin, but also acknowledging that true education prepares people to live for God in a broken world. The application to those students who are Christians, those in whom the Holy Spirit dwells, should be evident. Education, from this perspective, is designed to prepare people to engage in the glorification of Christ through participation in the process of reconciliation. It is learning how to be faithful to the obligations of stewardship in a fallen world. This perspective would correct the shortcomings of an education based in secularized Christian thinking. The obligations of stewardship, however, are expected of all who are created in the image of God. As such, the abnormalist perspective can also be extended to unbelievers, to those who do not have the transformative power of the Holy Spirit dwelling within. This prompts our asking to what extent the abnormalist view of education pertains to learning among students who are not believers.

Generally, the goal of education is to produce students who think in a particular way. The normalist and abnormalist perspectives are ways of understanding the world that, when applied to education, promote a particular way of thinking in students. When these two perspectives are applied to believers or unbelievers, they produce four general types of thinking in students: *Complete Secular Thinking*, *Secularized Christian Thinking*, *Unbelieving Religious Thinking*, and *True Christian Thinking*. These categories are summarized in figure 4.

Figure Four:
Characteristics of Normalist / Abnormalist Thinking

	Unbeliever	Believer

Abnormalist	**Unbelieving Religious Thinking**
	• Religious Education
	• Creates dissonant state
	• Understands that the world is not right and seeks a transcendent idea or ideal to restore
	• Lacks power of the Holy Spirit; thus leads to a gap between the ideal and the ability to implement or live it out in practice
		True Biblical Thinking
		• True Christian Education
		• Understands the world as abnormal and the need for a divine restoration / reconciliation
		• Recognizes that learning and living are responses to the abnormal state that the world is in
		  - Stewardship
		  - Reconciliation
		  - Cultivating / Restoring the Image of God
		• Views church / community of faith as a counter-cultural response (i.e., the abnormalist view confronting the predominant normalist perspective)

Normalist	**Complete Secular Thinking**
	• Naturalistic Education
	• Becomes unsustainable academically
	  - Natural Sciences—appeal to natural law
	  - Social Sciences—appeal to natural law or cultural norms as "truth"
	• Leads to fragmentation or the denial of truth to sustain
	• Attempts to normalize effects of sin
	• Appeals to natural state of unbelievers
		Secularized Christian Thinking
		• Incomplete / Disintegrated Christian Education
		• Creates dissonant state—a dualistic or fragmented Christianity that is not applied consistently to all areas of life
		• Creates Christian thoughts / behaviors that are in conformity and adaptation to the fallen culture (for comfort of individual rather than benefit of others)
		• Can lead to isolation (avoiding cultural engagement) or dualism (compartmentalization) of life (e.g., "secular / sacred" categories)

Of these four types of thinking, two alternatives apply to unbelievers, those students who do not possess the indwelling Holy Spirit. The first is a type of thinking that is promoted by an education that seeks to promote the normalist perspective. This can be identified as *Complete Secular Thinking*. It is based in a naturalistic education, where observing the physical world and its mechanisms are the exclusive means of knowing truth. It is an education consistent with philosophical materialism or naturalism, where the universe can be understood as the interworking of the variables of energy, time, matter, and probability. This type of education places an emphasis on the physical and social sciences to help discover and utilize natural laws or rules of probability to promote an efficient society. Because this perspective denies the social, moral, and spiritual design that is embedded in the creation, it eventually becomes academically and educationally unsustainable. By denying certain fundamental aspects of the created order, it produces knowledge that is fragmented—placing a particular emphasis on the physical world at the expense of the spiritual. As a result, it produces a fragmented view of humanity, reducing humans to physical beings whose social value (in the contemporary context) is defined economically. True secular thinking is the inclination of unbelief and is described by Paul in Romans 1:24–32, where the creation is worshipped above the Creator and the result is judgment. Ultimately it is a type of thinking that attempts to normalize the selfish tendencies of the sin nature.

Paul records in Romans 1:20–23, however, that there is a revelation of God in nature that unbelievers can see and an understanding of his existence that can be partially understood from reason. This type of system, labeled *Unbelieving Religious Thinking*, constitutes a theistic understanding of the world that can be obtained by an unbeliever. This type of thinking can be characterized by an understanding of God that, as the French philosopher René Descartes noted, is innately embedded in the mind of humans.[10] Directed by proper theology, unbelievers can also understand that the world is not as it is supposed to be, that it is abnormal from God's perspective. Education, from this perspective, goes beyond observing the physical design of the universe to understanding the social, moral, and spiritual components embedded in the creation. A theistic understanding of the world can be characterized as unbelieving religious education, where the student is provided a religious education but, because the Holy Spirit is not present in the life of the student, true spiritual transformation is absent. The result is an education designed not only to promote content acquisition but also to develop a moral character that is based in a religious tradition.

For students who are believers, those indwelled by and subject to the transforming power of the Holy Spirit, two different types of thinking are possible. The first type of thinking is promoted by a type of education that presents a normalist perspective of the world, labeled as *Secularized Christian Thinking*. This type of thinking can be cultivated by the student who attends a public school or a Christian school where the truth of the gospel is not extended to every aspect of life. It is a type of thinking that fails to appropriate the gospel message of reconciliation to all of creation. The result is a view of the world or a type of Christianity, like that of unbelieving religious thinking, that is incomplete and fragmented. This type of thinking can create a state of dissonance and helps cultivate a dualistic vision of life, where the Bible is explicit to certain areas and silent to others. This fragmentation can also create a division between the social, moral, and spiritual aspects of God's design for humanity, resulting in a view of education that is self-focused and self-empowering rather than directed toward the benefit of others.

A second type of thinking is promoted when the believer is educated in an abnormalist view of the world, one that fully appropriates the gospel message of reconciliation to every aspect of life. This position is identified as *True Biblical Thinking* because it seeks to integrate the physical, social, moral, and spiritual dimensions of creation into a coherent approach that appropriates the Lordship of Christ to every area of life. As abnormalist, it understands that the world is not as God intended and is in need of repair. It also understands that the reason for the abnormality in the world is sin so that repairs must be directed to every aspect of life. Since the process of repairing the damage of sin is active, this perspective of education goes beyond simple understanding to the application of truth, leading to a position that the biblical worldview is a world *and* life view. Learning and living are responses to the abnormal state of the world, and the obligations of stewardship and reconciliation require preparation for transformation and restoration

---

10. Descartes, *Meditations of First Philosophy*, 76–77. In his third meditation, entitled "Concerning God, That He Exists," Descartes attempts to demonstrate that, starting from his own reasoning, God must exist because the concept of God is innately embedded in his mind.

of Christ's Lordship to all of life. While acknowledging that Christ is the One who restores all things for his glory, this view of education also recognizes the believer's call to participate in restoration and reconciliation as a faithful disciple. Rather than engage in cultural adaptation, true biblical thinking promotes a view of the individual as fully human and a member of a community that is countercultural to the normalist practices of the world. Education for true biblical thinking should also prepare students to faithfully withstand the consequences that can result from living counter to or confronting a culture that seeks to make normal the tendencies of the sin nature.

The goal of all Christian education, whether the student is a believer or unbeliever, is to cultivate a full abnormalist view. The spiritual state of the learner, however, fosters various outcomes. Believers who fully understand the abnormalist perspective will cultivate learning and living that prepares them for stewardship and reconciliation. As image-bearers of God, they will also understand that their true humanity can only be experienced communally—in their relationship with God and with others. Consequently, they seek the advancement of Christ's kingdom through a community that seeks the betterment of others. For unbelievers, an abnormalist education promotes an ideal state or utopian view, one that should be pursued by the student. Without access to the Holy Spirit, these ideals become philosophical or ideological positions that are selfishly pursued. Lacking the Holy Spirit, the organic nature of community that is available to the believer is absent to the unbeliever. Communal relations are reduced to alliances or driven by shared individual goals. The students can understand that their talents, abilities, and resources should be used in a way consistent with stewardship, reconciliation, and promoting the image of God, which they may understand as the way things ought to be. They may also understand that the best way to accomplish these goals is in concert with others of similar motivation. The use of their abilities, however, is not obligatory. Any use of their talents to pursue these goals or their ideological position and any use of those abilities in a biblically consistent manner constitutes the operating of common grace in the world.

Outside of community, the unbeliever may pursue to promote his or her individual goals (which are subject to self-definition and interpretation). Apart from the Spirit, they become a means of self-glorification through the attainment of wealth, prestige, comfort, advancement, and so forth. While others may benefit from these actions, this benefit is secondary to the promotion of the individual's self-interest. The betterment of others is secondary to the primary goal of achieving their ideological or philosophical ideal. For this reason, the pursuit of the ideal can take precedence over the negative effects that can sometimes result in the lives of individuals. In either case, for the unbeliever such actions have no saving grace but can be viewed as having virtue (cf. Eccl 5:18–20) or incorrectly, as having saving effects. The promotion of self-interest by unbelievers can result in a disturbing phenomenon. Isaiah notes this tendency when he writes that "all our righteous deeds are like a filthy garment" (Isa 64:6). Whether for promotion in this life or in pursuit of salvation through works, unbelievers may pursue righteousness more vigorously than believers. The inability to realize their ideal can lead to a sense of dissonance in an unbeliever that permits opportunities for evangelism.

Unfortunately, not all Christian education conforms to the abnormalist perspective. Returning to figure 3, as education moves left from true biblical thinking, it also adopts an increasingly normalist or secularized perspective. This movement has two consequences. The first is to reduce the transformational power of the gospel to promote reconciliation in favor of a perspective that seeks to adapt to the culture. This adaptation, since it represents an accommodation to sin, is secular in its orientation. The second, since secularism fragments the image of God in humanity, is to exchange the dependent and communal nature of the image of God for a more autonomous and individual view. Educationally, evangelicals contribute to this movement by engaging in worldview change where worldviews are treated as synonymous with philosophies.

As discussed earlier in the book, philosophies are held individually; they are based on analytical or logical arguments and modified when a person determines they have been presented a more coherent or logical argument. Worldview education based in this model assumes that presenting a person with a more coherent argument will be persuasive enough to cause the individual to modify and align her thinking biblically. This approach reduces Christian thought and action to that which is rational and deemphasizes the roles of Holy Spirit and the church as the body of Christ. A philosophical or analytical approach to worldview transformation also assumes no difference between a student who is a believer and one who is an unbeliever. A rational argument will be rational whether the student is a believer or unbeliever for there is not a biblical logic that operates separately or differently from the logic of unbelief. Granted, there may be different presuppositions upon which the arguments are based, but if these presuppositions are accepted by the unbeliever (as in the case of unbelieving religious thinking), the logic and reasoning process can arrive at the same conclusions. If the Holy Spirit is considered in the equation, it is more to the extent that the Spirit increases the tendency of the believer to accept the biblical presuppositions and the inevitable conclusion more readily than an unbeliever.

This approach to worldview transformation assumes that a reorientation of one's life to God can be directed through reason. This approach to worldview transformation is based in the principles of evidentialist apologetics or the idea that the promotion of Christianity can be made based on facts supported and verified by historical evidence. Wolterstorff reports that Kuyper (and others) noted a problem in the fundamental assumption of this type of apologetics when he writes,

> It should come as no surprise now to learn that Kuyper had no use for evidentialist apologetics. He regarded such apologetics as committed to the thesis that even the most fundamental disagreements between Christians and non-Christians are not rationally intractable. Non-Christians, so the apologists assumes or claims, have it in their power to decide to attend with an open mind to the arguments displaying the evidence for Christianity: if they do so attend, they will be convinced. In fact, says Kuyper, "apologetics has always failed to reach results, and has weakened rather than strengthened the reasoner." That is so, at bottom, because evidentialist apologetics mistakenly assumes the truth of normalism. It assumes that the re-orientation of one's life toward God can be born of reason.[11]

11. Wolterstorff, "Abraham Kuyper on Christian Learning," 222.

What will result from an evidentialist apologetic, and a worldview education based in this apologetic, is that in attitude, thought, and behavior there will be little difference between normalist or secularized Christian thinking and unbelieving religious thinking that is grounded in the Christian tradition. This may help to account for why there is often little difference between Christian students in terms of goals, attitudes, and aspirations (once those have been stripped of evangelical jargon) and those of their nonevangelically churched or morally secular peers. Behaviorally, some differences may exist, but generally these can be attributed to the standards and reinforcement of the community of faith in which the believer identifies (i.e., more faith-based and communal) and less to the power of an evidentialist-based worldview education.

The introduction of normalism to Christian thinking also represents a threat to the coherence or internal consistency of the biblical worldview. The introduction of sin creates fragmentation in any worldview, leading to internal inconsistencies that cannot be resolved. Since worldviews always result in cultural behavior, the inability to resolve these inconsistencies forces proponents of a normalist worldview to adapt to culture rather than transform the culture in light of its ideals. These adaptations can take several forms. They can create forms of deception that allow proponents of a worldview to live comfortably with the inconsistencies and still gain some semblance of social approval or can create variations of the worldview that allow them to adjust to certain inconsistencies while ignoring others. For evangelicals, the introduction of normalist thinking has resulted in a fragmented and dualistic worldview that fails to connect biblical Christianity to all aspects of life. This has left the church in a position where it must adapt to culture rather than engage in its divinely mandated charge to transform it. In contemporary evangelical practice this adaptation has primarily taken two forms: isolation or dualism.

The first response, isolation, is an attempt to restrict involvement with the culture. From this perspective, the culture is permeated with the presence of sin. Since the introduction of sin into culture is believed to be both destructive and irreversible, any engagement in culture will lead to spiritually damaging effects in the life of the believer. Thus, the only legitimate response to culture is to avoid participation as much as possible. While this perspective correctly identifies the extent to which sin permeates culture, it fails to recognize the pervasive extent of sin; the fact is, sin has already affected even those who most faithfully attempt to adhere to this position. For example, since cultural engagement is to be avoided, there is little incentive in academic learning that prepares people for cultural transformation. Since education is no longer a preparation for cultural transformation, its benefit becomes utilitarian: preparing people to find jobs, which allows them to pursue their goals of supporting a family and contributing to ministry. This utilitarian approach to education is essentially no different from the reasons for pursuing an education given by secularists (minus the Christian terminology) where unbelievers pursue a quality education because it will allow them to achieve their individual goals. In both cases, the purpose for education is vocational; it is an economic argument that mirrors the dominant worldview of the culture, which the isolationists claim to avoid.

A second response, dualism, is characterized by a determination of what can or cannot be done culturally. From this perspective, individuals can freely engage in and enjoy culture as long as they are careful to avoid the spiritually damaging aspects of culture. While this perspective correctly acknowledges the graciousness of the gifts that God provides (including the gift of culture), it fails to grasp the extent to which sin permeates every aspect of cultural life. Objects can be viewed as value neutral, their moral and spiritual value determined by how they are used, which fails to account for the fact that the creation of any object is based in a particular worldview and, thus, is value-driven, and which tends to violate the expressed theology of those proponents who claim nothing is value neutral. This tendency to view certain aspects of culture as value neutral creates the secular-sacred problem: life is compartmentalized and certain aspects of life are viewed as intimately biblical while others are disconnected and not seen from a biblical perspective.

This position also introduces normalist tendencies to Christian thinking. By viewing certain aspects of culture as value neutral and, in essence, separating them from the direct authority and Lordship of Christ, not everything is abnormal nor does everything bear the effect of sin. As such, there are certain aspects of life that do not require transformation since their moral value is not inherent but determined by how individuals engage in that area of life. This can leave certain aspects of academic learning or cultural life insulated from biblical examination. For example, a Christian advertising executive can freely use the social and psychological techniques of his field to persuade people to buy a product as long as the product is not viewed as immoral, failing to consider the worldview values that helped to create these techniques and to discern whether the values from which those techniques derive may be at odds with the biblical worldview.

In essence, any type of education that aligns with either of these cultural adaptations produces a version of unbelieving religious education that is founded in the Christian tradition. By accommodating normalist tendencies, the system fails to fully embrace the abnormalist perspective upon which the biblical worldview and the divine mandate for cultural transformation are based. It also fails to extend the gospel to every aspect of life, compartmentalizing life in ways that create a tendency in believers to seek the vision of another worldview to fill the void. In addition, worldview education based in evidential apologetics reduces biblical Christianity to a set of rational propositions and logical arguments leading to a system of belief. This system can, and often does, produce a set of rules or behavioral expectations that are believed to be reasonable as well as morally and spiritually binding. The result is a type of individualistic Christianity where people can be "Christian" if their thoughts, attitudes, beliefs, and so on, are orthodox and if their behavior conforms to the standards set by the faith community. Eliminated from this type of Christianity is the transformational power of the Holy Spirit in the life of the believer to will and to do the good pleasure of God and to work for the benefit of others (Phil 2:1–13).

These effects can occur regardless of the quality of Christian education students receive. The spiritual condition of students is a significant variable relative to their acquisition and understanding of the content. Unbelieving students, without the power of the Holy Spirit to assist them, can only process and understand the world from a fallen perspective. Thus, even the most thoroughly biblical education will be processed in a manner consistent with unbelieving religious thinking. Similarly, believers who are more worldly, who possess the Holy Spirit but tend to think and act from motivations similar to an unbeliever, will also process their sound biblical content in a fashion similar to unbelievers. This does not, however, release the Christian school or the church from its responsibility to examine whether its approach to education helps to promote a type of thinking other than true Christian thinking. The church and the Christian school have a spiritual obligation to cultivate an abnormalist perspective and true biblical thinking in order to prepare and encourage a community to propagate the gospel to every aspect of life.

CULTURAL TRANSFORMATION AS SHALOM

Chapter 6 addressed the biblical concept of the Fall, the introduction of abnormality into the creation, and God's intended vision for reconciling the world from the effects sin. The Hebrew prophets called the return to normality God's instituted peace or *shalom*. While *shalom* is often translated to English as "peace," the term means so much more. Quoting Cornelius Plantinga, "In the Bible, shalom means *universal flourishing, wholeness, and delight*—a rich state of affairs in which natural needs are satisfied and natural gifts fruitfully employed, a state of affairs that inspires joyful wonder as its Creator and Savior opens doors and welcomes the creatures in whom he delights. Shalom, in other words, is the way things ought to be."[12]

Shalom is the time when all of creation is reconciled to God, when all the effects of sin are repaired, and when all humanity is restored to harmony with God, others, nature, and self. In relationship to the study of worldview, shalom is the time when all worldview dialogue will cease, for there will no longer be a need to describe the gap between what is and what ought to be. Shalom is not a utopian society, for utopians envision a world that has never been nor can ever be. Shalom is a restoration, a return to a world described by its Creator as good. Shalom is also not a return to Eden, for the original pristine Garden was simply the beginning of the creative process that was directed to the development of culture that would glorify God and serve others. Shalom, rather, is the state where culture is transformed to reflect the desire of God that was intended to direct human beings in their development of the creation. In shalom the talents, gifts, and abilities of all individuals are meaningfully employed to glorify God by serving others—enhancing the image of God in both the server and those being served.

The shalom of creation, the good that God intended, was disfigured and rendered abnormal by the Fall and the human introduction of sin into the world. The effect of sin was to corrupt shalom in every aspect of life in which human beings are related—to God, nature, others, and self. The effects of this corruption are easily noted in individuals as people think, desire, and act in ways contrary to God's will or original intent. Often, however, the corporate effects of this corruption are overlooked. If all aspects of life in which humans have contact are compromised by sin, then culture, as created by human beings, also bears the effects of corruption. As human beings engage in these cultural and communal aspects of life, they are socialized by them. The effect of this socialization is to

---

12. Plantinga, *Not the Way It's Supposed to Be*, 10 (italics in original).

view those aspects of life as normal, failing to see the corrosive effects of the institutions and the means of cultural engagement on the shalom of God.

Christ, as the Son of God, the Prince of Peace, comes to bring shalom to the world. It is God's promise of deliverance, the pledge of a Redeemer, that bestows to all creation both common grace and future restoration (cf. Gen 3:16; Rom 16:20). As the recipients of saving grace, Christians have begun to experience Christ's shalom. Through faith in Christ believers are indwelled with the power of the Holy Spirit so that they not only are reconciled to God positionally (justification) but can increasingly experience more of Christ's shalom as they grow in their relationship to him (sanctification). From this restoration, the Christian can now begin the process of being reconciled to others, to oneself, as well as to nature. As the "first fruits" of reconciliation (Jas 1:18), Christians are called to the "ministry of reconciliation" (2 Cor 5:18), to be "peacemakers" (Matt 5:9), so that the world can also experience the shalom of Christ. As the children of God grow in their relationship to God, they are to act as agents of shalom, just as the Lord Christ did in initiating and ensuring the process and completion of reconciliation. It is Christ, as the Son of God, who serves to bring peace to the world. Christians, when they act as peacemakers, are described by Christ as being the "sons of God." For Christians, the engagement in reconciliation should not be an unnatural act but an expression of who they are as disciples of Christ and children of God. As it is in the mind of Christ, seeking reconciliation and the betterment of others should govern and affect all that the believers think, desire, and do (Phil 2:1–8).

As the way the world was intended to be, shalom is the normal or uncorrupted state to which the creation groans to return. It is the state of affairs where the material and immaterial aspects of God's created order—the physical, psychological, social, and spiritual—all operate according to the design of God and in harmony with each other. As image-bearers of God, unbelievers may attempt to exercise shalom. They may act in ways that are benevolent or self-sacrificing. They may engage in behaviors or create institutions that seek the betterment of others. Such motivations and actions, however, are unnatural, as evidenced by the fact that societies must often create incentives to engage people to act in ways that promote the welfare of others. They are motivations and actions that violate the disposition of the sin nature to seek, protect, promote, and glorify the self. As a result, such ideas and actions become utopian, based in a vision and understanding that the world is not the way it should be yet destined to fail because such a vision cannot be sustained because of the presence of sin.

For believers, indwelled by the Holy Spirit and possessing a new nature free from the bondage of sin, shalom becomes a natural state. The attitudes and actions required to live shalom are natural (i.e., the way God intended) and constitute the normal Christian life. The characteristics of the Beatitudes (Matt 5:3–12) do not represent an idealized Christianity but are the qualities of Christ to be emulated by every disciple. For the Christian, however, these natural actions of shalom are to be performed in a world that has been rendered abnormal. For this reason, following the characteristics of the Beatitudes is Christ's command to his followers to be salt and light so that the world can see their good works and glorify the Father (Matt 5:13–16). When applied to an understanding of culture, shalom living requires a countercultural response to a corrupted culture created by fallen humanity intent on normalizing sin. This type of countercultural response must be applied to every area of life. To live counterculturally is demanding. It requires the Christian and the church to distinguish themselves from the rest of society by demonstrating the reality of the Creator by living harmoniously in his creation.

Failing to appropriate the power of the Holy Spirit and live in accordance with the new nature, the Christian will more closely resemble the image of God in unbelievers. This will lead believers to adapt to culture, to normalize it, rather than engage in the difficult process of living normally in an abnormal world. Like unbelievers, they may attempt to exercise shalom, but do so in such a way that protects, promotes, and glorifies the self. For many believers, this process may be characterized by identifying several points of disagreement with the culture while fundamentally ascribing to the rest of the values of the culture. The identification of such issues allows believers to maintain a sense of difference, which they can base on biblical standards, while still ascribing to the basic values of the culture that provide social acceptance and general ease of life. Such acceptance, however, can only be achieved by accepting as normal the abnormality of a sinfully created culture.

A person identified as mentally ill can serve as an illustration. This designation generally occurs when the thought process or actions of an individual deviate significantly from that which is defined as normal. The definition of normal, however, is subjective, that is, it is based on what is considered an appropriate thought process or behavioral pattern in comparison to the majority of people in the culture. If someone acts significantly different from the established patterns of the society, that person would be considered deviant. The source of that deviance might be linked to motivations or ways of thinking that are at odds with how others in the society are motivated or think. In lieu of an objective, transcendent standard, normal becomes defined either by the patterns of the majority or according to a sociological or biological standard.

Theologically, however, the world is abnormal; it is not as God intended it to be. A transcendent standard of normal is available and is based in what the Bible identifies as the image of God. Being fallen and out of harmony with the transcendent standard, the majority of people define normal in ways that are at odds with God's standard. As such, they are deviant and, theologically speaking, "insane," despite the fact that the majority of people may think and act in ways that are congruent with this abnormal standard. As a result, the abnormal is rendered normal by the majority, while God's intended standard for normal is branded as abnormal. In light of the majority, the person who thinks and lives according to the standards of God, who displays his full humanity as an image-bearer of God, appears deviant; his thoughts, motivations, and actions are incongruent with those of the surrounding culture. The insanity of the majority, however, is considered normal based on the institutionally legitimized standards of sin in the society.

Ultimately, the principle of shalom means that believers are to be motivated to make the world better for others. This motivation affects not only how believers think but also how they act as children of God in the world. The biblical worldview is a world *and* life view. It is the desire to live in harmony with God and with the creation. It is the reestablishment of shalom, working to make the world better through God's grace and the act of reconciliation by Christ on the cross. For evangelicals, the first and most critical reconciliation is that of working to restore the relationship of humanity to God, yet an understanding of grace in both its forms, common and special, means that evangelism is not the only act of reconciliation in which believers engage. Believers also work to restore shalom to every area of life and do so because they are motivated to make the world better for others and not simply more comfortable for themselves. It is the emulation of Christ, who came not to be served but to serve others (Matt 20:28; Mark 10:45). Working for shalom demands that believers use their knowledge, talents, gifts, abilities, and resources for the betterment of others. This is the principle of stewardship, manifested in a fallen world as stewards engage in the process of reconciliation. In so doing, believers can be a light to all humanity, both believers and unbelievers, in the common grace effects that demonstrate what true humanity, based in the image of God, is intended to be. Worldview transformation is, above all else, the act of preparing people to engage in this process.

ARNIE'S DRIVE HOME

Arnie mulled over the morning's conversation with Manfred and Barry in his mind most of the day. As he started his drive home, now able to spend a few quiet moments with his thoughts, he considered his earlier statement that if Christianity is objectively true, then its demands are applicable to all humanity, not just Christians. Even so, Arnie thought, the absence of the Holy Spirit in the lives of unbelievers makes obedience to the biblical commands impossible. Still, even believers struggle with obedience because of the continuing presence of sin. Given these two theological realities, Arnie returned to the original question—can all students benefit from a Christian education?

As he continued his drive home, Arnie began to formulate his answer. There are two types of students; therefore, two types of Christian education. While the goals may be the same for all, the presence of the Holy Spirit should make all the difference in terms of outcomes. The principles discussed in the teacher in-services—stewardship, reconciliation, and restoration of the image of God—are applicable to all humanity. They are biblical expectations for human behavior for which education should prepare all individuals, and they are the standards upon which all individuals will be judged by God. They are the goals of a biblically based Christian education. Even so, the state of students' spiritual condition—the absence or presence of the Holy Spirit, their bondage to the sin nature, or their experience with the freedom of the new nature—means that students cannot be treated as blank slates. While unbelievers and believers are both image-bearers of God, the indwelling Holy Spirit and the new nature renders the believers qualitatively different from their unbelieving peers. The curriculum content and instructional methodologies of Christian education should focus on preparing individuals to live biblically in a world that has been rendered abnormal by the presence of sin. Unbelievers and obedient and maturing believers, however, will process this content and respond to these methodologies in different ways. As a Christian educator, Arnie came to realize, he was serving two roles.

For his students who are unbelievers, the focus of Christian education is on content. Because of their spiritual condition, Arnie cannot rely on the influence of the Holy Spirit to lead unbelieving students to all truth. As a result, the impetus for integration rests exclusively on him. He must present content that is aligned biblically to the principles of stewardship, reconciliation, and the promotion of the image of God, but he must also explain and demonstrate for them why living in a way that appears unnatural is the way that they should conduct their lives. For his unbelieving students, Arnie must explain that the world is abnormal, refuting the claims of a culture that seeks to make the sin nature—the only nature the unbeliever possesses—normal. He must persuade them to realize that the way the world is and the way it should be as explained by the culture are wrong by God's standards, which is not in their best interest (despite all the competing claims to the contrary by the culture). He must refute the world's explanation for who the students are and its vision for who they should be, and, instead, he must embrace a biblical explanation and vision. Like the parable of the Sower and the Seed, however, the unbeliever lacks the fertile ground from which the biblical vision can be understood and bear fruit. They may receive the biblical vision, even receive it with joy and show signs of biblical fruit, but they are apt to have that vision snatched away or wither due to the influence of the world.

For his unbelieving students, Arnie realized, he can have two objectives. The first is evangelistic—to have his students see the world as fallen and abnormal, and thus themselves as fallen and abnormal, in need of a Savior to make them whole. Engaging in Christian education would not be a means to salvation, but it would serve to demonstrate to students their need of salvation. In addition, Arnie sees that he can help his unbelieving students to live morally, to try to align their actions, if not their thoughts, with the social and moral standards embedded in the created design of the world. He can demonstrate to them what it means from a biblical perspective to be fully human and explain that conformity to God's standards provides a life in which they can experience a fuller humanity. He also understands that for these students, the biblical standard will, at best, represent a utopian ideal, one imposed externally rather than one that is generated from within. Without the Holy Spirit, an external standard of conformity to righteousness is the only possible substitute for true righteousness.

For his students who are believers, Arnie comes to realize that Christian education must be something entirely different. In possession of a new nature and empowered by the Holy Spirit, the goal of Christian education is not simply learning content but learning construction—allowing the Holy Spirit to guide the student to the application of content according to his leading. The principles of stewardship, reconciliation, and promotion of the image of God apply to both believers and unbelievers, but their application is fundamentally different. Unlike content, with its emphasis on knowing, for the believer, Christian education is about construction and its emphasis on doing. It is not simply knowing the principles of stewardship but acting as a steward; not simply comprehending but engaging in the ministry of reconciliation. Understanding the biblical concept of the image of God is replaced with demonstrating and promoting it in others. This does not diminish his role as a teacher; he is still an authority and still responsible to lead and guide students. His role with believers, however, is not simply to make scholars but disciples, teaching them to be apprentices of Christ just as he himself is an apprentice of Christ.

Does this mean that all students can benefit from a biblically based Christian education? Arnie was now more convinced than ever that the answer to this question is yes—realizing that the expected outcomes for believers and unbelievers cannot necessarily be the same. Considering his own teaching, Arnie realizes that the content he teaches and the methods he uses to teach it had been directed more to his unbelieving students. Through his content emphasis and teacher-directed integration, he essentially denied the presence of the Holy Spirit and the reality of the new nature in his believing students. He essentially has played to the lowest common denominator, the sin nature, which he knows is present in all his students. He finds this insight disturbing; he has always been considered an excellent example of a Christian school teacher. His insight is even more distressing because his approach to teaching was similar to almost all his colleagues. In the process of teaching in a Christian school could he actually have been guilty of rendering a disservice to the very students whom his school sought to serve?

For Arnie, the conclusion was clear: he must gear his content and instructional methodologies toward the goal of creating apprentices and not simply scholars. As a social studies teacher, he must not only help students identify the results of sin in history, government, economics, psychology, sociology, or any other social science, but also help them recognize what living as a steward in a fallen world means in relation to these disciplines. They must not simply be able to know or identify sin, but they must also develop and participate in strategies, both individually and corporately, to help return those areas of life to the way God intended them to be. These are "doing" goals, requiring methodologies that encouraged apprenticeship and application. Granted, there will still be unbelievers in his classroom, even if Mt. Carmel did not formally admit unbelievers to the school. Arnie is not so naive as to think every student that professes Christ is indeed a true believer. Even so, the goal of a Christian school is to educate Christians, and the methods used must be geared, first and foremost, to that clientele.

Arnie is also convinced that he can no longer be a teacher who educates unbelievers well and who hopes that the Holy Spirit worked in the hearts of his believing students to apply the truth of Scripture to their lives. Rather, as one who is charged with making disciples, he wants to use methods that allow him to cooperate with the Holy Spirit to encourage growth and development in his students. Arnie is not sure how the Mt. Carmel board will vote regarding accepting vouchers and admitting unbelieving students. For Arnie, at least, the decision does not really matter. If unbelievers glean benefits from this instruction, he would praise God. He would work to reconcile them to God and, if nothing else, try to help them to live more moral lives. For Arnie, however, it is time to reevaluate his teaching in light of the spiritual realities of those he has been called to teach: who his students are in Christ and who God desires them to be.

10

Worldview as Worship

We have a generation coming up that doesn't speak the same language, doesn't go to the same places, doesn't have the same needs and isn't looking at Christianity to answer spiritual concerns. . . . We either change or we lose them.

—George Barna

IT IS THE END of May, and Arnie stands at the window of his classroom taking in the sights and sounds of a late spring afternoon. Over the last several weeks he has noticed the energy and excitement of his students build. For the seniors, it is the thought of graduation; for others, it is the anticipation of the upcoming summer break. While Arnie has work to do—lessons to prepare and papers to grade—he blissfully procrastinates, preferring to contemplate his own summer plans. Much like his students, he anticipates the summer break and time for family, friends, and activities.

Arnie's muse is broken by a voice greeting him from behind. He turns to find Polly Pureheart, a former student, standing in the doorway. Polly is home from college and has decided to visit a few of her former teachers. Arnie walks over, greets her with a hug, and invites her to sit down. Polly was one of Arnie's favorite students, a young lady of keen mind and exuberant passion for Christ. After leaving Mt. Carmel, Molly enrolled as a student at Reformation Christian College. Because she was both musically talented and academically gifted, Arnie is excited to hear how the Lord has worked in Polly's life to develop her gifts and talents since high school.

"Wow, finishing your junior year already," Arnie replies to statements from Polly. "It hardly seems possible. Refresh my memory, what are you majoring in again?"

"Instrumental performance," replies Polly. "I am so blessed by the instructors at college and the opportunities that I've had to use my talents for Christ. God has allowed me to go on several mission trips, both in the United States and abroad. I never envisioned the chances I would have to minister when I was still in high school."

"That is tremendous," notes Arnie. "So, you are starting your senior year in the fall. I have to ask—is there a young man in your life?"

Polly blushes for a moment, smiles, and extends her left hand to show Arnie the engagement ring on her finger. "Yes, Joshua. He is a wonderful guy and I am so excited.

He is a preseminary major and committed to ministry. We are planning our wedding for next June, and he is already looking towards seminary the following fall. Actually, one of the reasons I wanted to come and see you was to tell you about him and invite you and your wife to the wedding next summer."

"Well, I saw the ring so I had to ask," confesses Arnie. "I am very excited for you and we will be honored to share in your wedding day. You just seem to be full of excitement and joy. I know that you have always been very ministry minded, and I am so happy to see that the Lord has given you the desires of your heart."

"I am so happy and feel so blessed," says Polly. "Joshua loves the Lord, and I share his passion and aspirations for ministry. I am thrilled that God has given me the opportunity to use my gifts and talents to support him and the ministry that God will give him. I just want to share in his life and be a part of it. I know that the seminary years will be hard and that a life of ministry is not always financially comfortable, but I am looking forward to serving God with Joshua as long as the Lord sees fit."

As Polly continues, Arnie cannot help but notice the exhilaration in her voice and the sparkle in her eyes as she talks about Joshua and their future life. Arnie is struck by how her passion and her excitement are contagious. "You seem very happy," notes Arnie, "and I am happy for you."

"I know it may sound silly," says Polly, "but I get excited when I talk about Joshua and tell others about our plans. I love him and am elated that he loves me. My friends will sometimes jokingly tell me that when I am with them I still seem to be with Joshua. When I go places, like some of the small shops downtown from school, I will see things that remind me of him. Often I'll find little things at the store that I want to give him to make him happy. It may sound a little selfish, but it actually seems to increases my joy to do those little things for him or talk to others about him."

After a few more minutes of conversation and a commitment by Arnie to attend the wedding, Polly excuses herself to meet her parents. As Arnie replays the visit in his head, he is struck by one of Polly's last statements. Over the last several months Arnie has spent a great deal of time thinking about worldview transformation and biblical integration and attempting to make sense of the in-service sessions that have been a part of the school year. His reflections have centered on how to put the concepts of stewardship, reconciliation, and the image of God together in such a way that they would provide direction for his teaching and possibly serve as a model of transformation for the entire Mt. Carmel community. As Arnie considers Polly's "silly" comment, it occurs to him that the excitement and joy Polly experiences when she shares her love for Joshua with others provides an ideal analogy for the process of worldview transformation.

Increasingly, Arnie has come to appreciate the Christian life as more than simply claiming Christ as Savior but as a desire to make him Lord over every aspect of life. That God has placed all things under the authority of Christ has come to mean that, as a disciple of Christ, the believer should seek to evidence his Lordship in every area and aspect of life. During his morning devotions Arnie has been studying the book of 1 John and has come to realize that the evidence of the Christian life is love (1 John 4:7). This love is not simply the love that the believer has for God because God first loves him (4:19), but the extension of the grace and mercy extended to the believer by God to others so that the believer is called to love others (4:11–16).

Like the strongest earthly love, where lovers seek to be part of and participate in every aspect of life with the one they love, so the believer's love for Christ should also be evident in every aspect of life where Christ is evidenced. Arnie recalls how Polly continually sees things that remind her of Joshua and how she continually wants to do little things to make him happy. He then finds himself thinking of Polly's upcoming wedding day. Like a bride at a wedding, where the bride's love for the bridegroom is enhanced through the sharing of her love with those in attendance, so the disciple's joy in the Lord is experienced and enhanced not only by Christ's love for him or her but also by sharing Christ's love with others. More than simply a desire to express vows of love and loyalty, Arnie notes the excitement and joy she experiences in wanting to participate in Joshua's life; his desire to attend seminary, his aspirations and goals for ministry have become the focus of Polly's conversations with her friends. For the community of faith, the bride of Christ, its joy is also experienced and enhanced by sharing in the life and desires of Christ. For believers, both individually and communally, this joy is experienced not simply by affirming loyalty to Christ or by telling others about him, but through sharing the grace and mercy that characterizes their love and joy in Christ with others. Arnie can sense in Polly that the desires of Joshua's heart have become the desires of her heart, so that by sharing in Joshua's life her own desires are fulfilled. The same is true for believers: as the desires of their heart are aligned with those of Christ and as they share in Christ's desire to extend his grace and mercy, the believers' joy is enhanced by participating in Christ's ministry of reconciliation.

Suddenly, for Arnie, the whole idea of worldview transformation is no longer separate from the rest of the Christian life; it is centered on experiencing the love of Christ and actively engaging in the life of Christ by acting according to his love. Worldview transformation is no longer simply a philosophical endeavor or the embracing of a better logical argument but the active extension of the Lordship of Christ to every area of life. Similarly, integration is no longer merely the intellectual realignment of academic content with scriptural principles but the process of actively participating in the life of Christ by extending his Lordship into action and engagement—a life experienced through obedience to the Spirit of God and in concert with the community of believers.

THE PROBLEM OF WORLDVIEW TRANSFORMATION

A predominant feature of much of the evangelical literature on worldview transformation is that it treats the process as intellectual. That is, the transformation of the mind referred to in Romans 12:1–2 (a text that serves as the quintessential worldview transformation text for many evangelical writers) is a cognitive process. As Paul states in Ephesians 4:22–24,

> That, in reference to your former manner of life, you lay aside the old self, which is being corrupted in accordance with the lusts of deceit, and that you be renewed in the spirit of your mind, and put on the new self, which in the likeness of God has been created in righteousness and holiness of the truth.

As a result, the method most often cited for the changing of the soul is one similar to that used to change the mind—in essence spiritual transformation becomes synonymous with philosophical transformation. Ronald Nash typifies this approach in his book *Faith and Reason: Searching for a Rational Faith* when he writes, "A person's noetic structure [which Nash later identifies as a worldview] is the sum total of everything that a person believes. Since the objects of beliefs are propositions (statements that are either true or false), a complete inventory of a person's noetic structure would include all the propositions a person believes."[1] Nash goes on to note that, "when faced with a choice among competing worldviews, we should choose the one that, when applied to the whole of reality, gives us the most coherent picture of the world."[2] While less formally philosophical in nature, James Sire, in his influential book *The Universe Next Door*, advocates a similar criteria to Nash whereby individuals should select an appropriate worldview.[3] By associating world-views with philosophies, the characteristics of philosophies (i.e., analytically founded and subject to analytical change or qualification) are also attributed to worldview transforma-tion. The result is an approach to worldview transformation that is intrinsically individual and intellectually separated from the biblical message of community as the embodiment of the gospel. As Nancy Pearcey writes (quoting theologian Lesslie Newbigin) "The gospel is not meant to be 'a disembodied message.' It is meant to be fleshed out in 'a congregation of men and women who believe it and live by it'—who exhibit in their relationships the beauty of God's character."[4]

The philosophical approach summarized by Nash and Sire generally ignores or tends to deemphasize the role of community in the development and transformation of world-view expressed by Pearcey. While an emphasis on the role of community in worldview transformation can be found in a number of writers, the philosophical approach remains, for many, the primary view. The partiality to this approach can be attributed to a number of factors that can negatively impede the application of the gospel to every aspect of life. First, the individual orientation of the philosophical approach—where individuals choose their worldview based on a series of (essentially logical) criteria—is consistent with the values of personal autonomy and individualism, which are foundational to the culture of the United States. This emphasis on personal autonomy in the selection of a worldview is generally blind to the influence of culture on the individual in making the choice. That is, unless the culture in general promotes the value of personal autonomy and provides the social reinforcement to act in a manner consistent with that value, the emphasis on individual choice could not be effectively proposed in the first place. It is an orientation consistent with what psychologist Jean Twenge calls the "Me-generation," where people do not need to seek the approval of others and generally opt for those standards of thought and behavior that make them personally comfortable but require a cultural milieu in which such an approach to life is encouraged and reinforced in order for it to thrive.[5]

1. Nash, *Faith and Reason*, 21.
2. Ibid., 51.
3. Sire, *Universe Next Door*, 214–17.
4. Newbigin, cited in Pearcey, *Total Truth*, 378.
5. Twenge, *Generation Me*, 20.

The philosophical approach is not simply a phenomenon of the "Me-generation" (which Twenge attributes to people born since 1970), but finds it roots in the ideals of the Renaissance and European Enlightenment. Based in the tenets of fifteenth-century humanism, the Renaissance ideal promoted the autonomous individual who could do all things well. This person is one of immense intellectual abilities and physical skills—well educated and capable of embracing all areas of knowledge and developing his or her abilities fully and successfully, whether vocationally, artistically, athletically, and so forth. The ideal of the Renaissance individual or the universal person is exemplified in Leonardo da Vinci, whose accomplishments in science, mathematics, engineering, painting, music, and architecture are esteemed to this day. Applied to worldview transformation, the philosophical approach essentially maintains that as individuals develop their biblical approach to life, they also integrate their knowledge of the arts, education, family life, politics, environmental concerns, economics, and so on with their understanding of Scripture. In essence, it proposes that the individual develop sufficient expertise as a theologian and scholar in every area of life to sufficiently examine those areas logically so as to produce a systematic and theologically consistent whole that is also subjectively satisfying.

Such a view of worldview development and transformation ignores the reality that, for all but a very small minority of exceptionally gifted individuals, most people are reliant on others to develop biblically consistent models in a number of areas. Thus, Christian content area scholars, sufficiently trained in theology, can develop a biblical approach to their disciplines, which can then be taught to and integrated, into a systematic whole by the community of faith. The believing community can then use the biblical narrative to develop faith-based responses to realities of individual and social life. While such a view does not alleviate the responsibility of the believer to take every thought captive or to demonstrate the Lordship of Christ and bring glory to God in every aspect of life, it does acknowledge the dependency that individual believers have, one to another, to help them develop these responses. The philosophical approach to worldview transformation is generally mute with regard to the role that community plays in assisting the believer in developing and reinforcing a biblically integrated response to the whole of life.

Similarly, the European Enlightenment of the eighteenth century promoted the authority of reason and the importance of systematic thinking applied to all aspects of individual and social life. Proponents of the Enlightenment, sometimes called "the Age of Reason," sought to cultivate the rational mind and translate reason into behavior that would lead to the progress of the individual and the society as a whole. The Enlightenment model proposed that all human beings possessed reason (in the form of common sense) but that this reason had been corrupted by the cultural and institutional environments of the society. Through the development of the mind, this corruption could be overcome, and reason would align consistently with natural law.

Similarly, the philosophical approach to worldview transformation proposes that the renewing of the mind commanded in Romans 12:2 is achieved through the development of a rational and systematic approach that is both consistent and faithful to the reality of God and his created order. Both the European Enlightenment and the philosophical approach to worldview transformation assume that the character of transformation is one that corresponds to the general traits of a philosophy detailed in chapter 2, specifically, that reason provides a sufficient foundation for practice (analytically founded) and that reason can be used to inform increasingly better practice (analytically qualified). The philosophical approach to worldview shares this perspective in that renewal is achieved by demonstrating the weaknesses in the existing understandings of the individual (their analytical foundation) and then presenting the learner with the more systematic and rationally satisfying biblical argument (an analytical qualification).

The problem with such a perspective of worldview transformation is that it is based in an approach that violates one of its own fundamental assumptions—the idea that all people have a worldview. By proposing an approach to transformation that seeks to qualify a person's preexisting understanding of the world, it immediately excludes certain groups of people that are not essentially rational. For example, infants and certain individuals with severe cognitive disabilities who may not behave from an essentially rational foundation are excluded from having the existing prerequisites of a worldview. Even if this approach grants that such individuals have a worldview (which raises the question about the basis of their worldview) those individuals are unable to experience worldview transformation. Since worldview transformation requires the ability to logically analyze one's existing understanding and modify it in ways that make it more coherent and aligned with divine truth, those lacking this ability immediately lack the requisite abilities to participate in renewal. Arguably, the philosophical model of worldview transformation requires a type of critical reasoning ability that only those trained to think philosophically can hope to fully attain. In addition, this logically coherent type of thinking must be appropriately extended by the individual to all aspects of life.

This is not to deny that worldview transformation involves the integration of every aspect of human experience with the reality of God, the truth of his Word, and the general revelation of his creation. Integration does involve understanding the connection of all of life to God in a manner that seeks to demonstrate his Lordship over every aspect of life. For the believer, this understanding must lead to the aligning of one's individual goals and desires to correspond to the heart and mind of God. The impetus for this alignment, however, is not solely logical or rational. Nor can the result of integration and, by extension, worldview transformation simply be logical or rational. Rather, integration, and the greater goal of worldview transformation, must be based in the believer's love for Christ, a love that encompasses every aspect of his being and is made evident in relationships with others.

For believers, the love relationships they exhibit toward others are an expression of their ultimate love relationship and the preeminence of God in their life. It is obedience to the first commandment that there should be no others gods before him (Exod 20:3). Loving others, however, is also to acknowledge that the Lord is a jealous God (Exod 20:4). While the term "jealous" may appear selfish, suspicious, or mistrusting, in the case of God, jealousy expresses his desire to protect, preserve, and seek the best for those whom he loves. In the Bible the jealously of God is often expressed in terms his choosing, being a special possession (e.g., in the Old Testament toward Israel), or having the marital relationship that Christ has with his bride the church (cf. Ps 135:5; Hos 2:29; 1 Cor 10:22; 2 Cor 11:2).

In the marriage relationship the bride leaves her father and mother to be joined as one to the husband, a relationship in which she is submissive to his headship or authority. It is a relationship in which the husband seeks the best for his bride and the bride serves as a helper and an extension in seeking to accomplish the commands of God (cf. Eph 5:22–31; Gen 2:18). The community of faith, as the bride of Christ, must be known by the attributes of God—traits often expressed as the "fruit of the Spirit" (Gal 5:22–23) and summarized by the apostle John as "love" (cf. 1 John 4:8, 16). For this reason Paul closes his teaching on the marriage relationship by noting that "this mystery is great; but I am speaking with reference to Christ and the church" (Eph 5:32), and Jesus tells his followers, "By this all men will know that you are My disciples, if you have love for one another" (John 13:35).

Christ's desire is to be more than simply the Savior of the church; he wants to be her Lord in every aspect of life. As Christ has authority over every aspect of life, the church, as his faithful bride, must also demonstrate that authority to the world by being submissive to his authority in the disciples' lives—both individually and corporately. To love Christ as his bride is to be his helper—designed to share his goals, desires, and vision and to assist him to bring these about. As Paul instructs in 2 Corinthians, it is the love of Christ that controls believers so that they no longer live for self but for Christ (5:14–15). Like a bride, who leaves father and mother and takes on the name of her husband, the believer is a "new creature" in Christ (5:17), becoming like the bridegroom as part of his body. As a result, the goal of Christ to reconcile the world to himself (5:19) is given also to his bride, the church, so that the community of faith serves as ministers and ambassadors of reconciliation (5:18, 20). In sharing the work of her husband, the church's joy is made complete as she seeks to honor Christ by proclaiming his love and sharing what she has experienced with others in every aspect of life.

As his bride, the church seeks to bring glory and worth to Christ. Believers engage in honoring God and bring glory to him through the practice of worship and participation in his work. In worship, the individual believer and the church corporately express their love for God and their joy in Christ is made complete.

THE MEANING OF WORSHIP

Pastor and author A. W. Tozer, speaking to a convention of pastors in 1963, remarked, "Worship acceptable to God is the missing crown jewel in evangelical Christianity."[6] While noting that there existed a desire for theological intellectualism and passion for doctrinal orthodoxy, he believed the church was missing an all-encompassing, all-embracing expression or wonder of who God is. He compared the church in the United States at that time to the church of Laodicea as described in Revelation 3:14–22, paralleling the growth in attendance, construction of magnificent buildings, emphasis on personal piety and material well-being to the Laodiceans who were guilty of claiming "I am rich, and have become wealthy, and have need of nothing" (Rev 3:17). Tozer's desire for the church was for it to be so captivated with God that his thoughts and desires would be the church's

---

6. Tozer, *Whatever Happened to Worship?* 7.

thoughts and desires. For Tozer, the vision and goals that God is working to accomplish in the world should guide and direct the vision and goals of the church as well. The church should see the world in its entirety as God sees it. Beyond this, not only should the church see God in everything but it should also seek him in everything so that the life of the church, both individually and corporately, will be an expression of God's glory and the joy of the church will be made complete as believers find expression of their intended humanity before God.

Tozer was disturbed by a loss of the sacredness of worship, a trait he called "secularized worship."[7] For him, this type of worship was an acceptance of worldly secularism, which was more appealing to the church than a genuine desire for a spiritual life pleasing to God. This worldly secularism has led to a narrowing of the definition of worship, often leading to defining worship by the place where it occurs—where the building itself is the focus of worship—or worship has become more narrowly defined by style. As a result, divisions have been created, to the extent that many churches are characterized almost exclusively by the type of music (traditional or contemporary), type of preaching (expository or topical) or even the type of acceptable dress (formal or more casual). This narrowing of worship reduces it to a game where individuals learn how to dress, speak, and act or when to bow their head and not look bored. It can become a type of formalism, an external practice devoid of a genuine heart expression toward God. The result is that often churches engage in "family fights" over whether or not the particulars of the game bring glory to God. What ensues is the churches' compromising the criteria that Christ himself provided to establish the validity of his message: "by this will all men know that you are my disciples, if you have love for one another" (John 13:35) before a watching world.

True worship involves not only God's holiness but also his uniqueness. In worship believers see God's glory and its relationship to every aspect of life. In Isaiah's vision of God, his robe fills the temple and the "whole earth is full of His glory" (Isa 6:3). The Psalmist writes that "the heavens are telling of the glory of God; and their expanse is declaring the work of His hands" (Ps 19:1). The result is that the law, testimony, precepts, commandments, and judgments of the Lord are true and applicable to all of life (Ps 19:7–9). As worshippers of the Most High God, those whose lives are to be expressions of the life of Christ, Christians are to radiate back to God his glory and majesty in every aspect of life, but they are also to radiate that glory to others. To do so, notes John Piper, not only demonstrates the reality of God but also serves to make their own joy complete:

> We praise what we enjoy because the delight is incomplete until it is expressed in praise. If we were not allowed to speak of what we value, and celebrate what we love, and praise what we admire, our joy would not be full. So, if God loves us enough to make our joy full, he must not only give us himself; he must also win from us the praise of our hearts—not because he needs to shore up some weakness in himself or compensate for some deficiency, but because he loves us and seeks the fullness of our joy that can only be found in knowing and praising him.[8]

---

7. Ibid., 117.

8. Piper, *Desiring God*, 49.

The contemporary word *worship* is derived from the Old English *weorthscipe*, meaning worthy or meritorious. It projects the idea that worship gives to God the recognition and adoration that he deserves. In the Old Testament, two Hebrew words often translated "worship" are *histahawa* and *shachah*, "prostrate" or "bow down in reverential fear" (cf. Gen 18:2, 47:31; Isa 49:7). The Hebrew is often translated into Greek with *proskynein*, literally meaning to "kiss forward" or to fall down in submission to great authority. Thus, worship, as expressed in the Bible, never involves simply thought or observation of authority alone, but also involves the act of service and reverence. The Greek *proskynein* is used twenty-six times in the New Testament (in the Gospels and Revelation) and exclusively refers to the act of falling at the feet of Christ.

The apostle John provides the clearest expression of Jesus's teaching on worship in the conversation of Christ with the Samaritan women at the well. In John 4:20–24, Jesus uses the word *proskynein* ten times to detach worship from the externals of location or the formalism of temple ritual and to tie true worship to an expression of "spirit" (heart) and "truth" (understanding). For Christ, worship of God was not associated with a place or even the specific behaviors involved in that place but with acts of service or reverence that were expressions of a right heart and a proper understanding of who God is. In this way, Christ confronts the formalism of Old Testament sacrificial worship. Christ also underscores Samuel's condemnation of Israel when the prophet states "has the Lord as much delight in burnt offerings and sacrifices as in obeying the voice of the Lord? Behold to obey is better than sacrifice" (1 Sam 15:22). Christ's words are also reminiscent of David's words is Psalm 51:16–17 when he writes, "For you do not delight in sacrifice, otherwise I would give it; You are not pleased in burnt offering. The sacrifices of God are a broken spirit; a broken and a contrite heart, O God, You will not despise."

Christ teaches that worship is an expression of an inward heart experience (spirit) directed or based in a proper understanding of who God is (truth). Even so, when reading much of the New Testament, particularly the writings of the apostle Paul, there is no reference or use of the word *proskynein*—an omission that appears odd. As noted earlier, the word most often translated "worship" in the Old Testament is the Hebrew *histahawa* or to "bow down." A second Hebrew word, *abad* or *abowdah*, which is translated "service" or "servant," denotes worship or ministry and is often used to denote priestly service in the temple or uniquely religious activities (cf. Num 8:15; 1 Chr 23:28). This idea of service, which stems from an attitude of spirit and truth, dominates the New Testament teaching to believers regarding the practice of worship. This idea is expressed in the use of the Greek word *latreia* or "service as an act of worship." In terms of worldview transformation, Paul's best known use of the word can be found in Romans 12:1, when he commands believers to present themselves a living sacrifice, "which is your spiritual service [*latreia*] of worship."

Paul is a Hebrew writing to non-Hebrews in the Greek language, and he understands the concept of worship taught by Jesus in John 4. In John 4, Jesus detached worship from a place and made it a condition of the heart and mind that leads to action. As a Hebrew, Paul understands the relationship of spiritual service in the concept of *abad*, where worship is active. James, writing primarily to Hebrew readers, expresses this same idea when he notes that "faith, if it has no works, is dead," and that the proof of faith is works (Jas

2:17–18). Similarly, Paul admonishes his readers to make themselves a sacrifice (*thusia*), which is "living," and that their worship (*latreia*) should he both active and voluntary ("present your bodies"). Paul's model of worship is Christ, who presented himself a voluntary sacrifice to the Father by going to the cross in an act that brings benefit to others.

Paul's use of the word *latreia* is not attached to a place or liturgical form but is a nonlocalized type of engagement or action. Rather than an act done in a particular place or according to a specified pattern or order, *latreia* in Romans 12:1 is a decentralized act that is done as an extension of a particular mindset or heart motivation. Paul begins his command to the Roman believers noting that they should present their bodies, indicating a willingness of the heart and mind to serve. The result of presenting oneself to God is a living or active body that is able to extend itself to every aspect of life. To be living is not only to work to glorify God but also to be the glory of God to others. This seems to be Paul's meaning in Philippians 3:3 when he writes, "we are the true circumcision, who worship [*latreuo*] in the Spirit of God and glory in Christ Jesus and put no confidence in the flesh." For Paul, the life of a believer is one of worship that starts with a motivation of the heart and then extends to every aspect of life.

The idea that the purpose of worship is to glorify God or to be the representation of Christ to others is captured in a second word that Paul associates with worship. Paul's command is that believers be a living sacrifice or *thusia* to God. The term *thusia* is used twenty-nine times in the New Testament, five times by Paul, who links the word to self-sacrifice or service for the benefit of others. In Ephesians 5:1–2 Paul urges believers to be imitators of Christ and walk in love just as Christ "gave Himself up for us, an offering and a sacrifice [*thusia*] to God as a fragrant aroma." Paul compares his actions for the benefit of the Philippians as a drink offering poured out on their behalf (2:17). Likewise, the gift of the Philippians to Paul on his behalf is described as a sacrifice [*thusia*] acceptable and well-pleasing to God (4:18). In Romans 12:1 Paul describes worship as an act of service to God (*latreia*) that is done as sacrifice (*thusia*) intended for the benefit of others.

Romans 12:2 is often used as a text by evangelical writers when addressing the topic of worldview transformation and the imperative of the believer to engage in the process of renewing the mind. Paul's command for renewing of the mind results in the believer's ability to engage in doing the will of God in a manner that is deemed "good and acceptable and perfect." It should be noted that the renewing of the mind is not an end in itself; nor is it simply to know the will of God. Renewing the mind is tied to the goal of doing God's will. The context for the command is a life of service worship that benefits others, as introduced in Romans 12:1. The command to renew the mind in Roman 12:2 is inextricably linked to the process of worship described in the preceding verse. Thus, the process of renewing the mind allows the disciple to know the will of God so that service to others can be rendered in a manner that reflects a heart or spirit that has been renewed by God. In this respect, Paul's teaching on worship conforms to the teaching of Christ in John 4, where worshipping in both spirit and truth are the hallmarks of genuine worship. The willingness of the heart, guided by the truth, which discerns God, motivates action and allows every aspect of life to be done for the glory of God (1 Cor 10:31).

Paul notes that the life of worship is based on the mercies of God and becomes an extension of the mercies that God has shown to the believer. The commands of Romans 12:1–2 are introduced by the word *therefore*—a reference to everything previously discussed in Romans 1–11. In chapters one through three, Paul explains that the pagan world, the world of moral people, and even the religiously righteous Jews, leaves all condemned and sentenced to death. As a result, the Father sent Christ to die to pay the penalty of sin and pardon the believer (chapter 4). Salvation, however, is more than escaping the wrath of God. The benefits of salvation are peace with God (5:1) and the ability to stand before him in grace (5:2). The believer can glory in his tribulations (5:3) and know that he is loved by God (5:8), saved from the wrath of God (5:9), able to see the truth (5:5), and, as a result, the believer is empowered to live the truth (5:19–21). The result is that the believer is dead to the power of sin and able to live for Christ, who has provided everything necessary for a life of godliness and victory over the power of sin (chapters 6–8). All these benefits are provided to the believer because the sovereign grace of God has ordained the believer as a child of God, a chosen member of his family, like the nation of Israel in times past (chapter 9). The adoption of the believer by God is provided on the basis of faith and results in the extension of God's righteousness to the believer (10:9–10), a righteousness that reflects God's desire to extend mercy to his people (11:30–32).

The logic of Paul's argument through the first eleven chapters crescendos in Romans 12:1. "Therefore," based on the incredible grace extended by God, he writes, believers are called to take every aspect of their lives and lay them on the altar of God, a sacrifice that is their "reasonable" (KJV) or their "spiritual service of worship." This worship extends to every aspect of life so that the disciple of Christ is to be no longer conformed to the patterns and values of the world but is to see the world from the perspective of God—that is, to see every aspect of life through the truth of God and then live all of life in conformity to that truth. To worship in spirit is to live the reality of God's truth or, in contemporary parlance, his worldview. As Paul makes clear in Romans 12:1–2, the biblical worldview cannot be separated from a vibrant, all-encompassing expression of the believer's love for God that extends to every aspect of life.

For this reason Paul refers to the believer as a "living sacrifice"—not the dead sacrifices of the Old Testament, but lives that are holy and acceptable to God. Believers are no longer to present themselves as slaves to unrighteousness but to pursue lives of righteousness in the power of God. Just as the believer lived a certain way in his spiritual death, he is now to live a new way in his spiritual life. Just as the sin nature manifested itself in every aspect of life before coming to Christ, the redeemed believer must now seek to manifest the new life of Christ in every aspect of life as well. This extension to all of life is accomplished by actively engaging in the process of understanding God through the renewing of the mind. This renewal, however, is pursued not as an end in itself but for the purpose of proving the will of God before a watching world. The result is that the believer is to become the embodiment of the will of God, the physical manifestation of God's grace and mercy, to a world that he seeks to redeem. To a world that neither knows God nor sees fit to acknowledge him, the believer is to demonstrate the reality and glory of God. In essence, the believer is called to make God famous in every area of life.

MAKING GOD FAMOUS

The opening question of the Westminster Shorter Catechism reads, "What is the chief end of man?" The response is "Man's chief end is to glorify God and to enjoy Him forever." The writers of the catechism understood that human beings were made to be worshipers of God. Worship is seen in the fellowship that humanity enjoyed with God in the Garden and in the pursuit of stewardship before the Fall. The joy of fellowship and the pursuit of human activity to glorify God were lost in the Fall. From Genesis 3 onward, the Bible teaches that worship is a restoration of God's original intent to dwell with his people as he did in the Garden. As the Psalmist writes, "Splendor and majesty are before Him, strength and beauty are in His sanctuary. Ascribe to the LORD, O families of the peoples, ascribe to the LORD the glory of His name" (Ps 96:6–8). Humanity, in this regard, reflects back to God the glory of his worth, a glory that is reflected in everything God created (cf. Ps 48:7–9; Luke 19:40).

As image-bearers of God, humanity is given the privilege and responsibility of serving God as an extension of the pleasure received from fellowship with him. Philosopher J. P. Moreland captures this privilege and responsibility when he writes, "God is worthy of the very best efforts we can give Him in offering our respect and service through the cultivation of our total personality, including our minds."[9] By implication, the purpose of worship is not to attain the gifts or favor of God but to enjoy the presence of God himself. As John Piper writes, "In the end the heart longs not for any of God's good gifts, but for God himself. To see him and know him and be in his presence is the soul's final feast. Beyond this there is no quest. . . . Now what does this imply about the feast of worship? Surprisingly, it implies that worship is an end in itself."[10] To worship is to engage in the very thing that God created humanity for; in short, to worship is to be all that humanity was meant to be.

Evangelical Christianity dedicates much time, effort, and resources to the goal of redemption or leading people to salvation. The gospel message in this context provides escape from hell and allows the person to experience the joys of heaven. Avoiding hell and entering heaven becomes the end of the gospel; salvation is the end rather than the means to the end. While salvation is a part of the gospel it is not the whole of the gospel. The good news of Christ is that human beings can be restored to be worshippers of God, to experience the joy that comes from fellowship and service to the One for whom they were created. Reduction of the gospel to anything less is to minimize the richness and fullness of the mercies of God and the work of Christ to the purchase of entry into a paradise of the receiver's own definition. It allows individuals to conceive of heaven as a place where they will experience all the joys, pleasures, gifts, and perfect contentment in a world devoid of pain—but where Christ need not be present. Such a heaven would not be heaven at all, for it would continue to leave a gap between who human beings are and who they were created to be. Apart from God, humanity can never experience its true purpose, joy, or fulfillment, because only in worship can humanity experience the greatest good, the most precious beauty, the most infinite value—God.

9. Moreland, *Love Your God with All Your Mind*, 159.

10. Piper, *Desiring God*, 80–81.

This minimized view of the gospel is one reason that so few young people seem to embrace the joy of salvation. Heaven is viewed as something separate from life or done at the conclusion of life and not integrally related to life. Being taken to heaven is not celebrated; instead it is something that, if most people are honest, they wish to experience when they are done living life. Young people have dreams and aspirations. They wish to graduate college, marry, have sex, and raise children. They seek to demonstrate their skills and abilities in a career, to accumulate some of the world's goods—whether those are material, social, or psychological—and to experience all that this world has to offer. Heaven can wait for life to conclude, when the vibrancy and vitality of youth gives way to the physical, social, and emotional pains of aging. Salvation, from this perspective, becomes a refuge from life rather than the purpose of life. To understand worship, however, is to embrace its true purpose—to understand and extend the joy one has in God to every aspect of life.

Worship of God is the highest good. It starts in heaven and continues to earth. The book of Revelation, which chronicles Christ's restoration of all things to himself, has worship as its central theme. Revelation teaches that worship is eternal because God is eternal (4:8) and that all things have been created by God for the purpose of worship (4:9–11; 7:11–12). It is Christ who is worthy of all the glory given to him (5:8–14), glory that stems from thanksgiving for the mercy and deliverance from judgment he provides (14:6–7). The worship of God proceeds from every nation for the work of Christ (15:1–8)—a work that results in the rescue of creation from corruption and restoration of all creation to its intended design (19:1–6). The result is life in a new heaven and on a new earth (21:1), a world that strangely resembles the original one described in Genesis chapters 1–2 (cf. Rev 22:1–3).

This desire for worship from humanity does not make God an egotist. Rather, it is God's desire to have humanity value that which is ultimately the greatest value, to love that which is most worthy to be loved—God himself. God, as the greatest good and highest value, demands that God's actions be turned to glorying himself. To love anything more than himself would be to choose something of lesser value and thus to desire something other than the greatest good. It is the meaning of the parable of the Pearl of Great Price (Matt 13:45–46), where a man sells all he has for the sheer joy of possessing the pearl, not for its utility but for the sheer pleasure of its beauty. As John Piper writes,

> This is the same as saying: [God] loves himself infinitely. Or he himself is uppermost in his own affections. A moment's reflection reveals the inexorable justice of this fact. God would be unrighteous (just as we would) if he valued anything more than what is supremely valuable. But he himself is supremely valuable. If he did not take delight in the worth of his own glory he would be unrighteous.[11]

For this reason God the Father glorifies the Son who is the very likeness of the Father (Heb 1:3; 2 Cor 4:4) and in whom the soul of the Father delights (Matt 3:17; Isa 42:1). Because the Son is the very likeness of the Father, Christ is the highest good that can be given, for in Christ the Father can give himself to those he loves (John 3:16). In the act of giving the Son, God the Father seeks not his own betterment but seeks others' joy, for

---

11. Ibid., 43.

perfect love seeks benefit in the fulfillment of others (1 Cor 13:5). God, who exists in perfect sufficiency and fellowship from eternity past, does not need the praise or adoration of humanity. God has no deficiencies or needs that would motivate him to seek human worship, nor can human worship add to his glory and majesty (Acts 17:25); rather, God desires to share with those he loves the best that can be given, himself, which motives God to make himself available for worship. In this regard, God's uniqueness separates him from all of creation. As completely self-sufficient, God can promote his glory for human betterment and not be egotistical.

Augustine opens his classic work *The Confessions* by stating, "Thou movest us to delight in praising Thee; for Thou hast formed us for Thyself, and our hearts are restless till they find rest in Thee."[12] Humans, as created and dependent beings, find their deepest and most enduring happiness *in* God, not simply *from* God. This happiness in God finds its greatest consummation when shared with others, a love that is manifested by seeking their betterment. In seeking to work for the betterment of others, the believer serves as a conduit of the love of God toward others; the believer shares in the desire of God that all humanity would ultimately find its greatest happiness and greatest peace in God. Christ emphasizes this truth as he answers the question of what is the greatest commandment: "You shall love the Lord your God with all your heart, and with all your soul, and with all your strength, and with all your mind; and your neighbor as yourself" (Luke 10:27). This summary of the law forms the basis for Paul's transition to worship in Romans.

When Paul writes, "Therefore, I urge you brethren, by the mercies of God . . ." he refers to how God has acted for the betterment of humanity through his mercy previously recorded in chapters 1–11. As a result of God's mercy to believers, they are to present themselves as a "living and holy sacrifice"—a spiritual act of worship. The act of renewing the mind, commanded in Romans 12:2, provides the ability to discern the will of God so that believers can act in a manner that demonstrates the mercy of God to others. To avoid any question that the reader would have, Paul goes on to define the will of God that believers are to perform. Romans 12:3–8 focuses on the believers' relationships within the church and the use of gifts for the edification of the church. In Romans 12:9–21 the emphasis is on the believers' relationships to others in the society, even noting that believers should perform good works for those who persecute and oppose Christ and the church. Romans 13:1–14 highlights the believers' relationships to the state and governing authorities, to be obedient citizens and to love all people, for "Love does no wrong to a neighbor; therefore love is the fulfillment of the law" (Rom 13:10). In Romans 14, Paul returns to the believers' relationships with the community of faith, encouraging them to accept the weak (14:1), not to judge (14:10), nor to act in a way that hinders the spiritual development of another (14:13). In all things, Paul concludes, believers are to imitate Christ (Rom 15:1–13) or to make God famous by emulating him before a watching world. The essence of Romans 12–16 is that the truth of God's mercy must be acted on and that the renewing of the mind serves as a means of preparing the believer to act as Christ in the world.

As worshippers, God gives believers life so that the church, as the bride of Christ, can make Christ famous. The reason for each additional day is to provide the believer with

---

12. Augustine, *Confessions* 1.

additional opportunities to make Christ known to others. As stewards, believers are given time, energy, abilities, and resources, not for their own benefit, but so that they might glorify Christ by serving others. In Matthew 25:31–45 God is glorified in the physical acts the believers perform toward others. These acts are not simply telling others of the good news of Christ but actions that work for the betterment of others. The church, as the bride of Christ, becomes a minister of mercy to others just as Christ was gracious and provided the mercies of God to the community of faith. The believer, individually, and the church corporately need to act as a conduit that conveys the grace (both saving and common) and mercies of God to others. For this reason, worship needs to be connected to all aspects of life—worship is an expression of who the believer is and who he or she is to be.

When the world becomes *too* normal—that is, when the community of faith fails to see the world the way God does or, worse, becomes too familiar and comfortable with it— there is a tendency to rationalize individual actions. In this state believers or the church as a whole can lapse from a state where they find their joy *in* God to one where they seek to find their joy *from* God. Christ is no longer the goal of faith but serves as a means to their own goals, whether it is eternal life in a heaven filled with pleasure and no suffer- ing or a life on earth characterized by the same. In such a state, believers no longer seek Christ as the end but rather use Christ as a means to fulfill their own ends. Such a state provides opportunity for the sin nature to dominate the believers' thinking—regardless of the spiritual terminology or trappings they surround themselves with. James describes this state as adultery (Jas 4:4) and notes that a type of worldly wisdom can develop that seeks to rationalize behavior. James characterizes this wisdom in James 3:15 as "earthly" (or temporally based), "natural" (appealing to the senses), and "demonic" (anti-God). In such a state, believers may or may not find joy in God, depending upon how God provides according to their own temporal and sensual expectations. For this reason, James starts his letter by encouraging the believers to "consider it all joy" when they encounter trials for trials are what God uses to conform believers to the image of Christ. This conformity to the image of Christ is designed to bring believers their greatest joy (Jas 1:2–4).

Similarly, John describes those things that rival for the affections of the believer—the lust of the flesh and eyes as well as the pride of life—which seek to diminish or rob God of the glory that he deserves from the life of faith (1 John 2:15–17). This love for the world will ultimately push out the love for God. Paul summarizes what it means for believers to act in ways that love God and oppose the worldliness described by both James and John. In Romans 15:1–14, Paul gives three descriptors of the life of faith that glorify God and make him famous: The believer is to act sacrificially toward others in a way that seeks the benefit of others (vv. 1–5). This sacrifice is not done at the expense of truth but as an expression of the attitude that Christ also exhibited (Phil 2:5–9). The purpose of this interaction is not to develop community for community's sake but to demonstrate the reality of Christ in the life of the believer. Furthermore, the acting on behalf of others is not simply done by each believer individually, but it should characterize the corporate response of the church to the world (Rom 15:6–8). Finally, acting in this manner will cause even unbelievers to notice the reality of Christ and give him praise and glory.

THE AGAPE PRINCIPLE

The evangelical philosopher and theologian Francis Schaeffer wrote,

> As Christians we are not only to *know* the right world-view, the world-view that tells us the truth of what is, but consciously to *act* upon that world-view, so as to influence society in all its parts and facets across the whole spectrum of life, as much as we can to the extent of our individual and collective ability.[13]

For most evangelical worldview theorists the goal of worldview transformation is not simply to change the way people think but, ultimately, to evoke change in how they live based on that new thinking. Philosophically, the application of how people think to how they develop standards of morality and align their behavior to those standards is the study of ethics. Ethics or moral philosophy has traditionally been seen as practical. While theoretically based, it does not simply define the good life but emphasizes the importance of pursuing the good life in practice. In terms of evangelical Christian terminology, worldview transformation provides the basis to engage in the integration of faith, learning, and life so that, when fully complete, the believer will ask the question, how should we then live?

For the apostle Paul the question of application or the pursuit of righteous living is central to his biblical ethics. While Paul is often seen as the most logical apologist of the Christian faith, his letters to the churches in the New Testament always end with the application of the theology he discussed earlier in those letters. As an example, the question of proper living is central to his first letter to the Corinthian church, a church that was divided by many factions that did not reflect the unity that was to characterize the body of Christ. These divisions, Paul observes, stemmed from their lack of spiritual maturity, to the point that their thoughts and subsequent actions were more characteristic of the unredeemed or natural person than one who is redeemed or spiritual (1 Cor 2:14–15). The consequence of their spiritual infancy and natural desires was the practice and tolerance of sin that was not even seen among the unbelieving Gentiles (1 Cor 5:1). In chapter 5 Paul deals with the issue of incest within the church. In chapter 6 he addresses the problem of believers bringing lawsuits and taking other believers to court (vv. 1–8) and the general practice of moral laxity (vv. 9–20). As a result of this moral laxity, there were difficulties in their marriage relationships (7:1–24), a pursuit of their self-interest and personal rights (8:1–13), and a general sense of self-indulgence (10:1–3). These divisions among the members resulted in the very functions of the church being corrupted as the worship of Christ was compromised (11:1–34), and the edification of the body was reduced to personal exaltation at the expense of rest of the community (12:1–30).

Paul introduces his chastening of the Corinthians by noting that the problems he addresses in the letter result from their worldly thinking, a worldliness that was often expressed in spiritualized terms. As a result, Paul laments, "And I, brethren, could not speak to you as spiritual men, but as to men of flesh, as infants in Christ" (1 Cor 3:1). Paul, however, is not willing to allow these believers to remain in their spiritual infancy, with all of the subsequent problems that result from their spiritual condition, but begins to instruct them by stating, "and I show you a still more excellent way" (1 Cor 12:31b). The question

---

13. Schaeffer, *How Should We Then Live?* in *Complete Works*, 5:254 (italics in original).

to be asked is—more excellent than what? For Paul, the answer is the type of thinking that produced the various factions and instances of immortality in the Corinthian church that he was compelled to address. His desire to speak to them as spiritual men was thwarted by a state of spiritual immaturity in their thought and resulted in behaviors that were "carnal" (KJV). In essence, while acknowledging them to be believers, Paul notes that the thoughts and motives of their behaviors were more "worldly" than spiritual. In addressing the more excellent way, Paul instructs the Corinthians that they need to base their behaviors on a motive of love (*agape*) in order to be more mature in their faith (1 Cor 13:11). What Paul proposes is a radical notion of ethics that places Christian moral thought and behavior in stark contrast to that of unbelievers.

The concept of basing ethical thought and behavior in love would have been quite familiar to the culturally Greek Corinthians. In that sense, the love idea is neither new nor particularly radical. Many Greek moral theorists had used the idea of love as foundational to their ethical systems. Greek has three primary words for love—*eros*, *philia*, and *agape*—and Paul neither coins a new word for love nor uses one unfamiliar to the Corinthians. In the Greek use of these three terms, only the word *agape* had never been used as foundational to a system of moral or ethical thought or behavior. In Greek philosophy both *eros* and *philia* had strong traditions in moral thought. Thus Paul's use of the term *agape* and his promotion of an ethical system based on *agape* love prove to be unique and must have struck his Corinthian readers as revolutionary.

For example, Plato based his system of ethics on the notion of *eros*—a love characterized by passion, sensual desire or longing. In his work *The Symposium*, Plato discusses at length his notion of love and its ethical implications. According to Plato, *eros* represents an internal force that drives a person toward what they consider to be good, true, or beautiful. While subjective, erotic love is the desire to have the object that is loved and is often sensual because the desired object is believed to meet a deficiency that the person feels. As Plato writes, "Such a man, then, and everyone else who feels desire, desires what is not in his present power or possession, and desire and love have for their object things or qualities which a man does not at the present possess but which he lacks."[14] The idea of *eros*, including its sexual connotations, is the desire to have or possess the object of the individual's sensual desires (which forms the basis of the English word *erotic*).

For Plato, however, *eros* did not have to be sexual (as seen in the notion of platonic love) but one that was based in the sense or the way that human beings perceive the world around him. For Plato *eros*, properly directed by reason, would drive the individual from desiring the physical manifestations of the good (which could be found in the physical world around them) to the ultimate or ideal goods of which physical representations were only incomplete. The physical pleasure gained through the senses (i.e., a beautiful thing) should cause a person to desire that which is ultimately good (i.e., beauty itself). As Plato writes,

> This is the right way of approaching or being initiated into the mysteries of love, to begin with examples of beauty in the world, and using them as steps to ascend continually with that absolute beauty as one's aim, from one instance of physical beauty to two and from two to all, then from physical beauty to moral beauty, and from

14. Plato, *Symposium*, 77.

moral beauty to the beauty of knowledge, until from knowledge of various kinds one arrives at the supreme knowledge whose sole object is that absolute beauty, and knows at last what absolute beauty is.[15]

Even so, because it is based in desire, *eros* is always egocentric; that is, it seeks to possess the object of its desire. In this regard *eros* seeks to derive pleasure from the object it desires and longs to possess. To use the word in an English context, if I were to say "I feel *eros* for a hamburger" my desire would be to gain a sensual pleasure from the hamburger without feeling any particular moral obligation to provide the hamburger any pleasure in return. In this sense, the idea of *eros* has an objectifying effect on whatever becomes the object of desire—whether a hamburger, a person, or truth itself.

Aristotle rejected an ethical theory based in *eros* and believed that moral thought and action should be based in a virtuous love characterized as friendship or *philia* love. *Philia* love is the emotional bond between human beings that provides the basis of all forms of social organization, common effort, and personal relationships between people. While there can be variations in the degree to which a person experiences *philia*—for example, I can love my wife with a greater degree of intensity than I love social institutions, such as love for my country—both would be examples of the type of *philia* love found in Aristotle's thought. For Aristotle, natural desires like hunger, thirst, or sex were biological phenomenon and do not enter into the discussion of *philia*. For Aristotle such phenomena were involuntary passions, whereas virtue was a state of character based in reason and choice.

Aristotle's most complete discussion of the ethics of *philia* is found in his work *The Nicomachean Ethics*. For him the notion that the moral could be based on what was of benefit to the individual was too subjective and transient, based too closely on involuntary passions, making this an insufficient guide to a virtuous life. As Aristotle writes,

> Therefore, these who love for the sake of utility love for the sake of what is good *for themselves*, as those who love for the sake of pleasure do so for the sake of pleasure *to themselves*, and not in so far as the other is the person loved but in so far as he is useful or pleasant. . . . Such friendships, then, are easily dissolved if the parties do not remain like themselves; for if the one party is no longer pleasant or useful, the other ceases to love him.[16]

Rather, for Aristotle, the best life is achieved when there is mutual good will when each party seeks the benefit of and derives benefit from the other. It is a state in which actions that produce pleasure because of their desired results (utility or instrumental ends) are balanced by actions that produce pleasure simply from doing the action itself (intrinsic ends). For example, a man may exercise simply for the purpose of losing weight (utility end) or from the good feelings or joy he receives from strenuous activity (intrinsic end). When applied to ethical behavior between individuals and the society as a whole, this balance is achieved when individuals understand their own desires but also balance these with an understanding of the interest and needs of others. Applying this principle to friendship, Aristotle writes,

15. Ibid., 94.

16. Aristotle, *Nicomachean Ethics* 8.3, p. 195 (italics in original).

> As in regards to the virtues some men are called good in respect of a state of charac-
> ter, others in respect of an activity, so too in the case of friendship; for those who live
> together delight in each other and confer benefits on each other.[17]

In terms of ethics, the question of love revolves around the question, should a person live mostly for himself or for someone else? Aristotle views both as instances of self-love. Those who merely look to their own interest will have the tendency to "assign to them-selves the greater share of wealth, honours, and bodily pleasures; for these are what most people desire."[18] Such love (*eros*) is neither rational nor proper self-love. True self-love (*philia*) is based on a mutual give and take, not only expressed among friends but also extended (as part of justice) to all people. As Aristotle describes,

> But such a man would seem more than the other a lover of self; at all events he
> assigns to himself the things that are noblest and best, and gratifies the most au-
> thoritative element in himself and in all things obeys this; and just as the city or
> any other systematic whole is most properly identified with the most authoritative
> element in it; and therefore the man who loves this and gratifies it is most of all a
> lover of self.[19]

Plato builds his ethical system on the self-love of *eros* because he realizes that such love exists in human beings in the greatest abundance. While Plato understood that the erotic tendencies of human beings are to desire specific pleasures, he believed that for people to become ethical, they must learn to desire the higher or more universal pleasures (a process that can only be achieved through the development of reason). The develop-ment of a reasoned approached to ethics, however, appears antithetical to the desires of the flesh, which he notes are more characteristic of human nature. For this reason the pursuit of universal pleasures seems at odds with human sensual desires. Consequently, since the development of reason is necessary for ethical decision making based in univer-sal principles, Plato believed that few people could or would truly become ethical. For this reason Plato, in his work *The Republic*, chooses to put the moral leadership of the state in the hands of Philosopher-Kings.

For Aristotle, ethical behavior is also built upon reason and rational choice. In his case, however, what is ethical can be discerned by all human beings who learn that it is in their own interest to pursue the interests of others. In the end such choices work for the benefit of all parties. To act justly is to make a rational choice that could be applied to all members of the community in a way that seeks the benefit of all members of the com-munity. Since working for one's own benefit or self-interest is not antithetical to human desire, Aristotle believed that all human beings who were trained and exercised reason could act ethically. While differing from Plato in seeing that ethical behavior could be exhibited by more members of the community, Aristotle maintained that *philia*-based rational self-love is demonstrated by human beings to a lesser degree than the *eros*-based human passions seen in Plato.

17. Ibid. 8.5, p. 199.
18. Ibid. 9.8, p. 235.
19. Ibid. 9.8, p. 236.

Into this context of ethical thinking, Paul confronts the Corinthian believers and insists that spiritual behavior is based on *agape* love. Unlike the ethics of Plato or Aristotle, who both start from a principle of self-love, in the ethics of *agape*, the individual works for the interest or well-being of another without expectation of receiving anything in return. It represents a total commitment to sacrificial love to the one that is loved. In the New Testament *agape* is used to describe not only God as love (1 John 4:8) but also the relationship that believers should have toward God (Matt 22:37) and toward others (Matt 22:39). For the believer to love others with total commitment or self-sacrifice is an expression of the character of Christ that is to embody them. As Jesus states, "this is My commandment, that you love one another just as I have loved you" (John 15:12), to the extent that "greater love has no one than this, that one lay down his life for his friends" (John 15:13).

While the Greeks understood that such a love, or actions that would result from such love, was possible (hence their coining of the word), no ethical system was founded on such a principle. They believed *agape* love so scarce that basing an ethic on it would be futile. While neither Plato nor Aristotle acknowledge the corruption of human nature that is described in the biblical concept of the Fall, their observations regarding human nature and its propensity toward self-love provide an abundant source of natural motivation on which to base ethics. Because such a love is unnatural, Paul espouses *agape* as the basis of Christian ethical motives and behavior, such a love places individuals in a position of vulnerability, where they can be disappointed, hurt, or left broken-hearted. It becomes a radical basis for ethical behavior, one that confronts and contradicts a more rational but worldly understanding of human nature and, therefore, stands in opposition to the carnal ways of understanding that Paul confronts in 1 Corinthians 3:1. As C. S. Lewis writes in *The Four Loves*, "Christ did not teach and suffer that we might become, even in the natural loves, more careful of our own happiness."[20]

For Paul the relationship that the believer should have to the three loves is fundamentally different from that of the natural man, which so characterizes the ethical thought of Plato and Aristotle. When Paul states that "a natural man does not accept the things of the Spirit of God, for they are foolishness to him; and he cannot understand them, because they are spiritually appraised" (1 Cor 2:14), he declares that only the presence of the Holy Spirit in the life of the believer makes the more excellent way of *agape* possible. The radical nature of Paul's ethic in 1 Corinthians 13 is predicated on the presence and effectual working of the Spirit in the believer's life. Paul acknowledges that while the Corinthians were believers, their carnal state caused them to act as those natural or unbelieving individuals who saw the ways of *agape* as foolish. For Paul, the "filling" or effectual working of the Holy Spirit is critical and is to be considered normal in the life of the believer. When Paul addresses the issue of being filled with the Holy Spirit to the Ephesian church, he concludes his command to "be filled with the Holy Spirit" by noting that this filling will be evidenced by their being "subject to one other in the fear of Christ" (Eph 5:18, 21).

The effectual presence of the Holy Spirit in the life of the believer is tied to the previous discussion of making God famous and the character of true worship. This connection can be seen in noting the relationship that each of the members of the Trinity has toward

---

20. Lewis, *Four Loves*, 122.

the others. Jesus Christ, as the Son of God, serves to magnify and bring glory to the Father (cf. John 13:31; 14:13). The Father, in turn, glorifies the Son by giving him all power, dominion, and authority (cf. Matt 28:18) and also by verifying the message of Christ through the resurrection (cf. John 13:32; 1 Cor 15:1–4). Believers, as they are conformed to the likeness of Christ, are to live in the same perfect humanity that characterized Christ as he lived in this world. In so doing, the believer brings glory to the Father just as Christ brought glory to the Father by being subject and perfectly obedient to the will of the Father in his life (cf. Matt 26:39, 42). The term *Christian* is indicative of the believer's desire to be conformed to the teaching and practices of Christ in a manner that, like Christ, serves to bring glory to the Father. The practice of making God famous, however, also brings glory to Christ by verifying the authenticity of his message of justification and freedom from the bondage of sin (cf. Gal 2:20).

In emphasizing the importance of being "filled," Paul notes that conformity to Christ is predicated on the effectual presence of the Holy Spirit operating in the life of the believer. To live ethically, to live as Christ lived on the Earth, is to live in accordance to *agape* love—to love in a manner that expects nothing in return. This type of love is sacrificial, for "just as Christ loved the church and gave Himself up for her" (Eph 5:25), believers are to live in a way that is also sacrificial (cf. John 13:35). The importance of the effectual presence of the Holy Spirit in the practice of *agape* cannot be overstated, considering the role of each of the members of the Trinity to each other. As noted above, the Son brings glory to the Father and the Father brings glory to the Son. Nowhere in Scripture, however, does any member of the Godhead bring glory to the Holy Spirit. The Father is the one who loves and the Son is the one loved (cf. John 3:35; 5:20), but the Spirit is said to be love (cf. Gal 5:22; Eph 6:23). As the embodiment of *agape*, the Holy Spirit is content to glorify the Son (John 16:13–15) without finding it necessary to seek or bring glory to himself. As Paul consistently teaches, it is the Holy Spirit who indwells believers and empowers them to live according to the principles of Christ and the will of the Father. It is the character of the Holy Spirit, a character that seeks not his own way but seeks to work for the betterment of others without regard for himself, who is described in the passage on the fruits of the Spirit and is embodied in the description of love that Paul gives in 1 Corinthians 13.

The benevolent and humble character of the indwelling Holy Spirit in the life of the believer is foundational to understand Paul's teaching on the general gifts of the Spirit. The "fruits" of the Spirit are those general character qualities that allow the believer to live and act toward others in such a manner that conforms to the character of Christ. As Paul writes,

> Do nothing from selfishness or empty conceit, but with humility of mind regard one another as more important than yourselves; do not merely look out for your own interests, but also the interests of others. Have this attitude in yourselves which was also in Christ Jesus, who although He existed in the form of God, did not regard equality with God a thing to be grasped, but emptied Himself, taking on the form of a bond-servant, and being made in the likeness of men. Being found in appearance as a man, He humbled Himself by becoming obedient to the point of death, even on a cross. (Phil 2:3–8)

Similarly spiritual gifts—those specific talents, abilities, or dispositions assigned to each believer—are provided for the betterment and general welfare of the church as whole. As each believer is empowered by the Spirit with one or more spiritual gifts, those gifts are to be used for the edification of the community of faith as whole. Insofar as the community of faith, both individually and corporately, ministers to the world, spiritual gifts also empower the believer to serve the greater or common good of the whole community. As gifts that are both Spirit-given and Spirit-driven, they are to be used for the betterment of others without seeking one's own ends or reward. It was this perversion of the use of spiritual gifts that prompted Paul's condemnation of their practice in Corinth, where believers sought specific gifts to promote their own desire of appearing spiritual to the detriment of the unity of the community (cf. 1 Cor 12:1–30).

Furthermore, for every spiritual gift that Paul mentions in his writings there is a like command for all believers to be faithful in that particular area as a part of an overall routine of faithfulness. In this regard, the Holy Spirit not only empowers the believer for a particular area of ministry or service but is also the source of all power in regard to general obedience to Christ. As a result, every act of obedience is to be characterized by *agape* and brings glory to God, so even the acts of feeding the hungry, clothing the poor, or visiting the sick or imprisoned are acts that are done as unto God (Matt 25:34–40).

In this regard, the presentation of the self, a commitment to others that is based in the similar attitude or mind of Christ described in Philippians 2, is predicated on the renewal of the mind that Paul describes in Romans 12:1–2. As worship is characterized by sacrifice (i.e., *thusia*, or emptying of the self; *latreia*, or service), the character of such worship is consistent in the practice of *agape*. For Christian educators, as proponents of worldview transformation, to separate an emphasis on the renewal of the mind without also providing opportunities for engagement and practice of service, is to engage in a type of worldview transformation that is more philosophical than theological, more compartmentalized than holistic, and more individual than communal. Such an attempt to engage in worldview transformation will be separated from the ethics of *agape*, from the practical exhibition of love and service, and runs the risk of being divorced from the power of the Holy Spirit.

LEARNING AND THE CHRISTIAN COMMUNITY

Thomas Sergiovanni, who writes extensively on the topic of educational leadership, notes that "*Communities* are collections of individuals who are bonded together by natural will and who are together bound to a set of shared ideas and ideals."[21] While the theology of "natural will" can be challenged, with believers being bound together by the Holy Spirit, Sergiovanni's definition of community can aptly be applied to the community of faith. As demonstrated earlier, the community of faith is bound together by a common idea and ideal—to worship God and to make him famous by declaring Christ to a watching world. Francis Schaeffer identifies a similar idea in his book *The Mark of the Christian* when he writes,

> This passage [John 13:33–35] reveals the mark that Jesus gives to label a Christian not just in one era or locality, but at all times and all places until Jesus returns.

21. Sergiovanni, *Leadership for the Schoolhouse*, 48 (italics in original).

Notice that what He says here is not a statement or a fact. It is a command which includes a condition: "A new commandment I give unto you, that ye love one another; as I have loved you that ye also love one another. By this will all men know that you are my disciples, *if* you have love one to another." An *if* is involved. If you obey, you will wear the badge Christ gave. But since this is a command it can be violated.

The point is that it is possible to be a Christian without showing the mark; but if we expect non-Christians to know that we are Christians, we *must* show the mark.[22]

Loving God and loving others both proclaim Christ; they demonstrate his nature, the relevance of his word, and the applicability of how he lived to every aspect of life. These are the fulfillment of the new commandment given by Christ to his disciples, "that you love one another, even as I have loved you" (John 13:34). The reality of Christ will be known to the world, Jesus notes, through the relationships that believers have one to another. "By this will all men know that you are my disciples, if you have love for one another" (John 13:35). As the perfect man, the second Adam (1 Cor 15:45), Christ shows humanity how to live life. The teachings of Christ have more to do with living this life than the next, and the life that Jesus proclaims as the test of his validity is a life of unity within community. Human beings are created by God to live in closer relationships, to live in community. The first reference to humanity in Scripture is a communal reference, when God declares, "Let Us make man in Our image, according to Our likeness" (Gen 1:26a). This initial statement of human essence is related to the singular relationship of community found in the Trinity. Notice that this image is given purpose: "and let him rule over the fish of the sea and over the birds of the sky and over the cattle and over all the earth" (Gen 1:26b). Later, the biblical narrative records that God claims, "It is not good for the man to be alone; I will make a helper suitable for him" (Gen 2:18), so that the image of God is not complete or not fully realized without relationship to others. God gives the helper to achieve the common goal—community to serve in the roles God has given them.

The modernistic material worldview and its extension to market-based economism may serve to elevate the autonomous individual (i.e., the producer-consumer), but in the process it may also threaten or undermine the biblical image of God in human beings. This process is so aptly seen in advertising, where the science of psychology and the technology of media are used to identify (or create) desires in individuals and develop and provide products specifically catered to a particular need. In the end, human free will becomes focused and dedicated toward individually determined and self-promoting ends, which threaten to undermine the image of God by seeing others not as those whose welfare needs to be protected and promoted (even above one's own) but as competitors or threats to one's own interests. This process leads to the devaluing and, progressively, to the dehumanization of others, a process that is always the consequence of sin.

Humans, however, were not created to be autonomous individuals, so attempts to create such autonomy run counter to human nature. This divinely created human need for community is recognized even in advertising and is used to sell products by attempting to develop brand loyalties that will serve to create a type of pseudo-community.

---

22. Schaeffer, *The Mark of the Christian*, in *Complete Works*, 4:184 (italics in original).

Douglas Atkins, former marketing director for Proctor & Gamble states, "[the job of a brand manager] is now to create and maintain a whole meaning for people in which they get identity and understanding of the world. . . . People, whether they join a cult or join a brand, do so for exactly the same reasons. They need to belong and they need to make meaning. [We need] to figure out what the world is all about and we need the company of others."[23] The video documentary entitled *The Persuaders* identifies certain companies—specifically Nike, Coca-Cola, and Apple Computers—as having been particularly successful in cultivating a type of community among its consumers, a pattern that other companies seek to imitate. Wearing the right clothes, using the "hip" computer, or drinking the right drink, and so forth distinguishes consumers from those who are "outside" or not part of the shared idea or ideal. Such brand loyalty, however, takes away from true community by changing the focus from human relationships and interaction to identification with things.

The threat to community in a consumer culture takes two forms. First, human beings are less likely to be identified by who they are or what creeds they embrace but increasingly by the personal distinctions that come from product identity. In essence, the symbols individuals display—what they own, what they drive, what they wear, where they eat, etc.—permit them to stand apart from the crowd, to be noticed and admired. Even so, as film and media critic Stuart Ewen notes, these promises of individual distinction are being made simultaneously to a mass of people. The result, he concludes, is that

> This highly individuated notion of personal distinction—marked by the compulsory consumption of images [in advertising]—stands at the heart of the "American Dream." To a certain extent, this continuous offer of personal distinction may indicate an epic crisis of identity that lurks within the inner lives of many Americans. Nonetheless, the promise is also an essential part of the way of life that is anxiously pursued by people who are now, or wish to become, part of the great American "middle class."[24]

The second threat is that human relationships become increasingly patterned on how people interact with objects. The bond of social relationships changes from one emphasizing common ideas or ideals to one where the perceived needs of the individual are paramount. Just as old products are discarded when they become obsolete or fail to promote the identity or image the consumer seeks to cultivate, relationships risk becoming more transitory and subject to revision or divorce if they also fail to meet individual desires or perceived needs. This threat of mass consumerism to social relationships was identified as early as 1921 by the Hungarian social critic George Lukács, when he wrote,

> The essence of commodity-structure . . . is that a relation between people takes on the character of a thing and thus takes on a "phantom objectivity," an autonomy that seems so strictly rational and all-embracing as to conceal every trace of its fundamental nature; the relation between people.[25]

---

23. *The Persuaders* [DVD].

24. Ewen, *All Consuming Images*, 58.

25. Lukács, *History and Class Consciousness*, 85.

As a more consumer-oriented ethos infests the church, it leads to an ecclesiology that is more individual oriented and less communal. The same type of brand loyalty may exist, which creates a sense of doctrinal community but which serves as a replacement for true community. For example, when it comes to automobiles, a person may be a "Ford man." As a young man starting out in life, he may drive a small economy car. As he marries and starts a family, he may find his needs change and purchases a minivan. Later in life, as he approaches midlife and possibly has greater disposable income, he may purchase a sports car. As he eases into retirement, he may choose to drive a luxury sedan. Even though his individual or family needs change over time, his brand loyalty prompts him to start his vehicle search at his Ford dealer. Ford, in order to ensure that it keeps him a lifelong customer, seeks to create models that will cater to the buyer's needs in each stage or personal situation of life.

Christians can also have a sense of brand loyalty (Baptist, Presbyterian, Methodist, etc.). As a young person, the importance might be on a more contemporary worship style and vibrant singles group. With marriage and family, the emphasis might change to small groups for the couples and an active and engaging youth ministry for the children and teens. Some people prefer more traditional music, others more contemporary. Some people prefer chairs to pews. In each case, the perceived individual needs of the person or family drive the decision of where to attend, and often churches feel compelled, like successful car dealerships, to have diverse and sufficient models (i.e., programs) to accommodate the desires of the consuming public. The fear is that if the church (like the car dealership) fails to provide the programs the individuals believe they need, those individuals may switch "dealerships" (i.e., attend another church of the same doctrinal persuasion) or switch brands altogether. In the end, a consumer-oriented ethos creates an approach characterized by asking what the church can do for the individual rather than what the individual can do for the church. Such an approach to worship and community erodes the *agape* ethic and corrodes the fundamental purpose of spiritual gifts—to promote the edification of others. That contemporary American evangelical culture has coined the term "church shopping" underscores the effect of this consumer-oriented ethos on the church.

Of note is that many believers consider a church successful by such variables as attendance, building, budget, or the number of worship products or options, such as forms of music, niche group ministries, service types. While none of these are fundamentally negative in themselves, the success of the church is often attributed to the degree to which people find that these programs provide for their wants, desires, or expectations. Like good advertising, these programs can be labeled as addressing particular needs, but the true need, as identified by Scripture, is a relational community built around a proper common purpose—to worship God and to make him famous before a watching world. As Christ identified, the only legitimate test of the reality of his Lordship to the unbelieving world is whether there is love one to another.

The term *church* as well as the term *community* is singular. As Sergiovanni's quote previously indicated, a community is a group of individuals bound together by a common set of ideas or ideals. The church is a group of individuals grafted together by the Holy

Spirit. The analogies used to identify the church in Scripture reflect this unity. Individuals are grafted into the vine. which is Christ (John 15). The church is referred to as the body of Christ (1 Cor 12; Eph 4). It is a holy temple in the Lord (Eph 2:20–22) and the bride of Christ (Eph 5; Rev 19:7–10). This unity is achieved theologically through all believers being "in Christ" (Gal 3:28) and practically through the Holy Spirit enabling all believers by empowering them through the provision of spiritual gifts to minister to others. As Paul writes, spiritual gifts are given

> For the equipping of the saints for the work of service, to build up the body of Christ; until we all attain to the unity of the faith, and of the knowledge of the Son of God, to a mature man, to the measure of the stature which belongs to the fullness of Christ. (Eph 4:12–13)

These gifts, as Paul also notes, are given for the promotion of the "common good" (1 Cor 12:7), a good that will reflect the unity in love of the believers to the world. The church in Corinth, to whom Paul writes, experienced great divisions. It was a church where individuals were seeking their own status and agendas, leading to jealousy and strife. Paul mentions this most notably in their identification with different leaders rather than the common purpose of the gospel (1 Cor 3:1–9), the exclusion of the poor by the wealthy in the celebration of the Lord's Table (1 Cor 11:17–34), and the coveting and abuse of spiritual gifts (1 Cor 12). Paul summarizes the cause for all the divisions he identifies in Corinth as stemming from the fact that they were thinking and acting with the same motivations as unbelievers or as "men of flesh, as to infants in Christ" (1 Cor 3:1).

Stewardship, reconciliation, and the development of the image of God are principles of integration tied to biblical theology—they prompt the believer to ask what God has called each individual and the community of faith to do in demonstrating the reality of Christ to others. As such, they constitute principles of worship, for in acting on these principles, the believer and the faith community demonstrate their love for God through the self-emptying sacrifice (*thusia*) which is manifested in service to others (*latreia*) as evidence of the reality of Christ. Just as Christ was obedient to the Father and emptied himself, both in his incarnation and in his sacrifice on the cross for the benefit of humanity, all believers are called, individually and corporately, to take up their cross for the benefit of others. In doing so, the community of faith demonstrates the reality of the resurrected Christ by living their faith according to the ideas and ideals of the Lord of life (cf. Rom 1:16; Gal 2:20).

The reality of service worship underscores the importance of developing disciples of Christ, not merely believers in the message of the gospel. This distinction is often lost in contemporary evangelicalism where being a disciple means engaging in the study of Scripture. Once the truth is learned, the student takes it to heart and believes—creating a type of synonymous use of the terms *disciple* and *believer*. In contrast, to be a student in the context of first-century education was to engage in a relationship of apprentice to a master. That is, the student would not only know the teachings of the master but would also train to engage in the mission and the work of the teacher. This distinction can be clearly seen in James's injunction to "prove yourselves doers of the word, and not merely hearers" for hearers are those who simply "delude themselves" (Jas 1:22). James does not leave his readers to interpret for themselves what it means to engage in the doing of the word but concludes his admonition by stating, "Pure and undefiled religion in the sight of our God and Father is this: to visit orphans and widows in their distress and to keep oneself unstained by the world" (Jas 1:27). True holiness cannot be pursued apart from ministry. To pursue holiness in the practice of service to others is what is acceptable to God and is characteristic of those who are doers of the Word.

The emphasis from James, and the principle clearly stated by Paul, is that the *agape* ethic produces sacrifice to service (Rom 12:1). This sacrifice to service places the individual in the position to engage in practices that are countercultural to the world and will lead to the renewing of the mind (Rom 12:2a), which generally is associated with worldview transformation. As Paul delineates the process, it is an attitude of humility or self-sacrifice that prompts the believer to engage in service that leads to transformation, whereby the believer can now "prove what the will of God is, that which is good and acceptable and perfect" (Rom 12:2b). What Paul appears to say is that *orthodoxy*, or the pursuit of right doctrine, must be attached to *orthopraxy*, or right practice, for the type of worldview transformation sought in Romans 12:1–2 to be attained. James states as much when he notes that faith without works is dead (Jas 2:17) but observes that the types of works associated with living faith are the feeding and clothing of the poor and not simply speaking words of blessing (Jas 2:15–16).

The distinction between orthodoxy and orthopraxy highlights the fundamental difference between philosophic and worldview transformation. Since philosophies are analytically founded and qualified, they are most closely aligned with the importance and the pursuit of orthodoxy. It should also be reemphasized that a fundamental characteristic of philosophies is that they are individually held and are not distinctly connected to community. In contrast, while worldviews have a rational component, their psychic or perceptual foundation is more closely associated with how a person behaves in the world. As a result, worldviews are closely associated with orthopraxy. That is, individuals can be taught to do what is right even before they understand the logical, philosophical, or theological reasons for the behavior. Since behavior is fundamentally tied to the relationship of people one to another, orthopraxy and worldviews are more tied to the goals, aspirations, and action within community. As evidenced by the fact that children attain the worldview of their culture, each person's initial worldview is acquired in association with others who are older or more competent than the learner in the values and behaviors of the community. As learners seek both the association and approval of those perceived as more competent, and, over time, greater assimilation into the community, they seek to emulate the behaviors of those who serve as models. Eventually, they may learn and be able to articulate the foundational values, goals, or ideals that form the basis of their practice. If thoroughly educated, the student may become a defender of those foundational principles—a philosopher or theologian of orthodoxy—and provide an analytic basis for the orthopraxy that is part of the community.

This is the dynamic of transformation that Paul writes of in Romans 12:1–2 that the believer should present himself a "living" sacrifice to engage in worship service. As believers engage in service worship, they place themselves under the values, goals, and ideals of the community, which seeks to promote the teachings and practices of Christ. As they engage in these practices, they are open to having those foundational principles instilled into their way of seeing the world. Rather than seeing the practices of the world as normal, that which is perceived as normal is transformed to align with the values, goals, and ideals of Christ and the community of faith. Similarly, over time, the believer may come to "prove," through both action and word, the good, acceptable, and perfect will of God.

Paul never assumes that such transformation will take place in isolation; rather, service learning assumes a community in which older believers have the responsibility to model and disciple new believers. Mature believers serve as the models of faith and practice—living their faith in such a way that new believers can emulate their practices and grow in the faith. Of note is that Paul's teaching to mature believers deals exclusively with orthopraxy so that they will show "all good faith so that they [new believers] will adorn the doctrine of God our Savior in every respect" (Titus 2:8). In other words, sound doctrine will result from faithful practice.

Many Christian educators cite the principle of teaching found in Deuteronomy 6:7 as the foundation of parental responsibility to educate children; thus, the Christian school should be an extension of the faith and values of the home. As Moses is writing to the Israelites regarding the commands of God, he instructs parents, "you shall teach them diligently to your sons and shall talk of them when you sit in your house and when you walk by the way and when you lie down and when you rise up." The term used here for "teach" is literally "to impress," and the command is that as parents engage their children in the normal actions of life, they will impress upon them the reasons for why they are doing the things that they do. Of interest is that the command of the Law to which Moses refers is found in Deuteronomy 6:5, where he instructs Israel to "love the Lord your God with all you heart and with all your soul and with all your might." Noticeably absent from the command is the term "mind," indicating that Moses's instruction to parents is to instill the proper motivation for loving actions or worship rather than to simply provide a rationale. In Matthew 22:37–49 Jesus refers to Deuteronomy 6:5 as the summary of the Law but also adds the command of Leviticus 19:18, where the Israelites are commanded to love others as they love themselves. That Jesus adds "the second is like it," linking the command to love others to the command of loving God, denotes Jesus's emphasis that one cannot separate the two in the practice of faithful obedience. On these commands, Jesus states, "depend the whole Law and the prophets."

This is not to dismiss the importance of the mind in the process of faithful obedience (Jesus does add "mind" to the summary of the law as recorded in Luke 10:27), but to indicate that through actions and the development of proper motivations the mind will be open to the reasons for engaging in such actions. This pattern is also evident in Paul's command in Romans 12:1, where the presentation of one's body as a living sacrifice as an act of worship precedes the renewing or transformation of the mind that allows one to discern or prove the will of God commanded in 12:2. The difficulty that many Christian educators may experience in attempting to transform the worldview of students is engaging in a model that violates the principles outlined by both Moses and Paul. A philosophical approach to worldview transformation contends that changing the mind will lead to changed actions. In this respect it is a model of worldview transformation that owes more to an Enlightenment rationalism than biblical theology. It is a model that emphasizes orthodoxy over orthopraxy, the individual (and personal empowerment) over community and sacrificial service, and the metaphor of student over the concept of disciple or apprentice. By contrast, a model of worldview transformation that is more biblically based emphasizes service learning and action. This model seeks to create disciples who work with mentors to accomplish the Christian purpose of the church community—to glorify God and, in so doing, to experience their true humanity and enjoy him forever.

DISCIPLESHIP AS APPRENTICESHIP

As noted earlier, the identifying characteristic that Jesus placed on his disciples is not one of theological orthodoxy but one that corresponds to the *agape* ethic—that his disciples love one another. This command does not discount the need for good theology (believers are to worship God in both spirit and truth) but emphasizes the idea that theological orthodoxy is lifeless if not made alive by the Holy Spirit and love. The reality of this truth should have profound implications for educators interested in the process of worldview transformation. If the process is conceived as essentially synonymous with theological or philosophical change, it runs the risk of creating a lifeless form of orthodoxy in students. While an approach based in orthodoxy may be educating students for Christendom, that is, civic knowledge of the kingdom, it does not sufficiently prepare people for active participation in the kingdom. Moving away from a more rationalistic approach to worldview transformation and toward a more biblical one requires rethinking the process in light of orthopraxy and participatory worship. It is a process designed to encourage the commitment of people to become living sacrifices for the glory of God and the benefit of others people who desire to make God famous, people who desire to be like Jesus Christ.

The principles of stewardship, reconciliation, and developing the image of God are integrative themes that engage the student in the process of worldview transformation. The principles are not simply academic orientations that assist teachers and students to comprehend academic content differently. Rather, they are principles that direct learning toward active implementation and the ethical use of content knowledge in ways that can be aligned with the biblical mandates given by God to humanity. They are principles that, when properly implemented, require an engagement in *agape* thinking, a thinking that leads to worshipful action. In this regard, they are principles that require the active and direct engagement of orthopraxy rather than the potentially passive and impersonal acquisition of orthodoxy. What results from such an approach to instruction is that all learning and the ethical response to that learning is now brought under the Lordship of Christ.

The more traditional approach to worldview transformation has been to engage in a more rationalistic and apologetic approach. Under this approach, if the student accepts the logic of the biblical worldview, that is, if they concur that it provides a better rationale for life and practice than an alternative worldview, they will choose to live in a manner consistent with that logic. This approach assumes that people are rational beings and that assent to a superior set of logical propositions is sufficient to both change perception and motivate action. It also assumes the ability of the student to, in essence, step back or objectively evaluate the rational claims of each worldview and choose the option that best corresponds to the world she understands. This method leads to an impersonal approach to biblical truth, where Christianity is reduced to a superior set of propositional truth statements. This mode of instruction helps account for the synonymous use of *worldview* and *philosophy* in evangelical literature. A problem with this approach is that it cannot be assumed that students have the ability to objectively evaluate the claims of orthodoxy. As cultural beings, students come to the process of worldview transformation generally pre-disposed to assume the normalcy of the more dominant secular worldview. Born with a sin nature that will improperly mediate even the most thoroughly Christian environment, students will subjectively assess orthodoxy in light of the world they perceive as true or normal. The result is either a rejection of the biblical worldview or an accommodation of orthodoxy to cultural practice more characteristic of philosophical dualism.

What often results in churches and schools in an engagement in biblical integration and worldview transformation that more closely resembles indoctrination than genuine alteration or change. Students learn to recite the standard lines of doctrine, appropri-ate the proper memory verse, or apply the biblical principle that aligns with a particular content area or character action. As students' creedal responses are reinforced by their teachers, they quickly learn the relationship between their responses and the responses of the community of faith. This can lead, in a positive sense, to a greater conformity to the expectations of the community of faith to those creedal responses, and those students who are connected or seek to have their personal needs met within the faith community will often have sufficient motivation to maintain certain standards of behavior. For those students who do not find sufficient motivation or personal connection to the community of faith, the lack of reinforcement or punishment to conform may quickly drive them away from the expected standards of behavior. In either case, the majority of students will be insufficiently prepared to make the connection between faith and practice expected of genuine worldview transformation.

The traditional evangelical approach to worldview transformation has its roots in two aspects of the Western intellectual tradition, namely rationalism and rationality. The roots of rationalism (from the Latin *ratio* or "reason") go back to the ancient Greeks; simply stated, it is the idea that reason is to be given the primary role in explaining the world (which can also include spiritual truth). Rationality has its roots in the European Enlightenment and particularly in the philosophy of René Descartes, who believed that reason could be systematized into a method that would render truth objective and con-sensual to all rational beings. The predominance of science as *the* means of ascertaining truth in public discourse serves as testimony to the triumph of rationality. While reason and its proper use are critical to the education process, even in relation to the process of worldview transformation, the predominance of rationalism and rationality has certain drawbacks that have to be considered. Both rationalism and rationality center first on the individual and changing one's thought process. As a result, worldview transformation is seen as synonymous with a philosophical or theological change of thinking. This emphasis is seen in the metaphor of "student" rather than that of "disciple." Parker Palmer refers to this educational phenomenon as the "objectivist myth of knowing"[26]

For Palmer, the knowledge to be known is objective and is known by someone trained in both the content and the way of thinking about that content who is the expert. It is a hierarchical relationship in which knowledge stands above all knowers and is something to be reached for and attained by learners. To become an expert is not only to learn the content sufficiently but also to be able to approach it without allowing subjectivity or bias to interfere with proper knowing. The expert serves as a teacher to those who are less knowledgeable, people without training and full of bias who are dependent on experts to provide a true understanding of the object to be known. At each level greater expertise allows objective knowledge to flow downward while preventing subjectivity from flowing upward and corrupting what can be known.

In the case of worldview transformation, the objects to be known are biblical content and the content of the academic disciplines to be integrated. The academic content is treated as objective (i.e., something outside the learner) and, therefore, something to be mastered. The successful acquisition is measured by the amount of content the learner acquires rather than the way the knowledge is used. While the biblical content is often portrayed as part of the relationship that the learner has with Christ, the general approach to biblical content mirrors that of other academic content—it is treated as something to be known, and successful acquisition is also measured by the amount of content acquired. Biblical integration, from this perspective, not only requires sufficient expertise in an academic discipline but also sufficient content knowledge of the Bible in order that the two areas can be incorporated. Teachers, as experts, are those who have successfully acquired more content knowledge in each area and are separated from their students hierarchically. Since acquisition of content is the key variable, teachers become the only ones who can adequately engage in biblical integration and are also in a position to transmit integrated content to their students.

This rationalistic approach to biblical integration and worldview transformation has two significant consequences for biblical educators. First, students do not actually have to engage in the process of biblical integration; in fact, they may even be viewed as incapable of engaging in the process. Since sufficient content knowledge of both the Bible and an academic discipline is necessary to successfully engage in integration, students may be viewed as insufficiently knowledgeable to participate in the process. Until students have gained significant knowledge of the Bible and the content area to be integrated (which, from a worldview perspective, is every aspect of life), they are not ready to participate in integration independently. As a result, students are not full-fledged members of the learning community and are not in a position to legitimately engage, question, or independently practice integration apart from their teachers. Consequently, biblical integration becomes a teacher-centered process and mirrors any other educational process where rationalism and rationality reign as supreme.

---

26. Palmer, *Courage to Teach*, 100.

Second, the process of integration and, ultimately, worldview transformation becomes one of truth without spirit since what predominates is content and not the relationship of the student to the truth. In the end, this approach violates the spirit of worship that is integral to Paul's command in Romans 12 that believers should be a living sacrifice, and that being such is an act of worship. As integration is based in content acquisition and becomes essentially teacher-centered, the knowledge of integration is separated from application. This is not to suggest that biblical educators do not desire nor attempt to make content applicable to the student. Any biblical educators worthy of the title desire that their students will take the truth that is learned in the classroom and make personal applications outside the classroom. Even so, when the process of integration is based in instructional models founded on the principles of rationalism and rationality, it can easily violate the principles of worldview transformation stated in Deuteronomy 7 and Romans 12:1–2.

The problem with the objectivist model of instruction when applied to worldview transformation is that it separates that which is to be known from the knower. He who is intended to be known (Christ) and his purposes (to do his will) become objects (or objectives) to be acquired. For example, I can tell you about my wife. I can teach you that she is a dedicated runner and avid reader and has an outgoing personality, yet, unless you have interacted with my wife, you do not really know her. Granted, you now know some facts about her, and if you were to take a quiz about her you could answer some questions (and even receive a perfect score), but it is a process that has simply objectified her in your mind without engaging you on the levels of feeling or motivations. To truly know her at the level of relationship would require you to interact with her, to experience and participate in her outgoing personality, and to have your impressions and feelings, as well as your thoughts, influenced by that interaction. A similar danger occurs when worldview transformation is done in a primarily rationalistic manner. The student can be taught a great deal about Christ; the principles of the Bible can be reduced to a set of theological statements that can be known by the learner with certainty but reduce Christ to the sum total of the content knowledge that can be known about him. As a result, Christ himself can be objectified in the process, reduced to a set of doctrinal statements or theological propositions, all of which can be true but lacking in relational power or engagement.

For this reason, the psalmist tells believers to "taste and see that the Lord is good; How blessed is the man who takes refuge in Him" (Ps 34:8). To "taste" is to experience, and to take refuge "in Him" portrays a closeness that goes beyond objectified content knowledge. To know about a sweet, crisp apple is much different than the pleasure one has, both at the moment and in memory, of actually biting into and experiencing the apple. Similarly, to experience that pleasure of Christ, a pleasure that comes from relating to him in worship at levels beyond content knowledge, is to experience him at levels that will impact the heart as well as the mind. Likewise, factual knowledge of my wife has little impact on how you live; yet this knowledge is fundamental to how I live since I engage in daily experiences with my wife. It is interesting that Paul uses the marriage analogy, where the community of faith is said to be the bride of Christ, to portray this relationship. Adam was given a bride to be his helper, one who could assist him to accomplish the mandates of God to humanity. Similarly, Christ is given a bride in the community of believers to assist him to accomplish the will of the Father. For this reason, Paul explains, believers are "created in Christ Jesus for good works, which God prepared beforehand so that we would walk in them" (Eph 2:10b).

In contrast, the disciple as apprentice is more aligned with how the process of worldview transformation as presented biblically. When individuals become apprentices, they begin a journey designed to make them functional members of that community. To become an apprentice is to place oneself under the authority of and in a learning relationship with the master. Of interest is how many trade unions of skilled artisans name their associations as brotherhoods. This learning relationship normally involves progressively assisting the master until certain tasks can be performed independently. While it is important for the apprentice to know, it is critical that the apprentice learn to do, and much of the learning is done within the framework of learning to practice the discipline.

For example, to become a master carpenter requires a certain basic level of knowledge to become an apprentice, but once admitted to the guild of carpenters, one progresses from apprentice to journeyman to master by demonstrating the ability to perform the skills of a carpenter. This learning, however, is directed in the fulfillment of various tasks associated with the discipline. For example, if an apprentice carpenter were building a chair, he would learn certain skills and techniques from the master that would allow him to assist in building the chair. Over time, as the apprentice moved to journeyman status, he would not only learn more techniques but also learn to discern when one technique is more appropriate than another, what conditions require certain techniques, and why certain techniques are better than others. This development would progress as the master worked with the apprentice, sharing with him the skills, abilities, and knowledge the master had acquired from years of practice to bring to bear on the tasks in which the two were jointly engaged.

This relationship is described by Palmer as "the community of truth."[27] In this model, Christ and the truth that can be learned about him from the Bible are the center of the community, where even masters acknowledge that they are apprentices to the Master. As a result, all teachers in the community also acknowledge their relationship to Christ as they continue to learn from him. In addition, each teacher acknowledges that every apprentice has been given certain talents, gifts, and abilities from the Holy Spirit so that they can perform the work of Christ. The teacher also acknowledges that, as one with greater knowledge and maturity, it is their responsibility to prepare younger, less experienced apprentices to perform the work of Christ. Apprentice development is not simply the acquisition of factual knowledge but is fundamentally tied to learning to use one's talents, gifts, and abilities in the process of engaging in the work of Christ.

As the apprentices work with their teachers, they learn not only how to do the work of Christ but also how the principles of stewardship, reconciliation, and developing the image of God are integrated into achieving that work. Over time, these processes become the foundation for decision making, allowing the apprentice to demonstrate greater maturity and, consequently, greater stewardship authority over the use of his talents, skills,

27. Ibid., 102.

knowledge, and resources. In this manner, learning becomes both relational (centered on knowing both Christ and his will) and experiential or task-centered (a process that allows the apprentice to make Christ known to the world). In this model of instruction, the *agape* ethic drives the process of making God famous by actual engagement in stewardship, reconciliation, and developing the image of God for the benefit of others. In the end, the goal is to bring new members into the community of faith and to create new disciples, new worshippers, new apprentices—it is the process of making new God-followers and thus fulfills the mandates of the Great Commission of Matthew 28:19–20.

DEVELOPING APPRENTICE DISCIPLES

While the church is corporately the bride of Christ, the relationship that Christ has with his bride is personal, involving time and place as well as individuals and local groups of believers. As a result, this relationship reflects the individual character of the disciples or group of believers in a particular place and at a particular point in time. This reality has consequences for the process of engaging in worldview transformation. For biblical educators, whether they are at the Christian school, university, or church, three factors should be considered in framing an approach to worldview change. These factors are

- the content or subject area to be integrated;
- the developmental age/abilities of the student;
- the community context in which instruction will occur.

In developing the content of the subject matter and the presentation of the material in light of the developmental age or abilities of the students, utilizing sources outside the immediate community is appropriate and can be extremely beneficial in planning both curriculum and instruction. Those who could prove useful in the curriculum development process include academic content experts in the disciplines being studied. Theologians and biblical thinkers, expert in integrating academic content with biblical principles, could also be useful in formulating the curriculum process. On the instructional side, developmental psychologists as well as other educators with experience in crafting instruction to meet the needs and demands of students at various levels of maturity would also be invaluable. The third factor, the community context, however, is unique to a group of believers and can only be addressed by those who understand the greater community in which learning will occur. In this area educators should consider the level of spiritual maturity within the community of faith as well as issues that affect the church and the community at large.

In terms of biblical integration and worldview transformation, the third factor, the community context in which instruction will occur, may be the most powerful. It is within the community that the principles of stewardship, reconciliation, and developing the image of God take place. It is within the community that worship as service will be practiced and where the relevance of the academic disciplines to the Christian faith can be demonstrated. The ability to integrate academic learning not simply to faith but also to life requires an understanding of knowledge that goes beyond mere comprehension of facts. Academically, the ability to apply knowledge in meaningful ways requires students to engage in learning that moves them from a mere novice understanding of content to practices corresponding with expertise. That is, students move from simply knowing facts or concepts (i.e., declarative knowledge) or the ability to perform rudimentary functions (i.e., procedural knowledge) to knowing how and when to apply that understanding to solve problems (i.e., conditional knowledge). Biblically, utilizing knowledge in a practical context will require students to apply the *agape* ethic to their understanding in a way that serves to make God famous before a watching world.

The traditional approach to worldview transformation, generally speaking, has been to provide students with reasons for why they should choose to live in a manner consistent with the teachings of Christ. Biblical integration, in this context, serves as a means of showing how what is learned in the classroom has connection to the Bible in a way that seeks to make the content relevant within the larger goal of worldview transformation. The reasoning behind this approach to worldview transformation, it seems, is that a thorough understanding of biblical doctrine or theological reasoning can be applied to situations in ways that make both logical and practical sense. In essence, the belief is that the theological foundations of the biblical worldview are so consistently rational that any reasonable person would see their validity. It is only the presence of sin that keeps people from affirming the validity of the biblical worldview, a conclusion supported biblically by the idea that the "word of the cross is foolishness to those who are perishing, but to those that are being saved it is the power of God" (1 Cor 1:18). The consistency of the biblical worldview is contrasted with the dissonance evoked when one espouses an alternative worldview.

This approach, however, has proven generally ineffective in soliciting change in many young people, for it does not provide an alternative example of how the truth of the gospel is relevant to life nor provide an alternative community in which certain practices will be reinforced as the communal value. The result is that the teachings of the Bible are accommodated to the existing practices of the world in a manner that allows the student to assimilate comfortably into the values of the dominant, unbelieving community. While this may, upon close theological review, create a sense of dissonance between belief and practice, it is a dissonance that allows the perception that the student fits in with the dominant practices of the culture, even if the reasons for conformity in practice are different from those of unbelievers. Philosopher Nicolas Wolterstorff, commenting on this tendency in believers, writes,

> [This] strategy, scrutinized closely, proves to consist of giving the student, or helping the student discover, *reasons* for acting a certain way—reasons that go back to his or her deeply religious convictions. . . . But such reasons, though sometimes effective, also have their inadequacies. Through apparently it is a characteristic of human beings to prefer consonance between beliefs and action, sometimes the perceived benefits of continuing to believe as we do and act inconsistently with that is greater than our discomfort over dissonance; so we do what we can to remain in our unstable state of hypocrisy. Or alternatively, when dissonance between belief and action turns up we sometimes change our beliefs rather than our actions.[28]

28. Wolterstorff, *Educating for Shalom*, 149 (italics in original).

What appears necessary is an approach to teaching service—a model that engages students in the process of being a living sacrifice or practicing the *agape* ethic that encourages the type of worldview transformation outlined in Romans 12:1–2. The Pauline outline—commitment, service, understanding of the reasons for practice—differs foundationally from the more rational approach to worldview transformation generally practiced and will result in a different approach to both curriculum and instructional practice. Wolterstorff suggests four components of a model structured to connect students in ways that move from simple knowing to actual doing. Each of these four components for shaping embodied moral character seems aptly relevant to engaging students in ways that seek to produce worldview change. In introducing these four components he writes,

> What I discovered very soon was that throwing abstract disciplines at students has almost no effect on their actions. . . . I had proposed the study of academic disciplines as the means to the goal of equipping and training our students to live as Christians in the world; now I was made to see that it was an illusion to think that this means would achieve this goal.[29]

The first step is identified as *discipline*, or the process of shaping the students' embodied moral character by providing them the expectation of desirable or undesirable consequences for their actions. In raising young children, parents and teachers instruct them how to behave before providing children an understanding or reasons for those behaviors. Similarly, when apprentices enter into their new profession, they commit to the common practices and purpose (i.e., the knowledge and skills) of the group. In both cases, it is the process of discipline that allows each to enter into and become functional and contributing members of the community. It is this immersion in the discipline, both in terms of knowledge and practice that brings about the type of change in thinking desired by biblical educators interested in worldview transformation.

Cognitive psychologists have long noted that it is not simply knowing more that separates experts from novices; experts know differently, that is, they think about their discipline in ways that are qualitatively different from novices. For example, economists think like economists and engineers think like engineers. This transformation does not come about simply by contact with more information but through active engagement in the practice of economics or engineering. Similarly, to get Christians to think in a manner more like Christ requires an active engagement in the work of Christ, a process that requires practice, dedication, and commitment. The idea of discipline is predicated on the belief that the student desires the outcomes that will result from focused and dedicated behavior. This is the reason Paul frequently uses the analogy of an athlete and the discipline necessary to be an effective runner to the Christian life. The writer of Hebrews uses the runner analogy as well, placing the discipline of running within the context of the community of the great witnesses of the faith (chapter 11) to encourage believers to engage in the disciplines of the faith regarding the direction, drive, and duties of life (Heb 12:1–29). In learning to play a musical instrument, the inherent discipline becomes practice, that is, a coordinated set of procedures to be done rather than content simply to

---

29. Ibid., 160.

be learned. It is through discipline that people learn to be disciples. They place themselves under the direction of a coach for the purpose of achieving the goal they seek to attain. In this sense, discipline, unlike control, is for the benefit of the disciples—preparing them to perform at the highest level possible.

The second step is *modeling*—the shaping of embodied moral character by providing students with models they admire who act according to the principles of the disciplines. Psychologists have long noted that people are more disposed to act in ways that mirror the behaviors of the significant people around them. This is especially true when the learner identifies or admires the model (e.g., parents, teachers, pastors, etc.). Most children will tend to model their parents as they are growing up and, upon reflection, may find themselves acting according to the tendencies of their parents long into adulthood. As noted earlier, one's initial worldview is not developed analytically but more by perception and disposition. This development can best be explained through the process of modeling whereby understanding of the world is formed by acting in ways consistent with those modeled. These attempts at mimicking behaviors are reinforced, directly or indirectly, by those who seek to model or by those who actively engage in disciplining the child into the accepted behaviors and, ultimately, the values of the community. In order to transform the worldview of students, teachers must not only expose them to what the biblical worldview is and why they should choose it, but students must also observe their teachers committed to that worldview and committed to engaging in the acts consistent with it as well. Optimally, this will require that students become active participants with their teachers as those teachers model the practice of effective biblical integration rather than hoping their students notice and engage in the behavior indirectly. This modeling can occur as teachers actively engage in the process of stewardship, reconciliation, and developing the image of God within their academic disciplines in ways that effectively integrate faith and learning to life applications.

The third step is *casuistry* or motivation—providing students with reasons to act in the ways that they have been taught. The practices of discipline and modeling provide teachers with the context to give students reasons to engage in the behaviors they practice. In casuistry, the emphasis is on providing students a rationale *for* action rather than a reason *to* perform an action. In this sense, casuistry, which follows discipline and modeling, is consistent with the command to love God and the process of instruction to that end provided in Deuteronomy 6:1–7: during everyday actions parents instruct children in the reasons those actions are done. It is important to note that this model requires active engagement; the passive receiving of reasons or justifications for behaviors does not to lead to the meaningful connections required for transformational learning.

The fourth, and final step, is cultivating *empathy*—providing students the opportunity to identify with the joys, fears, happiness, or hardships of others. Empathy is developed by coming to know the other people, understanding how they think and feel and what their goals and aspirations are. Unlike sympathy, where individuals relate to another person through their own experiences, in empathy the identification with another person comes from sharing in the experiences with another. In sympathy, individuals project their perspective to another; in empathy the perspective is changed through active involvement with another. Through empathy individuals learn why others engage the world in the way they do and what reasons they have for their behaviors. Without empathy, people are inclined to understand the actions of others from their own perspective. The result can be that individuals are more likely to judge those actions from the context of their own standards, a situation that Jesus aptly described as resulting in having a log in their own eye (Matt 7:1–5). The author of Hebrews notes that Christ can serve as the believers' high priest, having been exposed to the same sufferings and temptations of all humanity, so that he can have empathy and intercede before the Father on their behalf (Heb 2:17–18). With believers, as well, developing empathy will enable Christ's disciples to more effectively minister to those whom God has called the community of faith to serve.

Empathy allows students to put a human face to those whom they seek to serve. Empathy also serves to counteract the potential feelings of superiority and the condescendence to judge those less fortunate and in need of assistance. With empathy the plight of those served is viewed as the consequences of sin, as victims of the enemy, in need of restoration and reconciliation. Lacking empathy there is a danger that the situations of others can be used by those serving to enhance their own sense of superiority or that ministry can serve to bolster the server's well-being. The result is that service without empathy can lead to pride and that ministry can be engaged without humility. In empathy, relationships are developed in ways that help to preserve, protect, and develop dignity and to respect the position of those being served as image-bearers of God. Such relationships seek to empower those being served, providing them the means to engage in stewardship and reconciliation themselves rather than dependency on others to continue to serve their needs. A result is development of the image of God in students as they learn to minister to others in ways consistent with the ethic of *agape* love.

Empathy also requires relationships that place the student in direct contact and interaction with those being served. Discipleship that seeks to develop empathy understands that true ministry requires those serving to know and identify with those they seek to serve. For example, Jesus consistently identified himself with the poor (Luke 9:58) and claimed that the gospel was liberation for the poor and oppressed (Luke 4:18–19). From this perspective, Christ's statement that "you always have the poor with you" (Matt 26:11; Mark 14:7) is not a statement of the intended natural order of things or the divine plan for resource allocation but a statement regarding the proximity of the church to those who are disenfranchised and who suffer (directly or indirectly) the effects of sin. Educating students about the causes and effects of poverty may develop their understanding and even enhance their sympathy for the plight of the poor, but until they interact with those affected by poverty (or any other social condition), student will fail to develop the sense of identification needed for true ministry.

At the risk of sounding cliché, when it comes to worldview transformation it can be said that worldviews are caught and not simply taught. Worldview transformation cannot be viewed as unique or different from the cost of true discipleship, nor is biblical integration simply an enhancement to general curriculum that can be found in any other school. Biblical integration becomes the core element of Christian education and worldview transformation when the making of disciples serves as the primary goal. It is the process of "taking every thought captive to the obedience of Christ" (2 Cor 10:5) and doing all things for "the glory of God" (1 Cor 10:31). Christian education that leads to worldview transformation leads to the fulfillment of the great commandment to "love the Lord your God with all your heart, and with all your soul, and with all your strength, and with all your mind; and your neighbor as yourself" (Luke 10:27). For Christian educators, worldview transformation involves engaging the heart, soul, mind, and strength to the *agape* task of loving God and others. This is done so that students will be able to "prove what the will of God is, that which is good and acceptable and perfect" (Rom 12:2b).

EPILOGUE: ARNIE'S NEW PREP

Arnie returns to his desk after visiting with Polly. He has papers to grade, but his conversation with Polly causes him to reflect on the past school year. He thinks back to the initial in-service sessions in August where Dr. Wise first challenged his ideas on worldview transformation and how his initial skepticism slowly turned to receptivity and acceptance. There were the sessions in late November where the biblical concepts of stewardship, reconciliation, and developing the image of God in students were presented and served as a means to help him place integration into a more meaningful context. Just two weeks earlier, teachers met in workgroups by subject area to discuss how to implement these biblical concepts across the curriculum. Over the past several months, Arnie notes, the principles of stewardship, reconciliation, and developing the image of God have seemed to become the language of integration throughout the school. Secondary teachers were seeing ways to make their disciplines more relevant to students biblically, as well as several elementary teachers reporting that biblical integration no longer seemed as intimidating or as contrived. As one teacher stated, the three biblical principles gave her goals for which to strive.

Arnie looks across his desk and sees the new economics textbook resting there. With Mt. Carmel growing, the administration decided to increase their course offerings, resulting in Arnie gaining a new prep for the fall. Normally a new course would cause him some consternation, but Arnie is actually looking forward to this summer and the opportunity to build a new course around the three integration principles he has learned to adopt. Having learned back in April that he would be teaching the new course in the fall, Arnie has already begun preparations. He also contacted Dr. Wise who placed him in contact with one of the economics professors at Reformation Christian College who supplied him with resources to help him with his work.

At first Arnie was fairly certain that economics would prove to be an easy prep and that apart from how people and societies tended to use goods and services (and the values that directed those decisions) that the basic mechanism of resource allocation would be simple and straightforward. The more he read, however, the more impressed he became with some of the fundamental differences between a biblical approach to economics and the more conventional approaches he found in the secular and even many Christian economics textbooks. He also began to realize that his own views of economics had been shaped by the surrounding culture and his American vision of the world, which he wants to avoid when teaching economics to his own students. Arnie is convinced that he wants to challenge his students to think biblically about issues in economics and that in order to do this he needs to make them sensitive to the influence of culture—both how it has influenced them and how to be responsive to the world in which God has called them to live.

Arnie notes that the fundamental assumption and first principle from which all economics textbooks start is *scarcity*—that people's material wants exceed the ability and resources to satisfy those wants. As a result, societies must determine what are the most fair and efficient ways to allocate limited resources. Arnie is struck by certain fundamental ethical questions: who defines fair, and what are the criteria used to determine fairness? In terms of biblical integration, doesn't the allocation of resources fall under the principle of stewardship? Would differences in resource allocation lead to problems of inequity and conflicts that would require a biblical understanding of reconciliation to address? Does the increasingly materialistic emphasis of the society, where the biggest questions and concerns of the society become economic ones, have an adverse effect on how people define themselves and others and thus pose a threat to a biblical understanding of the image of God? From the perspective of worldview transformation, Arnie is not simply content to teach economics as the study of the way things are but to also relate the discipline to the way things should be—an emphasis that brings the will of God onto focus.

As Arnie prepares to teach economics, he becomes aware that the natural and fundamental assumption of scarcity in secular economics, where resources are limited and the desires of human beings are unlimited, must be contrasted with a different set of assumptions foundational to God's approach to economics. Whereas secular economics starts from scarcity, biblical economics assumes an abundance that flows from an omnipotent God but also requires that humans limit their desires; that God promised Israel a "land flowing with milk and honey" (Deut 31:20) but that his expectation was also that there would be no poor among them (Deut 15:4). The promise of God was predicated on Israel living in obedience to God's commandments, adopting behaviors that reflected God's values and expectations of how he intended them to live. If Israel chose to follow its own sinful desires and live in accordance with how they believed things should be, there would be consequences in the ways that the society would develop and work, which would include economics. As Arnie develops his economics course, he desires to contrast how departing from God's assumptions and starting from human desires fundamentally affects how believers live in the world economically and how they can be more effective ministers and ambassadors for Christ to the society.

While Arnie wants his students to understand the discipline of economics, he also wants them conversant with its principles and ideas, prepared to engage in its study after high school if they so choose. He also desires to contrast biblical economics to the secular approach typically found in most textbooks. In order to do this, he decides on three themes that he will use to contrast secular economics to a more biblical approach and to show the consequences of departing from God's expectations. He hopes that these three themes will become principles that his students will adopt to form the basis for how they will begin to examine economic issues and formulate economic questions and develop biblical responses. The first is to contrast a biblical view of abundance with the idea of artificial abundance promoted by the culture. Here Arnie hopes to demonstrate that the God of abundance does not serve to meet the unlimited desires of humanity but requires the limiting of human desires so that there would be no poor among them. By contrast, starting from scarcity, where the satisfaction of demand is impossible, there results a system of manufactured abundance, where the appearance of hundreds of types of breakfast cereals, toothpastes, or soft drinks, for example, offer options for consumption that provide the appearance of material abundance. One consequence, among many, is that manufactured abundance can create a system predicated on waste. To incorporate stewardship, Arnie hopes to demonstrate the long-term ecological ramifications that stem from such a system and even has discussed a joint unit with his friend Byron Bunsen, the science teacher, examining ecological issues from both an economic and scientific perspective.

Arnie's second theme is to examine the phenomenon of winners and losers—how all economic systems produce people who are the beneficiaries of the system and others who, for reasons both individual and systemic, suffer from ill-effects. With this theme Arnie wishes to highlight the issue of reconciliation, how the community of faith can learn to respond to issues of economic inequality. Here Arnie seeks to demonstrate that the advantages of incentives in free markets combined with the sin nature of humanity, when left unregulated, lead to large concentrations of wealth in the hands of a few and growing disenfranchisement and possible poverty among others. Here Arnie wishes not only to incorporate a biblical understanding of economics but also to have students understand current events and eras studied in their past history courses. The economic system designed by God made sure that the poor were cared for both in the short term (e.g., the provision of gleaning, Lev 19:9–10) and long term (e.g., the year of Jubilee, Lev 25:8–55). To tie economic inequality to the biblical concepts of righteousness and judgment, Arnie will incorporate God's condemnation through the prophets, particularly Isaiah and Micah, to the political, economic, and religious leaders of Israel to show how their callousness to economic injustices resulted in the loss of God's blessings and Israel's eventual exile from the land.

Finally, to incorporate the concept of human beings as image-bearers of God, Arnie will develop the theme of the intrinsic worth of the individual and the threat to this view of humanity from a materialistic and economic view of the world. For example, he notes that human labor, like any other commodity in a market system, has no intrinsic worth or moral value but is only valuable in terms or what someone else is willing to pay. People with certain skills or abilities desired by the market can sell those to the highest bidder, while people buying labor have an incentive to devalue its worth in order to lower their costs and increase their profits. The result is that the image of God embedded in human activities of stewardship and reconciliation no longer has economic worth unless someone is willing to pay for such activity. Even what becomes defined as meaningful labor is subservient to market forces that determine its value. The result is that a professional wrestler can earn more than a school teacher or that the ability of individuals to provide sufficient food, clothing, shelter, and healthcare for their family is predicated on having the right set of skills (and not just simply working hard). These factors lead to an increased desire for those skills that are marketable (thus increasing their abundance resulting in lowering their value), and this system is ignorant of the fact that God's sovereignty in distributing talents and abilities to individuals is not bound by market forces.

While Arnie wants his students to think biblically about economics, he also desires them to be disciples of Christ with the ability to apply their developing understanding of economics to the world in which they live. He hopes that by emphasizing the three biblical themes, they will develop an understanding of economic content as well as shape their moral understanding of the discipline. Arnie also wants to model how to think and act biblically as a student of economics, cultivating casuistry or a motivation for students to act on what they know and to develop a sense of empathy so that they can be true disciples of Christ in the arena of economics. In order to do this, Arnie believes he not only needs to teach economic content well and contrast that content with sound biblical principles but also give this knowledge a "face" that will provide his students practice in both using economics and developing biblical compassion and empathy. He is limited, however, in what he can do outside of the school. While he would like his students to become more involved in the community and have them invest time in helping others, he realizes this is not something that can be done practically. His response to his limitations is to add two faces to their understanding of economics—their own experience (or that of their family) and others brought into the classroom to speak to them. In order to facilitate these objectives, he decides on two projects that will help his students to access and develop casuistry and empathy.

The first he entitles the *Manna Project*. This project will involve a biblical understanding of the provision of manna for the Israelites as they wandered in the desert after leaving Egypt. It involves taking no more than was needed and trusting in God's provision when they responded in obedience (Exod 16). For the Israelites, the desire for too much or to hoard caused the manna to breed worms and become foul (Exod 16:20). This assignment will have them evaluate their own possessions, clothes, or CDs, for example, and determine how these are excesses that become foul or rarely used after they are purchased. In the assignment, students will calculate how much they spent on clothing, entertainment, dining out, and so on in the last month and how they can justify these expenditures. He will then have them relate their justification to the values that are embedded in their explanations (e.g., desire for comfort, ease, control) and explain how these relate to their understanding of and trust in God.

The second project Arnie will have students complete is a *Sabbath/Jubilee Project*. Here Arnie will examine the principles of the Sabbath and the institution of the Year of Jubilee and how these would relate to contemporary economic practice. The assignment is to create a hypothetical society where the economic principles of the Sabbath year and Year of Jubilee are the prevailing economic laws of the land. It is a speculative project, designed to engage adolescents to think hypothetically and ideally to create a better world and to see the ramifications of their actions on economic and social policy. He desires to encourage his students to examine questions such as why God instituted debt forgiveness every seven years (Deut 15:1–2) or the return of all land to its original owner every fifty years (Lev 25:10). What would be the consequences of lending and borrowing if this were true today? What would be the effect on the consumption patterns of people in the

United States if they practiced Sabbath and Jubilee laws? Who benefits (and how) from not following the biblical pattern? Who is disadvantaged (and how) for failure to follows these patterns?

In order to add the face of others, Arnie will bring in periodic guest speakers—business people, labor leaders, professional people, working-class people, and those un-employed. He will also bring in those who loan money, those who have borrowed, those overburdened by debt, and those who have been affected by bankruptcy. His desire is to confront his students' perceptions and misperceptions of all these people and to ask questions that will incorporate their biblical understanding of economics with current real-life practice. Arnie also understands that he will need to model this process to his students so that he must also learn to think about economic issues in a manner that will allow him to demonstrate and model this type of thinking and compassionate responses to others for his students.

Arnie realizes these are small steps in developing or changing a course, but they are ones that have huge ramifications. He has come to understand that the process of biblical integration, incorporating the principles of stewardship, reconciliation, and developing the image of God, cannot be reduced to an easy formula and that the context of the student and the community is an integral part of the integration process. It also means that integration and worldview transformation are not simply issues of curriculum emphasis or alignment; they must fundamentally impact goals, instructional techniques, and the ways that students are evaluated. He has also come to realize that the process of biblical integration is one where the teacher works to create a climate in which students can take what they have learned and relate it to meaningful practice. Ultimately, the goal of such integration is to bring about worldview transformation.

Arnie has now come to understand that worldview transformation is not simply changing the way students think about content or even the way they relate what they know to the Bible or biblical principles. Worldview transformation involves seeing the world the way God's sees it—not only how it is but also how God intends it to be—and then, as an act of worship, working to bring about that vision of the world. It is the process of making disciples in the realm of academics who become productive citizens of the kingdom of God until the return of Christ.

Bibliography

Adler, Mortimer J. *The Paideia Proposal: An Educational Manifesto*. New York: Macmillan, 1982.

Athanasius. "On the Incarnation of the Logos." In vol. 4 of *A Select Library of the Nicene and Post-Nicene Fathers*, edited by Phillip Schaff and Henry Wace. Second Series Grand Rapids: Eerdmans, 1984.

Althaus, Paul. The *Theology of Martin Luther*. Philadelphia: Westminster, 1966.

Anderson, Walter Truett. *Reality Isn't What It Used to Be: Theatrical Politics, Ready-to-Wear Religion, Global Myths, Primitive Chic, and Other Wonders of the Postmodern World*. San Francisco: Harper & Row, 1990.

Aristotle. *The Nicomachean Ethics*. Translated by Sir David Ross. London: Oxford University Press, 1954.

———. *The Politics*. Translated by Thomas Alan Sinclair. New York: Penguin, 1962.

Atkinson, John William. *An Introduction to Motivation*. 2nd ed. New York: Van Nostrand, 1978.

Augustine. *City of God*. Translated by Henry Bettenson. New York: Penguin, 1984.

———. *The Confessions of Saint Augustine*. Translated by J. C. Pinkerton. Cleveland, OH: Fine Editions Press, n.d.

Barna, George. *Real Teens: A Contemporary Snapshot on Youth Culture*. Ventura, CA: Regal, 2001.

Barna Group. "Marriage and Divorce Statistics." March 31, 2008. Posting on Blisstree page of B5 Media Network. http://blisstree.com/feel/marriage-divorce-statistics-the-barna-group-232.

Barth, Karl. *Church Dogmatics*. Edited by G. W. Bromiley and T. F. Torrance. Edinburgh: T&T Clark, 1956.

Bavinck, Herman. *Reformed Dogmatics*, vol. 3: *Sin and Salvation in Christ*. Edited by John Bolt. Translated by John Vriend. Grand Rapids: Baker Academic, 2006.

Beane, James A. "Curriculum Integration and the Disciplines of Knowledge." *Phi Delta Kappan* 76, no. 8 (April 1995) 616–22.

Bellah, Robert N., Richard Madsen, Williams M. Sullivan, Ann Swidler, and Steve M. Tipton. *Habits of the Heart: Individualism and Commitment in American Life*. New York: Perennial, 1985.

Berger, Peter L. *The Capitalist Revolution: Fifty Propositions about Prosperity, Equality, and Liberty*. New York: Basic Books, 1986.

———. *The Sacred Canopy*. Garden City, NY: Anchor, 1969.

Berger, Peter L., and Thomas Lickmann. *The Social Construction of Reality*. New York: Anchor, 1966.

Berkhof, Lewis. "Common Grace." http://www.theologue.org/CommonGrace-Berkhof.html (accessed February 9, 2009).

———. *Manual of Christian Doctrine*. Grand Rapids: Eerdmans, 1950.

Bernard, Shelia Curran, and Sarah Mondale. *School: The Story of American Public Education*. Boston: Beacon, 2001.

Black, Ellen Lowrie. "The Teacher." In *Foundations of Christian School Education*, edited by James Braley, Jack Layman, and Ray White, 145–59. Colorado Springs, CO: Purposeful Design, 2003.

Blamires, Harry. *The Christian Mind: How Should a Christian Think?* Ann Arbor, MI: Servant, 1963.

Blomberg, Doug. *No Icing on the Cake*. Edited by Jack Michielsen. Melbourne: Brooks-Hall, 1980.

Brueggemann, Walter. *The Prophetic Imagination*. 2nd ed. Minneapolis: Augsburg Fortress, 2001.

Brunner, Emil. *Man in Revolt: A Christian Anthropology*. Philadelphia: Westminster Press, 1979.

———. *Revelation and Reason*. Philadelphia: Westminster Press, 1946.

Buber, Martin. *I and Thou*. New York: Touchstone, 1970.

Buechner, Frederick. *Wishful Thinking: A Seeker's ABC*. San Francisco: Harper, 1993.

Bush, George W. "Foreword." In *No Child Left Behind*. Washington, DC: United States Government Printing Office, 2001.

Calvin, John. *Institutes of the Christian Religion*. Translated by Henry Beveridge. 2 vols. Grand Rapids: Eerdmans, 1983.

Campbell, Marla. "Integration of Learning into Faith." *Christian School Education* 6 no. 4 (March 2003) 18–20.

Carnock, Stephen. *The Existence and Attributes of God*. Grand Rapids: Baker, 1979.

Clapp, Rodney. *A Particular People: The Church in a Post-Christian Society*. Downers Grove, IL: InterVarsity Press, 1997.

Cohen, Lizabeth. *The Consumers' Republic: The Politics of Mass Consumption in Postwar America*. New York: Vintage, 2003.

Coles, Robert. *The Spiritual Life of Children*. Boston: Houghton Mifflin, 1990.

Coulter, Ann. *FoxNews* interview, December 22, 2001.

Counts, George S. *Dare the School Build a New Social Order?* Carbondale: Southern Illinois University Press, 1932.

Deane, Herbert A. *The Political and Social Ideas of St. Augustine*. New York: Columbia University Press, 1963.

DeGraaff, Arnold H., Jean Olthuis, and Anne Tuininga. *Japan: A Way of Life*. Toronto: Joy in Learning Curriculum Development and Training Centre, 1980.

Descartes, René. *Discourse on Methods* and *Meditations on First Philosophy*. Translated by Donald A. Cress. Indianapolis: Hackett, 1980.

Dewey, John. *Reconstruction in Philosophy*. Boston: Beacon Press, 1957.

DeYoung, Alan J. *Economics and American Education*. New York: Longman, 1989.

Dooyeweerd, Herman. *Roots of Western Culture: Pagan, Secular, and Christian Options*. Toronto: Wedge, 1979.

Dray, W. H. "Holism and Individualism in History and Social Science." In *The Encyclopedia of Philosophy*, edited by Paul Edwards, 4:53–58. New York: Macmillan and Free Press, 1967.

Dreeben, Robert. *On What Is Learned in School*. Reading, MA: Addison-Wesley, 1968.

Durkheim, Emile. *Education and Sociology*. Translated by Sherwood D. Fox. Glencoe, IL: Free Press, 1956.

Edlin, Richard J. *The Cause of Christian Education*. Northport, AL: Vision, 1994.

Edwards, Jonathan. *The Nature of True Virtue*. Ann Arbor, MI: Ann Arbor Paperbacks, 1960.

———. *The Religious Affections*. Edinburgh: Banner of Truth Trust, 1986.

Egan, Kieran. *Getting It Wrong from the Beginning: Our Progressivist Inheritance from Herbert Spencer, John Dewey, and Jean Piaget*. New Haven, CT: Yale University Press, 2002.

Emerson, Michael O., and Christine Smith. *Divided by Faith: Evangelical Religion and the Problem of Race in America*. Oxford: Oxford University Press, 2000.

Emerson, Ralph Waldo. "Nature." In vol. 1 of *Collected Works of Ralph Waldo Emerson*. Cambridge: Cambridge University Press, 1971.

Erickson, Millard J. *The Postmodern World: Discerning the Times and the Spirit of Our Age*. Wheaton, IL: Crossway, 2002.

Erikson, Erik H. *Childhood and Society*. 2nd ed. New York: Norton, 1963.

Estes, Daniel. *Hear My Son: Teaching and Learning in Proverbs 1–9*. Grand Rapids: Eerdmans, 1997.

Ewen, Stuart. *All Consuming Images: The Politics and Style of Contemporary Culture*. New York: Basic Books, 1999.

———. *Captains of Consciousness: Advertising and the Social Roots of Consumer Culture*. New York: McGraw Hill, 1976.

Feinberg, Walter, and Jonas F. Soltis. *School and Society*. 3rd ed. New York: Teachers College, 1998.

Foster, Richard J. *Streams of Living Water: Essential Practices from the Six Great Traditions of Christian Faith*. San Francisco: Harper, 1998.

Fowler, James W. *Stages of Faith: The Psychology of Human Development and the Quest for Meaning*. San Francisco: HarperCollins, 1981.

Frazee, Randy. *The Connecting Church: Beyond Small Groups to Authentic Community*. Grand Rapids: Zondervan, 2001.

Freire, Paulo. *Pedagogy of the Oppressed*. New York: Continuum, 1970.

Gaebelein, Frank E. *The Pattern of God's Truth: The Integration of Faith and Learning*. New York: Oxford University Press, 1954.

Gaede, S. D. *When Tolerance Is No Virtue*. Downers Grove, IL: InterVarsity Press, 1993.

Galbraith, John Kenneth. *The New Industrial State*. Boston: Houghton Mifflin, 1967.

Gangel, Kenneth O. "Biblical Foundations of Education." In *Foundations of Christian School Education*, edited by James Braley, Jack Layman, and Ray White, 53–66. Colorado Springs, CO: Purposeful Design, 2003.

———. "Integrating Faith and Learning: Principles and Process." In *The Philosophy of Christian School Education*, edited by Paul A. Kienel, rev. [4th] ed., 29–42. Whittier, CA: Association of Christian Schools International, 1983.

Gardner, Howard. *The Unschooled Mind: How Children Think and How Schools Should Teach*. New York: Basic Books, 1991.

Garrett, James Leo. *Systematic Theology*. Vol. 1. Grand Rapids: Eerdmans, 1990.

Geertz, Clifford. *The Interpretation of Cultures*. New York: Basic Books, 1973.

Geisler, Norman, and William Watkins. *Perspectives: Understanding and Evaluating Today's World Views*. San Bernardino, CA: Here's Life, 1984.

Gilkey, Langdon. *Society and the Sacred: Toward a Theology of Culture in Decline*. New York: Crossroads, 1981.

Graham, Donovan L. *Teaching Redemptively: Bringing Grace and Truth into Your Classroom*. Colorado Springs, CO: Purposeful Design, 2003.

Grand Canyon [DVD]. Directed by Lawrence Kasdan. Central City, CA: 20th Century Fox, 1991.

Greene, Albert E. *Reclaiming the Future of Christian Education: A Transforming Vision*. Colorado Springs, CO: Association of Christian Schools International, 1998.

Guinness, Os. *The Dust of Death*. Downers Grove, IL: InterVarsity Press, 1972.

Gurian, Michael, and Kathy Stevens. *The Mind of Boys: Saving Our Sons from Falling Behind in School and Life*. San Francisco: Jossey-Bass, 2005.

Halterman, James. *Market Capitalism and Christianity*. Grand Rapids: Baker, 1988.

Hart, Benjamin. *Faith and Freedom: The Christian Roots of Religious Liberty*. Dallas: Lewis and Stanley, 1988.

Hasker, William. "Faith-Learning Integration: An Overview." *Christian Scholars Review* 21, no. 3 (March 1992) 231–48.

Hegeman, David Bruce. *Plowing in Hope: Toward a Biblical Theology of Culture*. Moscow, ID: Canon, 1999.

Hirsch, E. D. *Cultural Literacy: What Every American Needs to Know*. Boston: Houghton Mifflin, 1987.

Hoeksema, Herman. *The Protestant Reformed Churches in America: Their Origin, Early History and Doctrine*. Grand Rapids: First Protestant Reform Church, 1936.

Hoffecker, W. A. *Building a Christian Worldview*. Edited by G. S. Smith. Phillipsburg, NJ: Presbyterian and Reformed, 1986.

Hogan, Kathleen, Bonnie K. Natasi, and Michael Pressley. "Discourse Patterns and Collaborative Scientific Reasoning in Peer and Teacher-guided Discussions." *Cognition and Instruction* 17, no. 4 (1999) 379–432.

Holwerda, D. E. *Exploring the Heritage of John Calvin*. Grand Rapids: Baker, 1976.

Howell, Irving. "Ojiba Ontology, Behavior and World View." In *Culture in History*, edited by S. Diamond, 19–52. New York: Columbia University Press, 1960.

Hudson, Winthrop S. *Religion in America*. 4th ed. New York: Macmillan, 1987.

Hume, David. *Treatise of Human Nature*. Edited by E. C. Mossner. London: Penguin Classics, 1969.

Hunter, James Davidson. *Culture Wars: The Struggle to Define America*. New York: Basic Books, 1991.

———. *Evangelicalism: The Coming Generation*. Chicago: University of Chicago Press, 1983.

Jacoby, Susan. *Freethinkers: A History of American Secularism*. New York: Owl, 2004.

John Paul II. *Fides et Ratio: On the Relationship between Faith and Reason* [encyclical letter]. Boston: Pauline Books and Media, 1998.

Johnson, Greg. *The World According to God: A Biblical View of Culture, Work, Science, Sex and Everything Else*. Downers Grove, IL: InterVarsity Press, 2002.

Kant, Immanuel. *Critique of Pure Reason*. Translated by Norman Kemp Smith. New York: San Martin's, 1929.

Kienel, Paul A. *Reasons for Christian Schools*. Milford, MI: Mott Media, 1981.

Kohn, Alfie. *Punished by Rewards*. Boston: Houghton Mifflin, 1993.

———. *The Schools Our Children Deserve: Moving beyond Traditional Classroom and "Tougher Standards."* Boston: Houghton Mifflin, 1999.

———. "The Truth about Self-Esteem." *Phi Delta Kappan* 76, no. 4 (December 1994) 272–83.

Kuhn, Thomas S. *The Structure of Scientific Revolutions*. 2nd ed. Chicago: University of Chicago Press, 1970.

Kuyper, Abraham. *Abraham Kuyper: A Centennial Reader*. Edited by James D. Bratt. Grand Rapids: Eerdmans, 1998.

———. *Calvinism*. Grand Rapids: Eerdmans, 1943.

Labaree, David F. *How to Succeed in School without Really Learning: The Credentials Race in American Education*. New Haven, CT: Yale University Press, 1997.

LaHaye, Tim. *The Battle for the Public School*. Old Tappan, NJ: Revell, 1983.

Lakoff, George. *Moral Politics: How Liberals and Conservatives Think*. Chicago: University of Chicago Press, 2002.

Lewin, Kurt. *Field Theory in Social Science: Selected Theoretical Papers*. New York: Harper & Row, 1951.

Lewis, C. S. *The Four Loves: The Much Beloved Exploration of the Nature of Love*. San Diego, CA: Harvest, 1960.

Lewontin, R. C., Steven Rose, and Leon J. Kamin. *Not in Our Genes: Biology, Ideology, and Human Nature*. New York: Pantheon, 1984.

Litfin, Duane. *Conceiving the Christian College*. Grand Rapids: Eerdmans, 2004.

Locke, John. *An Essay Concerning Human Understanding*. Edited by A. D. Woozley. New York: Meridian, 1964.

Lubac, Henri de. *At the Service of the Church*. San Francisco: Ignatius, 1993.

Lukács, Georg. *History and Class Consciousness*. Cambridge: MIT Press, 1971.

Luther, Martin. "How Christians Should Regard Moses." In Word and Sacrament I, *Luther's Works*, 35:363–93. Minneapolis: Fortress Press, 1960.

Lux, Michael. *The Progressive Revolution: How the Best in America Came to Be*. New York: Wiley, 2009.

Malinowski, Bonislaw. "Culture." In *Encyclopedia of Social Sciences*, edited by Edwin R. A. Seligman, 4:621–46. New York: Macmillan, 1931.

Marsden, George M. *Fundamentalism and American Culture: The Shaping of Twentieth-Century Evangelicalism, 1870–1925*. Oxford: Oxford University Press, 1980.

———. "The State of Evangelical Christian Scholarship." *Christian Scholar's Review* 17, no. 4 (June 1988) 347–60.

———. *Understanding Fundamentalism and Evangelicalism*. Grand Rapids: Eerdmans, 1991.

Marzano, Robert J. *A Different Kind of Classroom: Teaching with Dimensions of Learning*. Alexandria, VA: Association for Supervision and Curriculum Development, 1992.

Marzano, Robert J., and Debra J. Pickering. *Dimensions of Learning: Teacher's Manual*. 2nd ed. Alexandria, VA: Association for Supervision and Curriculum Development, 1997.

McCleod, Donald. *Behold Your God*. Ross-shire, Scotland: Christian Focus, 1990.

McDowell, Josh, and Bob Hostetler. *Beyond Belief to Conviction*. Wheaton, IL: Tyndale House, 2002.

———. *Right from Wrong*. Dallas: Word, 1994.

Middleton, J. Richard, and Brian J. Walsh. *Truth Is Stranger Than It Used to Be: Biblical Faith in a Postmodern Age*. Downers Grove, IL: InterVarsity Press, 1995.

Milne, Bruce. *Know the Truth: A Handbook of Christian Belief*. Rev. ed. Downers Grove, IL: InterVarsity Press, 1998.

Mirandola, Pico della. *Oration on the Dignity of Man*. Translated by A. Robert Caponigri. Chicago: Henry Regnery, 1965.

Moore, G. E. *Principia Ethica*. Cambridge: Cambridge University Press, 1903.

Moreland. J. P. *Love Your God with All Your Mind: The Role of Reason in the Life of the Soul*. Colorado Springs, CO: NavPress, 1997.

Moreland, J. P., and William Lane Craig. *Philosophical Foundations for a Christian Worldview*. Downers Grove, IL: InterVarsity Press, 2003.

Morris, Henry M. *Christian Education for the Real World*. El Cajon, CA: Master Books, 1977.

Mouw, Richard J. *When Kings Come Marching In: Isaiah and the New Jerusalem*. Grand Rapids: Eerdmans, 1983.

Nash, Ronald. *The Closing of the American Heart: What's Really Wrong with America's Schools*. Waco, TX: Probe, 1994.

———. *Faith and Reason: Searching for a Rational Faith*. Grand Rapids: Zondervan, 1988.

National Commission on Excellence in Education. *A Nation at Risk*. Washington, DC: U.S. Government Printing Office, 1983.

Naugle, David K. *Worldview: The History of a Concept*. Grand Rapids: Eerdmans, 2002.

Neuhaus, Richard John. "Foreword." In *Springtime of Evangelization: The Complete Texts of the Holy Father's 1998 ad Limina Addresses to the Bishops of the United States*, by Pope John Paul II. San Francisco: Ignatius Press, 1999.

Newbigin, Lesslie. *Foolishness to the Greeks: The Gospel and Western Culture*. Grand Rapids: Eerdmans, 1986.

Newton, Isaac. "Letters." In *The Enlightenment: A Comprehensive Anthology*. Edited by Peter Gay, 64–70. New York: Touchstone, 1973.

Niebuhr, H. Richard. *Christ and Culture*. San Francisco: Harper, 1951.

Nietzsche, Friedrich. *The Gay Science*. Translated by Walter Kaufmann. New York: Vintage, 1974.

Noebel, David. *Understanding the Times: The Religious Worldviews of Our Day and the Search for Truth*. Eugene, OR: Harvest House, 1991.

Noll, Mark. The Rise of Evangelicalism: The Age of Edwards, Whitefield and the Wesleys. Downers Grove, IL: InterVarsity Press, 2003.

———. *The Scandal of the Evangelical Mind*. Grand Rapids: Eerdmans, 1994.

———. *The Work We Have to Do: A History of Protestants in America*. Oxford: Oxford University Press, 2000.

O'Donnell, James J. *Augustine*. Boston: Twayne, 1985.

Olthuis, James. "On Worldviews." *Christian Scholar's Review* 14, no. 2 (1985) 153–64.

Owen, John. *The Mortification of Sin*. Ross-shire, Scotland: Christian Focus, 1996.

Packer, J. I., and Thomas Howard. *Christianity: The True Humanism*. Vancouver: Regent College Publications, 1985.

Pai, Young, and Susan Adler. *Cultural Foundations of Education*. 3rd ed. Upper Saddle River, NJ: Merrill Prentice Hall, 2000.

Palmer, Parker J. *The Courage to Teach: Exploring the Inner Landscape of a Teacher's Life*. San Francisco: Jossey-Bass, 2007.

Palmer, Parker J. *To Know as We Are Known: Education as a Spiritual Journey*. San Francisco: Harper, 1993.

Paris, K. *A Leadership Model for Planning and Implementing Change for School-to-Work Transition*. Madison: University of Wisconsin-Madison, Center on Education and Work, 1994.

Patterson, C. H. *Humanistic Education*. Upper Saddle River, NJ: Prentice Hall, 1973.

Pazmiño, Robert W. *By What Authority Do We Teach? Sources for Empowering Christian Educators*. Grand Rapids: Baker, 1994.

Pearcey, Nancy. *Total Truth: Liberating Christianity from Its Cultural Captivity*. Wheaton, IL: Crossway, 2004.

Perkinson, Henry. *The Imperfect Panacea: American Faith in Education, 1865–1965*. New York: Random House, 1979.

Phillips, W. Gary, and William E. Brown. *Making Sense of Your World*. Salem, WI: Sheffield, 1991.

Piaget, Jean. *The Child's Conception of the World*. Totowa, NJ: Littlefield, Adams, 1968.

———. *Comments on Vygotsky's Critical Remarks*. Cambridge, MA: MIT Press, 1961.

———. *The Moral Judgment of the Child*. New York: Free Press, 1932.

———. "Piaget's Theory." In *Carmichael's Manual of Child Psychology*, edited by P. H. Mussen, 3rd ed., 1:703–32. New York: Wiley, 1970.

Pinker, Steven. *The Blank Slate: The Modern Denial of Human Nature*. New York: Penguin, 2002.

Piper, John. *Desiring God: Meditations of a Christian Hedonist*. Sisters, OR: Multnomah, 1986.

Plantinga, Cornelius, Jr. *Engaging God's World: A Christian Vision of Faith, Learning, and Living*. Grand Rapids: Eerdmans, 2002.

———. *Not the Way It's Supposed to Be: A Breviary of Sin*. Grand Rapids: Eerdmans, 1995.

Plato. *The Symposium*. Translated by Walter Hammond. New York: Penguin Classics, 1951.

Polanyi, Michael. *Personal Knowledge: Towards a Post-Critical Philosophy*. Chicago: University of Chicago Press, 1962.

———. *The Tacit Dimension*. Garden City, NY: Doubleday, 1966.

Postman, Neil. *Building a Bridge to the 18th Century: How the Past Can Improve Our Future*. New York: Vintage, 1999.

Ramm, Bernard. *Offense to Reason: The Theology of Sin*. San Francisco: Harper & Row, 1985.

Reich, Robert B. "Of Darwinism and Social Darwinism." Published online by CommonDreams.org, November 29, 2005. http://www.commondreams.org/views05/1129-28.htm. Also in *The American Prospect* 29 (December 2005).

Reinke, Robert W., Mark C. Schug, and Donald R. Wentworth. *Capstone: The Nation's High School Economics Course*. New York: Joint Council on Economic Education, 1989.

Richert, Rebekah A., and Justin L. Barrett. "Do You See What I See? Young Children's Assumptions about God's Perceptual Abilities." *The International Journal for the Psychology of Religion* 15, no. 4 (2005) 283–95.

Rifkin, Jeremy. *Entropy: A New World View*. New York: Viking, 1980.

Rodgers, Robert E. L. *The Incarnation of the Antithesis*. Edinburgh: Pentland, 1992.

Rodin, R. Scott. "Stewardship." In *Toward an Evangelical Public Policy: Political Strategies for the Health of the Nation*, edited by Ronald J. Sider and Diane Knippers, 265–83. Grand Rapids: Baker, 2005.

Roso, Calvin B. "Constructivism in the Classroom: Is It Biblical?" In *Faith-Based Education That Constructs: A Creative Dialogue between Constructivism and Faith-based Education*, edited by Heekap Lee, 37–44. Eugene, OR: Wipf & Stock, 2010.

Rowland, Randy. *The Sins We Love: Embracing Brokenness, Hoping for Wholeness*. New York: Doubleday, 2000.

Ryle, Gilbert. *The Concept of Mind*. London: Penguin, 1949.

Samuelson, William, and Richard Zechhauser. "Status Quo Bias in Decision Making." *Journal of Risk and Uncertainty* 1, no. 1 (March 1988) 7–59.

Schaeffer, Francis. *The Complete Work of Francis A Schaeffer: A Christian Worldview*. 5 vols. Westchester, IL: Crossway Books, 1982.

Schmiechen, Peter. *Christ the Reconciler: A Theology for Opposites, Differences, and Enemies*. Grand Rapids: Eerdmans, 1996.

Schultz, Theodore W. *The Economic Value of Education*. New York: Columbia University Press, 1963.

———. "Investment in Human Capital." *American Economic Review* 51, no. 1 (March 1961) 1–17.

Searle, John R. *The Construction of Social Reality*. New York: Free Press, 1995.

Sergiovanni, Thomas. *Leadership for the Schoolhouse: Why Is It Different? Why Is It Important?* San Francisco: Jossey-Bass, 1996.

Sider, Ronald J. "Justice, Human Rights, and Government: Toward an Evangelical Perspective." In *Toward an Evangelical Public Policy: Political Strategies for the Health of the Nation*, edited by Ronald J. Sider, 163–93. Grand Rapids: Baker, 2005.

Sire, James. *The Universe Next Door: A Basic World View Catalog*. 2nd ed. Downers Grove, IL: InterVarsity Press, 1988.

Skinner, B. F. *Beyond Freedom and Dignity*. New York: Bantam, 1971.

Smelser, Neil J. "Culture: Coherent or Incoherent." In *Theory of Culture*, edited by Richard Munch and Neil J. Smelser, 3–28. Berkeley: University of California Press, 1992.

Smith, Adam. *The Wealth of Nations*. Vol. 1. New York: E.P. Dutton, 1947.

Smith, David L. *With Willful Intent: A Theology of Sin*. Wheaton, IL: BridgePoint, 1994.

Solzhenitsyn, Aleksandr. *A World Split Apart: Commencement Address Delivered at Harvard University, June 8, 1978*. New York: HarperCollins, 1979.

Sommers, Christina Hoff. *The War against Boys: How Misguided Feminism Is Harming Our Young Men*. New York: Touchstone, 2000.

Spencer, Herbert. *The Principles of Psychology*. 3rd ed. New York: D. Appleton, 1897.

Spengler, Oswald. *Decline of the West*, vol. 1: *Form and Actuality*. New York: Alfred A. Knopf, 1996.

Spring, Joel. *American Education*. 12th ed. Boston: McGraw Hill, 2006.

———. *The Sorting Machine: National Educational Policy Since 1945*. New York: Longman, 1976.

Stormer, John A. *None Dare Call It Education*. Florissant, MO: Liberty Bell Press, 1999.

Stronks, Gloria Goris, and Doug Blomberg. *A Vision with a Task: Christian Schooling for Responsive Discipleship*. Grand Rapids: Baker, 1993.

Tanner, Kathryn. *Theories of Culture: A New Agenda for Theology*. Minneapolis: Fortress, 1997.

Tatum, Beverly Daniel. *"Why Are All the Black Kids Sitting Together in the Cafeteria?" And Other Conversations about Race*. New York: Basic Books, 1997.

The Ad and the Ego [DVD]. Directed by Harold Boihem. Los Angeles: Parallex Pictures, 1997.

The Persuaders: Americans Are Swimming in a Sea of Messages [DVD]. Directed by Barak Goodman and Rachel Dretzin. Produced by Rachel Dretzin, Barak Goodman, and Muriel Soenens. Boston: WGBH Educational Foundation, 2004.

Tillich, Paul. *Systematic Theology.* 3 vols. Chicago: University of Chicago Press, 1975.

Tozer, A. W. *Whatever Happened to Worship?* Camp Hill, PA: Christian Publications, 1985.

Twenge, Jean M. *Generation Me: Why Today's Young Americans Are More Confident,7 Assertive, Entitled—and More Miserable Than Ever Before.* New York: Free Press, 2006.

Tyack, David, and Larry Cuban. *Tinkering toward Utopia: A Century of Public School Reform.* Cambridge, MA: Harvard University Press, 1995.

Van Til, Henry R. *The Calvinistic Concept of Culture.* Grand Rapids: Baker Academic, 1972.

Vygotsky, Lev Semonovich. *Mind in Society: The Development of Higher Psychological Processes.* Cambridge, MA: Harvard University Press, 1978.

Wallis, Jim. *God's Politics: Why the Right Gets It Wrong and the Left Doesn't Get It.* San Francisco: Harper, 2005.

Walsh, Brian. "Worldviews, Modernity, and the Task of Christian College Education." *Faculty Dialogue* 18, no. 1 (Fall 1992) 13–35.

Walsh, Brian, and J. Richard Middleton. *The Transforming Vision: Shaping a Christian World View.* Downers Grove, IL: InterVarsity Press, 1984.

Watson, John B. *Behaviorism.* Rev. ed. Chicago: University of Chicago Press, 1930.

———. "Psychology as the Behaviorist Views It." *Psychological Review* 20 (1919) 158–77.

Wertsch, James V. *Vygotsky and the Social Formation of Mind.* Cambridge: Harvard University Press, 1985.

White, Leslie A., and Beth Dillingham. *The Concept of Culture.* Minneapolis: Burgess, 1996.

White, Lynn, Jr. "The Historical Roots of Our Ecological Crisis." *Science* 155 (1967) 1201–07.

Wilcox, David K. "Promoting Student Academic Integrity: Our Responsibility." *Christian School Education* 9, no. 1 (Fall 2005) 17–19.

Williams, Raymond. *The Sociology of Culture.* Chicago: University of Chicago Press, 1995.

Wink, Walter. "Unmasking the Powers: A Biblical View of Roman and American Economics." *Sojourners* 7 (October 1978) 14–17.

Winthrop, John. "City upon a Hill" [1630]. Posted on webpage of Vincent Ferraro, Mount Holyoke College, "Documents Relating to American Foreign Policy—Pre-1898." http://www.mtholyoke.edu/acad/intrel/winthrop.htm.

Wolters, Albert M. *Creation Regained: Biblical Basics for a Reformational Worldview.* Grand Rapids: Eerdmans, 1985.

Wolterstorff, Nicolas. "Abraham Kuyper on Christian Learning." In *Educating for Shalom: Essays on Christian Higher Education,* by Nicolas Wolterstorff, edited by Clarence W. Joldersma and Gloria Goris Stronks. Grand Rapids: Eerdmans, 2004.

———. *Educating for Shalom: Essays on Christian Higher Education.* Edited by Clarence W. Joldersma and Gloria Goris Stronks. Grand Rapids: Eerdmans, 2004.

———. "Justice as a Condition of Authentic Liturgy." *Theology Today* 48, no. 1 (April 1991) 7–21.

———. *Reason within the Bounds of Religion.* Grand Rapids: Eerdmans, 1976.

———. *Until Justice and Peace Embrace.* Grand Rapids: Eerdmans, 1983.

Woolfolk, Anita. *Educational Psychology.* 10th ed. Boston: Allyn & Bacon, 2006.

Wright. N. T. *The New Testament and the People of God: Christian Origins and the Question of God.* Vol. 1. Minneapolis: Fortress, 1996.